CISA
Certified Information Systems Auditor™
Study Guide

CISA

CISA
Certified Information Systems Auditor™
Study Guide

240 min
200 Qued?

David L. Cannon
Timothy S. Bergmann
Brady Pamplin

Wiley Publishing, Inc.

Acquisitions and Development Editor: Jeff Kellum
Technical Editor: Mike Gregg
Production Editor: Rachel Gunn
Copy Editor: Sharon Wilkey
Production Manager: Tim Tate
Vice President and Executive Group Publisher: Richard Swadley
Vice President and Executive Publisher: Joseph B. Wikert
Vice President and Publisher: Neil Edde
Permissions Editor: Shannon Walters
Media Development Specialist: Kate Jenkins
Book Designers: Judy Fung, Bill Gibson
Compositor: Craig Woods, Happenstance Type-O-Rama
Proofreader: Nancy Riddiough
Indexer: Nancy Guenther
Cover Designer: Richard Miller, Calyx Design

Sybex®
An Imprint of
WILEY

To Our Valued Readers:

Thank you for looking to Sybex for your CISA exam prep needs. The Sybex team is proud of its reputation for providing certification candidates with the practical knowledge and skills needed to succeed in the highly competitive IT marketplace. Just as the Information Systems Audit and Control Association (ISACA) is committed to establishing measurable standards for certifying individuals working in the field of information systems audit, control, and security, Sybex is committed to providing those individuals with the skills needed to meet those standards.

The authors and editors have worked hard to ensure that the Study Guide that you hold in your hands is comprehensive, in-depth, and pedagogically sound. We're confident that this book will exceed the demanding standards of the certification marketplace and help you, the CISA candidate, succeed in your endeavors.

As always, your feedback is important to us. If you believe you've identified an error in the book, please visit the Customer Support section of the Wiley web site. And if you have general comments or suggestions, feel free to drop me a line directly at nedde@wiley.com. At Sybex we're continually striving to meet the needs of individuals preparing for certification exams.

Good luck in pursuit of your CISA certification!

Neil Edde
Vice President & Publisher
Wiley Publishing, Inc.

For Kristine, the love of my life. I express my appreciation to my past employers and clients for the opportunities that led me down this path.
—Dave Cannon

For my parents, Harold and Nellie Bergmann, who taught me the right things. I also dedicate this book to my wife Alice, to Stephen, and to Heather — who make every day rewarding.
—Tim Bergmann

For my wife Charlene and our daughters Anita, Celeste, and Sharon.
—Brady Pamplin

This book is a tribute to the students who attended our class. Their infinite questions were instrumental in the creation of this Study Guide.

Acknowledgments

We would like to thank our Acquisitions and Development Editor Jeff Kellum for his vision and guidance. Our Technical Reviewer Michael Gregg was very helpful in providing his expert assistance during the writing of this book. We wish to thank Production Editor Rachel Gunn for keeping the book on track, and her tireless effort in ensuring we put out the best book possible. We would also like to thank Copyeditor Sharon Wilkey, Compositor Craig Woods, Illustrator Jeffrey Wilson, Proofreader Nancy Riddiough, and Indexer Nancy Guenther for their polished efforts to make certain this book became a reality.

Contents at a Glance

Introduction   *xix*

Assessment Test   *xxxvii*

Chapter 1   Secrets of a Successful IS Auditor   1

Chapter 2   Audit Process   47

Chapter 3   IT Governance   89

Chapter 4   Networking Technology   143

Chapter 5   Life Cycle Management   197

Chapter 6   IT Service Delivery   249

Chapter 7   Information Asset Protection   277

Chapter 8   Disaster Recovery and Business Continuity   339

Glossary   381

Index   *407*

Contents

Introduction   *xix*

Assessment Test   *xxxvii*

Chapter   1   Secrets of a Successful IS Auditor   1

Demands for IS Audit   2
   Understanding Policies, Standards, Guidelines,
     and Procedures   3
   Understanding the ISACA Code of Professional Ethics   4
   Understanding the Purpose of an Audit   6
   Understanding the Auditor's Responsibility   6
Auditor Role vs. Auditee Role   6
   Applying an Independence Test   7
   Understanding the Various Auditing Standards   8
   Identifying the Types of Audits   11
Auditor Is an Executive Position   12
   Understanding the Importance of Auditor Confidentiality   13
   Working with Lawyers   14
   Retaining Audit Documentation   14
   Providing Good Communication and Integration   15
   Understanding Leadership Duties   15
   Planning and Setting Priorities   16
   Providing Standard Terms of Reference   17
   Dealing with Conflicts and Failures   17
   Identifying the Value of Internal and External Auditors   18
   Understanding the Evidence Rule   18
   Identifying Who You Need to Interview   19
Understanding the Corporate Organizational Structure   21
   Identifying Roles in a Corporate Organizational Structure   21
   Identifying Roles in a Consulting Firm
     Organizational Structure   22
Managing Projects   23
   What Is a Project?   25
   What Is Project Management?   26
   Identifying the Requirements of a Project Manager   27
   Identifying a Project Manager's Authority   27
   Understanding the Project Management
     Process Framework   28
   Using Project Management Diagramming Techniques   37
Summary   38

	Exam Essentials	39
	Review Questions	41
	Answers to Review Questions	45

Chapter 2	**Audit Process**	**47**
	Establishing and Approving an Audit Charter	48
	Role of the Audit Committee	50
	Engagement Letter	51
	Preplanning the Audit	51
	Identifying Restrictions on Scope	53
	Planning Detailed Audit Objectives	54
	Risk Management Strategy	55
	Performing an Audit Risk Assessment	57
	Determining Whether an Audit Is Possible	58
	Performing the Audit	59
	Allocating Staffing	59
	Ensuring Audit Quality Control	60
	Defining Auditee Communications	60
	Using Data Collection Techniques	61
	Reviewing Existing Controls	63
	Identifying Audit Evidence	65
	Types of Evidence	65
	Grading Evidence	66
	Timing of Evidence	67
	Evidence Life Cycle	68
	Typical Evidence for IS Audits	70
	Using Evidence to Prove a Point	71
	Preparing Audit Documentation	71
	Selecting Audit Samples	72
	Identifying Audit Testing	73
	Using Computer Assisted Audit Tools	74
	Detecting Irregularities and Illegal Acts	76
	Reporting Your Audit Findings	78
	Identifying Omitted Procedures	79
	Conducting an Exit Interview	79
	Conducting Follow-Up Activities	79
	Traditional Audit Compared to Control Self-Assessments	80
	Summary	80
	Exam Essentials	81
	Review Questions	83
	Answers to Review Questions	87

Chapter   3   IT Governance   89

Strategy in Organizational Control   90
   Overview of the IT Steering Committee   91
   Selecting an IT Strategy   96
   Specifying a Policy   96
   Planning the IT Strategy   98
   Identifying Sourcing Locations   100
   Conducting an Executive Performance Review   103
   Understanding the Auditor's Interest in the Strategy   103
Overview of Tactical Management   103
Planning and Performance   104
   Management Control Methods   104
   Project Management   107
   Risk Management   107
   Implementing Standards   109
   Human Resources   111
   System Life-Cycle Management   112
   Continuity Planning   112
   Insurance   112
   Performance Management   113
Overview of Business Process Reengineering   114
   Why Use Business Process Reengineering   114
   BPR Goals   115
   BPR Principles   115
   BPR Steps   116
   Benchmarking as a BPR Tool   116
   BPR Project Risk Assessment   117
   Business Process Controls to Consider   118
   Knowledge Requirements for BPR   119
   The Practical Application of BPR   119
   Conducting a Business Impact Analysis   121
   Practical Selection Methods for BPR   123
   A Practical Approach to the BPR Project   124
Tactical Management   127
Operations Management   127
   Supporting IT Goals   127
   Sustaining Operations   128
   Understanding Personnel Roles and Responsibilities 128
   Using Compensating Controls   132
   Tracking Performance   132
   Controlling Change   133
   Understanding the Auditor's Interest in
     Operational Delivery   133

Summary   134
Exam Essentials   134
Review Questions   136
Answers to Review Questions   140

Chapter   4   Networking Technology   143

Understanding the Differences in Computer Architecture   144
Comparing Single Processor and Multiprocessor Systems   148
    Identifying Various Operating Systems   148
    Selecting the Best Computer   151
    Comparing Computer Capabilities   153
    Processing vs. System Control   154
    Dealing with Data Storage   155
    Protecting Port Controls and Port Access   157
Overview of the Open Systems Interconnect (OSI) Model   158
    Layer 1: Physical Layer   160
    Layer 2: Data-Link Layer   160
    Layer 3: Network Layer   162
    Layer 4: Transport Layer   164
    Layer 5: Session Layer   164
    Layer 6: Presentation Layer   165
    Layer 7: Application Layer   166
    Understanding How Computers Communicate   167
Physical Network Design   168
Overview of Network Topologies   169
    Identifying Bus Topologies   169
    Identifying Star Topologies   169
    Identifying Ring Topologies   171
    Identifying Meshed Networks   171
Network Cable Types   173
    Unshielded Twisted-Pair (UTP) Cable   173
    Coaxial Cable   174
    Fiber-Optic Cable   174
Network Devices   174
Network Services   177
    Domain Name Service   177
    Dynamic Host Configuration Protocol   177
Expanding the Network   180
    Wireless Access Solutions   183
    Summarizing the Various Area Networks   185
Managing Your Network   186
    Syslog   186
    Automated Cable Tester   187

Protocol Analyzer	187
Simple Network Management Protocol	187
Remote Monitoring Protocol Version 2	188
Summary	188
Exam Essentials	189
Review Questions	191
Answers to Review Questions	195

Chapter 5	**Life Cycle Management**	**197**
	Governance in Software Development	198
	Managing Software Quality	199
	Capability Maturity Model	199
	International Organization for Standardization	200
	Overview of Steering Committees	202
	Identifying Critical Success Factors	202
	Using the Scenario Approach	203
	Aligning Software to Business Needs	203
	Change Management	206
	Managing the Software Project	207
	Choosing an Approach	207
	Using Traditional Project Management	208
	Overview of the System Development Life Cycle	210
	Phase 1: Feasibility Study	212
	Phase 2: Requirements Definition	215
	Phase 3: System Design	218
	Phase 4: Development	219
	Phase 5: Implementation	227
	Phase 6: Post-implementation	230
	Overview of Data Architecture	231
	Databases	231
	Database Transaction Integrity	236
	Decision Support Systems	236
	Presenting DSS Data	238
	Using Artificial Intelligence	238
	Program Architecture	238
	Centralization vs. Decentralization	239
	Electronic E-commerce	239
	Summary	240
	Exam Essentials	240
	Review Questions	243
	Answers to Review Questions	247

Chapter   6   IT Service Delivery   249

IT Operations   250
Using the IT Balanced Scorecard   252
 Using Metrics   253
 Help Desk   256
 Service-Level Management   256
Monitoring Controls   257
 System Access Controls   257
 Data File Controls   259
 Application Processing Controls   260
 Maintenance Controls   262
Change Management   262
 Software Release and Patch Management   263
 Configuration Control   264
 Change Authorization   264
 Emergency Changes   264
 Management Controls   264
System Monitoring   266
Network Management   266
Capacity Management   266
Problem Management   267
IT Performance Indicators   268
Summary   268
Exam Essentials   269
Review Questions   270
Answers to Review Questions   274

Chapter   7   Information Asset Protection   277

Understanding the Threat   278
 Examples of Threats and Computer Crimes   279
 Identifying the Perpetrators   281
 Overview of Attack Methods   283
Using Administrative Protection   288
 Information Security Management   288
 IT Security Governance   289
 Authority Roles over Data   290
 Identify Data Retention Requirements   291
 Document Access Paths   291
 Personnel Management   292
Implementing Physical Protection   295
 Data Processing Locations   296
 Environmental Controls   296
 Safe Storage   302

Using Technical Protection 303
Technical Control Classification 304
Application Software Controls 304
Authentication Methods 305
Network Access Protection 311
Intrusion Detection 317
Encryption Methods 321
Public-Key Infrastructure 325
Network Security Protocols 327
Design for Redundancy 328
Telephone Security 329
Technical Self-Assessment 330
Summary 330
Exam Essentials 330
Review Questions 332
Answers to Review Questions 336

Chapter   8   Disaster Recovery and Business Continuity   339

Defining Disaster Recovery 340
Surviving Financial Challenges 340
Valuing Brand Names 341
Rebuilding after a Disaster 341
Defining the Purpose of Business Continuity 341
Uniting Other Plans with Business Continuity 344
Identifying the Business Continuity Planning Phases 345
Phase 1—Initiation 348
Phase 2—Risk Analysis 350
Phase 3—Business Impact Analysis (BIA) 354
Phase 4—Strategy Selection 356
Phase 5—Emergency Response 362
Phase 6—Plan Creation 365
Phase 7—Training and Awareness 369
Phase 8—Maintain and Test 369
Phase 9—Crisis Communications 370
Phase 10—Integration with Other Plans 372
Summary 372
Exam Essentials 373
Review Questions 375
Answers to Review Questions 379

Glossary   381

Index   *407*

Introduction

This book is designed for anyone interested in taking the Certified Information Systems Auditor (CISA) exam. The CISA certification is one of the hottest in the market, with annual growth in excess of 28 percent, according to the Information Systems Audit and Control Association (ISACA), the administering organization.

It is a trend worldwide for organizations to have to implement and prove the existence of strong internal controls. You may have heard of a few of these, such as the Basel II accord in banking, the Sarbanes-Oxley Act for public corporations, the Federal Information Security Management Act (FISMA), and the Health Insurance Portability and Accountability Act (HIPAA). These are just four of more than twenty high-profile regulations that demand audited proof of internal controls. Frankly, these result in a long list of opportunities for a CISA. This may be the opportunity that you have been looking for, especially if you come from a background of finance or technology.

What is the job market for certified IS auditors? The CISA world is exploding. Corporations are hiring more consultants than ever before in an effort to obtain compliance before they get caught short. Consulting companies are hiring as many people as they can represent as qualified in an effort to service the same corporations. Small organizations are finding themselves at a competitive disadvantage if they're unable to demonstrate the same level of internal controls to their larger customers. One of the fundamental rules of auditing is that participating in the remediation (fixing) of problems found during the audit would compromise the auditor's independence. Under the rules of independence, the independent auditor must remain independent to certify the results as valid. A second, unrelated auditor should work on the remediation. The requirements for regulatory compliance are ongoing, and that means remediation at some level will be ongoing too. This means that the auditor requirement is actually doubled. The opportunity for you is right now.

For many years, organizations have undergone the scrutiny of financial audits. As financial systems have become more and more complex, automation has introduced a situation in which the integrity of financial records may be in question. An organization would hire a certified public accountant to review their financial records and attest to their integrity. Larger organizations would hire certified internal auditors to assist with normal internal controls of the business. Now, the long list of regulations requiring internal controls has focused attention on the information systems. Computers are now the house in which the financial records live. The CISA is the top credential for auditing IS and related internal controls.

This book is designed to help you become a well-respected CISA. We have been teaching CISA classes for several years and have some truly outstanding success stories. The test alone is a stepping stone in your career. Our goal is to take you through the CISA test better than anyone else by showing you the "how and why" of IS auditing. If you are familiar with technology, this book will help you understand how the auditor must act to be successful. If you come from a financial background, we're going to take you through an introductory tour of technology. Our explanations are technically correct and designed to be simple to understand.

There are many opinions about how the information systems audit should be performed. This book covers the official auditing standards necessary for you to be successful. You'll find that this book contains the majority of information necessary to operate a successful consulting practice. Initially our focus is on helping you pass your exam. This information will help you earn a great deal more than just a paper certificate, if you apply it.

Each chapter in this book has been arranged in a logical sequence focusing on a practical application. ISACA produces fine materials written by committees of authors. We have chosen to take a different route. We have written the material in this book in the sequence that we would use to teach you prior to an audit engagement. Every point that you read will carry through to the subsequent pages of this Study Guide. The analogy is comparable to building a pyramid. You'll start with gaining a firm understanding of the basics and build your way up into the advanced material. We strongly suggest that you read the book in sequence, without skipping ahead.

One of our complaints about other study material is that it simply represents a brain dump of answers or contains excessive redundancy. We have tried our best to present the material in an orderly fashion and to provide supporting examples.

What Is the CISA Certification?

ISACA offers the most recognized certification in the world for IS auditors. The CISA certification is recognized worldwide by all corporations and governments. ISACA has more than 45,000 members in over 140 countries. ISACA is recognized as the leader in IT governance, control, and assurance. The association was founded in 1969, with an objective to develop international IS auditing and control standards. As a result, it has created the number one information systems audit certification in the world, the Certified Information Systems Auditor (CISA).

ISACA controls and administers the CISA exam worldwide. Over 40,000 professionals have earned their CISA to date. Still, the demand exceeds the supply.

Why Become a CISA?

So, why become a CISA? The answer: credibility and opportunity. Many people proclaim themselves to be IS auditors. The majority of uncertified auditors are no more than well-meaning individuals who habitually violate the official audit standards. Here is a short list of the benefits associated with becoming a CISA:

Demonstrates proof of professional achievement   The CISA certification provides evidence that you have prior experience and are able to pass a rigorous certification exam. The exam tests your knowledge of auditing practices related to information systems. The test itself is loaded with technical challenges that require a significant understanding of technology. The CISA certification shows that you understand the audit requirements and are able to lead a successful audit in accordance with widely accepted audit practices. The certification demonstrates to the world that your experience represents a significant value.

Provides an assurance of quality to your clients   Audit clients are a demanding breed of individuals. The fate of their organization may rest on the findings detailed in the auditor's report. There is little room for mistakes. The CISA credential indicates that you are a person who can be trusted to deliver accurate results. Who would you trust to represent yourself: a person with no proof, or someone who can demonstrate a measure of their credibility? The person reading the audit report needs to understand that your work is accurate. They will direct capital and resources to be expended according to the report you provide. The CISA certification represents a third-party audit of your personal knowledge. It helps prove your credibility.

Increases your marketability   The IS audit market is exploding at a phenomenal rate. The CISA credential helps separate you from the mass of self-proclaimed auditors. Many organizations regard the CISA as the hallmark of professionalism. There is no better way to attract the favorable attention of management. It does not matter if you're internal or external to the organization—the credential speaks for itself. The requirements called for in government regulations are becoming a growing concern for executives. Your customer may not understand all the details necessary to describe the job of an auditor; however, your client will recognize that an auditor with the CISA certification should be able to fulfill their needs.

Provides a greater opportunity for advancement   Every organization strives to hire good people who are motivated. What does the lack of certification say about someone? Is it that they are unmotivated? Could it be that they are not capable? Or is it simply that they are afraid to try? No manager in their right mind would promote an individual who has not proven their value. Taking the time to get trained and certified shows the world that you are motivated, that you are somebody who wants to get things done. That trait alone can get you promoted. Instead of using words to describe your ability, you can prove it with your CISA credential. People will know that you're serious about your job and will treat you accordingly.

Builds respect and confidence from other people   The world today is extremely specialized. Consider that many things of premium value in today's world are certified. We have certified used cars, certified mail, certified public accountants, certified travel agents, certified lawyers, and even certified Subway sandwich artists. The people you meet may not completely understand what is involved in being a CISA. However, they will understand that you have expended time and energy to obtain the certification. You will gain their respect because of the effort you've demonstrated. If given the choice, almost everyone would choose to use a person who is certified. The CISA is a major step toward the widespread credibility that you desire.

How to Become a CISA

The CISA designation is given to individuals who have demonstrated their ability to fulfill the following five requirements:

Pass the CISA exam   The CISA examination is offered two times a year, once in June and again in December. You have to register for the test three months before it is administered. You can register online at www.isaca.org or by mail. You take the test with pencil and paper in front of a live test proctor. The examination is 200 multiple-choice questions that will take approximately 4 hours. A grade of 75 percent is required to pass the CISA examination. There is a 4-hour time limit.

Professional experience in information systems auditing, control, or security   To qualify for certification, you must demonstrate five years of IS auditing experience. ISACA will accept up to two years of substitution toward the work experience requirement, as follows:

    Related experience substitution   You can substitute a maximum of one year of experience from financial or operational auditing, or from information systems experience.

College credit hour substitution   The equivalent of an associate or bachelor's degree can be substituted for one or two years, respectively (60 hours or 120 hours).

University instructor experience substitution   A full-time university instructor can substitute two years of on-the-job experience toward one year of the IS auditing control or security requirement.

Your CISA test results are valid for five years from the examination date. Even without any experience at this time, you can take the examination. Certification will be awarded only after you have provided verification of desired work experience (of five years or the equivalent). ISACA limits acceptable experience to that which has occurred within 10 years prior to your application date.

Continuous adherence to ISACA's code of professional ethics   Trust and integrity are paramount to the auditor's profession. You will be required to pledge your ongoing support for adherence to the IS auditor's code of professional ethics.

Continuing education in the profession   You are required to continuously improve your skills. Continuing education is the best method of maintaining an individual's competency. Learning new skills will improve your professional abilities. Demonstrating a commitment to continuing education differentiates qualified CISAs from those who have not fulfilled their professional responsibilities. You will be required to demonstrate a minimum of 20 contact hours of training each year, which must total 120 contact hours in a three-year period.

Adherence to well-established IS auditing standards   The purpose of auditing standards is to ensure quality and consistency. An auditor who fails to meet the standards places themselves and the profession in peril. ISACA provides excellent information to guide auditors through their professional responsibilities. The auditing standards are based on well-recognized professional practices applied worldwide.

Why Should I Buy This Book?

If you're serious about becoming a professional CISA auditor, you should buy this book to study for your exam. If you're curious about becoming an auditor, you should buy this book to learn how the job is actually done.

This book is unique in the field of IS auditing. You will benefit from this book by learning the methods necessary to be a successful auditor. Each chapter builds step-by-step toward obtaining your goal. This book provides important details about how to accomplish your job, the exam objectives for each chapter, and all of the most important auditing concepts.

How to Use This Book and CD

This book is organized into eight chapters. Each begins with a list of chapter objectives that relate directly to the CISA exam.

An "Exam Essentials" section appears near the end of every chapter to highlight the topics that you're likely to encounter during your exam. These exam essentials are intended to provide guiding thoughts rather than a laundry list of details. Our goal is to help you focus on the higher-level objectives from each chapter as you move into the next chapter.

At the end of every chapter are 20 review questions with explanations. You can use these review questions to help gauge your level of understanding and better focus your study effort. As you finish each chapter, you should review the questions and check whether your answers are correct. If not, you should really read the section again. Look up any incorrect answers and research why you may have missed the question. It may be a case of failing to read the question and properly considering each of the possible answers. It could also be that you did not understand the information. Either way, going through the chapter a second time would be valuable.

We have included several other testing features in the book and on the companion CD. Following this introduction is an Assessment Test that will help you gauge your study requirements. Take this test before you start reading the book. It will help you identify areas that are critical to your success. The answers to the assessment test appear after the last question. Each question includes a short explanation with information directing you to the appropriate chapter for more information.

Included on this book's CD are two bonus exams of 60 questions each. In addition, there are more than 150 flash cards. You should use this Study Guide in combination with your other materials to prepare for the exam.

Take these practice exams as if you were taking the real exam. Just sit down and start the exam without using any reference material. We suggest that you study the material in this book in conjunction with the related ISACA references on IS auditing standards. The official CISA exam is very challenging. Most individuals will barely finish the exam before time runs out. Fortunately for you, our students have a high success rate. You have it within you to become the next certified CISA.

You are ready for your CISA exam when you score higher than 90 percent on the practice examinations and chapter reviews.

A copy of this book is on the CD in Adobe Acrobat PDF format for easy reading on any computer.

 In addition to the materials on the CD, we have included some bonus materials on this book's page at www.sybex.com.

Test Taking and Preparation

The CISA examination is quite difficult unless you are prepared. Preparation requires good study habits and a well-planned schedule. You should review your notes at least 30 minutes per night, but not more than 2 hours per day. Cramming for this examination will not work.

Let's discuss preparations leading up to test day—specifically, the best method to arrange your schedule for that ace grade.

10-Day Countdown

Review each chapter in your Study Guide. Give extra attention to the subjects that you may have skimmed over earlier. The test is written from the viewpoint of an auditor, using directives from ISACA's world.

Number one hint: Make sure you are reading from the auditor's perspective.

You should review the flash cards on the accompanying CD. It is also an excellent technique to make your own flashcards by using 3 × 5 index cards. Take a dozen or two dozen to the office each day for random practice between meetings.

Be sure to run through the Bonus Exams on the CD. They are less difficult than the real test, but still a good resource to see where you stand. The value of these tests is in improving your resilience and accuracy.

Be sure to request a day of rest. Ask your boss for personal time. Use vacation time if necessary. Most employers will understand after you remind them of the limited testing dates.

3-Day Countdown

The exam location may be in a hotel, college, or convention center. It will save you a great deal of time and stress to drive over to visit the test site. You should do this even if you have been there recently. The room number for your test will be printed on your exam acceptance letter. Make it a point to locate the meeting room and physically walk up to touch the door. In colleges, it is possible that room 300 is a significant walk away from room 302. Arriving at the wrong building can ruin your day if it makes you late to the exam.

Convention centers are worse. Unknown to you, there may be a big trade convention over the upcoming weekend. Such an event will change the availability of parking in the area. It will also affect the long route you may have to walk in order to enter the examination room.

We suggest you scout the area for a nearby place to eat breakfast. Plan to eat healthy before the exam begins.

1-Day Countdown

The best aid to a high score is to take off early on Friday. Remember the exam is early on Saturday morning. Make a pact with your friends and family to leave you alone all day Friday. You may consider limiting your diet to simple foods, avoiding anything that is different than usual. This is not the time to experiment.

Make a pact with yourself: There are no errands or chores more important than passing the exam.

Go to bed earlier than usual. Do whatever it takes. You will need to be up and totally focused by 6 a.m. Try to go to bed by 10 p.m. Set two alarm clocks to get up on time. Put your favorite study materials together in a carrying bag. You will take them with you to the exam for a final glance before being seated for the test. The exam is a "closed book" test.

Do not attempt to cram on Friday night; it will work against you in a long test like the CISA. Just review your notes again. Be sure to run through the flash cards and chapter review questions.

We suggest people with a technical background review Chapter 2, "Audit Process," twice. If you have a financial background, the best advice is to reread Chapter 4, "Networking Technology," and Chapter 7, "Information Asset Protection." Practicing drawing the diagrams and models on a separate sheet of paper will help you understand the specific wording of questions and make it easier to select the correct answer.

Test Morning

Time to get up and get yourself moving. Be sure to arrive at the exam early. Test room locations have been known to change overnight, especially at college locations.

After arrival, you can sit in the hallway while you wait. This is an excellent time to make a final review of your notes. There is no advantage to being seated before 7:30 a.m. Just park yourself within a few feet of the door to ensure that you are not forgotten or missed. You can expect a long line at some test locations. Major cities may have 200–300 people sitting in different rooms.

Upon entering the room, ask if you can draw inside the test booklet. Tell the proctor you like to make longhand notes when solving problems. Usually the booklet will never be reused, so you can mark in it all day long.

You can make notes to yourself in the booklet and mark your favorite answer, and then just transfer the answer from the test booklet to the answer sheet. This technique really helps if you start jumping around or choose to skip a question for later. Consider drawing useful diagrams like the OSI model on the inside back cover of the booklet. The proctor will tell you that only answers on the answer sheet will count toward your score.

Plan on Using All Four Hours

You should expect the test to take the entire four hours. It is advisable to plan ahead for both pace and breaks. The exam proctor will usually allow you to take restroom breaks as long as you do not talk to anyone about the exam while out of the room. You might find it helpful to reduce fatigue by just taking a walk to the restroom and then splashing water on your face. One trip per hour seems to work for us.

Read the Question Carefully

Read each question *very* carefully! The questions are intentionally worded differently from this Study Guide. For overly confusing questions or ones that you are not sure of, try reading them twice or even three times.

On the first pass, circle the operative points in the question, such as the words *not, is, best, and, or,* and so on. Next, underline the nouns or the subject of the question. For example, if the question is "The purpose of controls is to…," you would underlining *purpose* and circle the word *is.*

On the second pass, ensure that you understand the implied direction of the question and its subject. Is the question a positive (*is*) or negative (*is not*) implication? Watch for meanings that are positive, negative, inclusive, or exclusive. A common test question-writing technique is to imply terminology associations that should not exist or vice versa. Do not violate the intent of the question or answer. Most people fail a question by misreading it.

On the third pass, dissect the available answers by using a similar method. Watch for conflicting meaning or wrong intent.

Place a star next to any question in the booklet when you have doubts about your answer. You can return to the question before turning in your answer sheet. (This keeps your answer sheet clean of any stray marks).

For your final check, you can compare the answers marked in the test booklet to your answer sheet. Remember that there is no penalty for wrong answers. Do not leave any blank. Just take a guess if you must.

Done! The Exam Is Over

Plan for a relaxing activity with your family or friends after the exam. We suggest you plan something that is fun and doesn't require mental concentration; you will be mentally worn out after the exam. Do not punish yourself by looking up the answers for a particular test question. The test is over.

You should receive your score from ISACA in about four to six weeks. It may be by email or a simple one-page letter.

We wish you all the best. Good luck on your exam.

Related Professional Certifications

Although this book focuses on ISACA's Certified Information Systems Auditor (CISA) certification, there are many more certifications you should consider for your professional advancement. This section offers a sampling of the more commonly known professional certifications that cover many of the same topics that the CISA does. This list is not inclusive of all certifications. It focuses only on vendor-neutral certification, which provides an unbiased view of the issues facing all vendors and customers

It is important to be able to separate performance claims (smoke) from truly effective function (results). Results are measured by highest effect on the ultimate need and not by the use of a particular computer software package. There is a big difference between managing and just being an application operator. Persons with the following certifications should be versed in the basics for success in their field.

Information Systems Security Practices

The following certifications are focused on IS security topics:

Certified Information Systems Security Professional (CISSP)   This exam, administered by the International Information Systems Security Certification Consortium, or (ISC)², covers the 10 knowledge areas of information security. Certification requires passing the exam plus five years of IS security experience. More information can be obtained from the consortium's website (www.isc2.org).

Systems Security Certified Practitioner (SSCP)   This exam, administered by (ISC)², covers 7 of the 10 knowledge areas of information security. Certification requires passing the exam plus two years of IS security experience. SSCP is a subset of the CISSP subject material. Cert-Test recommends you attend the CISSP course to ensure you receive all the training necessary for your future.

Certified Information Security Manager (CISM)   This exam, administered by ISACA, covers the risk management areas governing IS security. Certification requires passing the exam plus five years of experience in IS auditing, control, or security.

Security+   This exam, administered by the Computing Technology Industry Association, or CompTIA (www.comptia.org), is an entry-level security certification. It covers a fraction of the topics covered in the CISSP certification.

Auditing

In addition to the CISA, a few of the other certifications focus on auditing, include the following:

Certified Internal Auditor (CIA)   This certification, administered by The Institute of Internal Auditors (www.theiia.org), requires passing a four-part exam. The exams may be taken separately or combined in any order. Each part is 125 multiple-choice questions. In addition, candidates must have a bachelor's degree or equivalent, plus 24 months of internal auditing experience.

Certified Fraud Examiner (CFE)   This certification, administered by the Association of Certified Fraud Examiners (www.acfe.org), requires passing the exam plus a bachelor's degree and two years of fraud detection–related work experience in the areas of accounting, auditing, fraud investigation, criminology, loss prevention, or law.

Information Assessment Methodology (IAM)   This certification, administered by the US National Security Agency (www.nsa.gov), requires US citizenship with at least two years of experience in information system security and/or IS auditing. Originally created by presidential executive order and now mandated by US Homeland Security Directive/HSPD-7, the certification is designed for system administrators and auditors working on government systems, critical infrastructure, and commercial systems.

Information Evaluation Methodology (IEM)   This is a new certification that extends the IAM to include technical evaluation of IS systems by using the official NSA evaluation methodology. It is also administered by the US National Security Agency.

Disaster Recovery and Business Continuity

The following certifications focus on disaster recovery and business continuity topics:

Associate Business Continuity Professional (ABCP)   This certification, administered by the Disaster Recovery Institute International, or DRII (www.drii.org), covers the 10 best practices of disaster recovery and business continuity. The Associate covers the same material as the CBCP, but does not require any work experience.

Certified Business Continuity Professional (CBCP)   This certification, also administered by DRII, requires passing the CBCP exam, plus you must have two years of experience as a business continuity/disaster recovery planner.

Master Business Continuity Professional (MBCP)   This certification, also administered by DRII, requires participation in the DRII Masters program along with passing a qualifying exam and then the MBCP exam. You must also have five years of practical experience.

Fellow of the Business Continuity Institute (FBCI)   This certification, administered by the Business Continuity Institute (www.theBCI.org), is based on a points-scoring system.

Project Management

The following certifications focus on project management:

Certified Associate in Project Management (CAPM)   This certification, administered by the Project Management Institute (www.pmi.org), requires passing the CAPM exam plus 23 hours of formal PMI training and 1,500 hours of project management–related work experience. The CAPM test covers a reduced version of the PMP content areas. CertTest recommends the CAPM candidate follow the PMP study curriculum to ensure you receive the training necessary for your future success.

Project Management Professional (PMP)   This certification, also administered by the Project Management Institute, covers 44 process areas of project management. Certification requires passing the PMP exam plus 35 hours of formal PMI training and 4,500 hours of project management–related work experience. In addition, you must have a college degree, or 7,500 hours of experience and a high school diploma.

Project+   This entry-level certification is administered by CompTIA. Certification is obtained by passing one exam. No work experience is required.

Physical Building Security

The following certifications focus on physical building security topics:

Physical Security Professional (PSP)   This certification, administered by the American Society for Industrial Security (www.asisonline.org), requires passing the exam plus a high school diploma and five years of security-related work experience.

Certified Protection Professional (CPP)   This certification, also administered by the American Society for Industrial Security, requires passing the exam plus a bachelor's degree and nine years of security-related work experience, three of which must be in security management.

CertTest Training Center, the training center we teach at, offers many classes for a number of these certifications. In addition, we offer a SuperHERO course, which covers project management, IS security, and business continuity. For more information, visit our website at www.certtest.com.

CISA Exam Objectives

Objective	Chapter
Content Area 1: IS Audit Process	
1.1 Develop and implement a risk-based IS audit strategy for the organization in compliance with IS audit standards, guidelines and best practices.	2
1.2 Plan specific audits to ensure that IT and business systems are protected and controlled.	2
1.3 Conduct audits in accordance with IS audit standards, guidelines and best practices to meet planned audit objectives.	1
1.4 Communicate emerging issues, potential risks, and audit results to key stakeholders. 1.5 Advise on the implementation of risk management and control practices within the organization while maintaining independence.	1
1.5 Advise on the implementation of risk management and control practices within the organization, while maintaining independence.	2
Knowledge Statements	
1.1 Knowledge of ISACA IS Auditing Standards, Guidelines and Procedures and Code of Professional Ethics	1
1.2 Knowledge of IS auditing practices and techniques	2
1.3 Knowledge of techniques to gather information and preserve evidence (e.g., observation, inquiry, interview, CAATs, electronic media)	2
1.4 Knowledge of the evidence life cycle (e.g., the collection, protection, chain of custody)	2
1.5 Knowledge of control objectives and controls related to IS (e.g., CoBIT)	2
1.6 Knowledge of risk assessment in an audit context	2
1.7 Knowledge of audit planning and management techniques	2
1.8 Knowledge of reporting and communication techniques (e.g., facilitation, negotiation, conflict resolution)	2
1.9 Knowledge of control self-assessment (CSA)	2
1.10 Knowledge of continuous audit techniques	2
Content Area 2: IT Governance	
2.1 Evaluate the effectiveness of IT governance structure to ensure adequate board control over the decisions, directions, and performance of IT so that it supports the organization's strategies and objectives.	3

2.2 Evaluate IT organizational structure and human resources (personnel) management to ensure that they support the organization's strategies and objectives.   3

2.3 Evaluate the IT strategy and the process for its development, approval, implementation, and maintenance to ensure that it supports the organization's strategies and objectives.   3

2.4 Evaluate the organization's IT policies, standards, and procedures; and the processes for their development, approval, implementation, and maintenance to ensure that they support the IT strategy and comply with regulatory and legal requirements.   3

2.5 Evaluate management practices to ensure compliance with the organization's IT strategy, policies, standards, and procedures.   3

2.6 Evaluate IT resource investment, use, and allocation practices to ensure alignment with the organization's strategies and objectives.   3

2.7 Evaluate IT contracting strategies and policies, and contract management practices to ensure that they support the organization's strategies and objectives.   3

2.8 Evaluate risk management practices to ensure that the organization's IT related risks are properly managed.   6

2.9 Evaluate monitoring and assurance practices to ensure that the board and executive management receive sufficient and timely information about IT performance.   6

Knowledge Statements

2.1 Knowledge of the purpose of IT strategies, policies, standards and procedures for an organization and the essential elements of each   1

2.2 Knowledge of IT governance frameworks   1

2.3 Knowledge of the processes for the development, implementation and maintenance of IT strategies, policies, standards and procedures (e.g., protection of information assets, business continuity and disaster recovery, systems and infrastructure lifecycle management, IT service delivery and support)   1

2.4 Knowledge of quality management strategies and policies   3

2.5 Knowledge of organizational structure, roles and responsibilities related to the use and management of IT   3

2.6 Knowledge of generally accepted international IT standards and guidelines   1

2.7 Knowledge of enterprise IT architecture and its implications for setting long-term strategic directions   4

2.8 Knowledge of risk management methodologies and tools   3

2.9 Knowledge of the use of control frameworks (e.g., CoBIT, COSO, ISO 17799)   3

2.10 Knowledge of the use of maturity and process improvement models (e.g., CMM, CobiT)   3

2.11 Knowledge of contracting strategies, processes and contract management practices   6

2.12 Knowledge of practices for monitoring and reporting of IT performance (e.g., balanced scorecards, key performance indicators [KPI])   6

2.13 Knowledge of relevant legislative and regulatory issues (e.g., privacy, intellectual property, corporate governance requirements)   1

2.14 Knowledge of IT human resources (personnel) management   3

2.15 Knowledge of IT resource investment and allocation practices (e.g., portfolio management return on investment (ROI))   3

Content Area 3: Systems and Infrastructure Lifecycle Management

3.1 Evaluate the business case for the proposed system development/acquisition to ensure that it meets the organization's business goals.   5

3.2 Evaluate the project management framework and project governance practices to ensure that business objectives are achieved in a cost-effective manner while managing risks to the organization.   5

3.3 Perform reviews to ensure that a project is progressing in accordance with project plans, is adequately supported by documentation and status reporting is accurate.   5

3.4 Evaluate proposed control mechanisms for systems and/or infrastructure during specification, development/acquisition, and testing to ensure that they will provide safeguards and comply with the organization's policies and other requirements.   5

3.5 Evaluate the processes by which systems and/or infrastructure are developed/acquired and tested to ensure that the deliverables meet the organization's objectives.   5

3.6 Evaluate the readiness of the system and/or infrastructure for implementation and migration into production.   5

3.7 Perform post-implementation review of systems and/or infrastructure to ensure that they meet the organization's objectives and are subject to effective internal control.   5

3.8 Perform periodic reviews of systems and/or infrastructure to ensure that they continue to meet the organization's objectives and are subject to effective internal control.　5

3.9 Evaluate the process by which systems and/or infrastructure are maintained to ensure the continued support of the organization's objectives and are subject to effective internal control.　5

3.10 Evaluate the process by which systems and/or infrastructure are disposed of to ensure that they comply with the organization's policies and procedures.　5

Knowledge Statements

3.1 Knowledge of benefits management practices, (e.g., feasibility studies, business cases)　5

3.2 Knowledge of project governance mechanisms (e.g., steering committee, project oversight board)　5

3.3 Knowledge of project management practices, tools, and control frameworks　1, 5

3.4 Knowledge of risk management practices applied to projects　5

3.5 Knowledge of project success criteria and risks　5

3.6 Knowledge of configuration, change and release management in relation to development and maintenance of systems and/or infrastructure　5

3.7 Knowledge of control objectives and techniques that ensure the completeness, accuracy, validity, and authorization of transactions and data within IT systems applications　5

3.8 Knowledge of enterprise architecture related to data, applications, and technology (e.g., distributed applications, web-based applications, web services, n-tier applications)　5

3.9 Knowledge of requirements analysis and management practices (e.g., requirements verification, traceability, gap analysis)　5

3.10 Knowledge of acquisition and contract management processes (e.g., evaluation of vendors, preparation of contracts, vendor management, escrow)　5

3.11 Knowledge of system development methodologies and tools and an understanding of their strengths and weaknesses (e.g., agile development practices, prototyping, rapid application development [RAD], object-oriented design techniques)　5

3.12 Knowledge of quality assurance methods　5

3.13 Knowledge of the management of testing processes (e.g., test strategies, test plans, test environments, entry and exit criteria)　5

3.14 Knowledge of data conversion tools, techniques, and procedures   5

3.15 Knowledge of system and/or infrastructure disposal procedures   5

3.16 Knowledge of software and hardware certification and accreditation   5
practices

3.17 Knowledge of post-implementation review objectives and methods   5
(e.g., project closure, benefits realization, performance measurement)

3.18 Knowledge of system migration and infrastructure deployment practices   5

Content Area 4: IT Service Delivery and Support

4.1 Evaluate service level management practices to ensure that the level of service   6
from internal and external service providers is defined and managed.

4.2 Evaluate operations management to ensure that IT support functions   6
effectively meet business needs.

4.3 Evaluate data administration practices to ensure the integrity and   6
optimization of databases.

4.4 Evaluate the use of capacity and performance monitoring tools and   6
techniques to ensure that IT services meet the organization's objectives.

4.5 Evaluate change, configuration, and release management practices to ensure   6
that changes made to the organization's production environment are adequately
controlled and documented.

4.6 Evaluate problem and incident management practices to ensure that incidents,   6
problems, or errors are recorded, analyzed, and resolved in a timely manner.

4.7 Evaluate the functionality of the IT infrastructure (e.g., network   4
components, hardware, system software) to ensure that it supports the
organization's objectives.

Knowledge Statements

4.1 Knowledge of service level management practices   6

4.2 Knowledge of operations management best practices (e.g., workload   6
scheduling, network services management, preventive maintenance)

4.3 Knowledge of systems performance monitoring processes, tools, and   4
techniques (e.g., network analyzers, system utilization reports, load balancing)

4.4 Knowledge of the functionality of hardware and network components (e.g.,   4
routers, switches, firewalls, peripherals)

4.5 Knowledge of database administration practices   5

4.6 Knowledge of the functionality of system software including operating systems, utilities, and database management systems   4, 5

4.7 Knowledge of capacity planning and monitoring techniques   4

4.8 Knowledge of processes for managing scheduled and emergency changes to the production systems and/or infrastructure including change, configuration, release, and patch management practices   6

4.9 Knowledge of incident/problem management practices (e.g., help desk, escalation procedures, tracking)   6

4.10 Knowledge of software licensing and inventory practices   6

4.11 Knowledge of system resiliency tools and techniques (e.g., fault tolerant hardware, elimination of single point of failure, clustering)   4

Content Area 5: Protection of Information Assets

5.1 Evaluate the design, implementation, and monitoring of logical access controls to ensure the confidentiality, integrity, availability and authorized use of information assets.   7

5.2 Evaluate network infrastructure security to ensure confidentiality, integrity, availability and authorized use of the network and the information transmitted.   7

5.3 Evaluate the design, implementation, and monitoring of environmental controls to prevent or minimize loss.   7

5.4 Evaluate the design, implementation, and monitoring of physical access controls to ensure that information assets are adequately safeguarded.   7

5.5 Evaluate the processes and procedures used to store, retrieve, transport, and dispose of confidential information assets.   7

Knowledge Statement

5.1 Knowledge of the techniques for the design, implementation and monitoring of security (e.g., threat and risk assessment, sensitivity analysis, privacy impact assessment)   7

5.2 Knowledge of logical access controls for the identification, authentication, and restriction of users to authorized functions and data (e.g., dynamic passwords, challenge/response, menus, profiles)   7

5.3 Knowledge of logical access security architectures (e.g., single sign-on, user identification strategies, identity management)   7

5.4 Knowledge of attack methods and techniques (e.g., hacking, spoofing, Trojan horses, denial of service, spamming)   7

5.5 Knowledge of processes related to monitoring and responding to security incidents (e.g., escalation procedures, emergency incident response team)   6

5.6 Knowledge of network and Internet security devices, protocols, and techniques (e.g., SSL, SET, VPN, NAT)   7

5.7 Knowledge of intrusion detection systems and firewall configuration, implementation, operation, and maintenance   7

5.8 Knowledge of encryption algorithm techniques (e.g., AESRSA)   7

5.9 Knowledge of public key infrastructure (PKI) components (e.g., certification authorities, registration authorities) and digital signature techniques   7

5.10 Knowledge of virus detection tools and control techniques   7

5.11 Knowledge of security testing and assessment tools (e.g., penetration testing, vulnerability scanning)   7

5.12 Knowledge of environmental protection practices and devices (e.g., fire suppression, cooling systems, water sensors)   7

5.13 Knowledge of physical security systems and practices (e.g., biometrics, access cards, cipher locks, tokens)   7

5.14 Knowledge of data classification schemes (e.g., public, confidential, private, and sensitive data)   7

5.15 Knowledge of voice communications security (e.g., voice over IP)   7

5.16 Knowledge of the processes and procedures used to store, retrieve, transport, and dispose of confidential information assets   7

5.17 Knowledge of controls and risks associated with the use of portable and wireless devices (e.g., PDAs, USB devices, Bluetooth devices)   7

Content Area 6: Business Continuity and Disaster Recovery

6.1 Evaluate the adequacy of backup and restore provisions to ensure the availability of information required to resume processing.   8

6.2 Evaluate the organization's disaster recovery plan to ensure that it enables the recovery of IT processing capabilities in the event of a disaster.   8

6.3 Evaluate the organization's business continuity plan to ensure its ability to continue essential business operations during the period of an IT disruption.   8

Knowledge Statements

6.1 Knowledge of data backup, storage, maintenance, retention and restoration processes, and practices   8

6.2 Knowledge of regulatory, legal, contractual, and insurance issues related to business continuity and disaster recovery   8

6.3 Knowledge of business impact analysis (BIA)   8

6.4 Knowledge of the development and maintenance of the business continuity and disaster recovery plans   8

6.5 Knowledge of business continuity and disaster recovery testing approaches and methods   8

6.6 Knowledge of human resources management practices as related to business continuity and disaster recovery (e.g., evacuation planning, response teams)   8

6.7 Knowledge of processes used to invoke the business continuity and disaster recovery plans   8

6.8 Knowledge of types of alternate processing sites and methods used to monitor the contractual agreements (e.g., hot sites, warm sites, cold sites)   8

Exam objectives are subject to change at any time without prior notice and at ISACA's sole discretion. Please visit ISACA's website (www.isaca.org) for the most current listing of exam objectives.

Assessment Test

1. What are the qualifications of the incident commander when responding to a crisis?
   A. Member of management
   B. First responder
   C. Trained crisis manager
   D. First person on scene

2. Which of the following would be a concern that the auditor should explain in the audit report along with their findings?
   A. Detailed list of audit objectives
   B. The need by the current auditor to communicate with the prior auditor
   C. Undue restrictions placed by management on evidence use or audit procedures
   D. Communicating results directly to the chairperson of the audit committee

3. What are the different types of audits?
   A. Forensic, accounting, verification, regulatory
   B. Financial, compliance, administrative, SAS-74
   C. Information system, SAS-70, regulatory, procedural
   D. Integrated, compliance, operational, administrative

4. What indicators are used to identify the anticipated level of recovery and loss at a given point in time?
   A. RTO and SDO
   B. RPO and ITO
   C. RPO and RTO
   D. SDO and IRO

5. What is the principal issue surrounding the use of CAAT tools?
   A. The capability of the software vendor.
   B. Documentary evidence is more effective.
   C. Inability for automated tools to consider the human characteristics of the environment.
   D. Possible cost, complexity, and the security of output.

6. Which is *not* a purpose of risk analysis?
   A. Supports risk-based audit decisions
   B. Assists the auditor in determining audit objectives
   C. Ensures absolute safety during the audit
   D. Assists the auditor in identifying risks and threats

7. Which of the following answers contains the steps for business process reengineering (BPR) in proper sequence?

   A. Diagnose, envision, redesign, reconstruct

   B. Envision, initiate, diagnose, redesign, reconstruct, evaluate

   C. Evaluate, envision, redesign, reconstruct, review

   D. Initiate, evaluate, diagnose, reconstruct, review

8. Which of the following functions should be separated from the others if segregation of duties cannot be achieved in an automated system?

   A. Origination

   B. Authorization

   C. Correction

   D. Reprocessing

9. At which layer of the OSI model does a gateway operate?

   A. Layer 6

   B. Layer 3

   C. Layer 7

   D. Layer 5

10. What is the purpose of the audit committee?

   A. To provide daily coordination of all audit activities

   B. To challenge and review assurances

   C. To govern, control, and manage the organization

   D. To assist the managers with training in auditing skills

11. What does the third layer of the OSI model equate to in the TCP/IP model?

   A. Network

   B. Internet

   C. Data-Link

   D. Transport

12. What are three of the four key perspectives on the IT balanced scorecard?

   A. Business justification, service-level agreements, budget

   B. Organizational staffing, cost reduction, employee training

   C. Cost reduction, business process, growth

   D. Service level, critical success factors, vendor selection

13. Which of the following statements is true concerning asymmetric-key cryptography?

   A. Sender encrypts the files by using the recipient's private key.

   B. Sender and receiver use the same key.

   C. Sender and receiver have different keys.

   D. Asymmetric keys cannot be used for digital signatures.

14. How should management act to best deal with emergency changes?

   A. Emergency changes cannot be made without advance testing.

   B. All changes should still undergo review.

   C. The change control process does not apply to emergency conditions.

   D. Emergency changes are not allowed under any condition.

15. What is one of the bigger concerns regarding asset disposal?

   A. Residual asset value

   B. Employees taking disposed property home

   C. Standing data

   D. Environmental regulations

16. Which of the following is the most significant issue to consider regarding insurance coverage?

   A. Salvage, rather than replacement, may be dictated.

   B. Premiums may be very expensive.

   C. Coverage must include all business assets.

   D. Insurance can pay for all the costs of recovery.

17. Which of the following is required to protect the internal network when a wireless access point is in use?

   A. Wireless encryption

   B. Wired equivalent protection

   C. Wireless application protocol

   D. Network firewall.

18. Digital signatures are designed to provide additional protection for electronic messages in order to determine which of the following?

   A. Message deletion

   B. Message sender verification

   C. Message modification

   D. Message read by unauthorized party

19. What is the primary purpose of database views?

    A. Restrict the viewing of selected data.

    B. Provide a method for generating reports.

    C. Allow the user access into the database.

    D. Allow the system administrator access to maintain the database.

20. Which of the following indicates why continuity planners can create plans without the Business Impact Analysis (BIA) process?

    A. Management already dictated all the key processes to be used.

    B. Not possible—critical processes constantly change.

    C. Business Impact Analysis is not required.

    D. Risk assessment is acceptable.

21. Segregation of duties may not be practical in a small environment. A single employee may be performing the combined functions of server operator and application programmer. The IS auditor should recommend controls for which of the following?

    A. Automated logging of changes made to development libraries

    B. Procedures that verify that only approved program changes are implemented

    C. Automated controls to prevent the operator logon ID from making program modifications

    D. Hiring additional technical staff to force segregation of duties

22. The auditor is permitted to deviate from professional audit standards when they feel it is necessary because of which of the following?

    A. Standards are designed for discretionary use.

    B. The unique characteristics of each client will require auditor flexibility.

    C. Deviating from standards is almost unheard of and would require significant justification.

    D. Deviation depends on the authority granted in the audit charter.

23. What does the principle of auditor independence mean?

    A. It is not an issue for auditors working for a consulting company.

    B. It is required for an external audit.

    C. An internal auditor must undergo certification training to be independent.

    D. The audit committee would bestow independence on the auditor.

24. What are the five phases of business continuity planning according to ISACA, for use on the CISA exam? (Select the answer showing the correct phases and order.)

    A. Analyze business impact, develop strategy, develop plan, implement, test plan

    B. Analyze business impact, develop strategy, develop plan, test plan, implement

    C. Analyze business impact, develop plan, implement, test plan, write the plan

    D. Analyze business impact, write the plan, test strategy, develop plan, implement

Answers to Assessment Test

1. **D.** The first person on the scene is the incident commander regardless of rank or position. The incident commander may be relieved by a person with more experience or less experience, according to the situation. The incident commander will change throughout the crisis. For more information, see Chapter 8.

2. **C.** Undue restrictions on scope would be a major concern as would a lack of time or the inability to obtain sufficient reliable evidence. For more information, see Chapter 2.

3. **D.** All of the audit types are valid except procedural, SAS-74, verification, and regulatory (which are all distracters). The valid audit types are financial, operational (SAS-70), integrated (SAS-94), compliance, administrative, forensic, and information systems. A forensic audit is used to discover information about a possible crime. For more information, see Chapter 1.

4. **C.** The recovery point objective (RPO) indicates the fallback position and duration of loss that has occurred. A valid RPO example is to recover by using backup data from last night's backup tape, meaning that the more-recent transactions would be lost. The recovery time objective (RTO) indicates a point in time that the restored data should be available for the user to access. For more information, see Chapter 8.

5. **D.** Computer assisted audit tools are able to perform detailed technical tasks faster than humans and produce more-accurate data during particular functions such as system scanning. Cost, training, and security of output are major considerations. For more information, see Chapter 2.

6. **C.** The risk analysis does not ensure absolute safety. The purpose of using a risk-based audit strategy is to ensure that the audit adds value with meaningful information. For more information, see Chapter 2.

7. **B.** According to ISACA, the general steps in business process reengineering are envision the need, initiate the project, diagnose the existing process, redesign a process, use change management to reconstruct the organization in transition, and evaluate the results. For more information, see Chapter 3.

8. **B.** Authorization should be separate from all other activities. A second person should review changes before implementation. Authorization will be granted if the change is warranted and the level of risk is acceptable. For more information, see Chapter 3.

9. **C.** According to ISACA, the gateway operates at application layer 7 in the OSI model. The function of the gateway is to convert data contained in one protocol into data used by a different protocol. An example is a PC-to-mainframe gateway converting ASCII to mainframe Extended Binary Coded Decimal Interchange Code (EBCDIC). For more information, see Chapter 4.

10. **B.** The purpose of the audit committee is to review and challenge assurances made, and to maintain a positive working relationship with management and the auditors. For more information, see Chapters 2 and 3.

11. B.   The third layer of the OSI model is the Network layer. Use the memory tool of "Nor Do I Throw Apples" to remember the layers of the TCP/IP model. The third layer of the TCP/IP model is the Internet layer. For more information, see Chapter 4.

12. C.   The four perspectives on the IT balanced scorecard are the customer perspective, business process perspective, financial perspective, and the growth perspective. Each of these seek to define the highest return by IT. For more information, see Chapter 6.

13. C.   The sender and receiver each have their own public and private (secret) key pair. All the other statements are false. Asymmetric keys are definitely used for creating digital signatures. The sender would never use the recipient's private key, only the recipient's public key. For more information, see Chapter 7.

14. B.   All emergency changes should still undergo the formal change management process after the fact. The review determines whether the change should remain in place or be modified. For more information, see Chapter 6.

15. C.   Any standing data should be purged from the equipment prior to disposal. *Standing data* refers to information that can be recovered from a device by using any means. For more information, see Chapter 6.

16. A.   The insurance company may dictate salvage to save money. Salvage will increase the delay before recovery. Any replacement purchases by the organization may not be covered under reimbursement. For more information, see Chapter 8.

17. D.   The wireless network may be using wired equivalent protocol (WEP); however, a firewall is still required to protect the internal network. The WEP design has been broken and is considered insecure under all conditions. In addition, new CISP regulations of the Senate Banking Committee with VISA, Mastercard, American Express, and Discover place $100,000 penalties per occurrence for any loss due to noncompliance.

18. B.   Digital signatures provide authentication assurance of the email sender. Digital signatures use the private key of the sender to verify identity. For more information, see Chapter 7.

19. A.   Database views are used to implement least privilege and restrict the data that can be viewed by the user. For more information, see Chapter 7.

20. B.   It is not possible to create business continuity plans without a current Business Impact Analysis (BIA). The BIA identifies critical processes and their dependencies. The critical processes will change as the business changes with new products and customers. For more information, see Chapter 8.

21. B.   Procedures should be implemented to ensure that only approved program changes are implemented. The purpose of separation of duties is to prevent intentional or unintentional errors. A logical separation of duties may exist if a single person performs two job roles. The ultimate objective is to ensure that a second person has reviewed and approved a change before it is implemented. For more information, see Chapter 3.

22. C.   Standards are mandatory, and any deviation would require justification. Exceptions are rarely accepted. For more information, see Chapter 2.

23. B. The auditor must be independent of personal and organizational relationships with the auditee, which could imply a biased opinion. The auditor is not permitted to audit a system for which they participated in the support, configuration, or design. An auditor may not audit any system that they helped to remediate. For more information, see Chapter 1.

24. A. Notice that analyzing the business impact is always the first step. Then criteria are selected to guide the strategy selection. A detailed plan is written by using the strategy. The written plan is then implemented. After implementation, the plan and staff are tested for effectiveness. The plan is revised, and then the testing and maintenance cycle begins. For more information, see Chapter 8.

Chapter

1

Secrets of a Successful IS Auditor

THE OBJECTIVE OF THIS CHAPTER IS TO ACQUAINT THE READER WITH THE FOLLOWING CONCEPTS:

- ✓ Understanding the foundation of IS audit standards
- ✓ Understanding the auditor's professional requirements
- ✓ Familiarity of auditor skills necessary for a successful audit
- ✓ Understanding mandatory versus discretionary wording of regulations
- ✓ Knowing the various types of audits
- ✓ Knowing how to communicate with the auditee
- ✓ Understanding auditor leadership duties, including planning and setting priorities
- ✓ Understanding the organizational structure of corporations and consulting firms
- ✓ Understanding the methods of managing projects, including audit projects

Welcome to the world of information systems (IS) auditing. We congratulate you for having the foresight and ambition to enter one of the most challenging careers in the world. The business issues in our global economy have created tremendous opportunities for individuals such as yourself.

Imagine what the world would be like without the Internet. A world without electronic systems would feel prehistoric. The days of manual systems of bookkeeping are gone. All organizations, regardless of size, are being driven toward increasing levels of automation. This increasing dependency on electronic information systems has created the need for a new type of auditor: the information systems auditor.

Just as financial auditors verify monetary balances and bookkeeping practices, the IS auditor verifies the integrity of the electronic system. Information systems are used to maintain customer data, company files, inventory, and records of transactions. IS auditing can provide a fabulous opportunity for people with a financial or information technology background.

You may be asking yourself whether this opportunity would work for you. Becoming an IS auditor will expand your career options.

In this chapter, we will study the foundation of IS audit standards. The CISA establishes professional requirements and defines the auditor skills necessary for successful audit. Every IS auditor is expected to recognize the difference between mandatory versus discretionary wording in regulations.

The CISA candidate is expected to know the different types of audits. There is an established process for communication with the auditee. Every successful auditor must understand their leadership duties, including planning and setting priorities.

We will discuss the organizational structure of corporations and consulting firms. The auditor will need to evaluate the organization's governance structure to determine if IT objectives are aligned to organizational goals. This chapter will review methods for managing projects including audit projects.

This chapter is a foundation for the next chapter, which is about the IS audit process. Each concept we discuss will be in effect from now through to the end of this study guide to progressively build your knowledge.

Demands for IS Audit

New regulations for more stringent financial and internal controls are driving business leaders into a controlled frenzy. You may have heard of the following: Sarbanes-Oxley Act (corporations),

Gramm-Leach-Bliley Act (financial transactions), Federal Information Security Management Act (government), Health Information Portability and Accountability Act (HIPAA), Supervisory Control and Data Acquisition (utilities), Fair and Accurate Credit Transactions Act (credit processing), Federal Financial Institutions Examination Council regulations (financial), and numerous privacy laws worldwide. These are just a sample of the regulations and regulators facing today's businesses.

All of these regulations require businesses to possess two simple components:

- Evidence of business integrity
- Evidence of internal controls to protect valuable assets

An *asset* is defined as anything of value, including trademarks, patents, secret recipes, durable goods, data files, competent personnel, and clients. Although people are not listed as corporate assets, the loss of key individuals is a genuine business threat. We can define a *threat* as a negative event that would cause a loss if it occurred. The path that allows a threat to occur is referred to as *vulnerability*. Your job as an IS auditor is to verify that assets, threats, and vulnerabilities are properly identified and managed to reduce risk.

In the past, businesses were allowed to operate with fewer restrictions. The problem with past regulation (or lack thereof) was that many organizations were taking risks that would have been unacceptable to investors and business partners had they been fully informed of corporate actions. Financial auditors were focused on bank balances and transaction totals proving to be correct. Now increasing automation enables little mistakes to cascade into massive catastrophes. Stockholders, customers, and the government are looking for reassurance that management has taken the necessary precautions to prevent loss or corruption.

Our economy is founded on banking and investment. The majority of our global economy invests directly or indirectly in stock and financial markets. You may be an indirect investor through pension funds or bank accounts. Unfortunately there exists a group of individuals who view stock as their own private monetary system. How wonderful that must be to have our money at their disposal, without any terms of repayment, without interest or consideration, and without the requirement to ever pay the money back. Sounds ridiculous, doesn't it. But frankly, that is exactly how the stock market operates. You invest money with the hope that one day you will see something in return, knowing that you could lose it all.

One of the purposes of a controls audit is to ensure that there is reason to believe investors' money is protected from stupid mistakes. Our free enterprise strives to prevent another market collapse and protect the world banking system from crashing. We expect management to specify policies and to create procedures, processes, and safeguards to prevent loss and corruption. It is the job of management to design a solution that effectively protects corporate assets.

As an IS auditor, you must be familiar with the various policies, standards, and procedures that an organization or company you are auditing has. In addition, you must understand the purpose of your audit. You will look at those topics in this section.

Understanding Policies, Standards, Guidelines, and Procedures

A plethora of documentation exists in the operation of any organization. Management uses this documentation to specify operating and control details. Consistency would be impossible without putting the information into writing.

Organizations typically have four types of documents in place:

Policies   These are high-level documents signed by a person of significant authority (such as a corporate officer, president, or vice president). The policy is a simple document stating that their particular high-level control objective is important to the organization's success. Policies may be only one page in length. Policies require *mandatory* compliance.

Standards   These are mid-level documents to ensure uniform application of a policy. After a standard is approved by management, compliance is mandatory. All standards are used as reference points to ensure organizational compliance. Testing and audits compare a subject to the standard, with the intention of certifying a minimum level of uniform compliance.

Guidelines   These are intended to provide advice pertaining to how organizational objectives might be obtained in the absence of a standard. The purpose is to provide information that would aid in making decisions about intended goals (should do), beneficial alternatives (could do), and actions that would not create problems (won't hurt). Guidelines are often *discretionary.*

Procedures   These are "cookbook" recipes for accomplishing specific tasks necessary to meet a standard. Details are written in step-by-step format from the very beginning to the end. Good procedures include common troubleshooting steps in case the user encounters a known problem. Compliance with established procedures is *mandatory* to ensure consistency and accuracy. On occasion a procedure may be deemed ineffective. The correct process is to update the ineffective procedure using the change control process described later. The purpose of a procedure is to maintain control over the outcome.

Figure 1.1 illustrates the hierarchy of a policy, standard, guideline, and procedure.

Understanding the ISACA Code of Professional Ethics

The Information Systems Audit and Control Association (ISACA) set forth a code governing the professional conduct and ethics of all certified IS auditors and members of the association. As a Certified Information Systems Auditor (CISA), you are bound to uphold this code. The following eight bullet points represent the true spirit and intent of this code:

- You agree to support the implementation of appropriate policies, standards, guidelines, and procedures for information systems. You will also encourage compliance with this objective.

- You agree to perform your duties with objectivity, professional care, and due diligence in accordance with professional standards. You will support the use of best practices.

- You agree to serve the interests of stakeholders in an honest and lawful manner that reflects a credible image upon your profession.

- You promise to maintain privacy and confidentiality of information obtained during your audit except for required disclosure to legal authorities. Information you obtain during the audit will not be used for personal benefit.

- You agree to undertake only those activities in which you are professionally competent and will strive to improve your competency.

- You promise to disclose accurate results of all work and significant facts to the appropriate parties.

- You agree to support ongoing professional education to help stakeholders enhance their understanding of information systems security and control.

- The failure of a CISA auditor to comply with this code of professional ethics may result in an investigation with possible sanctions or disciplinary measures.

Ethics statements are necessary to demonstrate the level of honesty and professionalism expected of every auditor. Overall, your profession requires you to be honest and fair in all representations you make. The goal is to build trust with clients. Your behavior should reflect a positive image on your profession. All IS auditors are depending on you to help maintain the high quality and integrity that clients expect from a CISA.

FIGURE 1.1   The relationship between a policy, standard, guideline, and procedure

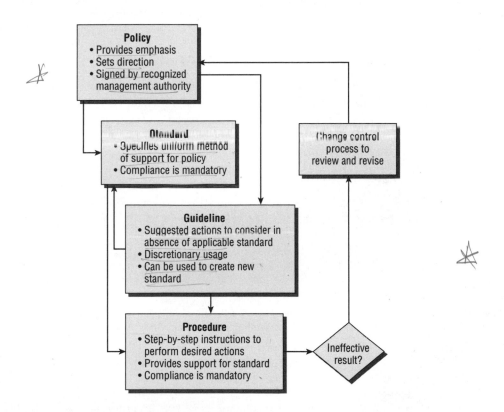

Every CISA should have a strong understanding of these objectives and how each would apply to different audit situations.

Understanding the Purpose of an Audit

An *audit* is simply a review of past history. The IS auditor is expected to follow the defined audit process, establish audit criteria, gather meaningful evidence, and render an independent opinion about internal controls.

If the assertions of management and the auditor's report are in agreement, you can expect the results to be truthful. If management assertions and the auditor's report do not agree, that would signal a concern that warrants further attention.

Your success as an auditor is to accurately report your findings, whether good or bad or indifferent. A good auditor will produce verifiable results. Nobody should ever come in behind you with a different outcome of findings. Your job is to report what the evidence indicates.

Understanding the Auditor's Responsibility

As an auditor, you are expected to fulfill a fiduciary relationship. A *fiduciary relationship* is simply one in which you are acting for the benefit of another person and place the responsibilities to be fair and honest ahead of your own interest. An auditor must never put the auditee interests ahead of the truth. People inside and outside of the auditee organization will depend on your reports to make decisions. The auditor is depended upon to advise about the internal status of an organization. This is a tremendous responsibility.

Auditor Role vs. Auditee Role

There are only two titles for persons involved in an audit. First is the *auditor*, the one who investigates. Second is the *auditee*, the subject of the audit.

ISACA refers to this as audit vs. nonaudit roles. Your purpose as an auditor is to be an independent set of eyes that can delve into the inside of organizations on behalf of management or on behalf of everyone in the outside world. *Independent* means that you are not related professionally, personally, or organizationally to the subject of the audit. You cannot be independent if the audit's outcome results in your financial gain or if you are involved in the auditee's decisions or design of the subject being audited.

When determining whether you are able to perform a fair audit, you should conduct an independence test. In addition, you must remain aware of your responsibility as an auditor under the various auditing standards.

Applying an Independence Test

Are you free of any conflicts, circumstances, or attitudes toward the auditee that might affect the audit outcome?

Is your personal life free of any relationships, off-duty behavior, or financial gain that could be perceived to affect your judgment?

Do you have any organizational relationships with the auditee including business deals, financial obligations, or pending legal actions?

If the answer is "yes," you are not independent. Only internal auditors (whose aim is improve internal performance) can answer yes and still possibly continue the audit. External auditors are required to remain independent during an independent audit.

 Real World Scenario

Being Fair and Objective

Early in my career, I learned a slogan that helped guide me through some difficult decisions: "The truth is the truth until you add to it." As an auditor, you are expected to report findings that are fair and objective. It is presumed that the auditor asked the right questions during the audit. In this book, we intend to teach you practical applications of the audit standards, including the right questions to ask.

What if the client asks you to provide advice to their design staff while you are engaged as their external auditor? The unknowledgeable auditor could create a conflict or lose the client's respect. A good auditor would remind the client of the need for auditor independence. Imagine the power of the following statement that you, as a professional auditor, could make:

Sir/Madam, In my role as external auditor, I must remain independent of design decisions; otherwise, I would not be able to provide you the independence and objectivity required. Providing design advice would be a violation of several standards governing auditor independence, including PCAOB audit standard AS-1, GAAP audit practices, ISACA professional standards, and Statement of Auditing Standards 1, 37, and 74 (SAS-1, SAS-37, and SAS-74).

 You are encouraged to explain what an auditor looks for during an audit. You must be careful not to participate in design decisions, detailed specification, or remediation during your role as the auditor. You may be hired to help with remediation; however, you will be disqualified from auditing any related work. The same principle applies to design work and system operation.

Auditors have the luxury of being able to rely on well-known accounting standards that have been accepted worldwide. The standards were originally developed for financial audits, but their spirit and intent also apply to IS auditing. Frequently, a minor adaptation will provide the foundation and detail necessary for use in IS audits. These standards allow you to render a fair opinion without fear of retribution or liability.

Understanding the Various Auditing Standards

There are two basic types of audits: one that verifies compliance (*compliance test*) and one that checks the substance and integrity of a claim (*substantive test*). Just how does an auditor know what to do in these audits? As an IS auditor, you are fortunate to have several credible resources available to assist you and guide your clients.

Among these resources are standards and regulations that direct your actions and final opinion. It would be quite rare to depart from these well-known and commonly accepted regulations. In fact, you would be in an awkward situation if you ever departed from the audit standards. By following known audit standards, you are relatively safe from an integrity challenge or individual liability. By adhering to audit standards, a good auditor can operate from a position that is conceptually equal to Teflon nonstick coating. Nothing negative or questionable could stick to the auditor.

You can learn more about auditing standards by reading and then implementing information provided by the following:

- Financial Accounting Standards Board (FASB)

- Generally Accepted Accounting Principles (GAAP)

- American Institute of Certified Public Accountants (AICPA)

- Statement on Auditing Standards (SAS), standards 1 through 101, which are referenced and applied by the AICPA.

- Committee of Sponsoring Organizations of the Treadway Commission (COSO), providing the COSO internal control framework that is the basis for PCAOB standards

- Public Company Accounting Oversight Board (PCAOB), issuing audit standards AS-1, AS-2, and AS-3

- U.S. National Institute of Standards and Technology (NIST), providing federal IS standards

- U.S. Federal Information Security Management Act (FISMA), which specifies minimum security compliance standards for government systems including the military

- IS Audit and Control Association (ISACA) and IT Governance Institute (ITG) issue COBIT guidelines that were derived from COSO with a more specific emphasis on information systems.

- International Organization for Standardization (ISO)

- Basel Accord Standard II (Basel II), governing risk in banking

- Organization for Economic Cooperation and Development (OECD), providing guidelines by participating countries promoting multinational business

Although this list may appear daunting, it is important to remember that all these examples are in fundamental agreement with each other. Each standard supports nearly identical terms of reference and supports similar audit objectives. These standards will have slightly different levels of audit or audit scope. The IT Governance Institute and ISACA have developed a set of IT internal control standards for CISAs to follow. These incorporate several objectives of the COSO internal control standard that have been narrowed to focus on IT functions. Let's look at a brief overview of the ISACA standards.

ISACA IS Audit Standards

The members of ISACA are constantly striving to advance the standards of IS auditing. CISAs should check the ISACA website (www.isaca.org) for updates on a quarterly basis. The current body of ISACA Audit Standards are organized using a format numbered from 1 to 11:

S1 Audit Charter   The audit charter authorizes the scope of the audit and grants you responsibility, authority, and accountability in the audit function.

S2 Independence   Every auditor is expected to demonstrate professional and organizational independence.

S3 Professional Ethics and Standards of Conduct   The auditor must act in a manner which denotes professionalism and respect.

S4 Professional Competence   The auditor must have the necessary skills to perform the audit. Continuing education is required to improve and maintain skills.

S5 Planning   Successful audits are the result of advance preparation. Proper planning is necessary to ensure that the audit will fulfill the intended objectives.

S6 Performance of Audit Work   This standard provides guidance to ensure that the auditor has proper supervision, gains the correct evidence to form conclusions, and creates the required documentation of the audit.

S7 Audit Reporting   The auditor report contains several required statements and legal disclosures. This standard provides guidance concerning the contents of the auditor's report.

S8 Follow-up Activities   The follow-up activities include determining whether management has taken action on the auditor's recommendations in a timely manner.

S9 Irregularities and Illegal Acts   This standard outlines how to handle the discovery of irregularities and illegal acts involving the auditee.

S10 IT Governance   This standard covers the authority, direction, and control of the information technology function. Technology is now pervasive in all areas of business. Is the auditee properly managing IT to meet their needs?

S11 Use of Risk Analysis in Audit Planning   This standard provides guidance for implementing a risk-based approach in audit planning.

 This chapter, as well as Chapter 2, "Audit Process" will thoroughly discuss all the objectives contained in ISACA's audit standards.

During the audit process, you will find clients are more receptive when your audit goals are linked to specific citations in the ISACA audit standards. You should aim to fill a known and defined point of compliance rather than provide a vague statement relating to something you may have read in a textbook.

Let's review the basic purpose of several major regulations (see Figure 1.2). These are predominantly US regulations with worldwide compliance implications due to global outsourcing.

FIGURE 1.2   Sample of sources for regulations and best practices

Sample of Regulations	Intended Purpose	Application
SOX US Sarbanes-Oxley Act of 2002	• Ehance integrity in public corporations. • Mandates full disclosure of potential control weaknesses to audit committee. • Creates officer liability.	• 906 Act, Signed attestation of integrity in financial statement. • 302 Act, Signed attestation of full disclosure to audit committee every 90 days of any potential control weaknesses and management commitment to find and remediate weaknesses. • 404 Act, Recommended internal controls.
GLBA US Gramm Leach Bliley Act 1999	• Create minimum processing performance requirements for financial institutions, collection agencies, and mortgage and real estate companies. • Outline privacy and data protection controls in banking. • Creates officer liability.	• Sets maximum service outages at 59 minutes for basic account functions. • Public disclosure of security breaches. • Mandatory verification of continuity plans by quarterly testing.
Basel II Basel Accord Standard II	• Outline risk management controls in banking.	• World banking consortium of the G-10 member countries to safeguard international banking.
FACTA US Fair and Accurate Credit Transactions Act of 2003	• Reduce fraud and identity theft by establishing information security requirements for merchants and credit card processors.	• More restrictive data retention. • Prohibit storage of account numbers. violation results if IT system fails to comply. • Data destruction requirements.
FFIEC US Federal Financial Institutions Examination Council	• Multiple government authorities. • Establish uniform principles, standards, and report forms. • Establish mandatory federal examination of financial institutions.	• Financial institutions • Banks • Non-banks, credit unions and thrifts • Subsidiaries • Holding and edge companies • Foreign banks and non-banks operating in US jurisdictions • Officers, employees, and certain other individuals
HIPAA US Health Information Privacy and Accountability Act of 1996	• Provide privacy for records in healthcare organizations and benefit managers. • Combat fraud, waste and abuse in health care.	• Insurance companies • Insurance processors • Healthcare providers • Custodian of records • Patient record handlers
FISMA US Federal Information Security Management Act of 2002	• Create security controls in all systems and information relied upon by the US government. • United Federal Information Processing Standards (FIPS)	• All US government federal systems including the military. • IT systems for US critical infrastructure in commerce.
SCADA US Supervisory Controls and Data Acquisition	• Enhance security for automated control systems in US critical Infrastructure.	• Utility industry, power generation and transmission, water, gas, communications. • Research facilities • Traffic control • Manufacturing • Other automated controlsSample of

Every regulation is designed to mandate the minimum acceptable requirements when conducting any form of business within that specific industry. The auditor must remain aware of two types of statements contained in all regulations:

 Recommended (discretionary)   These are actions that usually contain statements with the word *should*—for example, suggested management responsibilities, staffing, control mechanisms, or technical attributes.

Required (mandatory)   These are actions that contain the word *shall*. *Shall* indicates that the statement is a commandment of compliance. *Shall* is not optional. The auditor should remember that failing to meet a required Shall objective is a real concern. The regulations serve to protect the citizens at large. Incredible justification would usually be required to prove the organization's actions do not fall under the jurisdiction of the regulation. The regulator will accept no excuses without a major battle, and on almost every occasion will win any potential disputes. Most juries comprise individuals who will interpret claims using a basic common-sense approach without detailed knowledge of a particular industry. Almost all excuses for violating the regulatory objective have failed in court battles. Each organization in that market is required to meet the objective in spite of cost or revenue issues. In other words, the organization must comply even if it means that compliance will lose money. Failure to make a profit is not a valid exception from the law. The organization must strive to obtain compliance or they can be forced to exit the industry with fines and sanctions. The auditor may need to consult a lawyer for advice upon discovery of significant violations.

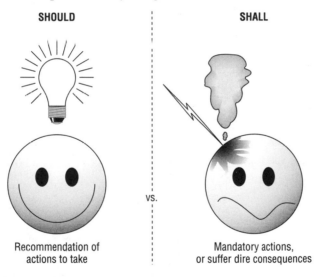

SHOULD   **SHALL**

vs.

Recommendation of   Mandatory actions,
actions to take   or suffer dire consequences

Identifying the Types of Audits

IS auditors may be engaged in a variety of audits. The only fundamental difference between internal and external audits is auditor independence. Although the focus and nature of the audit may vary from time to time, your audit function and responsibilities will remain constant.

NOTE Medium to large businesses undergo a quarterly audit for their financial statements.

Government interpretation of laws and regulations has determined that financial audits and internal controls are interrelated. You could not ensure the integrity of one without verifying the other. As an example, consider the requirements specified under the Sarbanes-Oxley Act of 2002 (SOX) for public corporations. There are two critical reporting functions that management must fulfill under SOX:

- Act 906 statement, in which management attests to the integrity of financials and indicates that no hidden or questionable transactions exist.

- Act 302 statement, in which management attests that full disclosure of the internal controls has been made to the audit committee, and that no deficiencies or weaknesses were withheld.

Management must make their assertions of compliance without reliance on the auditor. The intention of these two statements is to bind management with liability. SOX is essentially a disclosure law. Its purpose is to provide government authorities with a method of ensuring criminal prosecution of corporate officers if management misrepresents the truth.

As an IS auditor, you should be aware of the following types of audits:

Financial audit   Verifies financial records, transactions, and account balances. This type of audit is used to check the integrity of financial records and accounting practices compared to well-known accounting standards.

Operational audit   Verifies effectiveness and efficiency of operational practices. Operational audits are used frequently in service and process environments, including IT service providers. An operational audit is detailed in Statement of Accounting Standard 70 (SAS-70).

Integrated audit   Includes both financial and operational controls audits. An integrated audit is detailed in Statement of Accounting Standard 94 (SAS-94).

Compliance audit   Verifies implementation of and adherence to a standard or regulation. This could include ISO standards and all government regulations. A compliance audit usually includes tests for presence of a control.

Administrative audit   Verifies that appropriate policies and procedures exist and have been implemented as intended. This type of audit usually tests for the presence of required documentation.

Information systems audit   Verifies systems for certification and/or accreditation. Certification usually involves system testing against a reference standard, whereas accreditation represents management's level of acceptance.

Auditor Is an Executive Position

Many people are envious of the CISA auditor's position. They see nice cars, lunches with important people, expensive suits, and comfortable expense accounts. Nobody seems to pay attention to the humorous situation of six auditors sharing one folding table while sitting in a closet, balancing laptop computers with only one network jack and one telephone to share. Frankly, the auditor position grants you the luxury of being well-paid observers with professional benefits. Occasionally, your office and travel accommodations may not be the best. However, the reality is that most people look up to auditors with respect.

Your clients expect you to be authoritative and professional regardless of the circumstances. Your office is mobile, so you are depended on to handle decisions in the field. Your clients include the highest levels of management within an organization. Those clients expect you to assist them with your observations and occasional advice. You will deal with the challenges of providing advice in a manner that does not interfere with the independent audit. Remember the independence question raised a few pages ago?

Personnel at every level of your client's organization have an expectation of your appearance. You are going to be judged by your speech, mannerisms, clothing, and grooming. You should always wear professional attire to a level more formal than the attire of your client. Your neat and pressed appearance instills respect and confidence. Your courtesy of manner and speech dictates you should use reassuring words. Any humor by the auditor should always be restrained and professional.

Understanding the Importance of Auditor Confidentiality

The client entrusts the auditor with sensitive information. A good auditor would never betray that confidence nor allow sensitive information to be revealed at any time. Any breach of confidentiality would be unforgivable. It is conceivable that during your audit, you may discover information that could cause some level of damage to the client if disclosed. You should prepare for the possibility of detecting irregular or even illegal acts that have occurred.

To protect yourself, you must exercise caution and least privilege in all activities. The concept of least privilege refers to providing only the minimum information necessary to complete a required task. It is the auditor's responsibility to implement security controls to maintain confidentiality. An auditor's working papers contain details and secrets that need to be protected. The information you're privy to may be alarming to some, damaging to others, or trigger additional actions by a perpetrator.

To ensure confidentiality, the auditor should adopt the following operating principles:

- Sensitive information is the property of the owner and should not be removed from their office by the auditor.

- The auditor should contact legal counsel for advice concerning confidentiality and laws that would dictate disclosure to authorities. You should follow basic principles of confidentiality at all times.

- Many auditors use automated working papers (WPs) during an audit. Spreadsheets and report-writing templates are common tools to increase efficiency. The next level of automation is entering our workplace to aid even the smallest auditor. This includes database automation, checklists, evidence tracking, and report generation tools. The data must be protected with access control and regular data backup. Make sure to back up your work. It would be unforgivable to lose your audit work and client data by failing to implement your own controls.

- Every auditor should seriously consider using locking security cables and privacy viewing screens for laptops. You will gain respect by demonstrating your concern for maintaining confidentiality while protecting assets. The laptop could still be stolen with broken parts lying on the floor, but at least you would have some evidence that the theft was not your fault. At prior audit firms where I worked, these controls were mandatory.

- A document file archive is created during each audit. The archive is subject to laws governing records retention. Every auditor is advised to leave all records in the custody of the client unless criminal activity is suspected. The client shall maintain sole responsibility for the safe retention of the archive.

Working with Lawyers

There is much discussion concerning who should hire the auditor. Is it the client or is it their lawyer? At stake is the legal argument of confidentiality under attorney-client privilege. Most communication between lawyers and the client may be exempt from legal discovery (disclosure).

We suggest that you ask the client. If necessary, the lawyer could issue a letter authorizing the auditor's work on their behalf. As an auditor, you have to be able to do your job without intimidation in order for it to be fair and honest work. This should be spelled out in the audit charter or your engagement letter. A good auditor will leave the legal issues to the lawyers and focus on their job of performing a good audit. Truth often serves as an excellent defense.

Retaining Audit Documentation

In most cases, the archive of the integrated audit may need to be kept for seven years. Each type of audit may have a longer or shorter retention period depending on the regulations identified during audit planning. If the client loses the files, that would be their problem and not yours.

When I hear that a client does not have a complete archive, the first sound in my head is *chi-ching*! I get to charge them extra money for re-creating the missing documentation.

During an audit, you will be preparing reports and documentation on laptops belonging to members of your audit staff. All members of the audit team should practice good physical security, including using physical cable locks on the laptops and locking up sensitive files each evening or when not in use. You must be wary of prying eyes and big ears. It is advisable for the audit team to implement a designated "war room" as a secure work location. Meetings and interviews with all other persons should occur in a different location that is also safe from prying eyes and ears.

Providing Good Communication and Integration

Have you ever felt nervous, threatened, or intimidated? What are your own feelings when you're told an auditor is coming to visit? Nothing launches a person's defensive attitude faster than the threat of an audit. A good auditor understands client expectations and realizes it is necessary to take time to speak with customers who may be curious or nervous.

It is a good idea to alleviate fear and anxiety by implementing the following objectives with your client:

- The auditor's job is to be a second set of eyes and ask the right questions.

- Establish mutual respect. To be successful, mutual respect must exist between the auditees and auditor. When you find a problem, do not place blame on a specific individual, because the very person you are speaking with could be the one who made the poor decision. Do not insult your client; just stick to the facts. You could say the following: "Based on the information available at the time, it may have looked like an acceptable idea; however, it is time for you to consider…" A good auditor is always respectful of other people and their feelings.

As a former auditee, I always appreciated an auditor who took the time to explain to me what the audit would entail. Please keep in mind that the auditee feels at a disadvantage. It will be helpful to simplify your explanations. You can measure your own performance by the general attitude toward you at the auditee site. You are doing a good job if the client shows interest and is forthcoming with truthful answers.

Understanding Leadership Duties

A good auditor spends time planning and setting priorities before commencing an audit. You will need to make plans on how you will be working with your own team. Develop the leadership style you want to implement. The days of Captain Bligh shouting orders "lest ye be flogged" are gone.

Let's look at the characteristics of good leadership:

Your leadership style needs to clearly identify when your directions are mandatory and when they are open to feedback and comments. Team members should feel comfortable making comments and asking questions.

A good leader will develop specific requirements for success and then share those plans. A good leader will strive for the buy-in and cooperation of the staff. You cannot lead those who do not want to be led or those who do not understand the objectives.

An old and still valuable leadership lesson states the staff holds the fate of their manager in their hands. The manager will be promoted or disgraced by the performance of their staff. If your people believe the work is good, you will usually get good results. If they do not believe in what you're doing, it will become a failure. Your personal opinion of good or bad is not the pinnacle factor. What matters is what the staff believes. True believers can generate exceptional results.

Making time to educate your staff and demonstrating a willingness to take criticism are traits of a good leader.

The audit manager is responsible for creating clearly defined responsibilities and authority. There can only be one boss in order to prevent confusion. It is the responsibility of this one boss to make the hard decisions and answer for the choices made.

A regular schedule of briefings for both the auditee and the audit team are required. All client communication should be vetted before it is shared. *Vetting* is the process of evaluating and editing words to obtain the desired outcome.

Planning and Setting Priorities

Good auditing is the result of proper planning, not magic or luck. Every audit starts with an audit charter or engagement letter. The customer will define the focus and scope of the audit. It is the auditor's responsibility to gather pre-audit information and develop a schedule integrating the audit team functions with the customer's schedule. To be successful, a project management methodology should be used.

Let's look at a few of the auditor's responsibilities during the planning phase:

- Gaining an understanding of the customer's business
- Respecting business cycles (monthly, quarterly, seasonal, and annual)
- Establishing priorities
- Selecting an audit strategy based on risk and information known or observed
- Finding the people for your audit team
- Coordinating the logistics prior to the audit for resources, work space, and facilities
- Requesting documents (discovery requests)
- Scheduling people's time and availability
- Arranging travel and accommodations
- Planning for delays or nonperformance
- Considering rescheduling if recent downtime or risks warrant it
- Developing alternative strategies
- Developing a briefing schedule

We will be spending a significant amount of time on the subject of audit planning in the next chapter.

A professional auditor provides the auditee with a list of basic requirements and necessary resources well in advance of the audit team arrival.

We are astounded by how many times auditors fail to request sufficient desk space and access to IT resources prior to an audit team's arrival.

A good auditor gives plenty of notice as to what they need to perform their job. This includes documentation requests for manuals, policies, and procedures that will be included in the subject of the audit.

Providing Standard Terms of Reference

The auditor needs to remain fair and objective when executing an audit. As an auditor, you should be consistent and courteous to your clients. *Standard terms of reference* can be developed to promote respectful and honest interpretation. As an auditor, you should try using the following terms, or something similar:

- Auditee claim/statement
- Present
- Not present
- Planned
- Tested (how)
- Not tested (why)
- Observed
- Verified (how)
- Not verified
- New requirement
- Requirement changed
- Requirement cancelled
- Failed to meet requirement
- Resource not available
- Insufficient evidence
- Access denied
- Personnel unavailable
- Lack of time

Dealing with Conflicts and Failures

A good auditor recognizes some degree of conflict is inevitable and failures are always possible. IS auditors face the challenges of time, money, resources, and attitudes.

These challenges may be with the client or with the auditor. The auditor must always demonstrate professionalism. An exceptional auditor will exercise common sense with a quick response. An exceptional auditor uses past experiences and makes the job look effortless, especially when dealing with change or conflict.

Real World Scenario

What Exactly Does *Addressed* Mean?

A genuine pet peeve of many practitioners is the term *addressed*. Just what does it mean? Does it mean that we are working on it? Does it mean we scheduled it for a future meeting and nothing is happening at this time? Does it mean that you wrote down the details and put it in an envelope with the name of the person who should look at it?

Imagine how satisfied a mortgage company would be if you told them your payment has not been made yet, but it's in an envelope and addressed. That envelope is in your pocket, and you intend to mail it someday, but it's been addressed! A more specific explanation is required. Hopefully we can find something better than the word *addressed*.

Identifying the Value of Internal and External Auditors

In this Study Guide, we as authors are often implying an external auditor position. This is intentional in order to emphasize auditor independence. However, substantial opportunities exist for both internal and external auditors.

   External auditors are paid to be independent reviewers for an organization. *Internal auditors* can add enormous value to an organization by providing ongoing efforts that help prepare the organization for an external audit. The internal auditor could approach the situation with an attitude of independence even though they will be unable to certify or attest final results. Their expert audit skills could help guide design and remediation efforts at a substantially lower cost than that of their external counterparts.

In the internal auditor position I would focus my efforts on reducing a four-week external audit to only ten days. Depending on the organization, it may take a few years to reach this noble objective. In the meantime, my auditing services will definitely be adding value to the organization through emphasis and cost reduction. Internal auditors can aid every organization by improving evidence collection.

Understanding the Evidence Rule

The audit world revolves around the collection and review of reliable evidence. Without evidence, a claim or assertion is unverifiable and an auditor could not separate fact from fiction. Good evidence is intended to substantiate a claim or prove the existence of something you have interest in knowing.

   A good auditor will use sufficient evidence to formulate their *auditor's opinion*. No opinion can be formed when you lack evidence of acceptable quantity, relevance, and reliability. Your job is to be a professional skeptic and demand proof in the form of evidence you can verify. The best evidence will need little explanation to interpret. When more judgment is required to understand the evidence, that evidence has decreased value. Your job is to render a score based on the evidence captured during the audit. Having no evidence would warrant a zero score.

Let's suppose you are looking for evidence concerning an existing corporate policy. First, you would look for the policy itself. Is it a paper or electronic document? Documents that cannot be located within a couple of hours could be assumed not to exist. Inability to find the policy would indicate it is not actively used. Now assume the client has found a copy of the policy. Was it easily accessible or covered with dust?

The next step is to verify that you have the current edition. Your audit charter may or may not ask you to review (test) the contents of the policy. Either way, you will need to verify that the policy is actually in use by the client's organization. You might conduct a random survey of workers asking whether they can show you a current copy of the policy.

Next, you would ask questions to see whether the workers had actually read the document.

It is not uncommon for an auditee to respond that the policy is on their website. You should ask the person to show you the link and open the page. You want to know if the client can successfully demonstrate an ability to find the document.

However, existence of the policy alone does not meet the evidence rule. The auditee's score would improve as more persons demonstrate that they read the document.

Another method would be to look for notes containing the minutes of meetings where the policy was discussed. It is rare for a policy to exist without some form of questions being raised or argued. Challenges to the policy may exist in emails. You may also ask for a person to perform the tasks related to the policy and observe their actions. Direct observation is powerful evidence. Simply ask the client to reperform a task whenever you want to cut to the heart of a claim. The words *show me* can invoke either fear or pride depending on the truth of the situation. Once again, no evidence equals no score.

We will discuss evidence again in Chapter 2.

Identifying Who You Need to Interview

As an IS auditor, it is important for you to be cognizant of whom you should be interviewing, and how long those interviews should take. Every auditor will frequently face a time crunch due to the customer's schedule or other issues. You will need to pay particular attention to the value of the others' time. Consider the work outage created when you take someone out of their job role to spend time with you. Will it be necessary to backfill their position by providing a substitute during this time away?

Think for a moment of what it would cost the organization for a key executive to spend 15 minutes with you. This executive's time may be measured in personal compensation or by the revenue they generate for the organization. Top executives, such as the CEO, will have compensation packages that include both money and substantial shares of stock. Based on total compensation, the CEO may be receiving several thousand dollars per hour or more.

 Former Walt Disney CEO Michael Eisner received compensation equal to $27,000 per hour, which was equivalent to approximately 1 percent of the revenue generated under his leadership during the same time period.

The moral is that to justify 15 minutes of somebody's time, you better have something to discuss that is of greater value than his prorated value to the organization (greater than prorated revenue + compensation). Consider the cost for a meeting of high-level executives. You need to ensure that the time spent is relevant and remains focused on the audit objectives. The savvy auditor respects the value of a person's time.

Every system will have an inherent need for controls. The auditor needs to ensure that discussions occur with the correct individuals concerning appropriate controls. Three basic IT-related roles exist for every system: owner, user, and custodian. Table 1.1 shows examples of individuals with their associated roles and responsibilities.

TABLE 1.1 Responsibilities of Data Owner, User, and Custodian

Role	Example	Basic Responsibilities
Data owner	Vice president	Determine classification Specify controls Appoint custodian
Data user	Internal business user Business partner Business client (web)	Follow acceptable usage requirements Maintain security Report violations
Data custodian	Database administrator Production programmer System administrator	Protect information Ensure availability Implement and maintain controls Provide provisions for independent audit Support data users

These individuals don't have to work in the IT department. On the contrary, these roles exist regardless of the individual department boundaries. If someone performs the function, the responsibility of the role applies to that person. No exceptions. If a person performs two roles, two sets of responsibilities apply. If someone performs all three roles, either it's a one-person operation or you need to have a talk about separation of duties and the value of your data.

Understanding the Corporate Organizational Structure

It is always helpful for the auditor to clearly understand the relationships and responsibilities at different levels of an organization. The auditor needs to understand who holds the authority. Let's focus on some basics that will be pervasive throughout this book.

Identifying Roles in a Corporate Organizational Structure

Businesses are focused on generating money for investors. There will always be some type of management hierarchy in order to maintain control. Government and nonprofit organizations will use a similar control hierarchy; however, the titles will be different. For government and nonprofit organizations, the term *mission objectives* would be substituted for the term *revenue*.

Figure 1.3 illustrates a typical business *corporation*. Let's start at the top of the diagram and work our way down:

Board of directors The board of directors usually comprises key investors and appointed advisers. These individuals have placed their own money at stake in the hopes of generating a better return than the bank would pay on deposits. Board members are rarely—usually never—involved in day-to-day operations. Some members may be retired executives or run their own successful businesses. Their job is to advise the CEO and the CFO. Most organizations indemnify board members from liability; however, government prosecutors will pursue board members if needed.

Chief executive officer (CEO) The CEO is primarily focused on generating revenue for the organization. The CEO's role is to set the direction and strategy for the organization to follow. The CEO's job is to find out how to attract buyers while increasing the company's profits. As a company officer, the CEO is liable to government prosecutors. Corporate officers have signing authority to bind the organization.

Chief financial officer (CFO) The CFO is in charge of controls over capital and other areas, including financial accounting, human resources, and IS. Subordinates such as the CIO usually report to the CFO. As a company officer, the CFO is liable to government prosecutors.

Chief information officer (CIO) The CIO is subordinate to the CFO. The CFO is still considered the primary person responsible for internal control. A CIO might not be a true company officer. An exception may be the CIO in the corporate headquarters. The CIO title may bear more honor than actual authority, depending on the organization. The CIO has mixed liability depending on the issue and their actual position in the organization.

President/general manager The president, sometimes referred to as the general manager, is the head of a business unit or division. As a company officer, the president/general manager is usually liable to government prosecutors. Regulations such as SOX encourage management to require all divisional presidents and controllers to sign the integrity statements in an effort to increase divisional officer liability.

Vice president   The vice president is the second level of officer in a business unit or division. As a company officer, the vice president is usually liable to government prosecutors.

Department directors (line management position)   Typically directors are upper-level managers supervising department managers and do not have company officer authority. In large organizations, you may encounter a major-level director and minor-level director.

Managers and staff workers   Managers are responsible for providing daily supervision and guidance to staff members. Staff members may be employees or contractors working in the staff role. Managers and staff members are seldom held responsible for the actions of a company unless they knowingly participate in criminal activity.

Identifying Roles in a Consulting Firm Organizational Structure

Now we will look at the structure of a typical consulting firm. A *consulting firm* is a hybrid organization. Internal clerical and support functions are similar to those in a typical business. The consulting side of the firm uses functional management positions. The staff is allocated according to temporary project assignments. At the end of each engagement, the staff is reallocated by either returning to the available resource pool or becoming unemployed until the next engagement.

Figure 1.4 illustrates the organizational structure of a typical audit firm. We'll review the structure here:

Partner   A partner is equivalent to a divisional president or vice president and is responsible for generating revenue. Their role is to represent the organization and provide leadership to maximize income in their market segment. Partners are required to maintain leadership roles in professional organizations and to network for executive clients. Most partners have made financial commitments to produce at least $15 million in annual revenue along with supporting other business management functions. The partner and all lower managers are responsible for professional development of the staff.

Engagement manager   This is a director-equivalent position with the responsibility of managing the client relationship. The engagement manager is in charge of the audit's overall execution and the audit staff. The engagement manager is responsible for facilitating the generation of new income opportunities from the client.

Senior consultant   This is a field manager whose responsibilities include leading the daily on-site audit activities, interacting with the client staff, making expert observations, and managing staff assigned to the audit.

Consultant   This is a lead position carrying the responsibility of interacting with the client and fulfilling the audit objectives without requiring constant supervision. A consultant is often promoted by demonstrating an ability to fulfill the job of senior consultant or supporting manager.

Systems analyst   This is usually an entry-level position. Often the individual is selected for their ambition and educational background and may be fresh out of college. Systems analysts perform some lower-level administrative tasks as they build experience.

FIGURE 1.3   A typical business organizational chart

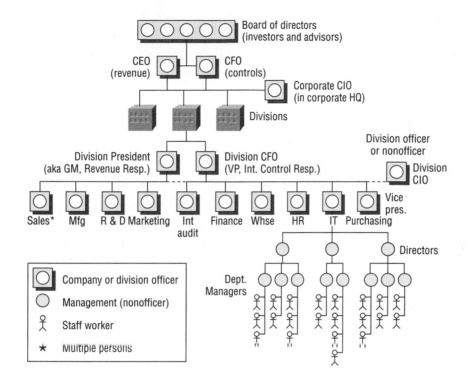

Managing Projects

A typical IS audit has many elements in common with projects and project management. We believe that the two disciplines go hand in hand. To excel in auditing, you must excel at project management. Through project management, you define what you strive to accomplish and the actions that will be taken as part of the project.

During our careers, we have worked with organizations using each of the different models for managing projects and quality. The project models are used for unique events or to refresh quality-control programs. The quality-control programs require every person in the organization to be trained and participate in support of every quality effort. Projects are typically run with less overhead, using smaller groups of people focused on a particular goal.

FIGURE 1.4   A typical auditing firm organizational chart

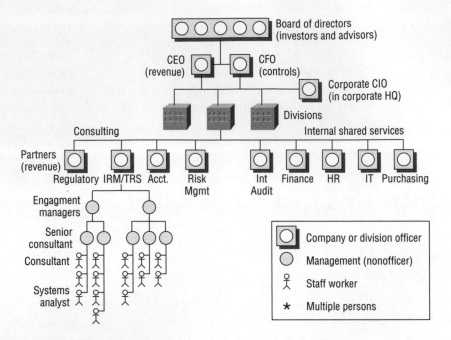

Table 1.2 shows the most common models for either managing projects or ensuring quality.

TABLE 1.2   Project Management and Quality-Control Models

Source	Focus	Structure
Project Management Institute (PMI)	Projects (International) Unique or repeating	44 process areas Well defined
Prince2	Projects (UK) Unique or repeating	9 process areas Less defined than PMI
Total Quality Management (TQM)	Quality control Repeating process control	Zero defects program Statistical process control Derived from works by Phillip Crosby and Edwards Deming
Six Sigma	Quality control Repeating process control	Reduce defects from 16,000 to 3.4 per million Motorola derivative of TQM
ISO 9001	Quality control Repeating process control	Revision of ISO 9000 quality standards International derivative of TQM

One organization stands above all others for defining project management and project management processes: Project Management Institute (PMI).

PMI has created a definitive standard for project management: *A Guide to the Project Management Body of Knowledge (PMBOK)*, which was originally published in 1987. This guide, which is in its third edition, informs project managers about basic processes that facilitate managing projects.

In this section, you will learn some basic information about the *PMBOK*, to prepare you for acquiring additional knowledge about project management and how to manage a specialized project. If you would like additional information, we suggest two sources:

- CertTest Training Center (`www.certtest.com`)—the company we work for—for training courses in project management. CertTest is a PMI global Registered Education Provider (REP).

- PMI (`www.pmi.org`) for additional information about the project management standard, ordering copies of the *PMBOK*, or information about becoming a certified Project Management Professional (PMP).

What Is a Project?

A project has three components that define it:

A project is temporary.   The project has a beginning and an end. The project is *not* an ongoing operation of the company.

A project is unique.   The project is done for a unique purpose or it creates a product or service that has unique characteristics.

A project is progressively elaborated.   The project gains details about its definition and purpose as interrelated processes are used to define and control the project.

Let's talk about each of these three project characteristics as they relate to security audits:

What defines a project as temporary?   Your project must have a beginning and a planned end. For example, although performing multiple security control audits of multiple departments over a calendar year may be an ongoing business operation, each individual security audit would probably be a separate entity with separate definitions (scope) and goals. The ongoing security audit function of the company should be considered an operation; the individual audits with specific scope would be projects.

What defines your project as unique?   Even if you are using the same processes and procedures for each audit, you will most likely have unique goals or outcomes. For example, to audit a new functional area that has never been audited before is certainly a project. To perform its evolutionary successor audit the following year is a unique project as well. Although each uses similar processes and has similar goals, the outcome and the data used are unique.

How do we define *progressively elaborated*?   In the *PMBOK*, PMI has defined 44 processes that fit into 5 process groups for managing a project. These processes take a project from a vision to an end product. The processes flow from one process to the next, acting as a framework to ensure proper definition and control. All or most of the processes interrelate to manage the outcome. As an example, in the first process—Develop Project Charter—you can create a project charter for the project. This basically authorizes the project to begin. Then you would use the project charter as input for the next process: Develop Preliminary Scope Statement. When you have a preliminary scope statement, you use this as input (along with the project charter) for the next process: Scope Planning. In Scope Planning, you create a scope management plan. And then you can use this information (as well as the previous documents) as input for the Scope Definition process, where you elaborate and document the total scope of the project in the scope statement.

We can relate this portion of the process to a security audit: getting authorization to audit (*project charter*), defining a high-level need (*preliminary project scope*), planning how to handle change to the audit scope (*scope planning*), and then setting the goals and objectives as well as documenting all items to be audited (*scope definition*).

This describes only four processes and their relationships. There are 40 more to consider for every project.

What Is Project Management?

Project management is defined in the *PMBOK* as "the application of knowledge, skills, tools, and techniques to project activities to meet project requirements." Logically speaking, the project manager has to use their knowledge of the project subject, their knowledge of project management, and available processes and procedures to fulfill the goals of the project as it relates to the audit.

A simple definition of project management is the management of competing demands. These demands are often defined as the following three competing values:

- Scope
- Cost
- Time

Think about it: You can satisfy all the items on your list of to-dos at what actual cost and what investment of time? Or you can finish the project in the time allotted and not fulfill all the to-dos. And while doing this, what effect will time or scope have on your project's budget? Managing competing demands determines whether a security audit is complete when it is due or when all necessary items (as defined in the scope document) have been audited.

The *PMBOK* states that the project manager will work with multiple stakeholders while managing the project and the competing demands. *Stakeholders* are defined as anyone with viable interest in the project. Stakeholders can be above the project manager in the organization, below the project manager, or peers. Stakeholders can also be outside the organization.

It is stressed that the project manager should concentrate on the defined scope of the project; "all the scope and only the scope" should be done. Sometimes the project manager will be required to make difficult decisions to balance the competing demands and meet the scope, time, and cost objectives for the project. Sometimes meeting these demands will require negotiation skills; sometimes it will require leadership skills to "sell" an unpopular decision.

 The CISA exam will expect you to understand project management. You need to be prepared to explain project management terminology and objectives. As practitioners, we have found that the PMI reference information provides an excellent fit in the audit world.

Identifying the Requirements of a Project Manager

A project manager must have several levels of knowledge and skills to be successful:

- Project management knowledge and skills
- General management knowledge and skills
- Interpersonal skills
- Application area knowledge and skills

Without all of these elements, PMI suggests strongly that the project manager will be less than successful in managing the competing demands of the project.

This reasoning is based on the tools defined as part of the 44 project management processes. Many times some form of "expert judgment" is used to define project needs. Without specialized application knowledge and skills, the project manager would not know what specific requirements were needed or specific tasks must be accomplished to fulfill the project goals.

To translate this specifically to a security audit, the auditor must have the following:

- Security auditing skills (and certification)
- Specialized application knowledge of the company processes and procedures
- Specialized application knowledge of the functional area being audited
- General management knowledge and skills
- Interpersonal skills

Identifying a Project Manager's Authority

Project managers are not created equal. Their level of authority and influence is dictated by the organizational structure and culture. The same issues exist in managing the audit as would exist when clients are managing their own projects.

Table 1.3 demonstrates the basic differences among management structures and cultures. Every auditor needs to understand the advantages and disadvantages of each.

TABLE 1.3   Differences in Project Manager Authority and Organization Structure

Organization Type	Advantages	Disadvantages
Functional	Project manager has no real authority; functional manager remains in charge. Good for recurring operations-oriented projects.	Usually a staff function with no formal project manager authority. Project manager may need to beg for resources or rely on personal influence. Project manager may hold positions of project leader, coordinator, or expediter.
Weak matrix	Project manager has little to no authority. There is no real advantage.	Project manager is part of the functional organization.
Balanced matrix	Project manager has both functional and minor authority that is shared with functional managers. Allows small efficiency in resource use.	Functional manager and project manager may wind up arguing over resources. Team may feel torn between two bosses.
Strong matrix	Project manager generally has an assigned team for a specific period of time. Authority level improves team dynamic and communications.	Competition for resources may still exist. Overall costs of project may increase due to inefficiency in resource allocation.
Projectized	Project manager is the formal authority and has the ability to decide project direction with little second guessing or interference.	Project manager succeeds or fails based on project results. Encourages hoarding of resources and competition with other project teams. May cause lack of focus toward end of project due to lack of future work; job positions end upon project completion.

Understanding the Project Management Process Framework

The PMI standard for project management as defined in the *PMBOK* is intended to be applied to all sorts of projects in all sorts of environments. The project manager may use all or some of the processes along with their inputs, tools and techniques, and outputs for the project they are managing. The use of these processes is need based. The PMI processes provide an excellent checklist to prevent errors and omissions in the project management of any specific project.

As previously stated, we look upon the PMI standard as a framework, a guideline for project management. You and your company define specific specialized processes and procedures to be used for project management within your enterprise. PMI provides this standard for you to measure your internal processes against.

In the *PMBOK*, there is a definition of the project life cycle. In brief, the *project life cycle* is defined by the organization in order to meet the demands of the specialized projects that are to be managed. There is also specific definition of a project phase. Briefly, (and paraphrased), a *phase*:

- Is defined by the organization
- Is part of the life cycle
- Is a subset of the overall project
- Has a measurable deliverable
- Ends with a review

PMI places the project management framework as defined in the *PMBOK* into the specialized life cycle and phases that are defined by the organization. The *PMBOK* focuses on process groups, processes, inputs to processes, tools and techniques used in processes, and outputs from processes.

A simple outline of this framework would look something like this:

```
 −  Project life cycle            (as defined by the organization)

    o   Phases                    (as defined by project need)

        ♣  Process groups         (defined in the PMBOK)
           •   Processes          (defined in the PMBOK)
           o   Inputs             (defined in the PMBOK)
           o   Tools              (defined in the PMBOK)
           o   Outputs            (defined in the PMBOK)

           ♣  Actions or tasks    (unique to project)
```

The five process groups as defined by PMI are as follows:

- Initiating
- Planning
- Executing
- Monitoring and Controlling
- Closing

Each process group has a general function and contains processes that have specific functions to be accomplished. The process groups are interdependent; changes made in one process group can generate cascading change into another group. Each of process group performs the functions indicated by its name:

Initiating   This process group begins the project or a phase of the project. This group contains two processes. One component sets the scope, the second component authorizes the project to begin.

Planning   This process group, which contains 21 of the 44 processes, is where the project scope, goals, and objectives are detailed and documented.

Executing   According to PMI, the largest portion of resources is used in executing activities. The seven processes within this group are used to create deliverables.

Monitoring and Controlling   As you might expect, in this process group you control the project. Specifically, you use the 12 processes in this group to measure performance and control changes.

Closing   When a phase or the project is completed, two processes are used within this process group to close out the project.

As we have said, PMI defines 44 processes that fit into these 5 process groups. The 44 processes also are part of 9 specific knowledge areas. The following information describes the knowledge areas and associated processes. You'll learn where each process fits in to a process group, the actions taken in the process, and the main output or result from the process.

 For further reference, a unified chart describing similar information exists in *A Guide to the Project Management Body of Knowledge, Third Edition* (PMI, 2004).

Project Integration Management

Project Integration Management is the knowledge area containing processes that tie all of the other processes together. Each process can feed iterative changes into the next process. This is why project management is referred to as an *iterative management process*. A change in scope or deadlines, for example, will trigger changes throughout the entire plan. As a result, each process would need to be updated to remain synchronized. Therefore, another iteration of the plan is created.

Table 1.4 shows the various processes of the Project Integration Management knowledge area.

TABLE 1.4   The Project Integration Management Processes

Process	Process Group	Action Taken	Main Output
Develop Project Charter	Initiating	Documenting intent of project and obtaining approval	Project charter
Develop Preliminary Scope Statement	Initiating	Elaborating project definition	Scope statement
Develop Project Management Plan	Planning	Combining all of the other project outputs into one collection of documents that defines the project	Project management plan
Direct and Manage Project Execution	Executing	Obtaining work results and identifying changes	Deliverables

TABLE 1.4   The Project Integration Management Processes *(continued)*

Process	Process Group	Action Taken	Main Output
Monitor and Control Project Work	Monitoring and Controlling	Identifying actions required to create work results	Recommended corrective actions, change requests
Integrated Change Control	Monitoring and Controlling	Updating defined project definition	Approved change requests
Close Project	Closing	Obtaining final approvals	Project archives

Project Scope Management

Project Scope Management contains processes that define the product created by the project and the work to be performed on the project. During this process, a structure is created that breaks each task into itemized details of work to be performed.

Table 1.5 shows the various processes of the Project Scope Management knowledge area.

TABLE 1.5   The Project Scope Management Processes

Process	Process Group	Action Taken	Main Output
Scope Planning	Planning	Documenting intent of project to define the scope	Scope management plan
Scope Definition	Planning	Elaborating preliminary project scope statement	Scope statement
Create Work Breakdown Structure (WBS)	Planning	Decomposing the scope statement into a work breakdown structure	Work breakdown structure and dictionary
Scope Verification	Monitoring and Controlling	Obtaining work results and acceptance of work	Accepted deliverables
Scope Control	Monitoring and Controlling	Identifying changes to project scope	Project scope updates

Project Time Management

Project Time Management contains processes that define and control the activities required to complete the project as well as resources for the project. In this knowledge area, the project manager defines the baseline schedule for the project.

Table 1.6 shows the various processes of the Project Time Management knowledge area.

TABLE 1.6   Project Time Management Processes

Process	Process Group	Action Taken	Main Output
Activity Definition	Planning	Decomposing WBS to create activity list	Activity list
Activity Sequencing	Planning	Identifying interactivity in logical relationships	Network diagrams (PERT or Gantt chart)
Activity Resource Estimating	Planning	Determining resource requirements for activities	Resource requirements
Activity Duration Estimating	Planning	Estimating a time duration for each task	Activity duration estimates
Schedule Development	Planning	Calendaring activity durations and sequences	Project schedule
Schedule Control	Monitoring and Controlling	Identifying schedule changes and variances	Schedule updates

Project Cost Management

Project Cost Management comprises three processes that define, specify, and control costs for the project. This knowledge area uses *earned value technique* to measure cost performance for the project. Earned value (EV) is the current value of work that has been performed in the project.

Table 1.7 shows the various processes of the Project Cost Management knowledge area.

Project Quality Management

The Project Quality Management knowledge area comprises three processes that define what quality definition will be applied to the project's product and performance. The project team audits project performance. Then the product that is produced by the project will be inspected for conformance to objectives. A determination will be made concerning the product created and its fitness for use.

TABLE 1.7 Project Cost Management Processes

Process	Process Group	Action Taken	Main Output
Cost Estimating	Planning	Using task estimates and resource estimates to create a cost estimate	Cost estimate
Cost Budgeting	Planning	Assigning cost estimates to work packages (from WBS)	Cost baseline
Cost Control	Monitoring and Controlling	Identifying changes and variances to baseline	Budget updates

Table 1.8 shows the various processes of the Project Quality Management knowledge area.

TABLE 1.8 Project Quality Management Processes

Process	Process Group	Action Taken	Main Output
Quality Planning	Planning	Documenting intent of project and product quality	Quality management plan
Perform Quality Assurance	Executing	Porforming project audits to determine project quality	Quality improvement
Perform Quality Control	Monitoring and Controlling	Inspecting outputs to ascertain quality	Acceptance or rejection of work results

Project Human Resource Management

Project Human Resource Management facilitates planning the organization, roles, responsibilities, and staffing for the project. A comprehensive staffing management plan is a key tool for managing resources and controlling project costs and schedules.

Table 1.9 shows the various processes of the Project Human Resource Management knowledge area.

TABLE 1.9 Project Human Resource Management Processes

Process	Process Group	Action Taken	Main Output
Human Resource Planning	Planning	Determining human resources required to complete the project	Roles and responsibilities

TABLE 1.9   Project Human Resource Management Processes *(continued)*

Process	Process Group	Action Taken	Main Output
Acquire Project Team	Executing	Negotiating or procuring staff	Project staff
Develop Project Team	Executing	Developing team competency, training	Performance improvement
Manage Project Team	Monitoring and Controlling	Obtaining work results and identifying corrective actions	Change requests, corrective action

Project Communications Management

Project Communications Management defines the communications needs of the project stakeholders, and then facilitates and controls communications distribution during the life of the project. A calculation of earned value (EV) is used to show stakeholders the value of work performed in the project. EV provides a financial measurement of the value created to date.

Table 1.10 shows the various processes of the Project Communications Management knowledge area.

TABLE 1.10   Project Communications Management Processes

Process	Process Group	Action Taken	Main Output
Communications Planning	Planning	Documenting communications needs of project stakeholders	Communications management plan
Information Distribution	Executing	Sending out info as per plan	Project records
Performance Reporting	Monitoring and Controlling	Measuring performance using earned value (EV)	Performance reports
Manage Stakeholders	Monitoring and Controlling	Managing stakeholder communication	Resolved issues

Project Risk Management

Project Risk Management comprises six processes that define the risk methods to be used, define the risks of the project, analyze the risks, and document responses to identified risks.

Through these processes, managing the risk becomes a high priority for the project and remains in the forefront of project activities.

Table 1.11 shows the various processes of the Project Risk Management knowledge area.

TABLE 1.11 Project Risk Management Processes

Process	Process Groups	Action Taken	Main Output
Risk Management Planning	Planning	Documenting intent of project regarding risk management	Risk management plan
Risk Identification	Planning	Reviewing project to identify risks	Risk register
Qualitative Risk Analysis	Planning	Analyzing risk impacts and probabilities	Risk register updates
Quantitative Risk Analysis	Planning	Analyzing risks numerically to predict outcomes	Risk register updates
Risk Response Planning	Planning	Identifying actions to respond to priori-tized risks	Risk register updates
Risk Monitoring and Control	Monitoring and Controlling	Monitoring for identi-fied risks and symp-toms, looking for new risks	Risk register updates

Project Procurement Management

Project Procurement Management defines the processes that are required to purchase resources (people, equipment, and materials) from outside your organization. This creates an orderly, documented method for contracting with vendors.

Table 1.12 shows the various processes of the Project Procurement Management knowledge area.

TABLE 1.12 Project Procurement Management Processes

Process	Process Groups	Action Taken	Main Output
Plan Purchases and Acquisitions	Planning	Deciding whether to make or purchase.	Procurement management plan

TABLE 1.12   Project Procurement Management Processes *(continued)*

Process	Process Groups	Action Taken	Main Output
Plan Contracting	Planning	Determining type of procurement document. Decision 1: Offer fixed price, cost reimbursable, or time and material. Decision 2: Use request for proposal (RFP), request for information (RFI), or invitation to tender (ITT).	Procurement documents
Request Seller Responses	Executing	Sending out procurement documents, holding bidders conferences.	Procurement packages
Select Sellers	Executing	Negotiating a contract.	Contract
Contract Administration	Monitoring and Controlling	Managing sellers work.	Contract documentation
Contract Closure	Closing	Giving seller formal acceptance.	Closed contract

 Real World Scenario

Why Is This Important?

Managing projects can become complex and exceed the ability of some individuals. The goal of the preceding framework is to ensure proper organization and control during the project life cycle. By understanding and following these techniques, the organization will be able to avoid costly mistakes.

Proper training will improve a person's understanding of the project management process. The next goal after training is to obtain proficiency. You can achieve proficiency by practicing the process. CISAs should exercise every opportunity to improve their skills and proficiency in project management.

We strongly advise every IS auditor to improve their project management skills. Major updates have recently been added in the field of project management. In fact, the PMI process model prior to September 2005 is obsolete and incompatible with the current PMI model. Your success in auditing is directly related to the ability to manage projects. It will help you advance in your career.

Using Project Management Diagramming Techniques

Effective project management requires a significant level of communication and integration. Two of the more common diagramming techniques include Gantt charts and PERT network diagrams.

Gantt charts (see Figure 1.5) are used to schedule and sequence activities in a waterfall-type representation (activities are shown flowing downward to completion). The figure shows both sequential and concurrent activities in a linear bar-chart style presentation. Milestones will be identified and progress reported against planned activities. Gantt charts are more simplistic than PERT diagrams. In a typical Gantt chart, the bars show tasks, and diamond symbols indicate milestones. The long dark overhead bars depict a phase or a section of the schedule.

Programmed Evaluation Review Technique (PERT) is used to illustrate the relationship between planned activities (see Figure 1.6). A PERT diagram shows multiple routes through the activities necessary for accomplishing a project. The advantage of PERT is the ability to demonstrate a critical path. A *critical path* represents the minimum steps necessary to complete a successful project. This path is the longest route in the diagram and the shortest time estimate for project completion.

FIGURE 1.5   A Gantt chart

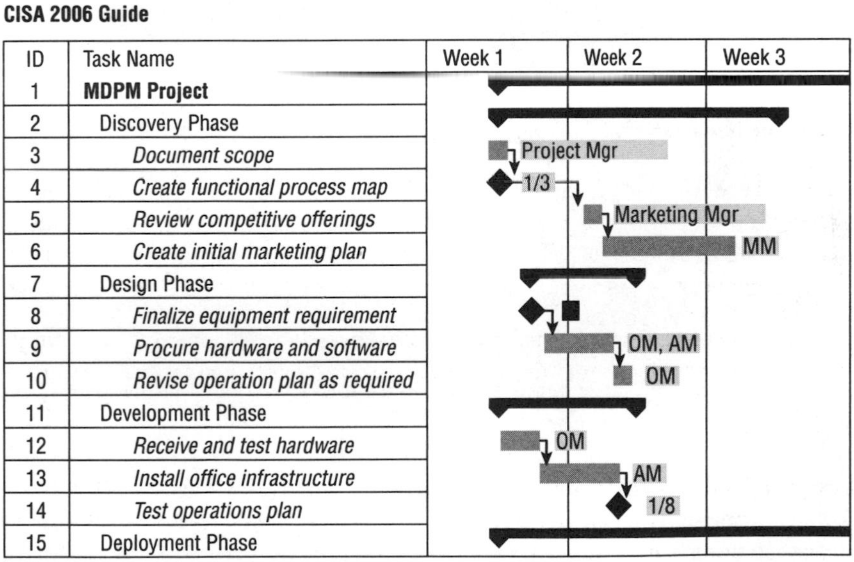

CISA 2006 Guide

ID	Task Name	Week 1	Week 2	Week 3
1	**MDPM Project**			
2	Discovery Phase			
3	*Document scope*	Project Mgr		
4	*Create functional process map*	1/3		
5	*Review competitive offerings*		Marketing Mgr	
6	*Create initial marketing plan*		MM	
7	Design Phase			
8	*Finalize equipment requirement*			
9	*Procure hardware and software*		OM, AM	
10	*Revise operation plan as required*		OM	
11	Development Phase			
12	*Receive and test hardware*	OM		
13	*Install office infrastructure*		AM	
14	*Test operations plan*		1/8	
15	Deployment Phase			

FIGURE 1.6 A PERT chart

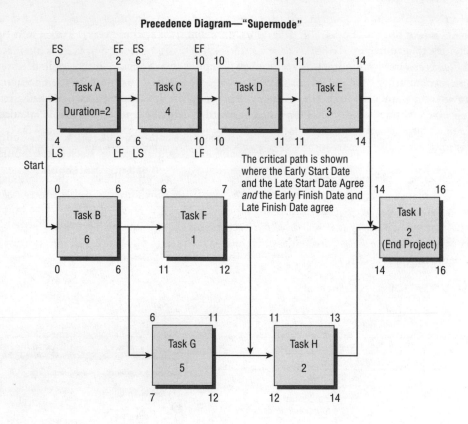

Precedence Diagram—"Supermode"

The critical path is shown where the Early Start Date and the Late Start Date Agree *and* the Early Finish Date and Late Finish Date agree

Summary

In this chapter, we covered the pervasive foundation of knowledge necessary for you to be a successful IS auditor. Our goal is to provide basic auditor knowledge to help guide your decisions. The secret of a successful auditor is to understand who to believe and their motivation. A successful IS auditor will follow industry-accepted practices while dealing with conflict and change in a manner that generates admiration from their clients. It is your responsibility as an IS auditor to demonstrate effective leadership skills in the pursuit of your work. A good leader will take control of the situation to direct all effort toward fulfilling the desired objective.

In the next chapter, we will discuss the audit process in detail.

Exam Essentials

1.1 Know the purpose of policies, standards, guidelines, and procedures.   Policies are high-level objectives designated by a person of authority, and compliance to policies is mandatory. Standards ensure a minimum level of uniform compliance to a policy, and compliance to standards is mandatory. Guidelines advise with preferred objectives and useful information in the absence of a standard. Guidelines are often discretionary. Procedures are a cookbook recipe of specific tasks necessary to implement a standard. Compliance to procedures is mandatory.

1.2 Know the ISACA standards governing professional conduct and ethics.   The auditor is expected to perform with the highest level of concern and diligence. Each audit should be conducted in accordance with professional standards and objectivity, and should implement best practices.

1.3 Understand the general purpose of the audit and the role of the IS auditor.   The purpose of auditing is to challenge the assertions of management and to determine whether evidence will support management's claims.

1.4 Understand an audit role vs. a nonaudit role.   There are only two roles in an audit. The first role is that of the auditor who performs an objective review, and second are the roles of everyone else. A person cannot be both an auditor and also involved in the design or operation of the audit subject.

1.5 Understand the importance of IS auditor independence.   It is unlikely that an auditor could be truly independent if the auditor were involved with the subject of the audit. Auditor independence is an additional assurance of truth.

1.6 Know the difference between discretionary and mandatory language.   In regulatory language, the word *shall* designates a mandatory requirement. The word *shall* indicates that there is no excuse for failing to meet the stated objective, even if compliance would cause a financial loss. The word *should* indicates a recommendation that could be optional, depending on the circumstance.

1.7 Know the different types of audits.   The types of audit are financial, operational (SAS-70), integrated (SAS-94), compliance, administrative, and information systems.

1.8 Understand the importance of IS auditor confidentiality.   The IS auditor shall maintain confidentiality at all times to protect the client. Sensitive information should not be revealed at any time. Your client expects you to protect their secrets whenever legally possible.

1.9 Understand the need to protect audit documentation.   The data must be protected with access controls and regular backup. Sensitive information is the property of the owner, and its confidentiality shall be protected by the auditor. A document archive is created during the audit and is subject to laws governing record retention.

1.10 Know how to use standard terms of reference.   The auditor should communicate by using standardized terms of reference to avoid misunderstanding or confusion. The standard terminology should be defined through a mutual agreement at the beginning of the audit.

1.11 Understand application of the evidence rule.   Audit evidence needs to be confirmed or verified to ensure it is actually used in the production process.

1.12 Identify who the auditor may need to interview.   The IS auditor needs to consider the roles of data owner, data user, and data custodian when selecting persons to interview. Data owners specify controls, data users are to follow acceptable usage requirements, and custodians protect the information while supporting data users.

1.13 Understand the organizational structure.   Officers of an organization are usually persons with the title of vice president or higher, up to the board of directors. Department directors, managers, and staff workers are seldom liable for the organization, unless criminal activity is involved.

1.14 Understand how to manage projects, including the audit project.   The IS auditor is expected to manage audit projects and be cognizant of project management techniques. The auditor is expected to be competent in evaluating the client's management of projects. Every project contains the three competing values of scope, cost, and time. A project manager in the projectized or strong matrix organization has more authority than a project manager in a weak matrix or functional organization.

Review Questions

1. What is the difference between a policy and a procedure?

   A. Compliance to a policy is discretionary, and compliance to a procedure is mandatory.

   B. A procedure provides discretionary advice to aid in decision making. The policy defines specific requirements to insure compliance.

   C. A policy is a high-level document signed by a person of authority and compliance is mandatory. A procedure defines the mandatory steps to attain compliance.

   D. A policy is a mid-level document issued to advise the reader of desired actions in the absence of a standard. The procedure describes suggested steps to use.

2. Which of the following in a business organization will be held liable by the government for failures of internal controls?

   A. President, vice presidents, and other true corporate officers

   B. Board of directors, president, vice presidents, department directors, and managers

   C. All members of management

   D. Board of directors, CEO, CFO, CIO, and department directors

3. What does *fiduciary responsibility* mean?

   A. To use information gained for personal interests without breaching confidentiality of the client.

   B. To act for the benefit of another person and place the responsibilities to be fair and honest ahead of your own interest.

   C. To follow the desires of the client and maintain total confidentiality even if illegal acts are discovered. The auditor shall never disclose information from an audit in order to protect the client.

   D. None of the above.

4. What are the different types of audits?

   A. Forensic, accounting, verification, regulatory

   B. Integrated, operational, compliance, administrative

   C. Financial, SAS-74, compliance, administrative

   D. Information systems, SAS-70, regulatory, procedural

5. What is the difference between the word *should* and *shall* when used in regulations?

   A. *Shall* represents discretionary requirements, and *should* provides advice to the reader.

   B. *Should* indicates mandatory actions, whereas *shall* provides advisory information recommending actions when appropriate

   C. *Should* and *shall* are comparable in meaning. The difference is based on the individual circumstances faced by the audit.

   D. *Should* indicates actions that are discretionary according to need, whereas *shall* means the action is mandatory regardless of financial impact.

6. Highest authority for a project manager is in the _____ organizational structure.

   A. Projectized, followed by the strong matrix

   B. Functional

   C. Cross-functional matrix

   D. Business corporation

7. Which of the following is *not* defined as a nonaudit role?

   A. System designer

   B. Operational staff member

   C. Auditor

   D. Organizational manager

8. Why is it necessary to protect audit documentation and work papers?

   A. The evidence gathered in an audit must be disclosed for regulatory compliance.

   B. A paper trail is necessary to prove the auditor is right and the auditee is wrong.

   C. The auditor will have to prove illegal activity in a court of law.

   D. Audit documentation work papers may reveal confidential information that should not be lost or disclosed.

9. Which of the following is a network diagram that shows the critical path for a project?

   A. Program evaluation review technique

   B. Gantt chart with activity sequencing

   C. Shortest path diagramming technique

   D. Milestone reporting

10. What is the purpose of standard terms of reference?

   A. To meet the legal requirement of regulatory compliance

   B. To prove who is responsible

   C. To ensure honest and unbiased communication

   D. To ensure that requirements are clearly identified in a regulation

11. What does the statement "auditor independence" relate to?

   A. It is not an issue for auditors working for a consulting company.

   B. It is required for an external audit.

   C. An internal auditor must undergo certification training to be independent.

   D. The audit committee bestows independence upon the auditor.

12. Which of the following is true concerning the roles of data owner, data user, and data custodian?

    A. The data user implements controls as necessary.

    B. The data custodian is responsible for specifying acceptable usage.

    C. The data owner specifies controls.

    D. The data custodian specifies security classification.

13. What is the definition of a work breakdown structure?

    A. A detailed staffing plan

    B. Sequence of steps with milestones in support of the project scope

    C. The levels of authority delegated by the project manager

    D. Decomposition of tasks

14. What is the definition of a standard as compared to a guideline?

    A. Standards are discretionary controls used with guidelines to aid the reader's decision process.

    B. Standards are mandatory controls designed to support a policy. Following guidelines is discretionary.

    C. Guidelines are recommended controls necessary to support standards, which are discretionary.

    D. Guidelines are intended to designate a policy, whereas standards are used in the absence of a policy.

15. Who should issue the organizational policies?

    A. Policies should originate from the bottom and move up to the department manager for approval.

    B. The auditor should issue the policies in accordance with standards and authorized by the highest level of management to ensure compliance.

    C. Any level of management.

    D. The policy should be signed and enforced by the highest level of management.

16. The auditor's final opinion is to be based on:

    A. The objectives and verbal statements made by management

    B. An understanding of management's desired audit results

    C. The audit committee's specifications

    D. The results of evidence and testing

17. What is the purpose of ISACA's professional ethics statement?

    A. To clearly specify acceptable and unacceptable behavior

    B. To provide procedural advisement to the new IS auditor

    C. To provide instructions on how to deal with irregularities and illegal acts by the client

    D. To provide advice on when it is acceptable for the auditor to deviate from audit standards

18. How does the auditor derive a final opinion?

    A. From evidence gathered and the auditor's observations

    B. By representations and assurances of management

    C. By testing the compliance of language used in organizational policies

    D. Under advice of the audit committee

19. What are the three competing demands to be addressed by project management?

    A. Scope, authority, and money

    B. Time, cost, and scope

    C. Requirements, authority, and responsibility

    D. Authority, organizational structure, and scope

20. What is the difference between a threat and a vulnerability?

    A. Threats are the path that can be exploited by a vulnerability.

    B. Threats are risks and become a vulnerability if they occur.

    C. Vulnerabilities are a path that can be taken by a threat, resulting in a loss.

    D. Vulnerability is a negative event that will cause a loss if it occurs.

Answers to Review Questions

1. C. A policy is signed by the person of highest authority to ensure compliance by the members of the organization. Compliance to policies, standards, and procedures is mandatory.

2. A. Officers of the organization will typically hold the title of vice president or higher. A CIO might not be a corporate officer, unless the position is located in the parent organization. A division-level CIO may or may not be a true corporate officer. Those holding the position of department director and below are seldom held liable by the government for internal control failure. A department director is a supporting manager to the vice president.

3. B. Accountants, auditors, and lawyers act on behalf of their client's best interests unless doing so places them in violation of the law. It is the highest standard of duty implied by law for a trustee and guardian.

4. B. All of the audit types are valid except procedural, SAS-74, verification, and regulatory. The valid audit types are financial, operational (SAS-70), integrated (SAS-94), compliance, administrative, forensic, and information systems. A forensic audit is used to discover information about a possible crime.

5. D. *Should* represents discretionary information in a regulation. *Shall* indicates that compliance is mandatory regardless of profit or loss.

6. A. The highest level of authority is in the projectized organization, followed in decreasing authority by the strong matrix, balanced matrix, weak matrix, and functional. In functional and weak matrix organizations, the project manager has almost no authority and relies on begging and personal influence.

7. C. Every role except an auditor is a nonaudit role. Anyone in a nonaudit roles is disqualified from being an independent auditor.

8. D. The auditor may discover information that could cause some level of damage to the client if disclosed. The information could trigger additional actions by a perpetrator. In addition, the auditor shall implement controls to ensure security and data backup of their work.

9. A. A Program Evaluation Review Technique (PERT) is designed to show the critical path of a project. A Gantt chart shows activity sequences and milestones without identifying the critical path. Answers C and D are distracters.

10. C. Standard terms of reference are used between the auditor and everyone else to ensure honest and unbiased communication. Without standard terminology, it would be difficult to know whether we were discussing the same issue or agreed on the same outcome.

11. B. The auditor must be independent. Having a personal relationship with the organization being audited could result in a biased opinion. The business relationship is also an issue if the organization has influence over the auditor. The goal is to be fair, objective, and unrelated to the subject of the audit.

12. C. The data owner specifies controls, is responsible for acceptable use, and appoints the data custodian. The data users will comply with acceptable use and report violations. The data custodian will protect information and ensure its availability. The custodian will also provide support to the users.

13. D. A work breakdown structure is the decomposition of tasks necessary to perform the required work for the project.

14. B. A standard is implemented to ensure a minimum level of uniform compliance. Guidelines are advisory information used in the absence of a standard. Compliance to standards is mandatory; compliance to guidelines is discretionary.

15. D. Policies should be signed, issued, and enforced by the highest level of management to ensure compliance by the organization. It is the responsibility of management (not the auditor) to implement internal controls.

16. D. The auditor is to be a professional skeptic who tests assertions of management and renders an opinion based on the evidence discovered during the audit.

17. A. This statement specifies that IS auditors are expected to fulfill their duties with the highest standards of honest and truthful representation. It is unacceptable to violate the fiduciary relationship with your client.

18. A. A final opinion is based on evidence gathered and testing. The purpose of an audit is to challenge the assertions of management. Evidence is gathered that will support or disprove claims.

19. B. Scope, cost, and time are the three constraints in every project. Scope includes authority, while cost includes resources and personnel. Time affects both cost and scope of the project to be completed as planned.

20. C. Assets are anything of value. Threats are negative events that cause a loss if they occur. Vulnerabilities are paths that allow a threat to occur.

Chapter

2

Audit Process

THE OBJECTIVE OF THIS CHAPTER IS TO ACQUAINT THE READER WITH THE FOLLOWING CONCEPTS:

✓ Developing and implementing a risk-based audit strategy

✓ Planning specific audits

✓ Conducting audits in accordance with standards, guidelines, and best practices

✓ Dealing with conflict, potential risks, and communicating audit results to stakeholders

✓ Implementing risk management and control practices while maintaining independence

The auditing process is based on a series of generally accepted procedures. Your job as an IS auditor is to provide reasonable assurance that audit objectives are accomplished using applicable professional auditing standards.

During an audit, it is important to remember that all decisions and opinions will need to be supported by evidence and documentation. It is the auditor's responsibility to ensure consistency in the audit process. An *audit quality control* plan should be adopted to support these basic objectives.

There are 10 audit stages to be aware of when performing an audit. A CISA will need to be aware of their duties in each of these stages:

- Approving the audit charter or engagement letter
- Preplanning the audit
- Performing a risk assessment
- Determining whether an audit is possible
- Performing the actual audit
- Gathering evidence
- Performing audit tests
- Analyzing the results
- Reporting the results
- Conducting any follow-up activities

In this chapter, you will look at each of these stages in detail along with various procedures used during the audit. Figure 2.1 illustrates a simple flowchart of the audit process. The actual execution of the audit will be more complex.

We will begin with the process of establishing an audit charter in order to gain the authority to perform an audit.

Establishing and Approving an Audit Charter

The first audit objective is to establish an *audit charter*, which gives you the authority to perform an audit. The audit charter is issued by executive management or the board of directors.

When we refer to management, we are referring to the auditee unless stated otherwise.

FIGURE 2.1   Overview of the audit process

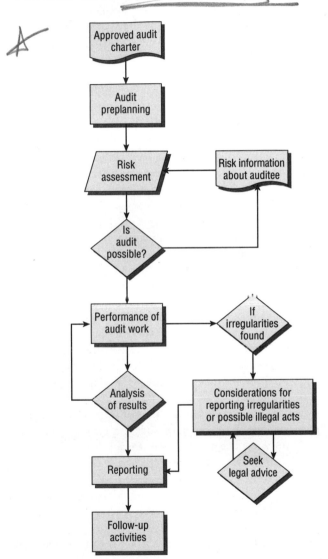

The audit charter should clearly state management's assertion of responsibility, their objectives, and delegation of authority. An audit charter outlines your responsibility, authority, and accountability:

Responsibility   Provides scope with goals and objectives.

Authority   Grants the right to perform an audit and the right to obtain access relevant to the audit.

Accountability   Defines mutually agreed actions between the audit committee and the auditor, complete with reporting requirements.

Role of the Audit Committee

Each organization should have an audit committee composed of business executives. Each audit committee member is required to be financially literate with the ability to read and understand financial statements including balance sheets, income statements, and cash flow statements. The audit committee members are expected to have past employment experience in accounting or finance, and hold certification in accounting. A chief executive officer with comparable financial sophistication may be a member of an audit committee.

The purpose of the audit committee is to provide advice to the executive accounting officer concerning internal control strategies, priorities, and assurances. It is unlikely an executive officer will know every detail about the activities within their organization. In spite of this, executive officers are held accountable for any internal control failures. Audit committees are not a substitute for executives who must govern, control, and manage their organization. The audit committee is delegated the authority to review and challenge the assurances of internal controls made by executive management.

The audit committee is expected to maintain a positive working relationship with management, internal auditors, and independent auditors. The committee manages planned audit activities and results of both internal and external audits. The committee is authorized to engage outside experts for independent assurance. Both internal auditors and external auditors will have escalation procedures designed to communicate significant weaknesses that have been identified. The auditor will seek to have the weaknesses corrected in order to give a positive assurance that the risk is appropriately controlled and managed. The head of the internal audit and the external audit representative should have free access to the audit committee chairperson. This ensures an opportunity to raise any concerns the auditor may have concerning processes, internal controls, risks, and limitations.

The audit committee should meet on a regular basis, at least four times a year, to fulfill this requirement. The Sarbanes-Oxley Act of 2002 requires executives to certify that all internal control weaknesses have been discovered, with full disclosure to the audit committee provided every 90 days.

The audit committee is responsible for issuing the audit charter to grant the authority for internal audits. The audit charter should be approved by the highest level of management as well as the audit committee. Authority also needs to be granted for an independent audit. A document called an engagement letter will grant authority for an independent external audit.

Engagement Letter

The audit charter allows the delegation of an audit to an external organization via an engagement letter. The *engagement letter* helps define the relationship to an independent auditor for individual assignments. The letter records the understanding between the audit committee and the independent auditor.

> The primary difference between an engagement letter and an audit charter is that an engagement letter addresses the independence of the auditor.

Engagement letters should include the following:

- All points outlined in the audit charter
- Independence of the auditor (responsibility)
- Evidence of an agreement to the terms and conditions (authority)
- Agreed-upon completion dates (accountability)

Preplanning the Audit

The second audit objective is to plan the specific audit project necessary to address the audit objectives. Analysis should occur at least annually to incorporate the constant stream of new developments in both the industry and the auditing field.

Your audit objectives will include compliance to professional auditing standards and applicable laws. The IS auditor needs to be prepared to justify any deviation from professional audit standards. Deviation is a rare event.

As an auditor, you will need to consider the impact of the audit on the business operation. You will need to gain an understanding of the business, its purpose, and any potential constraints to the audit. Let's look at the questions an auditor could ask to gain insight of the business operation:

Knowledge of the business itself   What are their specific industry regulations? For example, are they governed by the US Occupational Safety & Health Administration, any financial securities regulations, or the Health Insurance Portability and Accountability Act due to offering employee medical benefits?

What are the business cycles? The retail industry operates on a schedule that begins Christmas holiday activities in September. Their busy season is at the end of the year, whereas the construction industry is busy from January through May.

What are the reporting cycles? Is year-end on September 30 or December 31?

What are the critical business processes necessary for survival?

Are reports available from prior audits?

Will the auditors be able to tour the facilities? Which location and when?

Who should be interviewed? Will those people be available?

What are their existing plans? Any new products, clients, or significant changes?

Strategic objectives   What is the direction and structure going forward?

What is the organizational plan for IS?

What are the business objectives that IS is expected to fulfill?

What are the defined IS goals?

What is the strategic plan for the next 2–3 years?

What are the supporting tactical plan steps during the next 1–2 years?

What work is occurring from now to the end of the year?

Financial objectives   What is the rate of return (ROI) goal for capital investment and related expenses?

How are assets managed?

How are costs allocated to departments and projects?

What is the budget and forecasting process?

What are the financial reporting objectives? Will the client need an integrated audit for Sarbanes-Oxley reporting?

What are the business continuity plans?

Operational objectives for internal control   Any policies or procedures to be tested?

Will this be an administrative audit?

How are performance metrics managed?

What is the method used for capacity planning?

How have access controls been implemented?

What is the strategy and status of disaster recovery plans?

How is system administration managed?

What controls exist for managing network communications?

What is the nature of the last system audit? Are self-assessments used?

What are the staffing plans?

Figure 2.2 shows four basic areas related to the organization's business requirements.

FIGURE 2.2   Understanding the business requirements

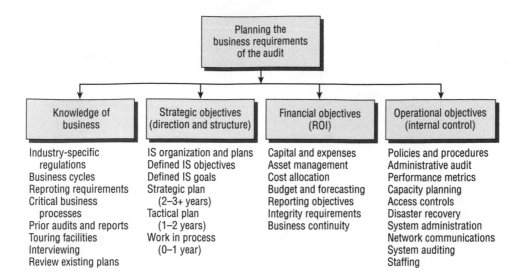

Identifying Restrictions on Scope

Every IS auditor will need to provide details any time significant restrictions have been placed on the scope of an audit. You will need to review your audit objectives and risk strategy to determine whether the audit is still possible and will meet the stated objectives. The audit report should explain specific restrictions and their impact on the audit. If the restrictions preclude the ability to collect sufficient evidence, you should render no opinion or no attestation in the audit.

Examples of restrictions include the following:

- Management placing undue restrictions on evidence use or audit procedures that could seriously undermine the audit objective

- Inability to obtain sufficient evidence for any reason

- Lack of resources or lack of sufficient time

- Ineffective audit procedures

Auditors have been known to terminate an engagement if the client places restrictions that are too severe on the audit. It is not unheard of for a client to discharge an auditor after receiving accurate findings that are distasteful to the client. The replacement auditor may need to inquire why a prior auditor is no longer being used by the auditee.

In some instances, the auditee will need to establish a level of communication between the previous auditor and replacement auditor. The purpose of this communication is to ensure that the client is not trying to obstruct truthful findings. Blackouts, or missing audit periods, would be a concern shared by more people than just the auditor. Statements on Auditing Standard 84 (SAS-84) will provide additional details if you ever encounter this situation.

Planning Detailed Audit Objectives

Each audit is actually an individual project linked into an ongoing audit program. Every audit should have a set of requirements and objectives in support of the ongoing program—for example, the controls and efforts necessary to comply with regulations such as Sarbanes-Oxley. It is not possible to test all the requirements in one monolithic audit, so we break down (*decompile*) the larger compliance requirements into a series of smaller audits (*modular stages*).

The auditee is responsible for working with the auditor to do the following:

- Identify critical success factors (CSFs) and measures of performance.
- Identify personnel roles and responsibilities.
- Provide access to information, personnel, locations, and systems relevant to the audit.
- Cooperate with the gathering of audit evidence.
- Provide access to prior audit results or to communication with prior auditors if necessary.
- Specify reporting lines to senior management.
- Make their assertion of controls and effectiveness independent of the auditor.

The auditor is responsible for the following:

- Plan each audit to accomplish specific objectives.
- Create a written project plan.
- Develop time and event schedules.
- Identify resources required.
- Document specific audit procedures linked to specific audit objectives.
- Use a risk-based audit strategy.
- Provide audit cost estimates.

The IS auditor may be asked to perform a variety of audits, including the following:

Product or service   Efficiency, effectiveness, controls, and life-cycle costs

Processes   Methods or results

System   Design or configuration

General controls   Preventative, detective, and corrective

Organizational plans   Present and future objectives

To be successful, the auditor needs to engage in a fact-finding mission. You will need to take into consideration business requirements that are unique to the auditee or common to their industry. Each business has its own opportunities, challenges, and constraints. Remember, the purpose of an audit is to help management verify assertions (claims). Proper planning is necessary to ensure that the audit itself does not disrupt the business, nor waste valuable resources including time and money.

As an auditor, you need to understand the nature of the systems your client desires to be audited. It would be nearly impossible to audit systems whose mission you do not understand.

Audit plans can change depending on whether the client is using a centralized or distributed system design. The location of IS facilities and personnel will need to be considered.

The auditor needs to demonstrate due care as a professional in both planning and execution. There are a number of definitions for the word *care*. *Basic care* is defined as the bare minimum necessary to sustain life without negligence. *Ordinary care* is better than basic and provides an average level of customary care in the absence of negligence. *Extraordinary care* is defined as that which is dramatically above and beyond what a normal person would offer or situation would entail. Various degrees of care could fall under the definition of *due care*. The degrees of care are proportional to the level of risk or loss that could occur. *Negligence* is the absence of care. A conscientious person will exercise due care in the performance of their job. Failure to exercise due care would be negligence.

Risk Management Strategy

After identifying a methodology for risk evaluation and control, the auditor will need to identify potential risks to the organization. The auditee will assist by providing information about their organization.

To properly identify risks, the auditor also needs to identify the following:

- Assets that need to be protected
- Exposures for those assets
- Threats to the assets
- Internal and external sources for threats
- Security issues that need to be addressed

Part of documenting risk data is for the auditor to identify potential risk response strategies that can be used in the audit with each identified risk. The four risk responses are as follows:

Accept   Take your chances. Ignoring a risk is the same as accepting it. The auditor should be concerned about the acceptance of high-risk situations.

Mitigate (reduce)   Do something to lower the odds of getting hurt. Most internal controls are designed to mitigate risk.

Transfer   Let someone else take the chance of loss by using a subcontractor or insurance. You can transfer the risk but not the liability for failure. Blind transfer of risk would be a genuine concern. This applies to outsourcing agreements and the reason for a *right to audit* clause in the contract.

Avoid   Reject the situation; change the situation to avoid taking the risk.

An assessment of risk will usually include a list of all possible risks that threaten the business and your evaluation of how imminent they are.

Figure 2.3 shows the basic process of responding to risks. A CISA is expected to understand the different types of responses. Risk management principles will apply to your audit planning. Your client will select from similar choices in their decisions about the risks faced by their organization.

FIGURE 2.3 Risk analysis process flowchart

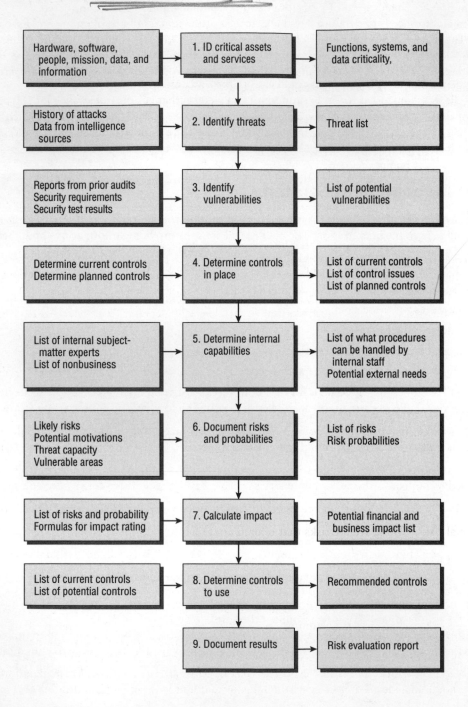

Performing an Audit Risk Assessment

Performing a risk assessment is the next step after the audit objectives have been identified. The purpose of a risk assessment is to ensure that sufficient evidence will be collected during an audit. We will add a new term to your auditor vocabulary: *materiality*. Materiality refers to evidence that is significant and could change the outcome.

While searching for evidence, it is important to remember that you are not looking for 100 percent of all conceivable evidence. You are interested in material evidence that will be relevant to the outcome of your audit. Please keep in mind that it is easy to be distracted during an audit. You should focus your efforts on material evidence that either proves or disproves your specific audit objective. Your findings and opinion will be based on this material evidence

An audit risk assessment should take into account the following types of risks:

Inherent risks   These are natural or built-in risks that always exist. Driving your automobile holds the inherent risk of an automobile accident or a flat tire. Theft is an inherent risk for items of high value.

Detection risks   These are the risks that an auditor will not be able to detect what they are looking to find. It would be terrible to report no negative results when material conditions (faults) actually exist. Detection risks include sampling and nonsampling risks:

Sampling risks   These are the risks that an auditor will falsely accept or erroneously reject an audit sample (evidence).

Nonsampling risks   These are the risks that an auditor will fail to detect a condition because of not applying the appropriate procedure or using procedures inconsistent with the audit objective (detection fault).

Control risks   These are the risks that an auditor could lose control, errors could be introduced, or errors may not be corrected in a timely manner (if ever).

Business risks   These are risks that are inherent in the business or industry itself. They may be regulatory, contractual, or financial.

Technological risks   These are inherent risks of using automated technology. Systems do fail.

Operational risks   These are the risks that a process or procedure will not perform correctly.

Residual risks   These are the risks that remain after all mitigation efforts are performed.

Audit risks   These are the combination of inherent, detection, control, and residual risks.

These are the same risks facing normal business operations. In the planning phase, an IS auditor is primarily concerned with the first three: *inherent* risk, *detection* risk, and *control* risk. All of the risks could place the business or audit in jeopardy and should be considered during some level of advance planning.

An auditor should create plans to allow for alternative audit strategies if an auditee has recently experienced an outage, service interruption, or unscheduled downtime. It would be unwise to pursue an audit before the business has ample time to restabilize normal operations. Plans should include an opportunity to reschedule without violating a legal deadline.

Determining Whether an Audit Is Possible

A good auditor remembers that setting priorities is their responsibility. You will need to assess the risk of the audit and ensure that priorities have been fulfilled. If you are unable to perform the necessary audit functions, it is essential that the issues be properly communicated to management and the audit committee. An audit without meaningful evidence would be useless.

The auditor will need to work with the auditee to define specific requirements and identify any third-party providers. You will need to review the auditee's organizational structure and to identify persons in areas of interest that are material to your audit.

Organizations with outsourcing contracts and labor unions could be particularly difficult unless you have sufficient cooperation. In the case of labor unions, it is often necessary for the shop steward to be present and involved in all plans and activities. Failure to do so may result in an operational risk of the union workers walking off the job.

Outsourced activities will present their own challenges with potential restrictions on access to personnel and evidence. It would not be uncommon for a service provider to decline your request for an audit. Most outsource providers will attempt to answer such requests by supplying you with a copy of their latest SAS-70 report, which is a standard report format for service providers. Occasionally, when a client requests and receives a SAS-70 report from a service provider, the value of content in the SAS-70 report may be overstated. The purpose of the SAS-70 is to eliminate multiple organizations from individually auditing the service provider. You can expect that several points of detailed evidence you requested will have been filtered or masked in the SAS-70 report. Your client's original outsource contract should have included a provision for the *right to audit* along with the service-level agreement. It must be clearly stated if the SAS-70 is acceptable or if individual audit is required. Performing your own audit adds cost but offers high levels of control. Be advised that some outsource providers run on a different business schedule than their clients.

 Real World Scenario

Working in Labor Union Environments

We are acutely aware of how seemingly trivial actions can have significant consequences in a labor union environment. Plugging in our own computers to a client's network resulted in a complete work stoppage after our actions were observed by an unhappy union worker. Every union worker in the plant stopped what they were doing. We were immediately summoned by management to explain our actions. After several agonizing minutes of begging forgiveness, the shop steward agreed that everyone could return to work. Your illustrious authors received a dire warning not to do this again. Fortunately, the client agreed to cover the cost of the work stoppage and we did not have the take money out of our own pockets.

Management has the ultimate responsibility for internal controls and holds the authority for delegation. Management may choose to delegate tasks to a third party (outsource). The outsource organization must perform the daily tasks as designated, but unfortunately management will still retain liability that cannot be delegated. Executive management will still be held responsible for any failures that occur with or at the outsource organization. The federal government has gone to great lengths to ensure that the decision maker (management) can be held fully accountable for their actions and liable for any loss or damage.

Performing the Audit

The next objective in the audit is to perform the actual audit. Here you will need to make sure you have the appropriate staff, ensure audit quality control, define auditee communications, perform proper data collection, and review existing controls.

Allocating Staffing

You will need to have personnel for the audit and to define the audit's organizational structure. You also will need to create a personnel resource plan, which identifies specific functions and skill sets necessary to complete your audit objectives. Individual skills and knowledge should be taken into consideration while planning your audit. Remember, it's impossible for the auditor to be an absolute expert in everything.

You will need to rely on the work of others, including your own audit team members, subcontractors, and possibly members of the client's staff. You should create a detailed staff training plan that is reviewed at least semiannually and before each audit. The time to train or retrain personnel is before the audit begins.

The auditor will lead persons with specialized skills, including the use of database scanners and other automated audit tools. A skills matrix should be developed, which indicates areas of knowledge, proficiency, and specialized training. Occasionally, finding a competent, independent expert in database administration for a particular vendor on your project may prove difficult. However, you might be able to train a member of the client's support staff to provide sufficient assistance to complete the audit.

Auditors frequently use the work of others as long as the following conditions are met:

- Assess the independence and objectivity of the provider.
- Determine their professional competence, qualifications, and experience.
- Agree on the scope of work and approach used.
- Determine the level of review and supervision required.

If these conditions are met, the auditor may choose to use the work of others. A CISA should have serious concerns if the work does not meet their audit evidence requirement for any reason. You can use only evidence of sufficient quality, quantity, and relevance. Failure to meet this requirement may require a change in the audit scope or cancelling the audit.

Ensuring Audit Quality Control

Quality does not happen automatically. It is a methodology that must be designed into your process and not just inspected afterward. Quality control is necessary in every audit.

Audit standards, guidelines, and procedures were developed to promote quality and consistency in a typical audit. The ISACA audit standards were developed to assist CISA auditors in performing audits. Additional guidance can be obtained by reading the ISACA audit guide at www.isaca.org/standards.

Your audit will need a variety of quality performance metrics to ensure success. When designing a quality control process, an auditor should consider doing the following:

- Use an audit methodology (documented plan and procedures).

- Gain an understanding of the auditee needs and expectations.

- Respect business cycles and deadlines.

- Hold client interviews and workshops.

- Use customer satisfaction surveys.

- Agree to terms of reference used (discussed in Chapter 1).

- Establish audit performance metrics.

- Measure audit plan to actual performance.

- Respond to auditee complaints.

Defining Auditee Communications

The auditor must work with management to define the auditee communication requirements.

As discussed in Chapter 1, the auditee often feels at a disadvantage to the auditor. Without effective communication, the auditee will feel disillusioned, confused, or disconnected from the audit. Each of these conditions would be undesirable; audits without client buy-in would be a major disaster.

It is your job to be a "second set of eyes" in reviewing the present condition at their organization. You are responsible for reporting accurate findings to senior management and the audit committee. The audit charter should assist you by defining the required level of auditee communication.

To be effective in your communication, you need to consider several points, including the following:

- Describing the audit's purpose, service, and scope

- Dealing with problems, constraints, and delays

- Responding to client questions and complaints

- Dealing with issues outside the scope of this particular audit

- Timing and scheduling

- Following the reporting process

- Obtaining an agreement of your findings with your client

- Implementing confidentiality, implementing principle of least privilege (need to know)

- Providing special handling for evidence of irregularities or possibly illegal acts

Nothing will replace the simple act of asking the client what level and frequency of communication they expect. The preceding points are simply a starting position. You should synchronize the auditee communication plan with your own internal audit team communication plans.

During the planning process, the auditor will need to gain approval from management for access to the appropriate staff personnel. A member of the audit team may be assigned to coordinate everyone's schedule.

Now is a good time to introduce some of the data collection techniques that auditors use in audits.

Using Data Collection Techniques

As part of the planning process, the auditor needs to determine how data will be gathered for evidence to support the audit report. To collect useful data, the savvy auditor will use a combination of techniques including the following:

- Observation of staff in the performance of their duties. Auditor observation is a powerful form of evidence.

- Review of existing documentation. Remember, the evidence rule will apply. Presence of a document does not mean it is actually in use. You should review the auditee documentation and any related legal documentation. Legal documentation may be either contracts or regulatory laws.

- Interviews of selected personnel appropriate to the audit. Be sure to structure the timing and questions for the interview. You need to ensure that the questions are consistent and to allow extra time to discuss any interesting points raised.

- Workshops to generate awareness and understanding. The audit committee may be a good audience for a workshop. Well-executed workshops can save time compared to individual interviews.

- Surveys.

Each technique has its advantages and disadvantages. For example, surveys offer an advantage of time but have the disadvantages of inconsistency and limited response. A survey cannot detect a personal mannerism such as hesitancy, surprise, or restlessness.

An auditor can observe an auditee during an interview and ask additional probing questions based on the auditee response. The auditor weighs each response in an attempt to create consistent scoring of answers by multiple interview subjects. Interviews consume more time but can gather additional information.

Real World Scenario

Familiarize Yourself with Their IT Environment

That old saying of "getting to know a person by walking in their shoes" certainly applies to IS auditing. You have to depend on the auditee to show you the design strategy and purpose of their IT environment. Their IT structure is supposed to be aligned to their business objectives.

Before you can determine whether that alignment exists, you will need to tour their facility. You should expect the client to provide a current network diagram. We prefer a schematic-level diagram rather than a high-level overview. The view from 3 feet away is a zillion times more informative than from 100 thousand feet. It does not matter whether the diagram is in digital format or hand drawn. What matters is that the diagram is accurate. We would accept a computer diagram with small handwritten changes, under the condition that the original document is updated before we finish the audit. Good detail would indicate that the auditee is actively working to manage their systems. We would ask the auditee to sign the document to certify that it is current and correct.

You should be particularly interested in understanding how transactions flow through the auditee's IS environment. You need to identify how transactions are authorized along with any potential routes for physical and logical access. Integrity cannot exist without access controls. A good auditor will take plenty of notes during a walk-through and will follow up with questions. Areas of significant interest to the auditor include the following:

- Hardware systems.

- Operating systems.

- Applications, database software, and special utilities.

- Monitoring and control systems (at the server, network, and application level).

- Relevant documentation, especially diagrams, flowcharts, and process diagrams.

- Personnel roles and specific duties. Job descriptions and a copy of the organizational reporting relationship will be helpful (org chart). Hopefully a skills matrix or training plan will exist.

- Relationship of the IT design to their higher-level business objectives. Is the design driven by strategic business requirements or technology favorites?

- Separation of duties pertaining to transaction authorization. This would apply to all significant transactions in the IT environment and within applications. The auditor would want to know who authorizes system access, changes, new transactions, deletions, and updates.

Surveys may execute quickly but carry extra administrative support burdens. It will take time and resources to create the survey, distribute the survey, track responses, provide answer assistance, ensure quality control, and tally the results. Because of human nature, people will seldom answer a survey in a manner that reduces their agenda and perceived value to an organization.

Most clients will be impressed if you demonstrate genuine interest and take good notes. It will help you obtain auditee buy-in and make them feel the audit report will contain statements of value. Just be sure to avoid the perception of an interrogation.

Reviewing Existing Controls

The next step in the planning process is to review the existing internal controls that are intended to prevent, detect, or correct problems. Management is responsible for designating and implementing internal controls to protect their assets. You can obtain initial information about existing controls by reviewing current policies and procedures, and later by interviewing managers and key personnel. All the basic controls can be classified into one of three categories:

Preventative   Controls that seek to stop the problem occurrence. A simple example is prescreening job applicants for employment eligibility.

Detective   Controls that are intended to find a problem and bring it to your attention. Auditing is a detective control for discovering information.

Corrective   Controls that seek to repair the problem after detection. Restoring data from a backup tape after a disk drive failure is a corrective control.

Controls from the three categories will be implemented by using one of three methods. The three implementation methods are as follows:

Administrative   Using policies and procedures.

Technical   Involving a software or hardware process to calculate a result.

Physical   Implementing physical barriers or visual deterrents.

The auditor should be concerned with the attitude and understanding demonstrated by the auditee. An excellent exercise is to ask the auditee to which category their control would best apply. You may hear some unique and often incorrect responses. The process of reviewing the controls to prevent, detect, or correct is an excellent awareness generator with your auditee.

Table 2.1 lists some examples of these control types.

TABLE 2.1   Controls and Methods of Implementation

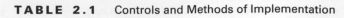

Control Type	Implementation Method	Some Examples
Preventative "stops"	Administrative	Hiring procedures, background checks, segregation of duties, training, change control process, acceptable use policy (AUP), organizational charts, job descriptions, written procedures, business contracts, laws and regulations, risk management, project management, service-level agreements (SLAs), system documentation
	Technical	Data backups, virus scanners, designated redundant system for high availability system ready for failover (HA standby), encryption, access control lists (ACLs), system certification process
	Physical	Access control, locked doors, fences, property tags, security guards, live monitoring of CCTV, human-readable labels, warning signs
Detective "finds"	Administrative	Auditing, system logs, mandatory vacation periods, exception reporting, run-to-run totals, check numbers, control self-assessment (CSA), risk assessment, oral testimony
	Technical	Intrusion detection system (IDS), High availability systems detecting or signaling system failover condition(HA failure detection), automated log readers (CAATs), checksum, verifying digital signatures, biometrics for identification (many search), CCTV used for logging, network scanners, computer forensics, diagnostic utilities
	Physical	Broken glass, physical inventory count, alarm system (burglar, smoke, water, temperature, fire), tamper seals, fingerprints, receipts and invoices
Corrective "fixes"	Administrative	Termination procedures (friendly/unfriendly), business continuity and disaster recovery plans, outsourcing, insourcing, implementing recommendations of prior audit, lessons learned, property and casualty insurance
	Technical	Data restoration from backup, High availability system failover to redundant system (HA failover occurs), redundant network routing, file repair utilities
	Physical	Hot-warm-cold sites for disaster recovery, fire-control sprinklers, heating and AC, humidity control

When you exercise this awareness game of preventative, detective, and corrective controls, it is interesting to notice how technology-oriented people will provide an overt emphasis on technology, while nontechnology-oriented people will focus on administrative and physical controls. If your background is technology, you will need to consider administrative or physical solutions to approach a reasonable balance of controls. Nontechnology-oriented people will need to force their emphasis to include technical controls and achieve a similar level of balance.

Identifying Audit Evidence

Every good auditor understands the necessity of collecting tangible and reliable evidence. You just read an introduction to the evidence rule in Chapter 1. Although you may really like or admire the people who are the subject of the audit, your final auditor's report must be based on credible factual evidence that will support your statements.

Consider for a moment something not related to IS auditing: police investigations or famous television courtroom dramas. Every good detective story is based on careful observation and common sense. A successful detective searches for clues in multiple places. Witnesses are interviewed to collect their versions of the story. Homes and offices are tirelessly searched for the most minute shred of relevant evidence. Detectives constantly ask whether the suspected individual had the motive, opportunity, and means to carry out the crime. The trail of clues is sorted in an attempt to determine which clues represent the greatest value and best tell the story. Material clues are the most sought after. From time to time, the clues are reviewed, and the witnesses re-interviewed. The detective orders a stakeout to monitor suspects. Ultimately, the suspects and clues of evidence are brought together in one place for the purpose of a reenactment. Under a watchful eye the materially relevant portions of the crime are re-created in an attempt to unmask the perpetrator. In the movies, the detective is fabulously successful, and the criminal is brought to justice.

Unfortunately, IS auditing is not so dramatic or thrilling to watch. A CISA candidate needs to possess a thorough understanding of evidence, because IS auditing is centered on properly collecting and reviewing evidence. Let's start with a short discussion on the characteristics of good evidence.

Types of Evidence

There are two primary types of evidence, according to legal definition:

Direct evidence   This proves existence of a fact without inference or presumption. *Inference* is when you draw a logical and reasonable proposition from another that is supposed to be true. Direct evidence includes the unaltered testimony of an eyewitness and written documents.

Indirect evidence   Indirect evidence uses a hypothesis without direct evidence to make a claim that consists of both inference and presumption. Indirect evidence is based on a chain of circumstances leading to a claim, with the intent to prove the existence or nonexistence of certain facts. Indirect evidence is also known as *circumstantial evidence*.

An auditor should always strive to obtain the best possible evidence during an audit. Using direct evidence is preferable whenever it can be obtained. Indirect evidence represents a much lower value due to its subjective nature. An auditor may find it difficult to justify using indirect evidence unless the audit objective is to gather data after detecting an illegal activity. An audit without direct evidence is normally unacceptable.

Grading Evidence

All evidence is graded according to criteria using four characteristics of evidence. This grading aids the auditor in assessing the evidence value. It is important to obtain the best possible evidence.

The four characteristics are as follows:

Material relevance   *Evidence with material relevance* influences the decision due to a logical relationship with the issues. Materially relevant evidence will indicate a fact that will help determine that a particular action was more or less probable. The purpose of material evidence is to ascertain whether the same conclusion would have been reached without considering that item of evidence. Evidence is *irrelevant* if it is not related to the issue and has no logical tendency to prove the issue under investigation.

Evidence objectivity   *Evidence objectivity* refers to its ability to be accepted and understood with very little judgment required. The more judgment required, the less objective the evidence. As you increase the amount of judgment necessary to support your claims, the evidence quickly becomes subjective or circumstantial, which is the opposite of objective. *Objective* evidence is in a state of unbiased reality during examination without influence by another source. Objective evidence can be obtained through qualitative/quantitative measurement, and from records or statements of fact pertaining to the subject of the investigation. Objective evidence can be verified by observation, measurement, or testing.

Competency of the evidence provider   Evidence supplied by a person with direct involvement is preferred. The source of their knowledge will affect the evidence value and accuracy. A secondhand story still holds value by providing information that may lead to the evidence the auditor is seeking.

An *expert* is legally defined as a person who possesses special skill or knowledge in a science or profession because of special study or experience with the subject. An expert possesses a particular skill in forming accurate opinions about a subject; in contrast, a common person would be incapable of deducing an accurate conclusion about the same subject.

Evidence independence   *Evidence independence* is similar to auditor independence, meaning the provider should not have any gain or loss by providing the evidence. Evidence supplied by a person with a bias is often questionable. The auditor should ask whether the evidence provider is part of the auditee's organization. Qualifications of the evidence provider should always be considered. A person with a high degree of detailed understanding is vastly more qualified than an individual of limited knowledge. Evidence and data gathered from a novice may have a low value when compared to data gathered by an expert. A person who is knowledgeable and independent of the audit subject would be considered the best source of evidence.

Table 2.2 lists examples of evidence grading. An IS auditor should always strive to obtain the best evidence, which is shown in the far right column.

TABLE 2.2   Example of Evidence Grading

	Poor Evidence	Good Evidence	Best Evidence
Material Relevance	Unrelated	Indirect (low relation)	Direct (high relation)
Objectivity	Subjective (low)	Requires few supporting facts to explain the meaning	Needs no explanation
Evidence source	Unrelated third party with no involvement	Indirect involvement by second party	Direct involvement by first party
Competency of provider	Biased	Nonbiased	Nonbiased and independent
Evidence analysis method	Novice	Experienced	Expert
Resulting trustworthiness	Low	Medium	High

Evidence is analyzed by using a structured test method to further determine the value it represents. The audit process itself represents a major portion of preparation work to support the analysis of actual evidence. Each test procedure must be documented to ensure that a duplicate test for verification will yield the same result. Each test execution should be well documented with a record of time, date, method of sample selection, sample size, procedure used, person performing the analysis, and results. It is often a good practice to use video recording to document the test process when the execution of the test method may be challenged—for example, to video-record a forensic computer audit if the results may be subject to dispute by individuals who are unfamiliar with the process.

The evidence grading effort aims to improve the resulting trustworthiness of the evidence. A competent IS auditor who can gather evidence and provide expert analysis with a High evidence trustworthiness rating is quite valuable indeed.

Timing of Evidence

An additional factor to consider in regard to evidence is timing. *Evidence timing* indicates whether evidence is received when it is requested, or several hours or days late. In electronic systems, the timing has a secondary meaning; electronic evidence may be available only during a limited window of time before it is overwritten or the software changes to a new version.

We have discussed the character of evidence, evidence grading, and timing. The next section will explain the evidence life cycle relating to the legal chain of custody.

Evidence Life Cycle

The evidence will pass through seven life-cycle phases that are necessary in every audit. Every IS auditor must remain aware of the legal demands that are always present with regard to evidence handling. Failure to maintain a proper chain of custody may disqualify the evidence. Evidence handling is just as important for Sarbanes-Oxley compliance is it would be for suspected criminal activity. Evidence handling is crucial for compliance to most industry regulations.

 Mishandling of evidence can result in the auditor becoming the target of legal action by the owner. Mishandling evidence in criminal investigations could result in the bumbling auditor becoming the target of both the owner and the alleged perpetrator of a criminal activity.

The seven phases of the evidence life cycle are identification, collection, initial preservation storage, analysis, postanalysis preservation storage, presentation, and return of the evidence to the owner. The entire set of seven phases is referred to as the *chain of custody*. Let's go down the list one by one:

Identification   The auditor needs to identify items that may be objective evidence lending support to the purpose of the audit. The characteristics of the evidence location or surroundings should be thoroughly documented before proceeding to the collection stage. All evidence shall be labeled, dated, and notated with a short description about its purpose or discovery. From this point forward, the evidence movements must be logged into a tracking record. Your client will not be happy if evidence is misplaced.

 It may be important to demonstrate how the evidence looked when it was discovered. Identification includes labeling and can include photographing physical evidence in an undisturbed state at the time of discovery.

Collection   The collection process involves taking possession of the evidence to place it under the control of a custodian. Special consideration should be given to items of a sensitive nature or high value. The IS auditor needs to exercise common sense during the collection process. Client records need to be kept in a secure location.

 For most audits except criminal investigations, the IS auditor should be cognizant of the liability created by taking the client's confidential records out of the client's office. We strongly advise that all records remain within the client's facility to relieve the auditor of potential liability. The best way to prevent accusations is to ensure that you never place yourself in a compromising position. Allow the client to remain responsible for evidence security. Just be sure to lock up each evening before you leave.

Criminal evidence should not be disturbed until after proper identification and labeling. It may be beneficial to have a nonbiased observer present as a witness to attest to the investigator's actions as observed during the collection activity.

Initial preservation storage   A major problem with evidence is the challenge of preserving it in its original state. The preservation and storage process is a vital component in the chain of custody. The custodian of the evidence must be able to prove that the evidence has been protected and no alteration has occurred. The slightest change will transform the evidence without changing its identity. Electronic evidence requires special handling procedures to overcome future claims that the evidence has been altered (evidence tampering).

 The chain of custody must remain unbroken to prevent evidence from being disqualified. In legal proceedings, a common method of disqualifying evidence is to argue that the custodian has failed the chain of evidence requirements. A related accusation is that evidence has been tampered with, which is often a plausible argument unless it can be proven that mishandling never occurred.

Analysis   In this phase, the evidence samples are examined by observation, scientific test, and qualitative and quantitative measurement. The entire process and results should be well documented. Individual tests may need to be rerun if errors are discovered with the test procedure, sample, or personnel executing the test.

In some instances, the test results may need to be duplicated by a second independent tester to validate the initial finding.

As you may recall, regulatory compliance is an ongoing requirement. The same internal controls will need to be tested at least once each year. The auditor should ensure that the testing process produces a reasonable degree of consistency in each subsequent audit.

Postanalysis preservation storage   After testing, the evidence and samples must be returned to preservation and secure storage. The evidence will continue to stay in storage except during presentation or retesting.

The auditor should be aware that proper handling is paramount for success in legal proceedings. Evidence used in legal trials may be retrieved and returned multiple times for use in court presentations prior to final release for return to the owner. The US legal process allows for trials in at least three separate courts as the case progresses through to final appeal.

 A bonded evidence storage facility might be used for storage when the evidence is used in legal cases lasting several years. An example would be a case of corporate fraud or theft.

Management may decide that the evidence used in routine compliance audits should be copied and bound into storage binders. Selected copies of those documents would be sent to storage with the client's financial records. This ensures the ability to demonstrate the evidence in a near original state for any future investigation by industry regulators. Initial evidence collection is a time-consuming process that might be difficult to duplicate in the future.

Presentation   The evidence and findings are be presented in support of the auditor's report. A variety of details may be included or omitted depending on the nature of the report. Reports of system performance offer little detail when compared to reports of criminal activity.

Return to owner   The evidence is returned to the owner after the audit test results are successfully evaluated, or after legal proceedings are officially concluded by order of the final court. It is important to notice the distinction. In noncriminal activity, the evidence is promptly returned when the audit is concluded. Evidence may be held in preservation storage for several years if situations of suspected criminal activity exist.

Figure 2.4 demonstrates the logical flow through the entire chain of custody. A CISA is required to be competent in this evidence life cycle.

Now we will discuss examples of evidence that an IS auditor will typically use during an audit.

Typical Evidence for IS Audits

You will attempt to gather audit evidence by using similar techniques as a detective. Some of the data you gather will be of high value, and other data may be of low value. You will need to continually assess the quality and quantity of evidence. You may discover evidence through your own observations, by reviewing internal documentation, by using computer assisted audit tools (CAAT), or by reviewing correspondence and minutes of meetings.

FIGURE 2.4   The evidence life cycle

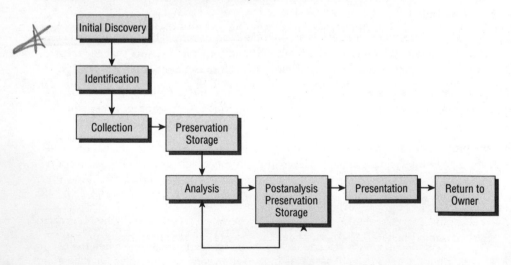

Examples of the various types of audit evidence include the following:

- Documentary evidence, which can include a business record of transactions, receipts, invoices, and logs
- Data extraction, which are details mined from data files or resulting from CAAT tools
- Auditee claims, which are representations made in oral or written statements
- Analysis of plans, policies, procedures, and flowcharts
- Results of compliance and substantive audit tests
- Auditor's observations of auditee work or reperformance of selected process

All evidence should be reviewed to determine its reliability and relevance. The best evidence will be objective and independent of the provider. The quality of evidence you collect will have a direct effect on the points you wish to prove.

Using Evidence to Prove a Point

Evidence will either prove or disprove a point. The absence of evidence is the absence of proof. In spite of your best efforts, if you're unable to prove those points, you would receive zero credit for your efforts. An auditor should not give any credit to claims or positive assertions that cannot be documented by evidence. No evidence, no proof equals no credit.

Preparing Audit Documentation

All auditors are required to prepare a thorough set of audit documentation at the start of each audit. This includes copies of the charter and scope, audit plans, policies, and specific procedures used during the audit. You should record both handling and test procedures.

Your job as an auditor is to provide consistency. All your findings should be repeatable by another auditor. Documentation should include auditor's working notes and evidence necessary to reperform the audit. During the audit, you should be preparing records to answer the following questions:

- Who was involved?
- What was audited and how the evidence was obtained, and the specific test procedure used?
- When it occurred?
- Where it occurred?
- Why, the purpose of the audit?
- How the audit plan and procedures were executed?

Later, the auditor's final working papers should be placed into an audit documentation archive, including copies of any reports that were issued.

The auditor should always remember that records of each audit may be needed again in the future. Integrated audits such as SAS-94 will have documentation retention requirements equal to the financial statement, typically at least seven years. Financial and internal control records for an integrated audit serve as a matched pair that should not be separated. Records for certain systems or processes may have a retention requirement specified in their service-level agreement or contract. Very specialized systems used in aerospace, life safety, hazardous materials, or the military may be retained for decades.

Let's look at the selection method for your audit samples and begin the move toward actual testing.

Selecting Audit Samples

Audit samples are selected for the purpose of collecting representative evidence to be subjected to either *compliance testing* or substantive testing (which are defined later in this section). The auditor should consider a selection technique that will provide the most relevant evidence supported by appropriate analytical procedures.

Two basic types of audit samples can be designed by the auditor to fulfill their requirements: statistical and nonstatistical. Figure 2.5 shows the various audit samples, as well as their testing methods Care is given to the selection process in order to avoid drawing the wrong conclusion from the wrong sample. This is referred to as a *sampling risk*. Let's look at each of these samples more closely.

FIGURE 2.5   Audit samples

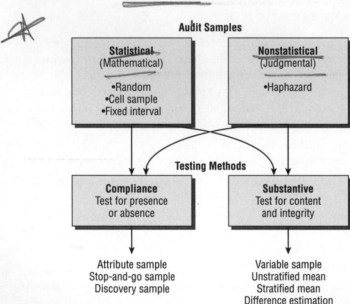

Statistical Sampling

Statistical sampling uses mathematical techniques that result in an outcome that is mathematically quantifiable. Statistical samples are usually presented as a percentage. The purpose of statistical sampling is to gain an objective representation. Samples are selected by an objective mathematical process. The auditor should be aware that if the client has strong internal controls, the sample sizes may be smaller because the odds of fraud or failure will be lower.

Examples of statistical sampling include the following:

Random sampling   Samples are selected at random.

Cell sampling   Random selection is performed at predefined intervals.

Fixed interval sampling   The sample existing at every $n +$ interval increment is selected for testing.

Nonstatistical Sampling

Nonstatistical sampling is based on the auditor's judgment (also referred to as *judgmental sampling*). The auditor determines the sample size, the method of generating the sample, and the number of items to be analyzed. This is a subjective process usually based on elements of risk or materiality. An example of nonstatistical sampling includes *haphazard sampling*, in which the samples are randomly drawn for testing.

After the samples are selected, the next step is to perform compliance tests or substantive testing.

Identifying Audit Testing

As stated earlier, the basic test methods used will be either compliance testing or substantive testing. Appropriate audit samples will have to be generated for the test.

Compliance testing tests for the presence or existence of something. Compliance testing includes verifying that policies and procedures have been put in place, and that user access rights, program change control procedures, and system audit logs have been activated. An example of a compliance test is comparing the list of persons with physical access to the data center against the HR list of current employees.

Compliance testing is based on one of the following types of audit samples:

Attribute sampling   Generally popular in compliance testing. The objective is to determine whether an attribute is present or absent in the subject sample. The result is specified by the rate of occurrence—for example, the presence of 1 in 100 units would be 1 percent.

Stop-and-go sampling   Used when few errors are expected. Stop-and-go allows the test to occur without excessive effort in sampling and provides the opportunity to stop testing at the earliest possible opportunity. It is a simple form of testing to reinforce any claim that errors are unlikely in the sample population.

Discovery sampling   Used to detect fraud or when the likelihood of evidence existing is low. This is an attempt to discover evidence.

Precision, or expected error rate   The precision rate indicates the acceptable margin of error between audit samples and the total quantity of the subject population. This is usually expressed as a percentage such as 5 percent. To obtain a very low error rate, it is necessary to use a very large sample in testing. The larger sample can yield a higher average.

Substantive testing seeks to verify the content and integrity of evidence. Substantive tests include verifying account balances, performing physical inventory counts, and executing detailed scans to detect effectiveness of a specific system configuration. Substantive testing uses audit samples selected by dollar value or to project a total for groups with related characteristics.

Substantive testing is based on one of the following types of audit samples:

Variable sampling   Used to designate dollar values or weights (effectiveness) of an entire subject population by prorating from a smaller sample. Consider the challenge of counting large volumes of currency by its weight. Variable sampling could be used to count currency by multiplying the physical weight of one unit by the total weight of the combined sample, and then multiplying by the face value printed on the bill or coin. A demonstration would be a single $50 bill weighing 0.8 grams, with the entire sample of $50 bills weighing 48 grams altogether. The combined sample weight would indicate a total quantity of 60 bills for an estimated dollar value of $3,000. This is a common technique for forecasting quantity and value of inventory based on particular characteristics.

Unstratified mean estimation   Used in an attempt to project an estimated total for the subject population.

Stratified mean estimation   Used to calculate an average by group, similar to demographics, whereby the entire population is divided (stratified) into smaller groups based on similar characteristics. Examples are teenagers from the ages of 13 to 19, people from the ages of 20 to 29, people from the ages of 30 to 39, and those who are male or female, smokers or nonsmokers, and so on.

Difference estimation   Used to determine the difference between audited and unaudited claims of value.

Tolerable error rate   Is the maximum number of errors that can exist without declaring a material misstatement.

Regardless of the audit sample and test method used, the auditor is presumed to have a high degree of confidence when the *audit coefficient* is 95 percent or higher. The *audit coefficient* represents your level of confidence about the audit results. It is also referred to as a *reliability factor*.

Using Computer Assisted Audit Tools

Computer assisted audit tools (CAAT) are invaluable for compiling evidence during IS audits. The auditor will find several advantages of using CAATs in their analytical audit procedure. CAAT tools are capable of executing a variety of automated compliance tests and substantive tests that would be nearly impossible to perform manually.

These specialized tools may include multifunction audit utilities, which can analyze logs, perform vulnerability tests, or verify specific implementation of compliance in a system configuration compared to intended controls.

CAAT includes the following types of software tools and techniques:

- Host evaluation tools to read the system configuration settings and evaluate the host for known vulnerabilities

- Network traffic and protocol analysis using a sniffer

- Mapping and tracing tools that use a tracer-bullet approach to follow processes through a software application using test data

- Testing the configuration of specific application software such as an SQL database

- Software license counting across the network

- Testing for password compliance on user login accounts

Many CAAT tools have a built-in report writer that can generate more than one type of predefined report of findings on your behalf.

Numerous advantages may exist, but they come at a cost. These expert systems may be expensive to acquire. Specialized training is often required to obtain the skills to operate these tools effectively. A significant amount of time may be required to become a competent CAAT operator.

Some of the concerns for or against using CAAT include:

- Auditor's level of computer knowledge and experience

- Level of risk and complexity of the audit environment

- Cost and time constraints

- Specialized training requirements

- Speed, efficiency, and accuracy over manual operations

- Need for continuous online auditing

- Security of the data extracted by CAAT

A CISA may encounter individuals who are self-proclaimed auditors based solely on their ability to use CAAT software. You should consider this when using the work of others. The ability to use CAAT tools alone does not represent the discipline and detailed audit training of a professional auditor.

Using CAAT for Continuous Online Audit

The new CAAT audit tools offer the advantage of providing continuous online auditing. You should be aware of the six types of continuous online auditing techniques:

Online event monitor   Online event monitors include automated tools designed to read and correlate system logs or transaction logs on behalf of the auditor. This type of event monitoring tool will usually generate automated reports with alarms for particular events.

A few examples include software that reads event logs, intrusion detection systems, virus scanners, and software that detects configuration changes, such as the commercial product Tripwire. (Low complexity.)

Embedded program audit hooks   A software developer can write embedded application hooks into their program to generate red-flag alerts to an auditor, hopefully before the problem gets out of hand. This method will flag selected transactions to be examined. (Low complexity.)

Continuous and intermittent simulation (CIS) audit   In continuous and intermittent simulation, the application software will always test for transactions that meet a certain criteria. When the criteria is met, the software will run an audit of the transaction (intermittent test). Then the computer will wait until the next transaction meeting the criteria occurs. This provides for a continuous audit as selected transactions occur. (Medium complexity.)

Snapshot audit   This technique uses a series of sequential data captures that are referred to as snapshots. The snapshots are taken in a logical sequence that a transaction will follow. The snapshots produce an audit trail, which will be reviewed by the auditor. (Medium complexity.)

Embedded audit module (EAM)   This integrated audit testing module allows the auditor to create a set of dummy transactions that will be processed along with live, genuine transactions. The auditor then compares the output data against their own calculations. This allows substantive integrity testing without disrupting the normal processing schedule. EAM is also known as *integrated test facility*. (High complexity.)

System control audit review file with embedded audit modules (SCARF/EAM)   The theory is straightforward. A system-level audit program is installed on the system to selectively monitor the embedded audit modules inside the application software. Few systems of this nature are in use. The idea is popular with auditors; however, a programmer must write the modules. (High complexity.)

Detecting Irregularities and Illegal Acts

It is management's responsibility to implement the controls and supervision necessary to detect irregularities and potentially illegal acts in their environment. Management is responsible for making written assertions as to their representation of internal controls. Audit plans should include provisions and procedures in the event an auditor encounters irregularities or possibly illegal acts.

Examples of illegal activities include the following:

Fraud   Any act of deception used to gain an advantage. Misrepresentation is a type of fraud. Examples include posting transaction records that are intentionally false and without genuine merit.

Theft   Taking or acquiring resources that are not rightfully yours. The legal term *conversion* is another name for theft. Embezzlement is a form of theft.

Suppression   Suppressing data or records and their effects in business transactions. This is related to *obstruction* and *willful omission*.

Racketeering   The process of repeated (pervasive) fraud or other crimes. Racketeering is governed by the Racketeer Influenced and Corrupt Organizations (RICO) Act, which carries dire consequences to those parties alleged to have participated.

Regulatory violations   Intentionally or unintentionally violating the law.

Indicators of Illegal or Irregular Activity

The IS auditor should understand that an organization's internal controls will not eliminate the possibility of irregular or illegal activity. Although it is not the auditor's job to detect these conditions, it is important to be alert to potential indicators. The auditor should be on the lookout for the following symptoms:

- Questionable payments. Examples include fees that appear to be excessively high or low, failed account reconciliation, payments to government officials, and payments for unspecified services.

- Unsatisfactory record control. Examples include poor record keeping in general, proper controls not in use, evidence of falsified documents, missing documentation, and the untimely shredding of documents in advance of corporate retention guidelines.

- Unsatisfactory explanations. Examples include large or unusual transactions, and especially transactions with related companies at the end of the financial reporting period such as month-end or quarter-end. Other examples include overbooked or underbooked sales, unexplained or unusual items, or unexplained funds held in suspense accounts.

- Other questionable circumstances such as an lifestyle of organization's executives and employees.

Responding to Irregular or Illegal Activity

If you discover any potentially irregular or illegal activity, the next step is to attempt a to determine whether management is aware of the situation or has participated in the suspected activities. The auditor should document all information, evidence, findings, and conclusions that led to the discovery of the suspected activities:

- The auditor should consider any unusual or unexpected relationships that could lead to material misstatements or misrepresentations.

- The auditor should maintain a position of professional skepticism.

- Upon learning of material irregularities or illegal acts, the auditor should promptly notify one level of management higher than where the suspected activities may have taken place.

- If the activities involve a person charged with internal controls or governance, reporting should take place at the highest level possible.

- The auditor should not contact law enforcement or regulators until advised to do so by the auditor's legal counsel. Special handling procedures may be required.

- The auditor should never become a party to the suspected activity. The auditor should seek competent legal advice if unsure about what actions to take. You may be advised to prepare for termination of the audit.

Reporting Your Audit Findings

After performing your audit, the next step is to prepare a presentation to report your findings. Reporting is the process by which the auditor conveys to management their findings, including the following:

- Audit scope
- Audit objectives
- Methods and criteria used
- Nature of findings
- Extent of work performed
- Applicable dates of coverage

In addition, the final report should state any restrictions, reservations, or qualifications (concerns) that the auditor holds in relation to the audit. The auditor may provide a final opinion or no opinion based on these potential limitations.

Statement of Auditing Standards (SAS), the COSO internal controls framework, and the IT Governance Institute (ISACA-ITGI) publish several points of information that should be included in the final report. You should consult their publications for specific details. In summary, the recommendations include the following:

- A title that includes the word *independent* (for an external audit)
- The applicable date of the report
- Identification of the parties and subject matter
- An executive summary
- Any visual representations, charts, graphs, or diagrams
- A statement of the standards followed during the audit
- A statement of the procedures performed, and whether they were agreed to by the specified parties
- Any necessary disclaimers
- A statement of additional procedures, if performed
- A statement on restrictions on the use of the report
- A statement of any auditor concerns, reservations, or qualifications to the audit
- Detailed findings and the auditor's opinion
- Auditor signature and contact information

The IS auditor's signature attests that the audit report and stated findings are true and correct. *Attestation* is the act of providing your assurance via a signature that the contents of a document are authentic and genuine.

You should keep your report easy to read. Simple graphics, tables, and color coding will be appreciated by your client.

After producing the final report, you will need to meet with the auditee and management to review the findings. The primary purpose of this meeting is not to change your findings, but to obtain acceptance and agreement by the auditee. This is the final quality-control check before issuing your final report. You want to ensure that the facts are correctly presented in your report. A final copy of this report and of your working notes will need to be placed into the audit archive for document retention.

Identifying Omitted Procedures

On the rare occasion that an auditor determines after issuing a final report that one or more auditing procedures have been omitted, it may be necessary to review some of the audit alternatives to compensate for the omission. If the omitted procedures present material bearing on the outcome, and the audit alternatives cannot compensate for the deficiency, cancelling the report and reissuing a new report (if appropriate) may be necessary. If the omitted procedures have tangible bearing on the outcome, the auditor should consult with their lawyer for advice concerning any possible avenues or potential legal actions.

Conducting an Exit Interview

After issuing a report, the auditor is required to conduct an exit interview with management to obtain a commitment for the recommendations made in the audit. Management is responsible for acknowledging the recommendations and designating whatever corrective action will be taken, including the estimated dates for the action.

In subsequent audits, you will check whether management honored their commitments to fix or remediate deficiencies found in a prior audit. Occasionally the deficiencies are left uncorrected because changes in the organization design or practice have eliminated the conditions of the prior control's weakness. Particular findings may apply to events that are no longer relevant. Otherwise, you expect management to act in a timely manner to correct the deficiency as originally reported.

Conducting Follow-Up Activities

Sometimes events of concern are discovered, or occur, after an audit has been completed. You would be concerned about the discovery of subsequent events that pose a material challenge to your final report. Accounting standards recognize these events and classify them as follows:

Type 1 events refer to those that occurred before the balance sheet date.

Type 2 events are those that occurred after the balance sheet date.

Depending on the type of audit, you may have additional reporting requirements or activities. These may require additional disclosures or adjustments to your report based on the nature of the event that was recently discovered or occurred. It is not the auditor's responsibility to detect subsequent events.

Traditional Audit Compared to Control Self-Assessments

A discussion of the audit process would not be complete without mentioning the benefits of using control self-assessments. The auditee can work to improve their audit score between audits by using these self-assessment techniques.

To employ the formal skills of a professional auditor is considered a traditional audit. In a traditional audit, the auditor manages the audit through the entire audit process and renders a final opinion.

A control self-assessment (CSA) is executed by the auditee. The auditee uses the CSA to benchmark progress with the intention of improving their score. This CSA process can generate benefits by empowering the staff to take ownership and accountability. With a CSA, the auditor becomes a facilitator to help guide the client's effort toward self-improvement.

A great deal of pride can be created by the accomplishment of CSA tasks and learning the detail necessary to succeed in a traditional audit. A CSA is not going to fulfill the independence requirement, so a traditional audit will still be required. A CSA will help your client understand the specific actions necessary to improve their audit performance. CSAs can be used to identify areas that are high risk and may need a more detailed review later.

Summary

This concludes our review of the IS audit process. A CISA is expected to have a thorough understanding of the entire audit process. You will be expected to understand the issues and motivation behind each step.

A violation of the audit process would be a concern and likely indicate the outcome is meaningless. As an IS auditor, you should always strive to honor the spirit and intent of the audit process. Conduct audits in accordance with recognized audit standards, guidelines, and best practices. It is your job to plan the audit around the business requirements by using a risk-based approach and to collect meaningful evidence. You are expected to produce an objective report based on the evidence you obtained during the audit. The final report will be communicated to management with the goal of gaining their commitment to resolve any weaknesses found. Your actions should be well documented and reproducible by another auditor.

In Chapter 1, we covered how the auditor should look, act and think. In this chapter, we discussed how the auditor should carry out the audit. In the next chapter, we will present the techniques used for IT governance.

Exam Essentials

Know how to develop and implement a risk-based audit strategy. The auditor should focus on areas of high value. The risk assessment will help to determine if the audit will yield meaningful information. Certain types of conditions may be very difficult to audit. It is important the audit is based upon meaningful evidence that is materially relevant.

Understand how to conduct IS audits in accordance with published standards, guidelines, and best practices. The auditor is expected to follow published audit standards to ensure thoroughness and consistency. Deviations from the standards and guidelines is very rare. Any deviation must be well documented, but results may not be accepted by the audit community. The purpose of best practices is to aid the auditor by identifying useful procedures and techniques. Every audit should be designed to adhere to standards.

Be familiar with how to plan for specific audits. The CISA needs to understand the constraints and requirements of individual audits. It is the auditor's job to identify the resource requirements, sampling requirements, test methods, and procedures to be used. The auditor will be to identify appropriate personnel to be interviewed. The interview process must be scheduled and implement predefined questions for the purpose of gathering data. An audit involving third-party personnel will present its own unique challenges.

Know the auditing practices and techniques. Well established IS auditing procedures ensure thoroughness and consistency necessary for a successful audit. Good audits will implement a well thought out sequence of procedures to evaluate materially relevant samples. ISACA provides the auditor with foundation knowledge that should be implemented during your audit. Effective sample selection of meaningful tests should yield materially relevant results.

Be familiar with IS control objectives and performing control assessment. The basic types of internal controls are preventative, detective, and corrective. Each control may be implemented using administrative methods, physical methods, and technical methods. The purpose of the controls are to prevent harm and protect an asset. The IS auditors responsible for evaluating the effectiveness of controls.

Know the techniques to gather information and manage the evidence life cycle. The auditor can collect information through traditional sources of business records, computer data files, and CAAT tools. Meaningful information can be obtained through personal interviews, workshops, and surveys. All information and evidence should be recorded and tracked. The evidence life cycle starts with identification, collection, preservation, analysis, safe storage, and finally return to the owner. Evidence used for criminal prosecution must be handled with the highest degree of care. Evidence that is mishandled will void legal claims and may result in punitive legal action.

Know the types of evidence and evidence grading. The best evidence will tell its own story. The best evidence will prove or disprove a point. Best evidence is both objective and independent. The timing of evidence must be considered when calculating its useful value. Evidence that is late and subjective will be of low value. Material evidence will have a bearing on the final outcome. Irrelevant evidence will not affect the final decision.

Familiarize yourself with the types of audit tests and sample selection.   Audit tests can be substantive or compliance based. It is important to select an appropriate sample in order to generate data to reflect the actual situation. Audit test procedures and sample selection methods must be well documented to ensure verifiable and reproducible tests. The sample may be selected upon physical characteristics, value, and size of population.

Know some of the various types of computer assisted audit tools (CAAT).   Computer assisted audit techniques are software tools that can provide detailed analysis of computer systems configuration, vulnerability, logs, and other information. The CAAT output should be kept confidential due to the potentially sensitive nature of its contents.

Understand the continuous auditing methods.   Continuous audit methods such as audit hooks or SCARF with embedded audit modules (SCARF/EAM) are used in environments where it is not possible to interrupt production.

Know how to deal with irregular and illegal acts.   It is possible that you could encounter evidence of irregular or illegal acts. The discoveries should be communicated to the next level of management higher than where the act occurred. Such a discovery involving persons responsible for internal controls must be reported to the absolute highest level of management. The auditor should consult their attorney for legal advice.

Know how to advise clients on implementing risk management and control practices while maintaining independence.   The auditor is encouraged to educate their client and help increase awareness of control issues. It is important that the auditor does not participate in specific discussions of design or architecture. The auditor must not work on fixing problems if the auditor is expected to be independent. A client may hire an auditor for remediation and use a separate, unrelated auditor for the audit. The auditor cannot be independent if they participated in the audit subject.

Be able to communicate issues, potential risks, and audit results.   The auditor is expected to communicate materially relevant issues to management through the audit reporting process. Issues of high significance should be communicated directly to the audit committee. The final results of each audit should be verifiable and reproducible. All communication must convey the facts without placing blame upon individuals.

Understand the role of traditional audits compared to control self-assessment (CSA).   Control self-assessments are designed to empower the customer's staff. The intention is to generate awareness and ownership of problems. A control self-assessment is an excellent way to improve the performance of an organization between traditional audits. The traditional audit is still necessary to the independence requirement.

Review Questions

1. Failing to prevent or detect a material error would represent which type of risk?

    A. Overall audit risk

    B. Detection risk

    C. Inherent risk

    D. Control risk

2. Which term best describes the difference between the sample and the population in the sampling process?

    A. Precision

    B. Tolerable error rate

    C. Level of risk

    D. Analytic delta

3. Which is not a purpose of risk analysis?

    A. Support risk-based audit decisions.

    B. Assist the auditor in determining audit objectives.

    C. Assist the auditor in identifying risks and threats.

    D. Ensure absolute safety during the audit.

4. Which of the following is not a type of quantitative sampling model?

    A. Difference estimation

    B. Stratified mean per unit

    C. Unstratified mean per unit

    D. Quantitative mean per unit

5. Which of the following is false concerning a control self-assessment?

    A. Empowers the user to take ownership and accountability

    B. Eliminates the need for a traditional audit

    C. May be used to identify high-risk areas for later review

    D. Will not have the level of independence provided by an external auditor

6. Which control classification attempts to repair the impact of a threat?

    A. Preventative

    B. Detective

    C. Corrective

    D. Deterrent

7. The two types of tests are referred to as _____ and _____ using _____ sampling methods.

    A. Substantive tests, compliance tests, variable and attribute

    B. Compliance tests, substantive tests, variable and discovery sampling

    C. Predictive tests, compliance tests, stop-and-go and difference estimation

    D. Integrity tests, compliance tests, stratified mean and unstratified mean

8. What is the purpose of the audit charter?

    A. To engage external auditors

    B. To grant responsibility, authority, and accountability

    C. To authorize the creation of the audit committee

    D. To provide detailed planning of the audit

9. Which of the following would be a concern of the auditor that should be explained in the audit report along with their findings?

    A. Detailed list of audit objectives

    B. The need by the current auditor to communicate with the prior auditor

    C. Communicating results directly to the chairperson of the audit committee

    D. Undue restrictions placed by management on evidence use or audit procedures

10. The concept of due care is best defined as which of the following?

    A. Proportional to the level of risk or loss that could occur

    B. Basic care providing a minimal level

    C. Ordinary care providing an average level

    D. Extraordinary care above and beyond average

11. What is the purpose of the audit committee?

    A. To assist managers with training in auditing skills

    B. To govern, control, and manage the organization

    C. To challenge and review assurances

    D. To provide daily coordination of all audit activities

12. What is the best data-collection technique the auditor can use if the resources are available?

    A. Surveys that create a broad sample

    B. Review of existing documentation

    C. Auditor observation

    D. Interviews

13. Which of the following types of risk are of the most interest to an IS auditor?

    A. Control, detection, noncompliance, risk of strike

    B. Inherent, noninherent, control, lack of control

    C. Sampling, control, detection, inherent

    D. Unknown, quantifiable, cumulative

14. Which of the following best describes the early stages of an IS audit?

    A. Documenting the IS environment

    B. Testing for compliance to applicable regulations as agreed

    C. Reviewing prior IS audit reports

    D. Commencing the planning process

15. Which of the following describes the relationship between compliance testing and substantive testing?

    A. Compliance testing checks for the presence of controls; substantive testing checks the integrity of internal contents.

    B. Substantive testing tests for presence; compliance testing tests actual contents.

    C. The tests are identical in nature; the difference is whether the audit subject is under the Sarbanes-Oxley regulation.

    D. Compliance testing tests individual account balances; substantive testing checks for written corporate policies.

16. What is the principal issue surrounding the use of CAAT tools?

    A. The capability of the software vendor.

    B. Possible cost, complexity, and the security of output.

    C. Inability of automated tools to consider the human characteristics of the environment.

    D. Documentary evidence is more effective.

17. An IS auditor is performing a review of an application and finds something that might be illegal. The IS auditor should

    A. Disregard or ignore because this is beyond the scope of this review.

    B. Conduct a detailed investigation to aid the authorities in catching the culprit.

    C. Immediately notify the auditee of the finding.

    D. Seek legal advice before finishing the audit.

18. The auditor is permitted to deviate from professional audit standards when they feel it is necessary because of which of the following?

    A. Standards are designed for discretionary use.

    B. Deviation is almost unheard of and would require significant justification.

    C. Deviation depends on the authority granted in the audit charter.

    D. The unique characteristics of the client will require auditor flexibility.

19. What are the proper names of the four methods of risk response?

    A. Avoid, accept, transfer, and mitigate

    B. Mitigate, accept, transfer, and reduce

    C. Ignore, accept, assign, and mitigate

    D. Analyze, mitigate, reduce, and assign

20. Audits are intended be conducted in accordance with which of the following ideals?

    A. Specific directives from management concerning evidence and procedure

    B. Reporting and communication

    C. Assessment of the organizational controls

    D. Adherence to standards, guidelines, and best practices

Answers to Review Questions

1. B. A detection risk is that you would fail to detect that a material error has occurred.

2. A. The compliance test uses *precision* to describe the rate of occurrence out of the sample population.

3. D. Risk analysis does not ensure absolute safety. The purpose of using a risk-based audit strategy is to ensure that the audit adds value with meaningful information.

4. D. Difference estimation, stratified mean, and unstratified mean are valid sample types for substantive testing. Quantitative mean is just a distracter.

5. B. All of the statements are true except B. A CSA is not a substitute for a traditional audit.

6. C. Corrective controls are designed to fix the damage caused by the threat's impact.

7. A. Answer B is incorrect because compliance testing uses discovery sampling to detect fraud. C and D are distracters.

8. B. The audit charter's purpose is to grant the right to audit and delegate responsibility, authority, and accountability.

9. D. Undue restrictions on scope would be a major concern as would the lack of time or the inability to obtain sufficient reliable evidence.

10. A. Due care is proportional to the level of risk or loss that could occur. Greater care is required for items of high value or greater impact due to loss.

11. C. The audit committee's purpose is to review and challenge assurances made, and to maintain a positive working relationship with management and the auditors.

12. D. Interviewing selected personnel is the best technique. Surveys, document review, and observations generate a lower yield.

13. C. The answers including risk of strike, lack of control, and unknown are distracters.

14. D. You start the planning process to identify objectives, resources, and the risk-based audit approach.

15. A. Substantive testing checks the substance or integrity of a transaction. Compliance testing looks for presence.

16. B. CAATs are able to perform faster than humans and produce more accurate data in functions such as system scanning. Cost, training, and security of output are major considerations.

17. D. Seek competent legal advice. It is not the auditor's job to detect potentially illegal acts; however, the auditor should seek the aid of a lawyer concerning liability and reporting requirements.

18. Answer B. Standards are mandatory, and any deviation would require justification.

19. A. The proper answer is avoid, accept, transfer to another party, and mitigate to reduce exposure. The other answers contain distracters.

20. D. Audits should adhere to standards, guidelines, and best practices. Answer A represents a restriction on scope. B and C are components of answer D.

Chapter

3

IT Governance

THE OBJECTIVE OF THIS CHAPTER IS TO ACQUAINT THE READER WITH THE FOLLOWING CONCEPTS:

- ✓ The fiduciary responsibility and security requirements that every organization must exercise to protect assets and information

- ✓ Accepted management practices that are in use to optimize allocation of available resources

- ✓ How management establishes adequate internal controls for the IT organization

- ✓ What management needs to do to protect the critical dependencies of information systems in economic transactions

- ✓ How an organization demonstrates that it has exercised the best available management options to protect itself

IT governance specifies the level of integration and control an organization has over its information technology investment. Information technology is pervasive in business today. The intrinsic value of information technology must be fully incorporated into every aspect of the business, rather than separated into a distinct IT function. The level of IT integration will have a dramatic effect on how the organization defines its mission, achieves strategic goals, and communicates its vision of growth. The auditing of the IT governance will include the highest levels of organizational management and cross internal boundaries between divisions and departments.

Strategy in Organizational Control

To be successful, management must define a strategy and provide for effective corporate governance. *Strategy* is defined as "an adaptation of behavior or structure with an elaborate and systematic plan of action." *Corporate governance* is "ethical behavior of corporate executives toward shareholders and the stakeholders to maximize the return of a financial investment."

Two high-level management objectives to be verified by the auditor are as follows:

- A process of monitoring assurance practices for executive management. The senior executives need to understand what is actually occurring in the organization.

- A strategic alignment between IT and the enterprise objectives. Proper planning is required to deploy resources in the right place for the right reason.

Each organization needs to develop a directional strategy. What direction should the business take to fulfill its goals? The strategy selected progresses to focus on client needs and how to fulfill that market. Critical success factors are selected. Marketing initiatives are designed to generate revenue with plans for fulfillment to the buyer. Figure 3.1 demonstrates the path of organizational requirements in conjunction with the IT requirements.

The revenue process entails a significant amount of administrative overhead and record keeping. The expectation in every business is to make money and not be hampered by a particular technology nor tied to a particular vendor. The IT department is looking for a clearly stated purpose that IT is expected to fulfill. The department looks at the demands and requirements necessary to be successful. A structured service-level agreement can be generated with this data, complete with staffing and technology growth plans. The technology plan has to fulfill a business objective. For instance, take Amazon.com. The bookseller isn't necessarily hung up on using Microsoft Windows or Unix. What the executives want to know is that all the money is processed and the product arrives on time to fulfill the customer expectations. Systems management and auditing on the back end will verify that all the bookkeeping and internal controls are functioning effectively.

FIGURE 3.1   IT alignment with organizational objectives

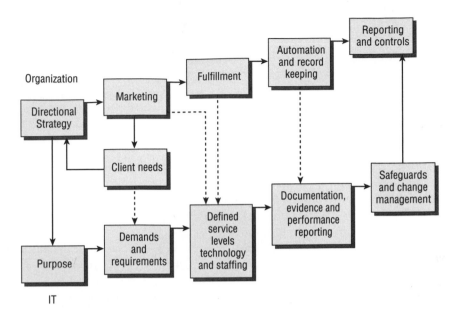

The principal mechanism for ensuring IT alignment is to implement an IT steering committee.

Overview of the IT Steering Committee

Most organizations use an IT strategy committee or IT steering committee. An IT steering committee is used to convey the current business requirements from business executives to the IT executive. The name of the committee is not as important as the function that it performs; a committee may perform more than one function. An IT steering committee may possibly be the same committee used for the purpose of a business continuity steering committee, but with a slightly different charter (focus). What's important is that the job of steering operations to business requirements is occurring.

Steering committees should have a formal charter designating the participation of each member. This charter grants responsibility and authority in a concept similar to an audit charter. An absence of a steering committee charter would indicate a lack of formal controls—a condition warranting management oversight review.

The steering committee is also discussed in Chapter 5 with the software development life cycle.

The steering, or strategy, committee is made up of quite a few individuals. Each individual is required to have the authority to act on behalf of their department. These members are vice president–level or higher in the organization so they can help align the IT efforts to specific business requirements. Figure 3.2 shows the basic organizational structure of the steering committee.

FIGURE 3.2 Organizational structure of a steering committee

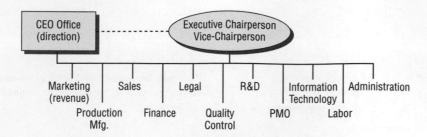

The committee is managed by an executive chairperson. The CEO is expected to provide directional guidance in person or via a representative to identify targeted sources of revenue. Each member of the committee is expected to participate in focus discussions concerning business issues. On occasion, the committee may invite trusted observers or presenters to the meeting to increase awareness of a particular area.

After the business objectives are identified, the next step is to determine the business objectives for IT to fulfill. The steering committee sticks to high-level objectives rather than dictating technical detail.

Let's look at the representation necessary on the steering committee:

Marketing   Marketing should be represented on the steering committee. The purpose of all marketing is to attract buyers for the organization's product or service. Even if the organization builds the world's finest product, it will not matter unless a steady stream of buyers make a purchase.

Manufacturing/Software Development   The input from manufacturing or software development is required to align production efforts to sales efforts.

Sales   The sales function is to convert interested prospects from marketing campaigns into closed sales. Sales executives are interested in using technology to facilitate more sales. The cooperation of manufacturing and technology is necessary to assist the sales effort.

Finance   Financial guidance and budgeting skills are essential to optimize the organization's investment. Obtaining funding approval for projects would be difficult without the cooperation of the finance comptroller.

Legal   The executive from the legal department should ensure compliance to the law. Qualified legal counsel advises management in areas of uncertainty. Expert legal counsel should help protect the company from excessive liability or undue risk as a result of a control failure.

Quality Control   The quality process provides consistency in operations, manufacturing, and risk mitigation. A well-run quality process is a major contributor to the organization's survival. Failures in quality control can damage market image or lead to liability problems.

Research and Development (R&D)   The Research and Development staff are constantly working on creating new products and improving existing products. The R&D effort is focused on developing products that will generate revenue six months to two years in the future.

 Depending on the organization, R&D may be suspended during times of financial shortfall. The planned R&D budget would be applied to projects with a faster return or to pay past-due obligations.

Project Management   The head of the Project Management office, if one exists, should be on the committee to advice members on current and proposed projects.

Information Technology   The chief information officer (CIO) or vice president of IT listens to business ideas and objectives raised by committee members. This person acts as a liaison to facilitate the involvement of IT. The IT member may delegate planning and research activities to members of the IT organization.

Human Resources   The management of personnel grows more complex each week. Compliance with federal labor standards is mandatory. International organizations require special assistance that is beyond the expertise most non-HR executives. Noncompliance can carry stiff penalties.

Labor Management   An executive representative from any labor organization, such as a labor union, may need to be involved in decisions concerning labor. This can be a touchy subject depending on the organization.

Administration   Office administration functions include bookkeeping, record keeping, and the processing of paperwork. Every executive would be handicapped without an administrative aide.

The steering committee reviews ideas and opportunities to make recommendations. Those recommendations go to the board of directors for review. If the idea receives preliminary approval, resources are allocated for project planning. The steering committee executives perform a final review of comparing the total cost and benefit to determine whether the project is a "go" or "no-go."

If a go decision is reached, the organization specifies details, charters the project, allocates funds, commits resources, and moves the plan into execution. If the project is scheduled to be a repeating event, the project is assigned to program status. Otherwise, it is managed as a project with a fixed time duration, and the assigned project team members will disband after project completion.

Figure 3.3 is a flowchart of the IT steering process.

FIGURE 3.3   The IT steering committee process

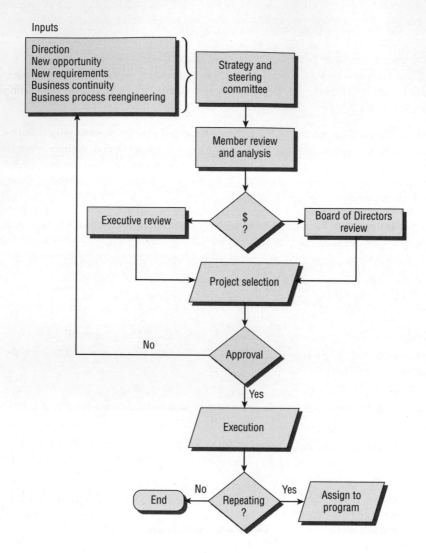

In strategic planning, plans generally run in a time frame of three to five years. A tactical plan is going to be carried out over six months to a year and it may go into two years. Daily plans are no more than steps in the tactical plan. When an organization projects three to five years, it is really developing a strategy. This strategy can be to run a streamlined low-cost airline operation like Southwest Airlines, offer the best market reach like eBay, provide competitive rate marketing like Progressive insurance, or use the shipping model of FedEx to assure your package is absolutely positively delivered overnight.

> ### 🌐 Real World Scenario
>
> #### How Many Hamburgers Do You Want to Sell?
>
> One of our famous awareness questions is to help people understand the issues of strategy and focus: If someone wanted to be in the hamburger business, *What is the number one critical factor that would be necessary for the hamburger business to be successful?* Interestingly enough, we have heard a lot of unusual answers, and none of them were correct.
>
> Claude Hopkins, the original master of marketing, would tell you the answer would not be menu, nor would it be location, nor would it be staffing, nor secret recipe. Although each of those points may offer support, the real answer is hungry customers. If we could establish where the hungry customers are, we could make money reselling cold cheeseburgers out of the back of a station wagon.
>
> In that regard, it is important to ask how IT is aligned to the organization. Does IT seek to satisfy the hungry customers, or is there an expectation for the customer to wander over on their own? Does IT provide repair-level support or is it truly strategic, carrying the company to their most noble objective? The reality is that when you build the world's best mousetrap, customers don't naturally come knocking at the door. The reality is that someone will need to find the customer and what the customer wants. Value is simply a perception of benefit and desire.

Table 3.1 shows a comparison of the differences between of strategic plans, long-term plans and operational plans.

TABLE 3.1   Differences between Strategic, Long-Term and Operational plans

Item	Strategic Planning	Long-Term planning	Operational planning
Time frame	3 years +	1–3 years	1 year or less
Question	What business are we in? Should we expand or contract?	What are major business components—what should we concentrate on now?	What specific tasks must be done to meet the long-term plan?
Output	General broad statement of what business the company is in.	What products and services planned? Financial goals. Market opportunities. Management organization. Next review period.	Assumptions for the period. Changes needing to be made. Production times. Responsibilities. Budget.

Now that we have discussed the definition of strategic planning, it is time to get specific about the IT strategy.

Selecting an IT Strategy

Executive management selects an IT strategy to fulfill their business objectives. The strategy should be approved from the top down. The strategy is then formalized into a policy and communicated throughout the organization. Figure 3.4 shows the executives involved at the strategy level (in policy making).

FIGURE 3.4   Executives involved at the IT strategy level

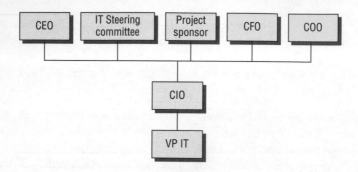

You should assume that the executives have already gone through the process of gathering requirements. Their strategy may be to insource or to outsource. However, one of their most important questions is to determine how the strategy will be funded. Each of the following methods of funding bears unique advantages and disadvantages:

Shared cost   It is common for the bulk of IT costs to be allocated as a shared cost across all members of the organization. This method is relatively easy for the finance department to implement. Unfortunately, it may lead to user dissatisfaction. Some users and their managers may feel that they are paying for a service that is not received.

Charge-back   Individual departments receive a direct charge for system use. This is designed to be a pay-as-you-go style of accounting for IT expenses. Charge-back schemes are quite effective if properly implemented.

Sponsor pays   This last type can present a significant challenge to IT governance. The project sponsor pays all of the bills. In exchange, the sponsor may demand more authority over decisions. This method is notorious for creating shadow support organizations. Additional conflicts may occur with IT management in disputes over implementing proper controls.

Specifying a Policy

Executive management has the responsibility of setting goals. Each goal should be supported with a defined set of objectives. A strategy should be in place to achieve those objectives. The next step is to specify a policy to communicate management's desires to the subordinates.

Every policy should be designed to define a high-level course of action. The purpose of the policy is to inform interested parties of a chosen solution. A well-designed policy is based on a statement by management of the policy's importance. The statement explains how this particular policy supports a business objective. The policy is signed by the most senior person available to prove authorization.

We discussed the role of policies, standards, and procedures in Chapter 1, "Secrets of an IS Auditor." Table 3.2 should serve as a memory refresher concerning the role of policies, standards, and procedures.

TABLE 3.2 Strategic Role of a Policy

	Strategic	Tactical	Operational
Goal objective	X		
Policy	X		
Standard		X	
Procedure			X

Successful policies are issued from the top down to all subordinates. The policy may designate a department director to create a standard in support of the policy. The final procedures are generated from the workers at the bottom of the hierarchy. Common procedures are intended to be implemented from the bottom up. The procedure is a lower-level person's response in support of the executive's policy.

Types of Policies

Policies are designed to inform interested parties about a particular situation. The policy may be advisory, regulatory, or informational:

Advisory policy An *advisory* policy explains the condition to be prevented by the policy and provides notice as to the consequences of failure. The interested party may be an employee. The subject could be acceptable use of the Internet. In the Internet example the advisory is to either comply or be fired.

Regulatory policy The term *regulatory* indicates that this policy is mandated by some type of law. All organizations under the jurisdiction of the regulation are expected to comply. Failure to comply will result in criminal liability.

Informational policy Informational policies inform the public of the organization's operating policies. Examples include the customer privacy policy, the customer refund policy, and the customer exchange policy.

  IS auditors should be aware that undefined policies indicate a lack of control.

After the strategy is selected and the goals are set and the policy is created, it's time to begin the planning process. In planning, the strategy moves closer to reality.

Planning the IT Strategy

IT strategy plans must be created to aid the organization in the fulfillment of long- and short-term business objectives. Each IT plan should correlate to a specific organizational goal. The business goal may be improvement in customer contact management, expand e-commerce services, or improve operating speed with better software integration. The supporting IT plan could define implementation and support for a new Customer Relationship Management system (CRM). IT's role is that of a requirements facilitator and custodian. The true strategic value will be determined in the minds of the business executives. There should be a concern if IT's influence is overriding other non-IT business objectives. The IT strategy will be composed of plans for data, software applications, technology, personnel, and facilities.

Data Plans

IT data plans are created in support of the organization's intended use of the data. An example is the creation of a new customer survey system or database marketing. After the intended use of the data is recognized, the next step is to define the application to manipulate the data.

Application Management Plan

Computer software applications are actually methods of accomplishing work. Therefore, a software management plan is necessary to define the type of work to be performed. A consumer bank may be in the same industry as a debt collection company, for example. However, both organizations use different software applications. Computer software applications need to be tailored to fit the client's needs. Computer software is not an advantage if the competitor uses the same software, unless the implementation is unique and highly customized.

It is possible to gain a competitive advantage by using a different product than the competitor uses. The advantage is attaining a higher level of business integration and/or lower operating costs. The cost argument is the very reason why some software applications use open-source MySQL for the database rather than the Oracle database. Both are fine products. The cost difference may allow for a significant investment in specialized customization by a guru to build highly integrated software which can create a competitive advantage with a lower overall operating cost. The resulting integrated software may perform a unique function the competitor will have difficulty obtaining due to required knowledge, lead time needed, or additional capital investment. Cost avoidance can be a competitive advantage. The application risk is that the integration does not occur or the intended application usage is flawed.

Computer application software represents a substantial investment in capital. Computer software creates business risks that must be managed. The risks include process failure, increased operating risk, ineffective results, waste of capital resources, lost time, and increased operating cost for the same effective output.

Technology Plan

Technology plans address an organization's technical environment by indicating the types of hardware and software that will be used. Unfortunately, some organizations start with the hardware technology first and attempt to force the data and application requirements into their desired technology. Putting the technology plans first may hinder the results.

Organizational Plan

The IT organizational structure needs to be designed to support the business strategy. Information technology is usually regarded as a function of internal administration. This would place IT under the head of internal controls (the CFO, VP of finance, or the comptroller). Figure 3.5 illustrates a typical IT organization. We will discuss the individual positions as we proceed through this chapter.

The objective of Figure 3.5 is to serve as a roadmap if you're unsure about the authority of positions we discuss in this chapter.

FIGURE 3.5   Typical IT organizational structure

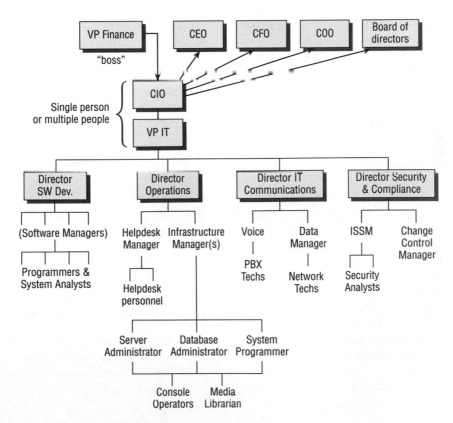

Facilities Plan

Finally, the strategy needs to incorporate a facilities plan. Where will the data applications and technology reside? Who will manage the environment? The final decision will be based on the desires of management. These desires can include increased control, insourcing, outsourcing, or a hybrid combination.

Identifying Sourcing Locations

The next step is to identify sourcing locations. The sourcing decision may be based on the operating cost for particular geographic locations. Operating cost is a combined factor of facilities, labor, regulations, and available resources. Organizations may choose to perform functions *on-site*, in their facility. Alternatively, there may be an advantage to performing functions *off-site*, at other offices or with an outside vendor. This is a common practice for customer support, employee payroll, and manufacturing. Cheap labor may influence management's decision to move the location *offshore*, to another country.

     Three popular offshore locations include China, India, and Russia.

Performing functions offshore introduces both opportunities and burdens. The opportunities include a potentially lower production cost. There is also an advantage for an organization to operate 24 hours a day to lower turnaround times. Disadvantages include the potential loss of control or the disclosure of proprietary intellectual property. In some countries, the culture, language, or level of education presents unique challenges. Cultural examples of potential challenges include India's caste system and Africa's ongoing tribal conflicts. Another example is the attitudes in some societies toward a woman in an authoritative role.

 Real World Scenario

The "Follow the Sun" Concept

Executive management may choose to service its customers by using a *follow the sun* concept, which in simple terms means that the organization moves daily support functions to an *off-site* location 8 to 12 hours away. The second (or third) office is starting their morning when the current office is closing at the end of the day. Each day, as one office closes, another office located in a different time zone takes over support (each time traveling to the west with the new day). Customers could always have a full staff available to help, regardless of the time of day.

A company might instead choose to schedule multiple shifts within the same office. As an auditor, you should inquire how the client retains full control with multiple shifts of personnel. What management controls are in place? Frequently the late-night staff has less supervision or greater access to shared work areas without detection.

Sourcing Practices

The world is growing smaller as transportation and communication services improve. Many of the old cultural barriers have been reduced by the global economy. This global economy also has increased the number of competitors in the fierce battle for revenue. An organization at one time worried only about servicing clients in a small number of local time zones. Now customers depend on businesses 24 hours a day, worldwide.

Most administrative and technical support functions can be performed from alternate locations. Some of the services that could be fulfilled from remote locations include the following:

- Accounting and bookkeeping
- Accounts payable (AP) and accounts receivable (AR)
- Data entry and transcription
- Live telephone support (including IT, customer service, order taking)
- Legal and medical records management and processing
- Human resources and benefits administration
- Creative advertising production
- Printing
- Software development
- Systems administration

In the following section, you will look at the various types of sourcing methods, what factors go into choosing a sourcing method, and why it is important for you as an IS auditor to be familiar with them.

Sourcing Methods

The decision of location is usually based on the cost of operation, market pressures, or a centralization vs. decentralization strategy. Management may choose to hire personnel by using a combination of insourcing and outsourcing. Services provided by internal staff are referred to as *insourced*. Services provided by an external vendor are referred to as *outsourced*. The insourced vs. outsourced decision may be based on a case-by-case or project-by-project requirement.

On occasion, an opportunity may present itself that exceeds the capability of the existing service provider. *Hybrid sourcing models* may be effective under a joint venture or to provide additional capability. The hybrid model combines insourcing and outsourcing on a function-by-function basis.

The advantage of outsourcing is that someone else may be able to perform the work better or cheaper, or frankly know how to do something others don't. Insourcing provides more control. The hybrid method retains control in selected area and uses the outsource contractor for collateral work. Outsourcing may allow the client to focus on what they do best, their core revenue generator. A potential disadvantage is losing control under the contract. Maybe the methods used by a subcontractor will cost less because they are cutting corners that, if known, a company might find unacceptable.

The basic decision may result from an executive thinking about the following:

- Is this something that the organization wants to do in-house?
- Is this something the company should outsource?
- Is there an advantage to sending this offshore?
- Is the organization bringing it back from offshore?
- Will local processing be a competitive advantage?
- Is the location here, in this building, or is it in another building?

Globalization Issues

Businesses may encounter a variety of globalization issues, including international regulation, local laws, tribal rivalries, or cultural class or caste systems. As an organization begins to look at opportunities for global outsourcing, they have to keep in mind the controls and the total costs related to that decision.

A business looks for inexpensive operating facilities with a high-quality labor pool willing to work for lower wages. If the business is going to decide whether to outsource, it needs to look at all the practices and strategies that are in place.

A business can run into problems over the differences in legal regulations between governments. Additional concerns can arise in different currency exchange rates and government taxation methods. Some of these requirements may indicate that foreign outsourcing would not provide any advantage.

Competitive advantage should be a factor in the sourcing decision. For example, American Apparel manufactures clothing exclusively inside the United States and pays better-than-average wages for their industry. Their advantage is a shorter cycle time from market idea to delivery and sale in their stores. American Apparel touts a one-day turnaround from a finished idea. Their competition has to contend with manufacturing and shipping delays measured in months.

In the last few years, Russia and the Baltic states have benefited from increased popularity, as companies reconsider India or choose to outsource for the first time. Increasing costs and US consumer rejection are troublesome to companies outsourcing to India. Additional reasons cited for Russian sourcing include a more convenient proximity to Western Europe, more positive consumer attitudes of acceptance, well educated population, financial savings in real estate prices, and the competitive low cost of labor.

Legal Compliance Issues

When dealing with outsourcing issues, companies need to be aware that what might be legal in one country might not be legal in another. Examples include the European Union (EU) privacy laws, which are much stricter than those of the United States, or the shortfall of intellectual-property laws in China, which frankly don't exist. In China the attitude is that if someone has a copy, they own it. This is where business management needs to understand: how does that country or culture see it?

As a primitive example, just compare the religious holidays and lifestyle that different counties observe. For example, the flow of harmony in the office is considered upset in Japan if everyone does not go to lunch at the exact same time, and return within a couple of minutes of one another. In Mexico the lunch hour is two hours and often includes drinking alcohol followed by a siesta (nap). It is not uncommon for employees to drink alcohol during the office lunch hour in the United Kingdom (referred to as having a few pints or getting pissed over a few drinks).

While management planned their labor strategy, there should be a provision ensuring continuity of operations for both insourced and outsourced activities.

Conducting an Executive Performance Review

The executive staff is subject to review by the audit committee. As you recall, it is this committee's job to challenge the assumptions and assurances in the organization. The audit committee is intended to provide management oversight and allow executives the opportunity to discuss confidential issues about the business. An effective audit committee will advise individual executives with an opinion for possible solutions to internal problems.

Independent auditors are hired by the audit committee to provide an impartial (independent) opinion as to the status of internal controls.

Understanding the Auditor's Interest in the Strategy

As an IS auditor, you need to find evidence of management governing IT and the enterprise. The composition and performance of the steering committee could be a powerful source of evidence. You may be able to review the plans and meeting minutes from the committee. The auditor's goal is to assess the performance of the CEO and executive management in developing and leading a successful strategy based on business objectives.

Overview of Tactical Management

By using tactical management, an organization selects a maneuver or technique that will render a better result. The goal of tactical management is to manage the return on investment for information systems. The successful manager will need to establish a requirement for the collection of performance metrics. The performance metrics are used to determine whether the results are improving or deteriorating against a baseline. The same metrics are used to demonstrate management success to the executives and stakeholders.

Figure 3.6 illustrates the tactical level in the organizational chart.

FIGURE 3.6   Tactical level in the organization

The individuals at the tactical level should be providing support to the strategic objectives. The majority of planning work accomplished at the director level is tactical in nature. Strategic plans are handed down from top management. The director level is expected to fulfill the strategic goals by providing solutions without the authority to make changes in other areas of the organizational structure. The director's authority outside of their own department is limited to requesting and negotiating.

Planning and Performance

Every IS organization has a number of functions that it should implement to fulfill its strategic plan, its tactical plan, and its daily plan. An auditor looks at any industry-standard benchmarks for performance optimization that have been adopted. Several are available, including the National Institute of Standards and Technology's controls matrix and the Federal Information Security Management Act (FISMA). In addition, the organization may use an organization planning maturity model such as the OPM3 of the Project Management Institute.

It is possible that the organization benchmarks its business continuity plans and disaster plans after the public domain version of the Business Continuity Maturity Model (BCMM). The organization may have an information assurance program and be using the ISO 17799 or Capability Maturity Model (CMM).

The value of benchmarking is to determine the organization's position and progress as compared to a recognized reference. There are several competitive advantages to benchmarking, the first of which is the ability to attract respect and more favorable terms from stakeholders. Every IS organization has an issue regarding financial management. The question comes up, what does IS pay for? What does the department pay for? What does the project pay for? Individual departments may be operating a shadow IT group funded by department budgets. This condition usually indicates some type of failure to align to the business objectives or the strategic plan.

Management Control Methods

All levels of management are responsible for providing leadership. Good leaders generate better performance from individual employees. The organization needs continuous evidence of performance. The minimum requirements of good management include the following:

- Performance reporting
- General record keeping
- Safeguards and implementation details of controls

The auditor needs to review a variety of documents, including the organization's strategic plan, policies, IT plans, and operating procedures. These include plans for training, system mitigation, system certification, disaster recovery, continuity, and the inevitability of change. As an auditor, you will need input from people besides IT management to ensure alignment with the enterprise objectives.

Performance Review

Performance review refers to the identification of a target to be monitored, tracked, assigned to a responsible party, and resolution of any open issues.

Existing systems require a regular review to determine the on-going level of compliance to internal controls and the next steps to take.

The Capability Maturity Model (CMM) is a method for evaluating and measuring the maturity of processes in organizations. A rating scale from 0 to 5 is used. A score of zero indicate nothing is occurring. Level 1 maturity indicates the initial activity was successful and may later progress up to level 5 when the activity is statistically controlled for continuous improvement. The CMM rating scale was developed by the Software Engineering Institute at Carnegie Mellon University and has been widely used for rating business process capabilities. Levels of CMM are as follows:

 The Capability Maturity Model is also discussed in Chapter 5 for the software development life cycle.

Level 0 = Nothing yet   The level of zero is implied in the CMM, but may not be noticed. This is important when evaluating process maturity. Missing processes and controls without evidence will be rated as zero. Many individuals assume that all controls are present when, in fact, some may be missing. A process or control must have occurred in order to reach a level of maturity (1–5).

Level 1 = Initial   Processes are unique and chaotic. The organization does not have a stable environment. Success is based on individual competencies and heroics. This level often produces products and services that work. However, output may exceed the available resources or be dependent on particular individuals.

Level 2 = Repeatable   Processes are repeatable. The organization uses project management to track projects. The project status is communicated by using milestones with a defined work breakdown structure. The basic standards process, descriptions, and procedures are documented.

Level 3 = Defined   Processes are well documented and understood. Level 3 is more mature and better defined than level 2. Processes have objectives, measurements, improvement procedures, and standards. The results in level 3 are predictable by qualitative measure.

Level 4 = Managed   Management can use precise measurement criteria to control the processes and identify ways to adjust the results. Processes at level 4 are predictable by quantitative measure.

Level 5 = Optimized   This is the highest level with continuous improvement of processes. Objectives for improvement are defined and continually revised to reflect business needs and objectives.

Figure 3.7 shows the five maturity levels of the Capability Maturity Model in a lateral view.

FIGURE 3.7   Capability Maturity Model

Frankly, attaining higher levels in the maturity model increases the likelihood that internal controls are successful. A higher CMM grade indicates a definition of maturity with a higher degree of control.

Consider the typical hooks in an outsource contract. The buyer is hooked to it, and so the following questions should be asked:

- Did the client give away resources, intellectual-property knowledge, or procedures of value that will not be recoverable?

- Has the client given away highly qualified personnel who will no longer be in-house?

- What will a contract change cost, if desired?

- Can the contract be cancelled?

- If a decision is made to cancel, what is it going to take to get the replacement function online?

This should be enough information for the prospective CISA. Let's take a look at two other sources of governance models. The first is the US National Institute of Standards and Technology.

National Institute of Standards and Technology

The US government has set forth standards for engineering, weights and measures, and even computer processing. Management of the standards is assigned to the National Institute of Standards and Technology (NIST). The NIST standards for information technology management are mandatory for government agencies and optional for nongovernment organizations. Many of the IT best practices were derived from NIST.

The US government passed new internal control regulations under the Federal Information Security Management Act of 2002 (FISMA) to unify the former Federal Information Processing standards (FIPS). The US internal control rating requirements for compliance are posted on the NIST website under the heading for special reports. NIST is an excellent resource with governance models that implement the CMM. Now let's look at an international standard.

International Standards

Not to be outdone by the United States, the British government enacted their own security standard for government systems in 1995. The standard for British information security is British Standard 7799-1 (BS-7799 part 1). This uses similar internal controls for governance of IS systems. The International Organization for Standardization (ISO) ratified the BS-7799-1 framework as ISO standard 17799. This new ISO 17799 standard contains numerous points that are identical to the US standards.

With so much attention on internal controls, the most important step an organization can take is the first, to implement controls. Any one of these best practices models should already be implemented.

Quality Management

We have already discussed the basics of quality management in Chapter 2 on quality control in the audit process. Every organization should have processes in place to ensure that people are taking steps to do the right job at the right time. Quality management is a pervasive requirement.

We will discuss quality further in Chapter 5 on software application development.

Project Management

In Chapter 1, we discussed a few basics of project management and the defined project management processes. Every organization should be following a well-defined project management methodology. Larger organizations will implement a Project Management Office (PMO). The PMO is composed of project managers for the organization. Their function is to manage the larger or more critical projects.

As a CISA, you should recall that each project will have at least four distinct phases. Recall that the Project Management Institute defines five phases of project management: Initiating, Planning, Executing, Monitoring and Controlling, and Closing. However, PMI considers the process of getting a sponsor as the phase of project initiation. Most employees will never be involved in the Initiating phase. Therefore, ISACA wants the IS auditor to understand the four common phases of Planning, Executing (scheduling), Monitoring and Controlling, and Closing.

Now let's look at risk management in IT governance.

Risk Management

Risks occur at all levels. There are strategic risks, tactical risks, operational risks, and inherent risks. We have discussed these definitions in Chapters 1 and 2. Now let's look one of the more common risk management formulas.

The first step in risk management is to calculate how much a single loss event would cost. This formula multiplies an asset value (expressed in dollars) by the percentage of loss for a particular event. For example, the percentage of loss of a stolen purse is likely to be 100 percent. In that example, the loss would be 100 percent of purse value. The loss due to data-entry errors may be equal to .007 percent of labor cost. This first formula is expressed as follows:

Asset value (AV) $ × exposure factor (EF) % = single loss expectancy (SLE)

The single loss expectancy can be multiplied by the number of related events that are likely to occur for the year. The final result would be the estimated annual loss, as shown in the following formula:

Single loss expectancy (SLE) × annual rate of occurrence (ARO) = annual loss expectancy (ALE)

Figure 3.8 is a graphical representation of calculating the annual rate of occurrence in the risk management process.

FIGURE 3.8   Calculating annual rate of occurrence

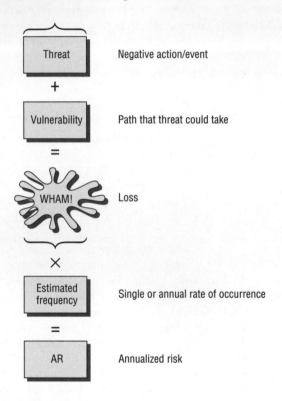

Threat — Negative action/event

+

Vulnerability — Path that threat could take

=

WHAM! — Loss

×

Estimated frequency — Single or annual rate of occurrence

=

AR — Annualized risk

Risk management should be pervasive in all areas of business, including the IT department. As you might recall, we covered risk management previously in Chapter 2. The choices are to avoid, mitigate, transfer, accept, or eliminate the risk, and the goal is to reduce the level of risk.

When developing a risk management program, the auditor wants to ensure that the risk management function has been implemented with an established purpose. Someone has been assigned responsibility, and risk management is a formal ongoing process, not just a review by lawyers.

Risks can involve many areas of the business. Impacts can be direct or indirect, but in either case will damage the organization's position, capital, or future opportunities. Typical assets include the organization's customer list, general information (which could be information about marketing or development), data, files, hardware, and software. Assets could also include the facility, a particular document, or services rendered. The risks, or threats, could be terror acts, malicious fraud, executing the wrong procedure, theft, or failure of controls.

It's interesting that criminals do not look at vulnerabilities the same way as an upstanding individual. To a criminal mind, a window becomes an entry or exit point to a building with the aid of a brick.

Risk management operates at a variety of levels: Management at the strategic level focuses on whether going forward with a particular strategy over a period of years is a good idea. Management could be at a project level—is the project on track? Or it could be at a daily or hourly or by-the-minute operational level to ensure that personnel are doing what they are supposed to do. Frankly, most major disasters are caused by a domino effect of a tiny failure multiplying into multiple failures that become catastrophic.

Overall, situations of high risk where high loss, high consequence, or high impact is possible will require a method to ensure the problem receives adequate consideration and the appropriate level of effort to prevent an unfortunate outcome. It is extremely common for IT staff to execute poor change control when dealing with interruptions, failures, theft, fraud, or just general risk while under pressure.

Personnel Risk

Determining the requirements related to hiring or terminating outsourced personnel can be challenging. Several companies have discovered way too late that certain organizations in the European Union have some rather stout requirements for expatriation and repatriation. The company may be liable for future employee benefits and the individual's cost of relocation. The requirements could also include severance plans that provide advance pay of up to about a year, include the company's purchase of the former employee's home because that person did not have time to sell it, and pay medical expenses for six months to a year. These requirements can make a huge difference if a company is planning changes such as layoffs or is trying to determine whether hiring a contractor is a good idea.

Information Security Risk

Every organization communicates sensitive data over delicate communication lines, which are not necessarily secure. In fact, every government has mandates to conduct surveillance for foreign intelligence to provide trade advantages for their citizens. News articles discuss the government organizations from competing countries attempt to bring the technology to native organizations that are residents of their country. It's the old game of economic espionage and political advantage. Data security is the number one concern when planning for trans-border communication. The next concern may be that infrastructure issues impede delivery or quality of service because of a geographically remote location.

Implementing Standards

IT governance is founded on the implementation of formal policies and standards. Each standard is supported by a matching procedure. The purpose of IT governance is to ensure that the risks are properly managed by mitigation, avoidance, or transfer. Let's review a short list of the policies required to address issues faced by IT governance:

Intellectual property   The term *intellectual property* refers to data and knowledge that is not commonly known. This information possesses a commercial value. The IS auditor should understand how the organization is attempting to protect its intellectual property. The rights of intellectual property can be destroyed by a failure of the organization to take preemptive action.

Data integrity   What mechanisms have been put in place to ensure data integrity? Does the organization have input controls? How is the data validated for accuracy? Are the systems formally reviewed in a certification and accreditation process? What level of security management and access controls are present? Internal controls for data integrity are required by most industries and government regulation. The goal of data integrity is to ensure that data is accurate and safely stored.

   Backup and restoration   What are the plans and procedures for data backup and restoration? The number one issue in IT is loss of data due to faulty backup. The failures can be procedural or technical.

   Security management   Without security controls, ensuring data integrity is impossible. Internal controls prevent unauthorized modifications. The Sarbanes-Oxley Act and FISMA mandate strong security controls.

Mandatory vs. discretionary controls   Every control is based on the human implementation. The organization needs to clearly identify its management directives for implementation of controls. Every control will be one of two fundamental types:

   Mandatory control   This is the strongest type of control. The implementation may be administrative or technical. A mandatory control is designed to force compliance without exception.

   Discretionary control   The weakest type of control is discretionary. In a discretionary control, the user or delegated person of authority determines what is acceptable.

Monitoring   The IT systems should be monitored throughout the entire life cycle and in daily operations. The monitoring process provides valuable metrics necessary to compare alignment to business objectives. The purpose of governance is to lead. It would be impossible to lead without understanding ongoing conditions. Monitoring may prove that the organization is well run for a ticking time bomb. Without monitoring, determining whether an incident needs attention would be impossible.

Incident response   A response is required for skilled individuals to deal with technical problems or the failure of internal controls. An incident may be major or minor depending on the circumstances. It is necessary to have an established policy, standard, and procedure for handling the incident response. At the beginning of an incident, it is impossible to accurately foretell the full impact of possible consequences. An incident response team should be in place to investigate suspicious situations. Care and diligence is necessary because it may later be determined that the initial response area is a crime scene. The mishandling of evidence could lead to forfeiture of the organization's damage claims. Unproven allegations against an individual or organization will frequently result in financial liability by the accuser.

Human Resources

IT governance is conjoined with requirements to properly manage people. Good management is founded on human resource management that is well defined, fair, and consistent. Let's take a look at a few of the HR-related policies that affect IT management:

Hiring   What are the organization's policies for selecting the best candidate? How should the interview process be handled? Quality management is required during the hiring process to ensure that the organization is in compliance with equal opportunity standards.

Termination   Personnel may be terminated via either friendly or unfriendly procedures. The requirements for layoffs are relatively clear. What are the procedures for terminating personnel over extended periods of time? A special procedure may be necessary in the case of an upcoming personal retirement. A different procedure may apply to an employee who will be returning as a contractor on the same project. A hostile termination could stem from workplace violence, a criminal act, fraud, or a dispute with other personnel.

Employee contracts   Many organizations use employee contracts to specify terms of employment. This technique is typically in effect in states with a Right to Work law. Right to Work laws are primarily about *union vs nonunion employment*—that people have a right to decide whether they want to be part of a union or not, that union membership can't be a condition of employment. The use of employment contracts is invaluable for identifying the ownership of new discoveries. The employment contract details that the individual is performing work for hire, to the benefit of the employer organization.

Confidentiality agreement   A standard practice is for employees and contractors to sign a confidentiality agreement. The purpose is to ensure that strategic, tactical, and operational details are not divulged outside the organization. Operating without a confidentiality agreement may be a significant risk.

Noncompetition agreement   The employer may implement a noncompete agreement to prevent the employee from working for a competitor. The terms of this type of agreement may be successful as long as they are not overly restrictive for the amount of money paid to the employee.

Ethics statements   The organization should provide a statement of what is acceptable and unacceptable behavior. The best method for preventing a problem is to explain to an individual what actions are acceptable. Unacceptable behavior includes any activities for personal gain at the expense of the organization.

Performance evaluation   A standardized process should be in place for reviewing an employee's performance. Each employee in the same basic role should be judged by their manager on defined criteria, pertinent to their organizational role. A quarterly or annual review is customary. The results of this review fall under HR record retention requirements for several years.

Promotion policy   What is the organization's promotion policy? Is it based on job performance, education, or something else? The organization is required to demonstrate a fair and objective promotion policy in order to meet equal opportunity compliance.

Work schedule   Work schedules and vacation schedules should be clearly defined. In some financial organizations, the vacation schedule is implemented as a detective control. An individual is forced to take vacations in one- or two-week increments. During their absence, another individual performs that job and a discovery audit may take place to ensure that no irregular or illegal acts have been committed by the employee.

Corrective counseling   What are the organization's policies for corrective counseling after poor performance from the employee? Care must be taken to prevent discrimination. An improper termination can create a financial liability. An employee may collect monetary damages if able to prove wrongful termination.

These are just a few of the many policies and procedures necessary to manage human resources. The IS auditor should be concerned about activities that increase the organization's level of risk. This includes Human Resources activities.

System Life-Cycle Management

All computer systems need to be managed through their entire life cycle. Each system will go through a series of phases starting with a feasibility study. Next, requirements are generated and followed by system design. Systems are tested for integrity and their fitness of use is determined. The life cycle continues into system implementation. After successful implementation, the system can migrate into production use. Each year of production, the system should undergo a review. The annual post-implementation review focuses on the system's present condition compared to the more current requirements. A system may be upgraded to the new requirements or retired. This is just a summary.

The CISA is interested in understanding how the organization manages each phase of this process. Evidence should be obtained to support the auditor's conclusions.

    We will cover the system life cycle in more depth in Chapter 5.

Continuity Planning

Information technology systems are so pervasive today that most organizations would cease to operate if their computers were unavailable. IT governance requires continuity planning for systems and data. Any disruption to operations could have far-reaching effects. Members of the media can be merciless in their quest to report an interesting story. The damage to an organization's reputation and brand can be fatal. ISACA wants every CISA to be aware of the need for continuity planning. We have expanded coverage on the subject of business continuity in Chapter 8.

Insurance

Adequate insurance is the minimum response for asset protection. This is a corrective administrative control. There are issues concerning insurance including the cost vs. actual benefits received. Insurance does not replace lost market share, nor damage from unauthorized disclosure of confidential information. Acts of god, war, and terrorism are exempt from coverage in most insurance policies. Proper risk management reduces the organization's exposure. Risk reduction efforts, combined with insurance, are a good practice.

The CISA should be aware that there is a difference between real insurance and self-insurance. Normally, the term *self-insurance* implies a level of protection that does not exist. Self-insurance usually means that the organization is accepting the risk with full liability for any consequences.

Performance Management

Performance management serves to inform executives and stakeholders as to the progress of current activities. A fair and objective scoring system should be used. Scores may be based on a current service-level agreement. Another method is to use key performance indicators (KPIs), which tend to represent a historical average of monitored events. Unfortunately, a key performance indicator may indicate a failing score too late to implement a change. A perfect example of a KPI is the high-school report card. By the time the score is reported, the target child may not be eligible to graduate.

A process should exist to report the performance of IT budgets and noncompliant activities. Executive management should encourage the reporting of issues without punishing the messenger. Some effort is necessary to ensure the accurate and timely flow of information upward to the executives. False information can be very damaging.

Instead of just having a qualitative assessment of good or bad, or high, medium, or low, this should be an accounting exercise using a quantitative measure. It could be a semiquantitative, using a ranking scale similar to scoring in a school: 70 to 79 is a C, 80 to 89 is a B, 90 to 100 is an A, and then percentages such as A– or A+. This technique will convert a subjective decision into a more objective review. The Capability Maturity Model is very effective for communicating performance metrics.

Figure 3.9 shows a brief glimpse of the CMM used to report metrics.

FIGURE 3.9   Excerpt of CMM to report metrics

Metric	CMM process maturity	Change	% Compliance
Help desk support	0 ———— 3.9 —— 5	▲	100%
Laptop security plan	0 —— 2.9 ———— 5	▲	73%
Laptop data encryption	0 ——— 3.4 ——— 5	●	67%
New user security training	0 ——— 3.4 ——— 5	▲	58%
Existing user security training	0 — 1.5 ————— 5	▼	19%
Vulnerability scan users	0 — 1 ————— 5	▲	8%

Managing Outsourcing

When an organization decides to consider outsourcing, one of the concerns is that the organization may lose the visibility necessary to effectively operate the processes. The outsource contract should require a *right to audit* the service provider. Occasionally the response is that they cannot be audited by everyone because they do not have the time or the money, but will give you a copy of the SAS-70 service providers audit report, which is a standard audit format.

Unfortunately, the report may be insufficient to management needs, because the report is probably vetted and groomed to ensure it states the level of information the service provider wants to convey, not necessarily what may be observed during your own audit. Our suggestion is that if a company is considering outsourcing, the auditor could ask, "Why not run a controls audit and an SLA audit using the client's auditor, or a full audit before signing the contract?", The goal is to determine whether the service provider is fulfilling their entire obligation before signing a contract. Why risk the time and money to sign a contract while silently hoping and praying that the requirements are met?

Besides the control issue, and an excellent idea to implement a business process review before outsourcing.

Overview of Business Process Reengineering

One of the principles in business that remains constant is change to processes and procedures. Most periodicals, manuals, and guidelines published today contain discussions of the planning necessary for implementing change in an organization. The concept of change must be accepted as a fundamental principle. The organization that does not change is destined to perish.

As a CISA, you must be prepared to ensure that changes to processes within the organization are accounted for with proper documentation. All internal control frameworks require that management be held responsible for safeguarding all assets of the organization. Management is also responsible for increasing revenue. Let's discuss why business process reengineering (BPR) review is important.

Why Use Business Process Reengineering

Authors and consultants Michael Hammer and James Champy, as cited by ISACA, define BPR as "the fundamental rethinking and radical redesign of business processes to bring about dramatic improvements in critical, contemporary measures of performance."

BPR is often concerned with reducing costs of the existing process while increasing performance. Three of the major areas for improvement are as follows:

Business efficiency   Efficiency will increase as workers become more proficient in their tasks (a.k.a. *learning curve*). In the very beginning, work progresses slowly with multiple test inspections required. After several iterations, the inspections may be reduced if the quality becomes consistent.

Improved techniques   During the regular course of production, new improvements may be discovered for existing techniques. An updated technique may eliminate previous steps that become unnecessary because of higher consistency. Efficiency may be gained by eliminating these unnecessary steps. If quality is diminished, it may be necessary to increase the number of steps in the business process.

New requirements   The existing business process may need to be reworked to comply with new requirements. The requirements may be in response to a regulation, business need, or customer.

BPR activities are performed as a unique project. The BPR project designs new or improved processes to replace outdated, outmoded, or inefficient processes.

You may want to refer to Chapter 1 for a quick refresher on project management.

The BPR processes will be reviewed for effectiveness, governance, and strategic value to the organization. Let's investigate the BPR goals.

BPR Goals

The principal issue is that business rules may have been generated from previous assumptions that no longer apply. The current business processes were designed around constraints that may not exist any longer. BPR investigates existing processes to determine whether a better course of action is available. The goal is to accurately identify all the nuances of the current process. The next step is to determine process relationships with the level of modification that is available. Any modifications made should generate strategic results that increase capabilities or reduce operating costs. BPR is also used to modify an existing process for compliance to a new requirement. Now we will discuss the BPR principles of operation.

BPR Principles

ISACA expects every CISA to understand the operating principles used in the BPR project. The principles suggested by BPR experts can vary considerably depending on their viewpoint, but some suggested principles include the following:

- Review of existing processes to determine whether several jobs can be combined
- Empowering workers to make operational decisions
- Determining a logical order for processes to use
- Reviewing and eliminating superfluous or multiple overlapping processes
- Applying the most efficient and effective controls to ensure governance
- Performing work where it makes the most sense
- Simplifying processes in use
- Standardizing processes, procedures, methods, products, and tools

- Integrating several processes into one, or integrating manual processes into automated methods
- Establishing parallel processes to ensure continuity

Remember, the primary goal is to increase efficiency while reducing operating costs. BPR projects should be undertaken only when the business value can be demonstrated. Three simple demonstrations are to increase capabilities, reduce operating costs, or obtain compliance with a new requirement. It is time to commence the BPR process after the business value can be demonstrated.

BPR Steps

Let's start with an overview of the six basic steps cited by ISACA in their general approach to business process reengineering (BPR) projects:

Envision   Envision a need, gain sponsorship from the organization, define areas to be reviewed.

Initiate   Assign a BPR project team, set goals, plan the BPR project, establish an approved project plan.

Diagnose   Document existing processes, identify requirements and value, gain understanding of existing processes.

Redesign   Develop and document the new process, ensuring that it meets strategic objectives.

Reconstruct   Use change management to transition, train, and implement the new process.

Evaluate   Monitor the new process to ensure that it works and has strategic value, establish continuous improvement goals and processes.

 You will look at each of these steps in more detail later in this chapter, in the section "A Practical Approach to the BPR Process."

As a CISA, you should remain cognizant that the focus of IT governance is to provide effective leadership and to control change. Let's investigate some of the ways BPR could be used.

Benchmarking as a BPR Tool

Benchmarking may be used to evaluate business processes being considered for reengineering. Benchmarks may be obtained by using control self-assessment and auditing for compliance to a published standard. ISACA identifies several general guidelines for performing benchmarking comparisons:

Plan   Create a plan of what will be benchmarked. Identify critical processes and measurement techniques for these processes.

Research   Collect baseline information about the process and collect baseline information about the comparison process.

Observe Gather data, visit a benchmark partner (internal or external) to gather comparison data results.

Analyze Use predefined tools to measure the collected data from all sources.

Adapt Translate the findings into documented results. Document how the findings affect strategic business goals.

Improve Implement new processes by using change management. Measure process results, establish procedures for continuous improvement.

The benchmarking process is a valuable step toward self-improvement. Figure 3.10 illustrates the benchmarking process.

FIGURE 3.10   Benchmarking process

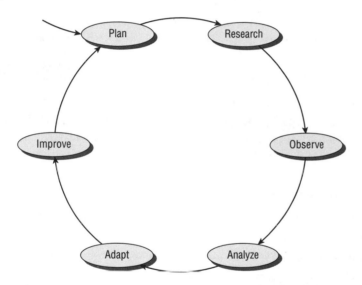

The next area in BPR is to conduct a project risk assessment.

BPR Project Risk Assessment

During the BPR project, risks associated with changing an existing process must be identified. ISACA cites several risk areas to consider in the *ISACA Audit Standards, Guidelines, and Procedures*. The subject is broken down into three broad areas of the BPR project with multiple categories in each area:

Design area risks A process design failure would be the doom of any BPR project. New projects require dedicated resources and the time and attention necessary to ensure a quality solution. This may entail more money and time than is available from key personnel. The following are risks that may occur in the design category:

Sponsorship risks   Senior management not supportive of the effort, the wrong person leading the project, poor communication of need

Scope risks   Project not related to strategic need, scope improperly defined, protected processes excluded from the project

Skill risks   Failure to fully explore potential solutions, closure to new ideas, project beyond ability of participants to define

Political risk   Sabotage, fear, cultural resistance

Implementation area risks   The implementation risks represent potential failures that could occur during the project. Four common risks are as follows:

Leadership risks   Failure to support the project, ownership disputes, management personnel change during BPR project, failure to prove a need

Technical risks   Beyond capability of IT to create, delays in implementation, capabilities of software insufficient, definition disputes, project is too complex, scope changes during implementation.

Transition risks   Loss of focus during implementation, loss of key personnel

Scope risks   Excessive costs, schedule variance, scope improperly defined

Operation/rollout area risks   After careful planning, it is still possible for the BPR project to fail in normal use. Common types of failure include human attitudes and technical shortfall. Other problems include cultural risks, management risks, and technical risks.

Culture/human resource risks   Resistance in the organization not overcome, training problems, outcomes not understood, no buy-in

Management risks   Ownership/power struggles not resolved, poor communications, active or passive resistance and sabotage, insufficient training

Technical risks   Insufficient support, operational problems, software problems, inadequate testing, data integrity problems

Business Process Controls to Consider

When considering changes to business processes or implementing these changes, the CISA should consider the use of multiple tools that will help define and document the processes being changed:

Process maps   Business processes can be diagrammed by using flowcharts, influence diagrams, and fishbone diagrams to assist in the definition and documentation of the process.

Process controls   Documentation of the current process with clearly defined checkpoints and/or checklists are used to ensure that the entire process is being performed.

Risk assessment   Look at the process by using the preceding risk categories as well as other categories. External risk and organizational risk should be assessed. Tools for risk identification such as interviewing experts, brainstorming, holding risk identification roundtable sessions, and using the Delphi technique should be considered. The Delphi technique uses a blind interaction of ideas between members of a group. Each member provides suggestions without knowledge of the other suggestions by other participants. The exercise continues until a consensus is reached. We covered some of the other methods of performing a risk assessment in Chapter 2, "Audit Process."

Benchmarking   Compare your process to another process that is the same or similar.

Roles and responsibilities   Define and document who is responsible for what process or what portions of the process. Many times the auditor will discover through interviews that several people know a portion of the process but no one knows the whole process.

Tasks and activities   Defining tasks and activities works in conjunction with defining roles and responsibilities. The purpose is to define who performs what work and how it affects the overall process. The results may be documented in a work breakdown structure (WBS).

Data process restrictions   This is a definition of data available for the process. This includes defining contributory sources and defining all data available from the process being considered for review.

Knowledge Requirements for BPR

As a CISA, you must have a working knowledge of auditing standards and the control frameworks such as Control Objectives for Information and related Technology (CoBIT). For auditing BPR projects, the competent auditor must possess the following:

- Information systems auditing skills
- Specialized CISA audit standard knowledge
- Specialized application knowledge of the company processes and procedures
- Specialized application knowledge of the functional area being audited
- General management knowledge and skills
- Interpersonal skills

The Practical Application of BPR

One practical way to attack the BPR project is to apply the principles of project management, as defined by the PMI. As stated in Chapter 1, you should look on this as a framework for project management. You may use all or some of the processes along with their inputs, tools, and techniques, and outputs for the project you are managing. The use of these processes is on an as-needed basis. The PMI processes provide an excellent checklist to prevent errors and omissions in the management of any specific project.

We suggest some practical basics for BPR:

- If it's not broken, don't fix it.
- If it is broken, make sure you understand the process before you try to fix it.

- When you fix it, make sure that there is value in fixing it. The return on investment (ROI) for the effort should be calculated before investing any resources.

- After you fix it, make sure you don't have any leftover parts. Every item should be reused, modified, or formally retired.

Let's discuss what each of these practical application guidelines mean to BPR.

"If It's Not Broken, Don't Fix It"

It is best to understand the process totally before you try to fix it. Some processes are put in place for a specific reason. If you fix the process without a total understanding, you run the risk of changing the condition and the results of the process. It is suggested that any process be thoroughly reviewed before it is selected for reengineering.

Many organizations install processes or change processes based on nonbusiness-related need. In our experience, we have seen many cases in which processes that were working were changed for nonprocess-related reasons: for example, standardization, outsourcing, or reorganization. Processes that are changed for nonprocess-related conformance issues are often changed back to the old process when the new conforming process fails to work.

"If It Is Broken, Make Sure You Understand the Process Before You Try to Fix It"

Even if the process is suspect and you think it is faulty, you should make every effort to fully understand what the process is doing and what the expected outcomes are before you begin reengineering.

A practical way to determine what the process does is to perform a Business Impact Analysis (BIA). The BIA is done by interviewing subject matter experts to determine what the process does. Part of the BIA is to document the process as the interviews occur. The result should identify what the process does, who does it, what the outcome of the process is, and what other processes it interacts with. Diagramming the process flow and process influences or interdependencies may be appropriate to fully define and understand the process.

"When You Fix It, Make Sure That There Is Value in Fixing It"

These BPR practical guidelines should not suggest in any way that processes should remain static. But, in any organization, there needs to be practical value in doing process reengineering. During the "good old, bad old days" of Y2K or the "dot-bomb" era, many projects were undertaken and many processes were reengineered without due diligence and without a return on investment.

Process reengineering should absolutely, positively, have a return for the money invested to do the reengineering.

One problem is determining what the value of the process is today to the enterprise. This can be solved by using a Business Impact Analysis.

🌐 Real World Scenario

Misunderstood Details in a BPR Project

An experienced purchasing manager had worked for a large retailer for many years. Over time, the manager developed—and personally performed—a manual process of sending packing materials to stores that were slated for closing. As circumstances changed, this job title (purchasing manager) was outsourced to an external company.

The new manager reviewed all of the processes he was to perform and determined that the manual process of sending packing materials to closing stores could be automated. After all, the materials sent all had an individual SKU and those SKUs could be combined into one unique SKU so that a single entry in the order system could speed all of these materials on their way. So the process was changed and automated.

The first time the new process was used, the reasoning behind the manual process became apparent. Under the old process, the purchasing manager closely controlled the date that the packing materials would be received in order to ensure that they were received on the date the store was informed that they were closing. With the new process, the materials automatically shipped when the confidential notification was received that the store would be closing sometime in the future. This informed the store personnel weeks before the store closing and created a security issue that resulted in the loss of many expensive merchandise items.

Although this situation could be remedied, the lesson learned is that the new person who decided to change the process was not adequately informed before making that decision. This created a governance problem, rather than protecting against such a problem.

"After You Fix It, Make Sure You Don't Have Any Leftover Parts"

When you disassemble a bicycle or lawn mower or other device and then put it back together again, one of the long-running jokes is that you always have leftover parts. When you disassemble your business process, you have to be sure that you don't have leftover parts—things that used to be performed under the old process that were missed when creating the new process.

Conducting a Business Impact Analysis

The Business Impact Analysis (BIA) is a discovery process. Its purpose is to uncover the inner working of any process. The BIA will answer questions about actual procedures, shortcuts, workarounds, and the types of failure that may occur. Armed with this knowledge, it is possible to assess priorities.

Part of the BIA is to determine what the process does, who performs the process, and what the output is. The BIA also determines the value of the process output to the organization. The BIA interviewer will ask key managers and key workers a series of questions to discover the low-level details of current processes. Some sample BIA questions that might be asked of key personnel in a BPR process review include:

1. What processes do you perform?

2. Who do you perform these actions for?

3. What tools, equipment, and systems do you use?

4. What request, event, or system provides indication for you to start work on the subject (input)?

5. Get/show examples of the work the person performs (processes). Do multiple processes exist? If so, be sure to document each process for later review.

6. Who is the key vendor and alternate vendor?

7. What is the time sensitivity of the process?

8. What is the basic priority of the process?

9. Where do you record your work (output)?

10. Who uses the output of your process next, and who depends on your output?

11. What happens if the process is

    - not used?

    - not available?

    - not performed?

    - not accepted?

12. What other methods could you use to accomplish the process? Are there workarounds or alternate processes that might already exist?

13. Would the alternate procedure really work?

14. How can you test it, or has it already been tested?

15. Who else knows this process and could do this in a crisis?

16. Who is the ultimate customer for this process?

17. How much revenue does this process create or support?

18. Is there documentation on this process readily available?

19. Is documentation on the technical requirements for the process readily available?

20. Are there previous audit reports about this process that can be examined?

21. What is the projected lifetime of this process? Will the process be used in perpetuity, or is this process being made obsolete by a future process or projected change in business?

Questions 17 and 21 provide key information for determining the true value of the process. Determining how much revenue the process creates or supports will help define its true value to the enterprise. Determining how long the process may be used is another measurement for value.

For example, an organization can afford to spend $100,000 to reengineer a shipping process if they intend to use the process in perpetuity and show savings or cost avoidance of some amount per year to pay for this effort. But if that process is slated to end in one year, the cost payback must be more carefully evaluated.

Another practical guideline would suggest that processes must have a lifetime in excess of one year or more to provide value for the time and effort expended to reengineer them.

 Real World Scenario

BIA Provides Improved Awareness

Consider a retail distribution company with over $1 billion in annual sales. When the Business Impact Analysis (process review) was done, it is determined that 95 percent of all product flows through only one branch of the supply chain. The key to process reengineering for this company will be to examine the processes that are now proven to support 95 percent of all of the company's revenue.

Proper planning of the process reengineering project will provide for documentation of the process to be modified. If the process has been correctly documented with all outputs and all interrelated activities, the chances of having "leftover parts" is minimized.

Practical Selection Methods for BPR

We suggest that processes that are being considered for inclusion in a BPR project be selected based on some predefined criteria. Each organization is unique and each may choose to define unique selection criteria and selection processes. Processes must be evaluated and will generally fit into one of the following categories:

- Working process
- Marginal process
- Nonworking process
- Excluded process

In addition to these categories, you need to consider the value equation. Does process reengineering have a return on investment? You may consider placing your processes being considered for reengineering into a table similar to Table 3.3.

 You should remember that your goal during BPR is to ensure that the organization is properly managing the entire process.

Let's discuss each of these of these categories in more detail:

Working process   This type of process has documentation associated with it, meets the requirements that the business has for its output, has controls in place that meet governance

TABLE 3.3   BPR Return on Investment and Priority

Category	No ROI Anticipated (Probably Not Selected for BPR)	ROI Anticipated	Priority for BPR
Nonworking process	*Insert your process names without ROI*	*Insert your process name having ROI*	1
Marginal process	"	"	2
Working process	"	"	3
Excluded process	"	"	4

and audit specifications, and has ongoing support from the IT organization. A working process conforms to business requirements, budget requirements, quality requirements, and is efficient as defined by the organization. Working processes should reach at least level 2 on the CMM (which means it's a repeatable process).

Marginal process   This means one or more of the elements are compromised. Outputs, business requirements, budgetary need, quality requirements, or efficiencies are compromised. A marginal process may not pass appropriate controls and audit reviews.

A process could be classified as a marginal process if it falls to level 1 of the CMM (which is the initial level, meaning chaos and heroics). Marginal processes need to be closely reviewed to determine whether there is a need for reengineering and whether there is value associated with the completed reengineering output.

Nonworking process   This is a process that has one or more elements that are simply not working. The process might be manual, and no controls exist to ensure that the process is executed on time. A nonworking process should have the highest level of priority for process reengineering. Like every other BPR effort, a nonworking process must consider the value equation.

Excluded process   This is a process that is exempt from the BPR consideration for some valid reason. Value could be a primary reason for exclusion. Frequency of using the process, the process being planned for elimination in the near future due to obsolescence, or being a temporary process could all be reasons to categorize a process as "excluded." Process owners who are resistant to change and political alliances are not good reasons for causing a process to fall into this category.

A Practical Approach to the BPR Project

To effectively manage the BPR project, you may combine the foundation steps of the BPR process with the processes and process groups defined by the PMI standard for project management. In the following sections, you'll look at the various phases of the BPR project and the PMI processes that they relate to.

Envision

This portion of the project identifies the BPR need. Begin the project by obtaining sponsorship. In the PMI model, the project manager—you in this case—must obtain formal approval to start the project. This formal approval comes in the form of a project charter. The project charter identifies several key elements of the project:

Project title   Name as well as a brief description of project goals and objectives.

Product description   The specific deliverables from this project.

Project manager   Name of the project manager and the level of authority that this person holds. Is the additional authority in the form of a support committee for the project?

Business case   Why we are doing this project and the estimated return.

Signature   Formal authorization.

Initiate

This portion of the project approximates the Planning process group in the PMI model. During this portion of the project, you need to set goals, plan the project, and obtain buy-in for the plan. A formal project plan document is prepared and approved. There are 21 processes that contribute to the planning/definition portion of the project. You need to understand the following functions in ISACA's BPR Initiate phase:

Identify the scope of the project   The BPR project manager documents specific BPR deliverables with business goals and objectives. Milestones are identified to measure progress.

Create a budget   The BPR project manager compiles an estimate of costs. The estimate is refined to create the formal budget. The details are presented to executive management with the goal of obtaining budget approval.

Create a schedule   The BPR project charter has a high-level estimate of time. Now the estimate will be refined to match the approved scope of work (SOW). Resources can be identified and allocated to the BPR project.

Create a staffing plan   Estimate people requirements for the project, assign roles and responsibilities, and assign specific tasks based on the work breakdown structure (part of the scope definition).

Define the quality plan for the project   Determine what quality tenets and processes are to be deployed on the BPR project. Determine how quality will be measured and documented.

Define the communications plan   Define what needs to be communicated, to whom, and at what frequency. The BPR usually has a large project team and a large group of project stakeholders. Communications is an essential part of the overall plan. Stakeholder buy-in for the project will not be ensured without adequate communications.

Create a procurement plan   Define the resources that will be acquired from external sources (people, equipment, and materials). If external procurement takes place, contract types must be determined, procurement documents prepared, and a solicitation process conducted to get proposals from perspective providers.

Identify project risks   Risks for the project need to be identified. Many different forms of risk identification can take place; in the end, a risk register is created for the project and prioritized based on potential for risk occurrence and impact.

Diagnose

In the Diagnose phase, you and the project team must identify the specific processes to be focused on during the BPR project. This is a planning process, focusing on scope definition for the project. It is important that the existing process is fully documented and fully understood so that BPR occurs in a well-informed environment. The ROI, or the value that the reengineered process can bring to the organization, should be defined at this time. This provides the BPR team with information with which to obtain buy-in for the project from diverse groups in the organization.

Redesign

This phase of the BPR project can be compared to the Executing process group in the PMI model. At this point, the BPR focuses on creating deliverables—the reengineered process. Communications with project stakeholders is essential during this period so that everyone is fully informed of the new process and what it will accomplish.

Performance measurement occurs in this area as well. As deliverables are accomplished, the practitioner/project manager measures whether the deliverables have been produced on time and within budget and task parameters. Performance reports should be shared with stakeholders to keep all parties fully informed. Poor performance will usually affect ROI and must be carefully tracked so that it does not decrease the effectiveness of the BPR.

Reconstruct

This phase approximates the Monitoring and Controlling process from the PMI model for project management. Here you utilize change control to carefully implement the reengineered process in the enterprise. Failure to use proper change control during implementation can create a cloud of confusion and distress that may prevent the reengineered process from being accepted by the users.

Evaluate

The Evaluate step of the ISACA model for BPR approximates the Closing process group of the PMI project management model. In this area, you need to monitor the reengineered process that has been implemented. The goal is to identify lessons learned, identify value received, and then get formal acceptance and sign-off for the implemented process. At this time, goals for continuous improvement—which were presumably previously identified during the Diagnose or Redesign steps—would be activated. The Evaluate step is an ongoing review that can occur over some period of time (as defined in the original plan).

If improvements to the implemented process are required, the six-step process for BPR and project management processes is repeated to fully define, design, and implement new reengineering efforts.

NOTE Additional information on business process reengineering can be found under the BPR guideline G-26 in the ISACA *Audit Standards, Guidelines, and Procedures.*

Tactical Management

Tactical management should be performed during weekly and monthly performance reporting with senior-level executives. Tactical performance is frequently included during a regular audit.

As an IS auditor, you will be interested in learning the scope and extent of project management methodologies in use. Your interest will include gaining an understanding of the management tools in use and application of management controls. Tactical management should be using a change control process that exercises advance planning, risk management, and due diligence. The auditor should seek materially relevant evidence demonstrating management's efforts in support of the strategic objectives. The auditor's opinion should include a determination of the effective level of IT integration with various stages of project management. Is tactical management well integrated with measurable performance?

Operations Management

We start the discussion of operations management with a simple definition. An *operation* is a "procedure to set forth or produce a desired result."

The objective of operations management is to promote consistency with an effective response to the user requests. Operations management represents support for issues faced in day-to-day business. The operations support is sometimes referred to as firefighting or user support. In this section, you will look at the IT goals and operations management.

Supporting IT Goals

The goal of operations management is to sustain the daily business needs. The strategy was set forth by executive management, a technical response was created by middle management, and the actual hands-on work is performed by operations managers and support staff. The work performed should be in direct support of the higher-level business objectives.

As a CISA, you should remain observant of the difference between personnel who are *busy* and those who are *effective*. The volume of work performed is not a single measure of success. IT personnel must be focused on specific business objectives and have the necessary skills to be effective.

Sustaining Operations

Every organization faces the challenges of sustaining operations. You will investigate whether the IT staff has the capability to sustain current operations. Three areas of interest are immediately identifiable. The auditor should seek evidence to discover whether the following three sustaining factors are met:

- Adequate staffing
- Written procedures
- Level of staff integration

It would be practically impossible to sustain regular operations without documented procedures executed by an adequate number of well-trained IT staff members. The staff members must be able to interact and communicate effectively inside the IT organization and with the business organization. To ensure these objectives, each member of the IT team will need to have specified roles and responsibilities.

Understanding Personnel Roles and Responsibilities

During any dispute over control, it can be challenging to determine who is actually in charge. The client's organizational chart can render a great deal of valuable information. The contents indicate who is in charge at each level, where each person reports to, and a clue about the basic job functions. It is not an uncommon practice to walk into an organization and find that the organization does not have a current copy of their own organizational chart.

You should recognize that the lack of a current organizational chart is a concern. All positions must have matching job descriptions that are accurate and reflect current responsibilities. Anything more than a small discrepancy in either of these documents would indicate a lack of proper internal control. We included a sample organizational chart in Figure 3.5 earlier in this chapter.

Let's take a quick look at several of the more common IT positions that should be of interest to you. Each of these roles has a unique degree of authority and influence in IT operations:

IT director The IT director has the day-to-day responsibility of managing IS/IT managers and executing the executives' plan. He or she is an upper-level manager with the authority to make decisions for their group. IT operations managers will receive orders directly from the IT director.

IT operations managers IT operations managers are in charge of their own IT staff working in software development, on the help desk, in server and network administration, and in information security. These managers are the first line of authority for the users. Each manager is responsible for the creation of effective procedures for their work area. IT operations managers are responsible for handling or delegating any issues that arise.

Systems architect   This individual reviews the data compiled from the systems analyst and then determines the preferred design for new systems. A systems architect's role is to create the overall system layout, whereas the systems analyst works with the end user and helps to create the ideas of what the business users require to fulfill their job or to align IT to their ultimate objectives. The true objective is to create a system that facilitates the generation of revenue for the organization.

Information security manager (ISM)   The information security manager (ISM) should be an individual with training—such as a Certified Information Systems Security Professional (CISSP) from the International Information Systems Security Certification Consortium or an ISACA Certified Information Security Manager (CISM) or an equivalent credential. The ISM specifies security standards to be implemented for all computer systems. The ISM will review procedures for compliance to security policies. Security management requires special software and tools to perform effective tests and review. The ISM specifies control settings to be implemented by the server and network administrators. An ISM should be a very busy person working on security monitoring, security policy compliance, individual system security certification, and systems accreditation. The information security manager is supported by information security analysts.

It is important to ensure that the ISM function is fulfilled by using a balanced set of security metrics such as NIST 800-53. The auditor would like to see that the organization is paying full attention to internal security controls (instead of management just saying yes and then turning a blind eye toward the implementation). The ISM function is impossible without full management support.

Change control manager   This position is a quality assurance requirement. An individual or a committee of managers may fill this function. The change control manager ensures that the staff is following proper procedures, controls, and plans as agreed to.

Applications programmer   Applications programmers write computer programs to solve problems for users. Their role is to create an automated solution for the business end-user. The applications programmer is supported by the systems analyst.

Systems programmer   The systems programmer writes programs to change the behavior of the operating system or its design. Do not confuse this position with an enhanced operator. An enhanced operator selects settings, whereas a programmer writes software functions from scratch. The systems programmer role is different depending on the environment.

In a Microsoft Windows environment, the systems programmer is Microsoft Corporation unless the client hired a programmer to re-write functions in the Microsoft operating system. Does the client have programmers to re-write the internal functions of the XP operating system? If not, the client organization is no more than a user and their systems administrator is a glorified operator of enhanced authority who simply selects predefined options from a menu.

In the Unix and mainframe environments, the systems programmer rewrites or modifies the operating system kernel, support utilities, and Job Control Language (JCL). In a nutshell, the systems programmer focuses on modifying or improving the operating system internal functions.

Network administrator   This person is the network router technician who handles data communication between devices on the network. The duties include supporting system administrators, managing Internet Protocol (IP) addresses, and monitoring networked devices (usually via Simple Network Management Protocol, or SNMP). The network administrator may be delegated the daily maintenance responsibility of network security devices such as intrusion detection systems, vulnerability scanners, firewalls, and gateways. A network administrator's primary job is to keep data communications working across the network.

Server administrator   The server administrator maintains the server hardware and software settings. In a Microsoft environment, the server administrator is an enhanced operator whose role is to select appropriate settings from a GUI interface or predefined menu. The Unix and mainframe administrator counterparts are usually skilled as script programmers or operating system programmers. The Unix or mainframe administrator will frequently write their own support utilities or customize the program code of existing utilities to enhance system integration.

Database administrator   This is the custodian of data who maintains the database systems. This is usually a role fulfilled by a person with prior experience as senior system administrator or systems programmer.

Computer operator   This is a junior server technician who assists the system administrator and database administrator. The computer operator functions include starting and stopping software, changing job prioritization, and identifying possible problems during normal processing. A computer operator acts as the eyes, ears, and hands under the direction of the administrator. Computer operators provide clerical assistance on issues of error and log reporting. Operators escalate problems to the attention of more-senior personnel.

Systems analyst   A systems analyst works with the business end-user to develop requirements. After the requirements are developed, the systems analyst works with the user to define screen layouts and report layouts. The systems analyst then communicates this information to the systems programmer. The systems analyst provides support for business methods to be implemented in technology.

Data entry staff   Data could be entered by a professional data entry staff for a large volume of data, or it could be entered by the end user. These days, with web forms and the online atmosphere of IT, data entry by the end user is quite common. If that has been the decision, we of course like to see compensating controls to ensure the integrity of that input.

Media librarian   A media librarian is a critical role even though it's a junior role. We will refer to this IT position by the short name of *librarian*. The librarian is responsible for keeping track of all of the media, no matter what it is on (tape, cartridge, CD, or even a Zip drive or a portable USB memory stick). The librarian is responsible for data storage and its tracking history including creation date, current storage location, last time accessed, and what data is claimed to be contained on the media. The data may be referred to as a *data set*.

Backup media is sent to an off-site storage company for safe off-site storage. The librarian is required to track when the media was sent and when it arrived at the destination. Every tape and label must be accounted for at all times. Loss of a backup media (tape) may constitute a breach of law or require mandatory public disclosure of loss, depending on contents.

The librarian assists with regular self-audits to verify that the property is still in safe storage with the off-site vendor. Media is recalled from storage by the librarian. Media containing old data is recycled by the librarian in accordance with the organization's reuse policy. The librarian is also responsible for proper disposal and destruction of old media.

Help desk   Every IS organization will have a help desk of some type to support computer hardware or particular software applications. This is where users initially call for first-level support; the caller is asking for IT assistance. The help desk person handles the most basic needs and then escalates problems to the appropriate personnel. The help desk follows the policies and procedures that are specified by management.

Staff on the help desk usually hold a junior role. This support role provides an interface with IT customers. Each help desk person should be trained to recognize problems that need to be escalated to more-senior IT staff. The customer interface serves the business person—the end user. The business end-user's job is to make money, and the help desk is intended to help the business user work more effectively. The help desk must keep performance metrics for all requests, including metrics of escalation and problem delegation.

Each of the roles we discussed has a particular function that is necessary to sustain normal operations. It is important that each transaction is properly authorized before it is executed. A physical or logical separation of duties is necessary to provide proper authorization. With separation of duties, you look at who holds custody of the assets and what compensating controls are present.

Figure 3.11 illustrates separation of duties and authorization in the IT department.

FIGURE 3.11   Separation of duties

Job Role	Authorize Changes	Production Library Access	Development Library Access	Security Administration Configuration	Execute Production Changes
System User (End user)	Approve	✓ Use	No	No	No
System Administration (Custodian)	Request	✓ Monitor-Control	No	Implement	✓ When Approved
Security Administration (Custodian)	Approve	No	No	✓ Specify Control	No
Programming/ Development	Request	No	✓ Create Software	No	No
Change Testing	Test only	No (Use Isolated Test)	No (Use Isolated Test)	Test only	No
Change Control	✓ Approves	No	No	No	No

The purpose of separation of duties is to segregate authorization so that no one individual can execute an action or have direct access to assets by bypassing control. Authorization is the most important element to separate from job roles. Every position should require authorization from another person before changes are made or before sensitive transactions are executed. The separation of duties is a control mechanism that separates the person doing the job from the person who renders authorization. The goal is to prevent stupid mistakes or possibly fraudulent activity.

Using Compensating Controls

Compensating controls are used to reduce the impact of an error or omission. As you will recall from Chapter 2, controls may be implemented using a physical method (barrier), technical method (logical), or administrative method (policy and procedure). Compensating controls are used whenever there is a lack of segregation of duties. Examples of compensating controls include the following:

Job rotation   Rotating individuals between job functions reduces the potential of questionable activities. A collateral benefit is having more than one trained person capable of performing the function.

Audit   Auditing is an essential component of internal control. It is imperative that audit logs are functional and well preserved. The audits may be internal self-assessments or independent audits.

Reconciliation   Reconciliation is a type of audit in which records are compared to ensure that a balance exists. Reconciliation is used in financial reporting, project management, scope verification, computer processing batch verification, and other instances where an answer should be verified. Proper reconciliation increases the level of confidence.

Exception report   On occasion, an error or exception will exist in computer processing and audit logs. Exception reporting should be made to the next level of supervisor. The supervisor collects a review of evidence of the event and determines the action required. The goal is to ensure that exceptions are handled properly in accordance with the organizational goals, policies, and standards for internal control.

Transaction log   Transaction logs provide audit trails which are designed to alert the user about a particular condition. The IS auditor needs to understand how the client reviews transaction logs along with what action is taken. The absence of a transaction log would represent a major concern. A similar concern would exist if the transaction logs are not reviewed on a regular basis.

Supervisor review   The supervisor should review each of the compensating controls through observation and inquiry. Failure to do so may constitute negligence. The supervisory review is the last level of compensating control.

Tracking Performance

Performance of all operations should be tracked and reported by using metrics developed for the user's needs. These metrics should be based on best practices of NIST, Committee of Sponsoring Organizations of the Treadway Commission (COSO), ISACA's CoBIT, and other industry standards. It is the responsibility of tactical management to develop the metrics. Operations management is required to report the detail necessary to generate a score.

 We'll cover metrics in detail in Chapter 6, "IT Service Delivery."

Controlling Change

Change control is an organized process for making sure the best possible decision is reached. The reality is that any change introduces new variables. A person can execute a minor change that does what it intended, but then also has unintended consequences such as disabling or invalidating a previous control setting or a processing method. So change control must be a methodical process.

The change process should be evidenced by supporting policies and procedures. One employer, for example, had a policy that changes would occur only on Tuesdays and Thursdays in the evening. Users were required to provide their work-acceptance test procedures along with a competent user from their department. The user would run their own tests to prove whether the evening change had an impact. Positive impacts were desired. Negative impacts signaled the need to rerun the intended change procedure or restore the system to its earlier condition. Management allowed changes over the weekend if the requirement was so broad as to exceed an 8-hour window. Their preference was to avoid scheduling changes that would result in the next work day being on Monday. Problems occurring on Monday tend to set a negative tone for the entire week.

Internal auditors should be involved in change control meetings. The visibility and experience of the internal auditor present a valuable opportunity for the client. Internal audit should review requested changes to ensure that each change complies with the best practices of change management. You can bet that the staff will become more alert when they realize that the internal auditors are watching.

Understanding the Auditor's Interest in Operational Delivery

The auditor will need to evaluate if the organization has provided effective daily support in accordance with the IS strategy. What is IT expected to deliver? Taking that into consideration, what are the issues considering fulfillment and capacity to supply this need? There should be a systematic decomposition of how each business objective is translated down into specific needs, which are fulfilled by specific tasks. If there is no stated requirement in a business objective, there should not be a specific need, only a request. The IT alignment concept is to dedicate all efforts toward bona fide goals identified in the business strategy, not requests.

The auditor's job is to ensure that proper controls are in place and are appropriate to the unique risks of each source and location.

Summary

In this chapter, we have reviewed the authority levels in the organization and controls used for IT governance. A short definition of IT governance is to effectively lead and monitor performance of the information technology investment. IT governance exists at three levels: strategic, tactical, and operational management. Top executives are responsible for providing the strategic guidance with policies and decisions to define objectives; department directors provide tactical management with standards and plans for their subordinates. The operational functions and procedures are controlled by the managers with execution by staff workers.

Exam Essentials

Know how to evaluate the performance and effectiveness of the IT governance structure. Does IT support the organizational objectives? You will investigate how the IT management decisions are made. After a decision is reached, it is important to understand how the directions are communicated to ensure that the decision supports the desired outcome. Does evidence indicate that management is leading the activities necessary to fulfill the business strategy?

Understand that the organizational structure must be designed to support the business strategy and objectives. Does the client have a well-documented organizational chart with accurate job descriptions? How does the client handle problem reports, user complaints, and staff member concerns? Is there a mechanism for management oversight?

Be aware that the IT policy, standards, and procedures must be developed under the supervision of management. A formal process should exist to ensure that each policy is in support of legal requirements and fulfills a business objective. You need to understand how the client determines policies and standards. Who approves the adoption and implementation? Do the policies and standards directly support the business strategy? Do the standards and procedures support the resulting IT strategy?

Know that management is responsible for ensuring compliance with policies and standards. Operating procedures must be developed to promote compliance and consistency. Have policies, standards, and procedures been formally implemented? How does management monitor compliance? How are violations detected, corrected, and prevented?

Understand that risk management practices should be in use at all times. Risk management applies to decisions concerning vendors, operational support, and projects. Is an effective risk management practice in use? Does the evidence show that risks are properly managed?

Know that quality management requires the use of generally accepted IT standards. A benchmarking process should be in use, with a control framework such as CoBIT, ISO 17799, COSO control framework, and the OECD security guidelines. A maturity model such as CMM should be in use to show progress or regression in regard to internal controls.

Understand that IT performance and IT vendors should be tracked by using key performance indicators. The goal of IT governance is to align IT resources to support the business strategy. The role of IT is to solve support problems faced by business users. The IT steering committee is designed to identify business support issues to be resolved by IT. Key performance indicators are based on business needs and used to determine the IT return on investment.

Review Questions

1. Which of the following would be included in an IS strategic plan?

    A. Brochures for future hardware purchases

    B. At least a six-month list of goals from the IT manager

    C. Target dates for development projects

    D. Plans and directives from senior non-IT managers

2. What is the primary purpose of the IT steering committee?

    A. Make technical recommendations.

    B. Identify business issues and objectives.

    C. Review vendor contracts.

    D. Specify the IT organizational structure.

3. Which of the following functions should be separated from the others if segregation of duties cannot be achieved in an automated system?

    A. Origination

    B. Authorization

    C. Correction

    D. Reprocessing

4. The Software Engineering Institute's Capability Maturity Model (CMM) is best described by which of the following statements?

    A. Measurement of resources necessary to ensure a reduction in coding defects

    B. Documentation of accomplishments achieved during program development

    C. Relationship of application performance to the user's stated requirement

    D. Baseline of the current progress or regression

5. What would be the area of greatest interest during an audit of a business process reengineering (BPR) project?

    A. Steering committee approves sufficient controls for fraud detection.

    B. Planning methods include Program Evaluation Review Technique (PERT).

    C. Risk management planning with alignment of the project to business objectives.

    D. Vendor participation including documentation, installation assistance, and training.

6. If separation of duties cannot be achieved, which of the following is an acceptable alternative?

    A. Compensating controls.

    B. Mandatory hiring of additional personnel.

    C. Change control review board.

    D. Separation of duties is required.

7. What is the correct sequence for benchmark processes in business process reengineering (BPR) projects?

   A. Plan, research, observe, analyze, adapt, improve

   B. Research, test, plan, adapt, analyze, improve

   C. Plan, observe, analyze, improve, test

   D. Observe, research, analyze, adapt, plan, implement

8. Which of the following statements is true concerning the steering committee?

   A. Steering committee membership is composed of directors from each department.

   B. The steering committee focuses the agenda on IT issues.

   C. Absence of a formal charter indicates a lack of controls.

   D. The steering committee conducts formal management oversight reviews.

9. What is the primary purpose for running a lights-out data center?

   A. Save electricity.

   B. Reduce risk.

   C. Improve security.

   D. Reduce personnel expense.

10. The Capability Maturity Model (CMM) contains five levels of achievement. Which of the following answers contains three of the levels in proper sequence?

   A. Initial, Managed, Repeatable

   B. Initial, Managed, Defined

   C. Defined, Managed, Optimized

   D. Managed, Defined, Repeatable

11. Segregation of duties may not be practical in a small environment. A single employee may be performing the combined functions of server operator and application programmer. The IS auditor should recommend controls for which of the following?

   A. Automated logging of changes made to development libraries

   B. Hiring additional technical staff to force segregation of duties

   C. Procedures to verify that only approved program changes are implemented

   D. Automated controls to prevent the operator logon ID from making program modifications

12. Which of the following is the best example of mandatory controls?

   A. User account permissions

   B. Corporate guidelines

   C. Acceptable use policy

   D. Government regulation

13. What is the objective of incident response?

    A. Ensure that the problem is reviewed by appropriate personnel using an established procedure to protect evidence.

    B. Reduce the impact of a virus outbreak without inconveniencing users.

    C. Provide an immediate estimate as to the consequence or impact of the damage.

    D. Fix the user's problem as quickly as possible. The final resolution should be reported to the help desk.

14. An IS auditor is auditing the controls related to employee termination. Which of the following is the *most* important aspect to be reviewed?

    A. Company staff members are notified about the termination.

    B. All login accounts of the employee are terminated.

    C. The details of the employee have been removed from active payroll files.

    D. Company property provided to the employee has been returned.

15. Which of the following is *not* true concerning the process of terminating personnel?

    A. The company must follow HR termination procedures.

    B. Any company property in possession of the employee must be returned.

    C. The employee must be allowed to copy any personal files from their computer.

    D. The employee's recent history of login account activity should be reviewed in the audit log.

16. Which of the following represents the best explanation of the balanced scorecard?

    A. Provides IT benchmarking against standards

    B. Ensures that the IT strategy supports the business strategy

    C. Measures IT help desk performance

    D. Specifies procedures for equal opportunity employment

17. What is the primary business purpose behind business process reengineering (BPR)?

    A. Eliminate jobs.

    B. Reduce steps to improve business efficiency.

    C. Change management direction.

    D. Increase stockholder value.

18. Which of the following business process reengineering (BPR) risks are likely to occur during the design phase?

    A. Transition risk, skill risk, financial risk

    B. Management risk, technical risk, HR risk

    C. Technical risk, detection risk, audit risk

    D. Scope risk, skill risk, political risk

19. Which of the following answers contains the steps for business process reengineering (BPR) in proper sequence?

   A. Diagnose, envision, redesign, reconstruct

   B. Evaluate, envision, redesign, reconstruct, review

   C. Envision, initiate, diagnose, redesign, reconstruct, evaluate

   D. Initiate, evaluate, diagnose, reconstruct, review

20. What is the purpose of job descriptions and the change control review board?

   A. Provide optimum allocation of IT resources.

   B. Eliminate disputes over who has the authority.

   C. Identify the hierarchy of personnel seniority.

   D. Provide guidance to the IT steering committee.

Answers to Review Questions

1. D. The IS strategy must support business objectives from senior managers in other departments of the business. The IT plans should be designed to support the strategic business plans of the organization.

2. B. The purpose of the steering committee is to bring the awareness of business issues and objectives to IT management. An effective steering committee will focus on the service level necessary to support the business strategy.

3. B. Authorization should be separate from all other activities. A second person should review changes before implementation. Authorization will be granted if the change is warranted and the level of risk is acceptable.

4. D. The Capability Maturity Model provides a baseline measurement of process maturity. The CMM begins with no process defined and progresses through five phases of documentation and controls. The fifth phase represents the highest level of maturity.

5. C. The steering committee provides guidance to IT concerning business objectives. A risk management plan must be in use for every BPR project. The purpose of risk management is to determine whether the project can actually fulfill a business objective. The second part of risk management is to determine whether the organization will be able to complete the project and generate the desired results.

6. A. Compensating controls may be used when separation of duties cannot be achieved. Compensating controls include supervisory review, audit trails, exception reporting, and job rotation. An auditor would recognize that the lack of separation of duties is a control failure unless compensating controls are in place. Lack of compensating controls is also control failure.

7. A. The business process reengineering sequence is to plan for change, research possible implications, observe the current process, analyze potential opportunities for improvement and verify key performance indicators, adapt to the new/updated process, and work to improve the results.

8. C. The steering committee should be authorized by a formal charter. The lack of a steering committee indicates IT is not governed by formal alignment to business objectives. The technology investment is not properly managed as an investment portfolio should be managed. The purpose of the steering committee is to convey business issues that IT should consider and objectives to fulfill. Membership of individuals on the steering committee should be formally designated.

9. B. The primary purpose of a lights-out operation is to reduce the personnel risk and environmental risk. Errors can be eliminated by separating equipment from the support IT personnel. Environmental risk is reduced by eliminating contamination from liquids, food particles, and debris. Maintenance and support personnel enter the lights-out operation for a short duration to perform any required functions.

10. C. The five levels of achievement in the Capability Maturity Model (CMM) are level 1 Initial, level 2 Repeatable, level 3 Defined, level 4 Managed, and level 5 Optimized.

11. C. Procedures should be implemented to ensure that only approved program changes are implemented. The purpose of separation of duties is to prevent intentional or unintentional errors. A logical separation of duties may exist if a single person performs two job roles. The ultimate objective is to ensure that a second person has reviewed and approved a change before it is implemented.

12. D. A government regulation is a mandatory control that forces compliance. Mandatory controls are the strongest type of control. Permission is explicit or it must be denied.

13. A. Incident response is intended to ensure that the problem is reviewed by appropriate personnel. Personnel should be properly trained and should execute an established procedure to document the condition, protect evidence, and resolve the problem. During the incident response, the problem will be analyzed to determine whether it was malicious or unintentional.

14. B. The former employee's access to information systems should be terminated immediately. The accepted practice is to terminate access while the employee is being informed of the termination in the HR department.

15. C. Employee access should be disabled upon termination from the organization. All of the other statements are true.

16. B. The balanced scorecard is used in management to ensure that all projects and activities are in direct support of the organization's strategy and objectives. The IT balanced scorecard is a subset of the organization's overall scorecard.

17. B. The purpose of BPR is to improve efficiency by reducing unnecessary steps or to implement improved techniques. Business process reengineering may be implemented to reduce operating costs or to achieve compliance with requirements.

18. D. The primary risks during the BPR design phase are improper scope, lack of necessary skills, political resistance, and a failure by management to support the project.

19. C. According to ISACA the general steps in business process reengineering are to envision the need, initiate the project, diagnose the existing process, redesign the process, use change management to reconstruct the organization in transition, and evaluate the results.

20. A. Job descriptions specify the roles of each individual to ensure proper allocation of personnel. The change control review board ensures that changes and related activities are properly managed.

Chapter

4

Networking Technology

THE OBJECTIVE OF THIS CHAPTER IS TO ACQUAINT THE READER WITH THE FOLLOWING CONCEPTS:

- ✓ Computer hardware terms, and advantages of different types of system architecture
- ✓ Functional introduction to the OSI model and its relationship with TCP/IP
- ✓ Different types of networking equipment and their functional purpose
- ✓ An introduction to network management

In this chapter, you will study networking technology equipment and concepts. ISACA expects every auditor to understand the functionality of the IT infrastructure. The infrastructure comprises a unique architecture of computer hardware and special-purpose software. You will study the advantages of implementing different types of system architecture.

A functional introduction of the OSI model will be presented with its relationship to the TCP/IP model used in the real world. Using the OSI model as the backdrop, we will discuss the functions of different types of network equipment. It is important for CISAs to understand the purpose and capabilities presented by the operating systems, routers, switches, firewalls, and other peripherals. The goal of this chapter is to provide a general understanding of how the infrastructure could be assembled in a manner that fulfills most of the internal control requirements.

We'll wrap up the chapter with a discussion on network management because auditors are expected to understand network analyzers, capacity planning, and monitoring techniques. Several of the points regarding network security are covered again in Chapter 7, "Information Asset Protection." The purpose of this chapter is to provide you a firm foundation in networking technology.

Understanding the Differences in Computer Architecture

All computers are not created equal. The differences in architecture have a substantial impact on performance and system security. However, every computer has three basic types of components.

The first component group centers around the central processing unit, also known as the CPU. The *CPU* performs mathematical calculations with the assistance of an internal arithmetic logic unit, a high-speed memory cache, and working memory space known as random access memory (RAM). Data stored in random access memory will be erased when power is turned off.

The second component group provides input and output. This input and output channel is used to transmit data to and from the CPU for processing. Computers with a simple architecture may use a common channel for all communication with the CPU. This channel may be an individual connector or a shared data bus of several devices.

The third component group is data storage. Every computer requires additional storage space, such as a hard disk. Data storage may be fixed in a semipermanent location or removable. When a computer is turned on, the initial startup process is executed from internal programmable chips and data storage disks. This startup function is called *boot strapping (boot)* or *initial program load (IPL)*. The operating system is loaded from data storage, along with device driver information for the Basic Input/Output System (BIOS). The system is available for use after completion of the boot, or IPL, process.

Figure 4.1 is a general diagram illustrating the architecture of a computer. Notice the CPU on the upper left. The CPU is the brains of the system and is attached to all of the other components with a string of electrical conductors. This string of conductors is called the system *data bus*, which is represented as the lines drawn across the middle of the diagram. The term *bus* is an electrical term that means a shared electrical path. The CPU could not run effectively without the support of solid-state memory, known as *random access memory (RAM)*. Random access memory is not as fast as the CPU. A special type of superfast memory is used to buffer between the CPU and RAM to help the CPU run at maximum speed. This high-speed CPU buffer memory is known as *cache*. The heart of computer processing occurs between the CPU, cache, and RAM. Other devices are attached to the data bus through computer expansion slots and interfaces. The disk drives and network each have their own electronic interface or add-in card connected to the data bus. This is how the information flows to and from the electronic components.

FIGURE 4.1   Computer hardware architecture

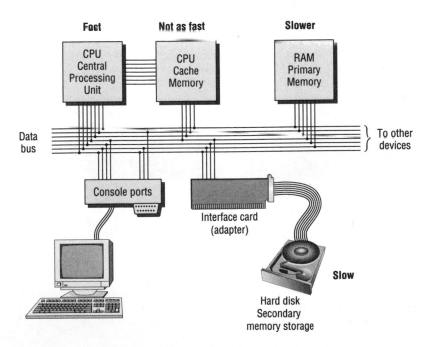

Integrated circuits of the CPU can perform mathematical calculations faster than we can think or act. In fact, a computer with a single CPU will spend a great deal of time waiting for human input. The CPU can therefore support light processing for several users at one time with little delay. The process of CPU sharing for multiple users is called *time-sharing* (see Figure 4.2). Each user or system process receives a tiny segment of time for processing their request. Only one request is processed at a time. All other processing requests are parked in memory, awaiting their turn. Each processing request is serviced by generating a system interrupt. The CPU halts on interrupt and swaps processing with the task stored in memory. This process is similar to how you handle interruptions during the day when the telephone rings. The computer is presumed to be running so fast that the other users do not notice any significant delay.

Computers with single processors have two major drawbacks. The first issue is related to systems security. Each system interrupt halts any security software that is running and allows the task to be processed before restarting the security software. The second drawback is the CPU bottleneck created by processor-intensive activities of database- and graphics-rendering software.

Multiprocessor computers are designed to deal with the demands of process-intensive applications, or systems designed for high-security environments. The processor may still perform time-sharing functions for multiple users; however, the load is allocated across multiple CPUs. Figure 4.3 shows a typical multiprocessor architecture.

When the multiprocessor system is booted, the first processor accepts the responsibility of running system functions for control, input, and output. The first CPU schedules tasks across to the other CPUs.

The operating system becomes resident on CPU 1 and performs hardware checks for input and output. The second processor loads as a task processor only. Each additional processor does the same. This allows the first CPU to have uninterrupted control of the system while the other CPUs perform problem-solving tasks in response to user requests.

FIGURE 4.2   Single CPU system with multiple users (time-sharing)

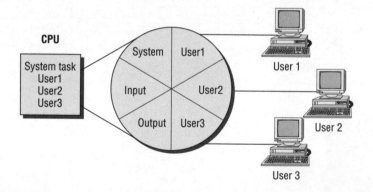

FIGURE 4.3   Multiple processor architecture

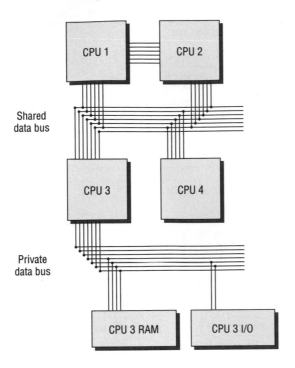

Figure 4.4 shows how the workload is stacked and processed through the CPUs. Notice that each CPU has a small stack of tasks that are each a different phases of processing. This stacking of tasks is referred to as *pipelining*. Think of it as a pipeline full of people standing at your door and wanting you to do work for them. A single CPU would be maxed out with a small pipeline. The multiprocessor system, on the other hand, designates one CPU to be the equivalent of a manager, while the other CPUs each process their own pipeline full of requests. In the real world, this could look like a room full of people talking on the phone, smoking cigarettes, drinking coffee, and answering email all at the same time. As you're aware, a group of people can smoke a lot more cigarettes and get a lot more email than one person. The same can be said about computers with multiple processors.

Multiprocessor systems can perform high-security processing with a separation of duties. Individual processors could be dedicated to perform security functions without interruption. The CPU can be programmed to ignore interrupt requests. Ignoring a processing request is referred to as *interrupt masking*. Interrupt masking is useful for ensuring that high-priority tasks are not interrupted.

FIGURE 4.4   Multitasking systems (single processor and multiprocessor workload)

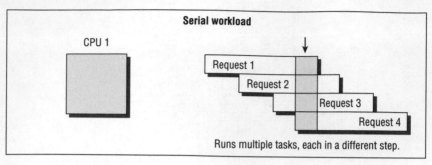

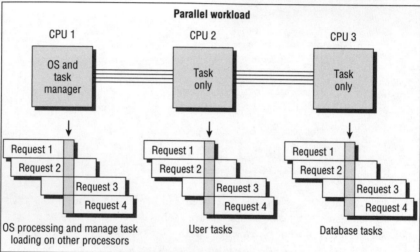

Comparing Single Processor and Multiprocessor Systems

In this section, you will look at various computer operating systems, as well as how to determine the best computer for you. In addition, you will compare some of their capabilities and look at supervisory vs. problem states. Finally, you will look at data storage and port controls more closely.

Identifying Various Operating Systems

Every computer uses some sort of operating system to control the hardware. Each make and model of computer is slightly different. For example, the processor type might be different, or the computer might use a specialized disk drive subsystem.

Computer programs of the 1950s and 60s were not as portable as they are today. The old computers required the programmer to write a unique program for each model of system. As time progressed, computer software evolved with the development of new programming languages and then new operating systems.

The Unix operating system was created by Ken Thompson to run a computer program called Space Travel. Each time he attempted to move the program from one computer to the next, it was necessary to rewrite the program to accommodate differences in hardware. Thompson and Dennis Ritchie began working on project portability and created a series of programming languages known as A, B, and then C. This is the same C programming language that you hear about today.

Modern computers use a more-refined operating system. You will typically use an operating system designed for the type of hardware you intend to use. IBM's OS/MVS is common in the IBM mainframe world, whereas Unix is run on a variety of systems. Microsoft Windows is popular for its relatively low initial cost and widespread availability. The Apple Mac OS holds a smaller market share with a devoutly dedicated following in the graphics industry.

Each of these operating systems holds common traits. The operating system vendor works with the hardware manufacturer to create specialized hardware support within the operating system. The application programmer simply compiles their program for a particular operating system. All the user needs to do is to match their desired application software to the operating system, and then match the operating system to the available hardware.

Figure 4.5 shows what a common computer operating system looks like.

FIGURE 4.5   Computer operating system

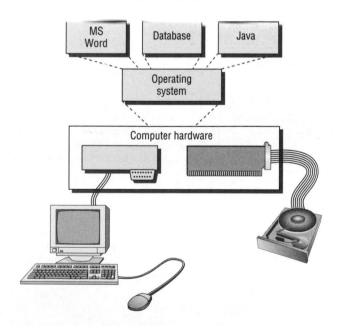

Every commercial-grade computer operating system provides at least the following functions:

- Provides a user interface to the computer. The interface is often called a *shell*. This is the command line or graphical interface supporting the directions to the computer.

- Manages security and event logging during the interaction between a user and the computer hardware.

- Provides a common software platform to run application programs. Computer programs run on top of the operating system.

- Provides a file system to store and retrieve data.

- Provides a method of input and output to various devices, including disk drives, network connections, printers, and video displays.

- Coordinates internal communications between programs and processing of tasks by the CPU.

Operating systems can be designed to support a single user or multiple users. You can run software in slow batch mode or fast batch mode to simulate real-time transactions.

Computers can function in an ever-increasing variety of roles. Some computers are designed for special-purpose functions, for example, the Palm handheld or new 3G integrated wireless phone. Many computers are designed for general-purpose use as a desktop or laptop computer. Table 4.1 lists some of the typical functional roles that computers fulfill.

TABLE 4.1   Typical Computer Roles

Role	Function	Examples
User workstation	Runs applications to solve problems	Microsoft Office, personal spreadsheets, email client, web surfing. Usually desktop or laptop.
File server	Stores data files for shared user access	Microsoft and Novell shared network drives (usually labeled F: through Z:), Unix file mounts (/usr/home/~your_name), mainframe file share to PC (letters or links).
Website server	Same as file server	http://www.CertTest.com
DNS server	Converts web server domain names into their matching IP address	77.93.217.38, which is an IP address of www.certtest.com. Uses Domain Name Service program to find the IP address matching the name you entered. DNS works like an automated phone book.

TABLE 4.1   Typical Computer Roles *(continued)*

Role	Function	Examples
Database server	Stores raw data and organizes it in tables for authorized users to access	Accounting software, sales automation, and online shopping carts. Can exist on a file server, web server, or dedicated machine. May be internally developed or built using a commercial product such as Oracle SQL, MySQL, IBM Informix, or IBM DB2.
Appliance or special-purpose device	Performs dedicated processing	Web cache, proxy server, email server, network router, or gateway. *Appliance* refers to a preconfigured computer designed to support a single need. Built from a general-purpose computer or unique hardware and configured to run a special-service program. Your home satellite receiver for the Dish Network or DirecTV is a PC hardware appliance running Linux.

Selecting the Best Computer

Computers come in a variety of sizes and prices, based on their processing power and throughput. (*Throughput* is a measure of how much information passes through the system in a specific period of time.) There are four major classes of computer systems, which we discuss in the following sections. The classes are supercomputers, mainframe computers, minicomputers, and personal computers.

Supercomputers

Supercomputers are designed for intense scientific calculations. A supercomputer would be used to calculate the incredible details of a nuclear reaction and to trace the particles through their life cycle, for example. Supercomputers are not measured in size, but instead by the lightning speed at which transactions can occur. They tend to be very specialized systems designed for a particular mission.

Mainframe Computers

Mainframe computers are large, scalable, general-purpose systems designed to support incredible volumes of data. These are the large boxes you would see in a traditional data center. A single mainframe computer could be as small as a filing cabinet or as large as a roomful of refrigerators, all depending on its configuration.

Mainframes have the advantage of being able to process massive amounts of data in parallel, with incredible throughput. These systems are capable of multithreading thousands of programs simultaneously. *Multithreading* allows programs to be executed in parallel to minimize idle time within the processors. Mainframe computers have provided the role model for other systems to follow.

Prices range from $50,000 to tens of millions of dollars. A mainframe offers several advantages to those who can afford one, including the following:

- Rock-solid virtual machine that can partition resources into smaller environments. You can easily set up one mainframe to act as 300 to 5,000 PC servers, without the administrative headache.

- Outstanding security. The internal system-partitioning controls have built-in segregation of duties with multiple layers of security. Internal system control reporting is excellent.

- Excellent financial-reporting controls. Most mainframes were designed to bill individual usage as a profit center. You can practically charge the user for each electron in the processing of their job across each device used.

- Very high throughput with stability that is measured in years.

- Mature 40-year arsenal of system support programs.

IBM is the dominant vendor in the mainframe market, with 90 percent of the market share. Sales of mainframe systems are increasing in response to issues of control and economies of scale. For large operations, the mainframe is proving again to be an economical choice. Its high-volume parallel throughput cannot be matched by smaller systems.

Midrange and Microcomputers

Midrange computers, also referred to as *minicomputers*, are designed to be operated by individual departments or smaller organizations. The IBM AS/400 and zSeries are designed to be either a mainframe or midrange computer, depending on the configuration selected by the buyer.

Unix is also popular as a midrange operating system. Unix lacks several of the partition and security controls of a mainframe environment, but it does have many of the important job-processing features at a lower cost.

Microcomputers are small systems that can be implemented as a PC, notebook, or personal digital assistant (PDA). Most microcomputers are designed to service the needs of an individual user. Their operating system may have multiuser capability if running on sufficient hardware to support the requirement.

Microcomputers can run a variety of general-purpose operating systems, including Unix, Microsoft Windows, and the Apple Mac OS. Microcomputers were invented to meet users' demands for more control over their individual processing needs. At the time, mainframes were dedicated to large-volume batch processing and ignored many of the user requests for processing.

The explosion of microcomputers has created a growing awareness of all the internal security controls that are missing. The biggest problem with microcomputers is the lack of mainframe-grade controls.

As an IS auditor, you may hear the term *MIPS*. MIPS is an acronym for *millions of instructions per second*. It is often used as numerical claim of system performance with little regard for the real-world environment. MIPS is actually a highly subjective number used to hype a particular computer. The true measure of performance is system throughput, measured in the total volume of transactions processed from end to end.

Comparing Computer Capabilities

It is your job as an auditor to determine whether the IT environment is aligned to the business requirements. Figure 4.6 is a simple graphical representation of the differences in capabilities among mainframes, minicomputers, and microcomputers.

The dominant criteria used for system selection is the desired throughput. Another area of interest is the level of internal control required by the user.

 Chapter 6, "IT Service Delivery," covers capacity and workload management issues.

Figure 4.7 demonstrates the simple hierarchy of the classes of computer systems and their market share.

At the top of the pyramid is a mainframe, which has the highest level of capability. Mainframes have fewer clients because of initial purchase cost. In the middle is the midrange computer for individual departments or a smaller organization. Midrange-processing computers are extremely popular for running databases such as Oracle Financials, SAP manufacturing, or the PeopleSoft HR database. At the bottom are the vast number of PC users with a lower-end processing requirement.

FIGURE 4.6   Comparing mainframes, minicomputers, and microcomputers

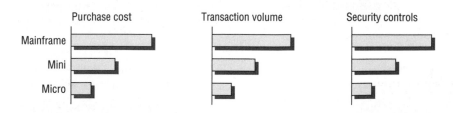

FIGURE 4.7   Computer processing market share

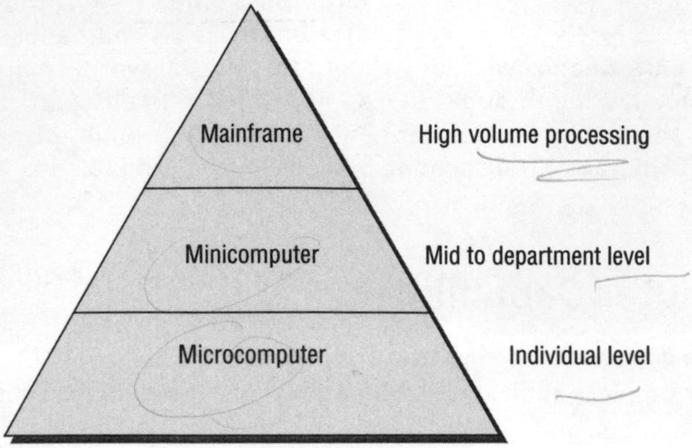

Processing vs. System Control

With all this computer processing, it is necessary to ensure adequate management controls.

The first level of control in the computer is the privileged *supervisory user*. Every computer needs a user representing the highest level of authority, for the purpose of controlling change. This supervisory user is also known as the superuser, root user, or administrator. The names may be different, but the purpose is the same. This privileged user is responsible for configuration, maintenance, and all ongoing administrative tasks. The supervisory user is often exempt from the internal controls imposed on other users. This exemption poses a unique challenge to system control.

The other type of user spends their day trying to get the computer to solve problems. This common user has limited access and is subject to a variety of system controls. All office workers fall into this second category.

The technology world has created simple terminology to illustrate the differences between the supervisory user and everybody else. The terms to describe these differences are supervisory and user problem. All computers operate in these two basic operating states:

Supervisory   *Supervisory state* is when the system security front-end is not loaded. All processing requests are run at the highest level of authority without any security controls.

Problem   *Problem state* is when security is active and the computer is supposed to be solving problems for the user.

The goal of a computer hacker is to gain problem state access (user access) and then convert it into supervisory state access (supervisor access). After the hacker gains access to the system, they will use a variety of attempts to break into supervisory control. The hacker may use invalid parameters to cause a supervisory-level program to fail. Some programs such as password change utilities or print queue management may default to a supervisory-level command prompt upon failure. This allows the hacker to bypass the normal security front-end.

Software parameter control is important for multiple reasons. As stated, invalid software parameters may be used by a hacker. The other risk is valid software parameters that should be run only for a special administrative purpose. For example, the command `mysql -i` instructs the system to reinitialize the database tables, which would erase any current data. Access to the command line should be restricted. It is much safer to design menus or restricted user interfaces to ensure security.

Dealing with Data Storage

Adequate data storage is an important issue in a production environment. Controls need to be in place to ensure safe storage of data. The auditor is concerned with how many copies of the data exist and the controls that are in use. It is amazingly easy to lose control over electronic data. As an auditor, you would be concerned about both the integrity and security mechanisms in use by the client.

Tape management systems (TMSs) and disk management systems (DMSs) are used to help retain control over data files. These automated systems can provide label and tracking management. The security of the data is always an issue. Good media management practices include the ability to rapidly identify every version of data under the organization's control with the label, location, and status of each piece of media that data is stored on. This is the job function of a good tape or media librarian.

The following are some of the common types of data storage media:

Magnetic hard disk   These rigid, metal disks mounted inside a sealed disk drive are high-speed devices that are designed for permanent installation. Capacity can go from megabytes through gigabytes to terabytes. Hard disks are the most common method of online data storage. By using special software, you can cluster drives into high-availability storage arrays. An example is RAID. Depending on who you ask, the definition is either *Redundant Array of Inexpensive Disks* or *Redundant Array of Independent Disks*. A vendor might use the latter to facilitate a higher sales price.

You are expected to understand a few basic differences between RAID levels. Table 4.2 covers these basic differences. You could copy and then cut out the table to be used as flash cards for memorization.

TABLE 4.2   Description of RAID Operating Levels

RAID Level	Operating Mode	Issue
RAID 0	Striping across multiple disks	Not fault-tolerant. This design simply makes several small disks appear as one big disk.
RAID 1	Mirroring	Excellent way of creating two live copies of the data. Most expensive way to implement; cuts disk space in half.

TABLE 4.2   Description of RAID Operating Levels *(continued)*

RAID Level	Operating Mode	Issue
RAID 2	Hamming error correcting code (ECC)	Interweaves data across multiple drives with error-correcting parity code. Too resource intensive.
RAID 5	Block-level distributed parity	This method is commonly used in disk arrays. The design uses less disk space than RAID 1 for the same amount of usable storage.
RAID 7	Optimized asynchronous	Uses independent, asynchronous transfer mode of very high transfer rates. Rather expensive.
RAID 0+1	High transfer rate	Combining two sets of RAID 0 disks with a RAID 1 mirroring design. The objective is to increase performance. Unfortunately, a two-drive failure can cause major data loss.

Magnetic soft disk   This includes floppy, Zip, and Jaz drives. They are designed with a soft read-write disk inside of a hard shell. This highly portable media is available in capacities from 1MB to more than 4GB.

Magnetic tape   Available in either reel or cartridge design, magnetic tape is the most common method of long-term data storage. Its original use was in 2400bpi (bits per inch) tape mounted on a reel. Capacities have grown dramatically. With higher capacity came the cartridge version. Cartridge tapes can have an internal design similar to a reel-to-reel cassette or a single-reel design like the old 8-track tape. Examples include DLT digital linear, 4mm–8mm DDS, 9-track reel, 3480 and newer 3590 cartridge, VHS video, DVD video, and others. Tapes can be expensive and require very particular hardware devices with special software. The media is portable only to identical tape drives with identical software from the same manufacturer. A malfunctioning tape drive can permanently destroy the tape and all the data it contains.

Read-only memory   Programmable read-only memory (ROM) is used to permanently record software programs on integrated circuits (chips). The advantages are lightning-fast program loading and solid-state nonvolatile storage without moving parts. Programming is accomplished by using specialized equipment to burn or fuse microscopic links inside the semiconductor chip. Once programmed, the software becomes permanent and cannot be changed or erased. This can be either a product limitation or security advantage depending on the intended purpose. To upgrade, you must physically replace the ROM chip. These chips are not portable between devices.

Flash memory   A special type of electronically erasable programmable read-only memory (EEPROM) is used in computers for flash BIOS, video cameras, USB handheld removable memory sticks, and newer portable devices. These are designed to supplement or replace magnetic disks. Unfortunately, the flash devices are easily lost or stolen. The small size and high capacity can be a real security concern. Some of these devices are bootable and can bypass your security controls. They have limited portability but are improving daily.

Optical CD-ROM   Used to store read-only data or music, optical CD-ROMs have a typical capacity of 80 minutes of audio or 700MB of data. This is an excellent method for archiving files or data backup when using a CD disk burner. It is a highly portable media. Blank disks are inexpensive. May be referred to as WORM (write once, read many).

Optical CD-RW   A rewritable version of the old CD-ROM design, these disks can be erased and rewritten just like all other magnetic disk media. If you used the old WORM nomenclature, this would be called a WMRM disk (write many, read many). Today nobody calls them anything but CD-RW.

Optical DVD   This is a newer variation of the optical CD with higher capacity measured in gigabytes. DVD is commonly used for video or data storage. This is a highly portable media.

Protecting Port Controls and Port Access

Every security professional is acutely aware of how physical access can bypass logical security controls. Physical input/output ports (I/O) provide an avenue for an individual to gain a higher degree of system access. The simultaneous connection of a modem and network card creates an unregulated pass-through opportunity that can circumvent perimeter defenses. As an auditor, you would want to see what controls have been implemented regarding physical access to input/output ports.

Microcomputers are particularly susceptible to port access via the keyboard, USB, RS-232, or network connection.

> The ISACA CoBIT contains a section covering physical security controls for servers, routers, and other high-value network devices.

Figure 4.8 shows the basic computer ports. Notice the PC ports for keyboard, video, printer, and serial attached devices. The mainframe has similar ports that are distributed between several large equipment chassis. No matter where they're located, all of the ports must be protected.

Computers communicate over these I/O ports to a variety of storage devices. Physical security controls are intended to protect the physical ports. Logical controls are used to protect data communications. A logical control is usually implemented as a software program control. This brings us to a discussion of the OSI communications model.

FIGURE 4.8   Input and output ports

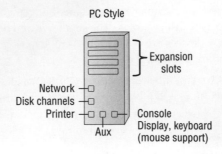

PC Style

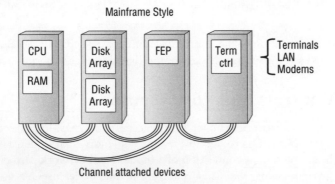

Mainframe Style

Channel attached devices

Overview of the Open Systems Interconnect (OSI) Model

In the early 1980s, the International Organization for Standardization (ISO) was busy creating a new data communications model. Its intention was to build the next generation of communications protocols to replace both proprietary protocols and the de facto TCP/IP protocol. In the end, the cheaper TCP/IP protocol won the battle.

Many customers had no interest in paying for the cost of developing the Open Systems Interconnect (OSI) protocol. The OSI model is still used as a network training tool. The model stratifies data communication into seven distinct layers. Each layer provides a unique function in support of the layer above.

We are going to walk through the OSI model layer by layer and compare each function to the TCP/IP protocol model. The seven layers of the OSI model are as follows:

- Physical layer
- Data-Link layer

- Network layer
- Transport layer
- Session layer
- Presentation layer
- Application layer

Let's start with a simple memory trick to remember each of the OSI layers in proper order (see Figure 4.9). My favorite mnemonic is "Please Do Not Throw Sausage Pizza Away" (PDNTSPA).

 We have been using this mnemonic for two decades. This mnemonic holds a unique association with a TCP/IP memory aid.

FIGURE 4.9 Mnemonic for seven layers of the OSI model

OSI memory aid

Away	= (Application)	Layer 7
Pizza	= (Presentation)	Layer 6
Sausage	= (Session)	Layer 5
Throw	= (Transport)	Layer 4
Not	= (Network)	Layer 3
Do	= (Datalink)	Layer 2
Please	= (Physical)	Layer 1

Each of the first letters relates to the first letter of an OSI layer, working your way up from the bottom. It is in your best interest to learn how to draw the OSI model and these layers from memory. You will find it helpful on your CISA exam. You will also find it helpful during discussions when you're trying to uncover the details about a particular product. It will impress clients.

The second half of the mnemonic (see Figure 4.10) is "Nor Do I Throw Apples" (NDITA). Once again, each letter refers to a layer of the Transmission Control Protocol/Internet Protocol (TCP/IP) model, working up from the bottom.

Let's review the basic OSI process for handling data. The top layer is where your application is running. The lower layers process the request and prepare the data for transmission as it works its way down to the bottom. When it reaches the bottom of the OSI model, the data has been broken down into electrical signals.

These electrical signals will be received by the other computer. Upon receipt, the transmission headers are stripped off. The remaining data message is passed to the application software running on the other computer. Figure 4.11 shows how this looks.

FIGURE 4.10   Mnemonic for TCP/IP layers

OSI		TCP/IP memory aid	
Application	Layer 7		
Presentation	Layer 6		
Session	Layer 5	(Application)	Apples
Transport	Layer 4	(Transport)	Throw
Network	Layer 3	(Internet)	I
Datalink	Layer 2	(Datalink)	Do
Physical	Layer 1	(Network)	Nor

FIGURE 4.11   OSI processing of headers and data

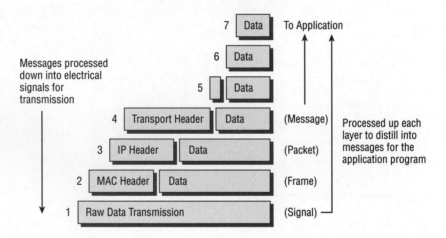

Now that you understand in general how data is transmitted when using the OSI and TCP/IP models, let's go inside the individual layers, one by one.

Layer 1: Physical Layer

The Physical layer (see Figure 4.12) defines physical requirements in the cables and voltages. This layer specifies functional specifications for creating, maintaining, and deactivating an electrical link between systems.

Layer 2: Data-Link Layer

The Data-Link layer (see Figure 4.13) focuses on establishing data communications via hardware device drivers and their transmit/receive function. Communication in layer 2 is established between each network card's Media Access Control (MAC) address. A *MAC address* is a burned-in serial number that is unique to every network card ever manufactured. The address is unique because it uses the manufacturer's ID and the board serial number. Each computer uses the MAC address for "to" and "from" communications within the same broadcast domain (layer 2).

Broadcast domains are no more than a noisy shouting match between computers on the same subnet. Every computer in that segment will hear every conversation from all the computers. For example, Microsoft NetBIOS is a layer 2 protocol. Dynamic Host Configuration Protocol (DHCP) is also a layer 2 protocol.

  We will talk about DHCP again later in this chapter.

FIGURE 4.12   OSI Physical layer

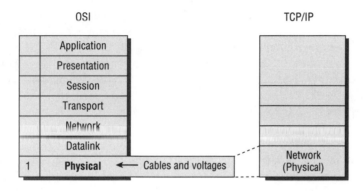

FIGURE 4.13   OSI Data-Link layer

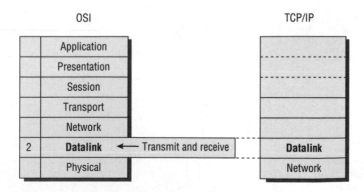

If too many computers were talking at the same time, we would have a congestion problem. This is referred to in Ethernet as a *collision*. Too many collisions will render the data link unusable.

 Ethernet networks can rarely sustain traffic loads over 45 percent. The rule of thumb for Ethernet is that you budget for network upgrades at 35 percent sustained utilization, and get out the boss's credit card to place an order for overnight delivery at 50 percent sustained bandwidth utilization. Ethernet will not run dependably over 50 percent. The 100 percent mark is both theoretical and unattainable.

Layer 3: Network Layer

The Network layer (see Figure 4.14) defines networking. Computers are stupid. The computer simply follows the directions of the person who programmed its settings or loaded the detailed list of instructions (a program). Your network administrator uses a numeric grouping of addresses to identify systems within the network.

Networks can be administratively divided into logical groups or segments. We refer to this grouping as IP *subnetworks (subnets)*. Each system has its own individual network address that is unique on the network.

Your computer acquires an IP address from either a static configuration or a dynamic configuration by using DHCP/BOOTP. The computer ties the IP address to its MAC address. Routing decisions are based on the IP address. The computers and routers implement the Address Resolution Protocol (ARP). The purpose of ARP is to match the IP address with the correct MAC address. The system may need to match the MAC to the IP by using Reverse ARP, known as RARP.

FIGURE 4.14   OSI Networking layer

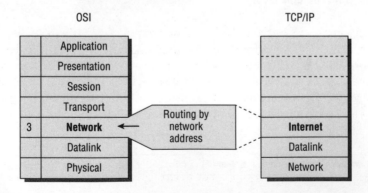

If you recall, the problem in layer 2 is that all the systems are transmitting so much that it is creating noise across the subnet. The issue is similar to noise in a school cafeteria. Some conversations are broadcast with everyone listening, while a few are discreet between a couple of users. With a layer 3 network address, it is possible to reduce traffic noise by unicast transmission to an individual address. *Unicast* is a method for point-to-point communication. So what if you need to send a message to more than one address, but not everyone? You could use *multicast* to deliver communication to a group of addresses. Multicast is similar to a conference call and is the basis of virtual networking.

 Real World Scenario

Technical Trivia

Internet Protocol (IP) uses a four-position numerical address. This IP address structure is similar to your postal mail routing address in reverse. If you used your mailing address in IP format, the result would look like Country.State.City.Street-number. IP version 4 uses addresses that are 4 bytes, or 32 bits, long. The new IP version 6 is designed for 8-byte, or 64-bit, addresses to give the expanding world more addresses.

Computers use a method of grouping IP v4 addresses, starting with 000.000.000.000 through 255.255.255.254.

Network routing is the process of directing traffic to the intended destination.

Static routing uses specific TO-FROM mappings of IP addresses created by the network administrator. The mapping is manually typed into the router and stored in the routing table of each router. The settings will not change unless the network administrator manually changes them. Static routes are good for security and are used when the network traffic is both predictable and relatively simple.

Dynamic routing uses a protocol algorithm to automatically adjust the path to the intended destination. This method uses a special router information protocols like RIP and OSPF to signal available paths (routes), dead routes (unroutable), and other changes. The routers will monitor routing updates and signal other routers to reconfigure their routing tables as changes occur. Dynamic routing is easy to enable. It removes the complexities of building an advanced configuration. To some individuals, this seems like the best answer; however, dynamic routing can be both beneficial and dangerous. Dynamic routing changes can be initiated by the following:

- Router equipment failure
- Addition of new networked devices
- Incorrect configuration of a network-attached device, including a common workstation

Figure 4.15 shows how a false network route can be accidentally created through a user's PC. The user's computer software caused the problem by transmitting a route that should not exist.

FIGURE 4.15 False network route via user PC

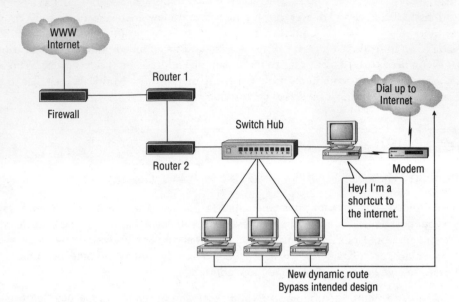

New dynamic route
Bypass intended design

By default, all network devices will listen to route updates. This can create a nightmare if left to default settings. Poor administration of computers and routers can cause traffic to be misdirected into a dead-end route or bandwidth bottleneck.

Proper design of the network usually includes implementation of both static and dynamic routing. Static routes can provide a designated *router of last resort* if prior dynamic routes fail. For higher security, the routers should be configured to accept updates from only a trusted router. The trusted router update is similar to an access control list (ACL) and will accept updates only from routers the network administratorknows and can trust.

Layer 4: Transport Layer

The Transport layer (see Figure 4.16) specifies the transport delivery method. There are two basic methods: confirmed and unconfirmed delivery. *Confirmed delivery* uses a TCP connection to the destination. This is similar to requesting a return receipt and sending certified mail from the post office. *Unconfirmed delivery* operates on a UDP connectionless datagram, which is normally broadcast across the network like a shout in a dark room. Even if transmissions are unicast between two stations, the higher level software application would have to confirm delivery, because UDP does not offer delivery confirmation. There is no guarantee of its receipt on the other end. UDP transmissions have less overhead. It is the responsibility of the recipient program to detect errors.

Layer 5: Session Layer

The Session layer (see Figure 4.17) governs session control between applications. This is where you initiate communications to a system and establish, maintain, and terminate a communication session. Examples include Network File System (NFS), SQL*net database sessions, and Remote Procedure Call (RPC).

FIGURE 4.16   OSI Transport layer

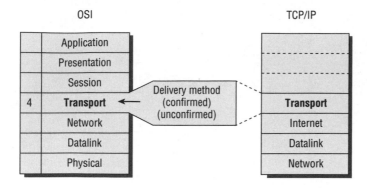

FIGURE 4.17   OSI Session layer

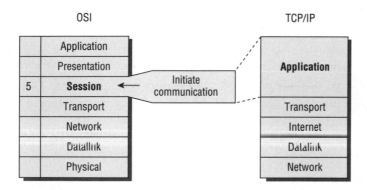

Layer 5 functions of session and error control are handled in TCP/IP by the user's application software. Under TCP/IP, it is the responsibility of the user application to manage the functions of session, presentation, and application.

Layer 6: Presentation Layer

The Presentation layer (see Figure 4.18) defines the presentation format. This is where you specify the format and data structure to be used for programs. Layer 6 will specify the differences between a PDA, VT100 terminal, or a word processor with What-You-See-Is-What-You-Get (WYSISYG) display capabilities.

Layer 6 converts data received from the Session layer into a format that can be handled by the upper-level Application layer (layer 7). It also works in the opposite direction, receiving application data from layer 7 and reformatting it for the underlying layer 5. For TCP/IP, the presentation function is combined into the TCP/IP Application layer.

FIGURE 4.18   OSI Presentation layer

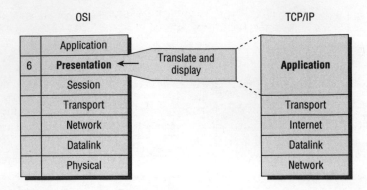

Layer 7: Application Layer

The Application layer (see Figure 4.19) is where the problem-solving calculations of the computer software program run. Various types of computer application software execute in the Application layer, including the following:

- *SNA gateways*, which convert the ASCII 7-bit data structure into IBM Extended Binary Coded Decimal Interchange Code (EBCDIC) 8-bit data structure for the mainframe

- *Domain Name Server (DNS)*, which is the program that associates a domain name to the matching IP address (for layer 3)

- File, print, and web servers

- Databases and office automation software (such as OpenOffice and Microsoft Office)

FIGURE 4.19   OSI Application layer

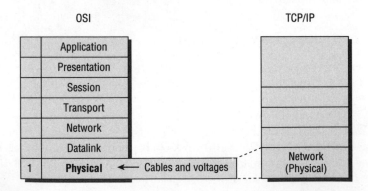

It is important to remember that a gateway will run at the Application layer, which is the highest level of the OSI model.

Understanding How Computers Communicate

Now that we've covered all seven layers of the OSI model, let's take a finished look at the communication between two computers across the network using the OSI model. We will assume that a router is being used in the communication path.

First, the user makes their request in their application software on layer 7. That request is passed down through each layer on its way to the bottom. Along the way, each layer performs its function to ultimately transform the request into a series of electrical signals for transmission on layer 1 (the physical layer of cable and voltages).

Next, the network hub (or network switch) on layer 2 passes the signal up to the layer 3 network router. The router executes a static or dynamic route directing the user's request to the intended destination computer.

Then the request is received as a series of electrical signals on layer 1 of the other computer. The request is passed through each layer of the OSI model and processed accordingly. The request is then received by the other computer in its Application layer, where it is executed. The response is packaged and sent back through the OSI model in reverse, until it reaches the computer display screen.

An example of how this looks is displayed in Figure 4.20.

FIGURE 4.20   OSI communication between systems

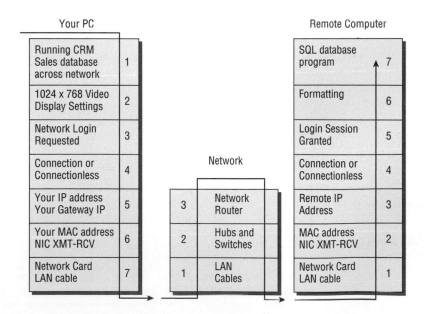

Congratulations, you have now learned the secrets of the OSI model. You'll need to be sure to review its relationship with the TCP/IP model. The OSI model will be used as a discussion tool, while the TCP/IP model is the de facto standard of the real world.

Now we will move into discussing the physical side of networking. We will begin with a simple illustration of physical networks.

Physical Network Design

The first computer networks were created by connecting serial ports between two computers. This primitive design used modem software to handle file transfer between systems.

Networks evolved with the invention of token passing and broadcast transmissions. The invention of the hub, or shared media access unit, created the opportunity to connect multiple computers together on the same segment (referred to as a subnet). The concept of a network *bridge* was created to connect two subnets into the same, single subnet. A layer 2 bridge allows all traffic to pass from one side to the next. The bridge could be configured to allow broadcast across it or configured to filter broadcasts and reduce noise—it depended on the bridge manufacturer's design.

Later, it became apparent that it would be necessary to connect two separate networks together without merging them into a single subnet as a bridge would. Many people complained that too many systems were creating too much traffic when all the computers were located within one giant subnet.

Thus came the development of a *router*. Early routers were simply a computer with two interface cards. Interface 1 serviced a connection to LAN 1, and interface 2 provided a connection to LAN 2. A software-routing program was then loaded to be run on the computer's CPU.

The routing program basically determines whether individual traffic requests need to cross to the other side. If so, the router passes the request through the other LAN interface to reach its destination. If the destination is within the same subnet (LAN 1 to LAN 1), the router will not pass the traffic. This protects the other subnet from unnecessary data transmission noise (LAN 2). That is the basic function of a router. Routers forward data traffic when necessary and insulate users on other subnets.

Figure 4.21 shows what some of the networks would look like.

FIGURE 4.21   First computer networks

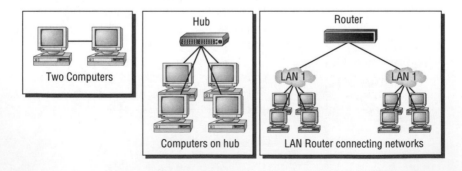

In modern networks, the routing function can be loaded onto a router card installed in the network switch chassis. Traditional routers are usually a dedicated device in their own chassis.

Overview of Network Topologies

As networks grew, creating a standardized topology for all the connections became necessary. Early networks were very proprietary. It was difficult to mix equipment from different vendors. Although this was good for the manufacturer, it drove computer users nuts. Over the years, three basic network cable topologies have become widely accepted: bus, ring, and star. You will look at these three topologies in this section.

Identifying Bus Topologies

One of the first topologies was the *bus topology* (see Figure 4.22). This presented a relatively inexpensive method for connecting multiple computers.

In a bus topology, each computer is daisy-chained to the next computer. A single coaxial cable passes through the connector on the back of each computer on the network. This cable runs through the office like a single rope, which ties all of the systems together.

The design has one major drawback: a break in the bus cable would interrupt transmission for all the computers attached to that cable. Cabling a bus topology can also be cumbersome.

FIGURE 4.22   Bus topology

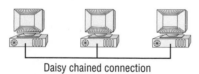

Daisy chained connection

Identifying Star Topologies

The star topology (see Figure 4.23) is the most popular topology in use today. In a *star topology*, each computer is a dedicated cable connection running to a network hub (or switch). This design offers the most flexibility for placement of workstations. It also offers the highest degree of cable redundancy. The cable redundancy ensures that other computers are not affected by a failure of an individual workstation connection.

This is the design of most data networks. It is also used by the PBX telephone switch to connect individual telephone stations. The primary drawback to the star topology is the cost of all the additional cable required to make connections for each station.

Figure 4.24 demonstrates the practical application of the star topology. Notice that each workstation has a connection to a nearby wiring closet. This design ensures that you do not exceed the maximum recommended cable length. The acceptable length of cable varies depending on the cabling type used. Normally it is 100 meters on unshielded twisted-pair (UTP). The star topology helps reduce the cabling cost by shortening the cable distance to reach each user. The hubs and switches are located in the wiring closet to connect users to the network. Every cable is terminated at the wall plate next to the user and a patch panel in the wire closet. A patch cord connects the building cable from the patch panel to the ports of the hub/switch. A backbone connection is then run from the data center to the wiring closet to establish a complete path for network communication. Figure 4.24 shows the real-world implementation of a star topology, complete with wiring closet and backbone to the data center.

FIGURE 4.23   Star topology

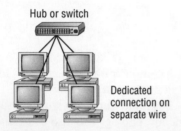

FIGURE 4.24   Practical application of the star topology

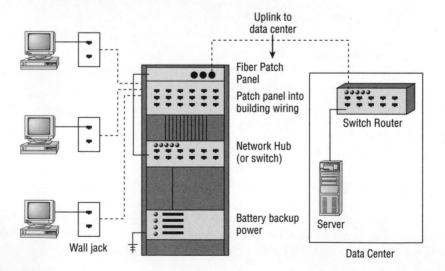

Identifying Ring Topologies

The most famous token-passing LAN protocol is IBM's ring topology (see Figure 4.25). Each LAN computer is connected to a media access unit (MAU). Each MAU is connected to both an upstream MAU and downstream MAU to form a backbone loop. Network traffic can be transmitted in either direction. This bidirectional loop is referred to as the *ring*.

A network ring topology has the advantage of built-in redundancy. Should the ring break, then all traffic will travel through the ring in the opposite direction, thereby avoiding the break point. The individual workstations are then connected into the ring by using a star topology.

FIGURE 4.25   Ring topology

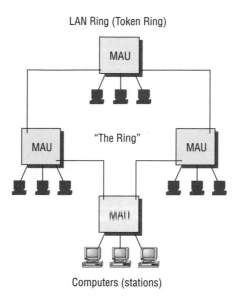

The phone company uses a ring technology in their fiber optic networks. This design allows the redundant path necessary to create a fault-tolerant network.

Identifying Meshed Networks

The important network links can have alternate path connections to increase redundancy. The meshing of star networks is a common method of providing redundancy similar to the approach used by a ring topology. The principal difference is that a meshed network is a series of point-to-point connections between critical backbone connections. The router determines which link to use based on a predefined routing criteria. A network administrator defines the best link and the alternate path link to use if the best link is down.

There are essentially two types of meshed networks:

Full mesh   A fully meshed network has alternate connections for every major backbone point on the network (see Figure 4.26). The primary obstacle to this design is the cost of implementation.

Partial mesh   When you cannot afford a full mesh network, you may decide to implement a partial mesh for the most critical links (see Figure 4.27). Occasionally, the critical link may not be determined by the overall value of traffic. The additional link may be determined by the ability of the sponsor to pay the additional cost. A partial mesh is better than no redundancy at all.

FIGURE 4.26   Full mesh network (N-1 design)

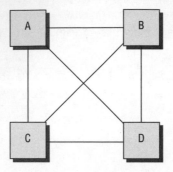

FIGURE 4.27   Partial mesh network

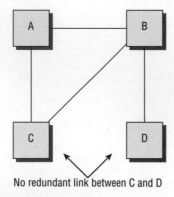

No redundant link between C and D

🌐 **Real World Scenario**

N-1 = Full Mesh Networks

Network designers refer to full mesh networks as the *N-1* design. This design gives the highest possible redundancy. *N* stands for the number of points to be connected, and the *-1* refers to the total number of additional connections necessary to achieve a full mesh. The notation *N-1* therefore denotes a full mesh network.

Network Cable Types

IS auditors are fortunate to have the guidance of industry cable standards provided by the Institute of Electrical and Electronics Engineers (IEEE) and the Electronic Industries Alliance/ Telecommunications Industry Association (EIA/TIA) building wiring committee. Several methods have been developed to use a variety of cables to create a network. Each type of cable has its own unique characteristics of construction or transmission capability. Some cables are better suited for voice, for example. Others are designed for the high demands of data.

You are is not expected to design the cabling system used in a network. That is the job of a Registered Communications Distribution Designer (RCDD), a certified expert in the layout of cable systems.

Cable installations are commonly referred to as *cable plants*. The cabling system for data and voice can be very complex, depending on the requirement. A CISA is required to have a basic understanding of the three most common cables used to build a network. You should understand the description and limitations of each type.

Unshielded Twisted-Pair (UTP) Cable

Unshielded twisted-pair (UTP) cable is the most popular for connecting computers to a network. *Unshielded* means that the wire does not have any protection from electrical interference. The twisting creates an electrical cancellation to prevent the wire from broadcasting like an antenna. Untwisted wire will create magnetic fields of interference that can swing a compass needle, whereas twisted wire will be invisible to the same compass.

UTP is an inexpensive, twisted, four-pair wire used for 10/100M Ethernet. Pairs are twisted to reduce EMI interference. Each wire is home run to a hub/switch in the wiring closet.

There are three common categories of UTP:

- CAT-3 (Category 3) is for voice only.
- CAT-5 (Category 5) for voice and data.
- CAT-5e (enhanced) for 1GB, 100Mhz data.

Higher-rated CAT-6 and CAT-7 are also available. Fire codes in commercial buildings specify that two types of jackets for twisted-pair cabling will be used. The cheaper twisted-pair cabling uses PVC as the covering jacket. Unfortunately PVC burns like a fuse when lit. Fire codes call for plenum grade Teflon jacketing to be used in plenum spaces to prevent the spread of fire.

UTP is used in distances less than 200 feet and is commonly used in star topologies. Special types of UTP are used for distances of up to 100 meters. Coaxial is used for longer runs or where some electrical interference may be an issue.

Coaxial Cable

Early networks used a form of *coaxial* (or *coax*) cable with mesh shielding to prevent electrical interference. The wire is similar to antenna cable or the cable for your television set. Coax has been replaced by UTP for indoor environments. You can still use coax in areas prone to electrical interference or for outdoor connections.

Coax is an older and slower design than UTP. It contains two electrical conductors (copper center, metal outer shielding covered in PVC). It was common in Ethernet networks with a bus topology. It's often used in distances up to 185 meters, but can be extended by using a repeater.

Fiber-Optic Cable

A fiber-optic cable is constructed of tiny strands of glass fiber. Lasers or light-emitting diodes (LEDs) are used to flash signals through the glass strands. Fiber-optic cable is commonly used for backbone connections and long-haul installations. You can send multiple streams of data concurrently through the same strand of glass by using different color wavelengths. The process is called *dense wave multiplexing*. The drawbacks are price and the fragile glass strands, which break easily.

Fiber-optic cable has unlimited bandwidth. It can support concurrent transmission of voice, video, and data traffic. Each laser color is a separate channel, allowing 12, 24, and 64 lasers to share one fiber without degradation. Speed, based on equipment used, is between 1G and 1,000GB. Is it also very difficult to tap.

It is important to understand when you would use copper twisted pair and when you would use fiber-optic cable.

Network Devices

Now that you understand the OSI model and cabling, it is time to discuss the various devices necessary to build a network. Every CISA is expected to understand the purpose of common networking equipment.

Let's begin from the bottom up. The first thing you need is the customer requirements. What do they intend to connect to the network? The next question, what is their intended usage while on the network? We are constantly amazed at how many times the client expects a network to magically be all things to all people. Proper identification of requirements will go a long way toward aligning the network to their organizational objectives.

We can start with the number of user connections. Each user will need to plug into a network hub or switch. A *network hub* is an electrical connection box that amplifies and retimes the electrical signals for transmission. A hub is similar to an electrical junction box. All traffic is shared across each port.

A network switch performs the functions of a hub and contains an intelligent processor capable of running logic programs. Switches separate traffic between ports to create the appearance of a private communications line. This is the same design that is in PBX telephone switches and in LAN switches.

The network architect may encounter a problem with the distance between network devices. The solution may be to use a special cable type for that run, or to add another device to compensate for the distance. A *network repeater* can amplify the tiny electrical signals to drive longer distances. Repeaters receive a signal and then repeat the transmission down the next link. We could also use fiber-optic cable from that particular leg of the run. Fiber optics are popular for use in long runs across the building or across the globe.

Maybe the issue is that wires are not acceptable for your intended usage. For example, it would be difficult to use a wire-line connection for counting inventory in a warehouse. The users would be unhappy, and the heavy steel wheels of the forklift would not be kind as they ran over the fragile cable.

Wi-Fi radio is good for communication over short distances. This will work in a warehouse. It will also work within a building for connecting handheld devices such as a PDA. Another wireless method includes infrared light (IR), which requires line-of-sight access. This is good for limiting communication to the immediate area, but still needs security.

 Wireless security is always a major issue. Chapter 7 covers this topic.

There may be a need to divide a network into small sections because of the sheer number of systems. Maybe you want to divide the network to put each group into their own subnet. Subnetting could protect the Accounting department from the Research and Development traffic, for example. This is performed by segmenting the big network into smaller groups of subnetworks (subnets).

You can subnet by using a *router* to provide access across the subnets while eliminating unnecessary traffic. As you will recall, a router will insulate subnets from traffic conversations that do not involve their systems. Just connect the router to the switch/hub for each subnet and set up the router configuration.

We can also implement virtual subnets known as *virtual LANs (VLANs)* to divide the users. A VLAN is like an automatic conference calling list configured on the network switch (layer 2). A VLAN will simulate one subnet for all the target computers (that's where the term *virtual* comes into the name). The VLAN methods vary depending on the comprehension of the installer and the capability of the manufacturer. The basic methods of creating a VLAN are to use specific ports, to associate MAC addresses into a VLAN, or to create policy rules if the switch hardware has that capability. Let's discuss each of these methods here:

Port-based VLAN (layer 1)   The administrator manually configures a specific port into a specific VLAN. Works well for uplinks, systems that don't move, and small networks.

MAC-based VLAN (layer 2)   Ties the MAC address into a VLAN by reading the network traffic and then automatically reconfiguring the network port on your switch.

Policy- or rule-based VLAN (layer 3 with layer 2 supporting)   A high-quality network switch reads the IP header in your traffic and executes an administrator's rule to join a VLAN based on protocol or by IP address. When correctly implemented, the process is automatic and does not require any software on the workstation. Switch ports will reconfigure automatically when the system is moved.

No matter what, every VLAN needs a router to access the other subnets. This router may be a physically separate device or a router CPU inside the same chassis. Now add the network servers and you will have a working computer network. Just be sure to include enough network-attached printers to make everyone happy.

Table 4.3 provides a summary of the various local area network devices that you will encounter.

TABLE 4.3   Local Area Network Equipment

LAN Equipment	Purpose
Router (layer 3)	Connects to separate subnetworks or adapts connection to different transmission media. Routers decide whether the traffic needs to pass through along another route or should just stay in the original subnetwork. This relieves traffic congestion across the network. Examples include LAN 1–to–LAN 2 and LAN-to-WAN circuits. Routers can also convert between Ethernet, token-ring, and telephone company communication protocols.
Switch (layer 2)	Provides intelligent process of creating discreet communication on each port. Same function as the PBX telephone switch, which creates the illusion of private communication lines for each user. Network virtual LANs (VLANs) are similar to administrator-designated group conference calling. Requires a router (layer 3 router function) to communicate with a different subnetwork or between VLANs.
Hub (layer 2)	Connects individual cables to share data between ports. Amplifies and retimes the tiny electrical signals. Similar to an electrical junction box for networking cables.
Bridge (layer 2)	Connects two separate networks by using the same network addressing in one subnet. Intelligent bridge is the same as layer 2 switch.
Repeater (layer 1)	Designed to boost the signal strength across a cable to overcome distance limitations.
Wi-Fi transmitter (layer 1)	Short-range wireless transmitter receiver to connect laptops and PDA devices to the LAN. (May be integrated into an all-in-one router offering both layer 1 and layer 3 functions.)

To connect different networks, you need a router.

Routers provide intelligent decisions about routing traffic down particular links. The router is like a traffic cop directing traffic in the direction it needs to travel. Routers come in a wide variety of shapes, sizes, and capabilities. An Internet router needs at least one Internet port and one LAN port. The type of router port depends on the type of circuit you need to connect.

We will also need a firewall to protect our network. We will discuss firewalls in depth in Chapter 7.

Network Services

Several pages ago, we discussed the OSI model with examples of network services running on layer 7. In the example, we mentioned network servers with a few of the services they provide. Let's discuss two common network support services that relate to everyone using a network: DNS and DHCP.

Domain Name Service

Computers like to use hexadecimal numbers, network administrators like to use IP addresses, and all of us who run computers like to refer to machines by name. Names are so much easier to remember. Even names can get confusing, so the Internet is designed to allow fully qualified domain names (FQDNs). A *fully qualified domain name* is what you see on the left side in the URL portion of the browser as you surf the Internet. Have you ever wondered how the web browser finds the website you typed? The answer is by using the Domain Name Service (DNS).

Routers have tables of IP addresses, along with the routes to take to reach those addresses. DNS servers are a layer 7 software application that contains a list of alias names and their associated IP addresses. DNS is how you end up reaching a website without knowing its IP address.

DNS offers additional flexibility. You can change the IP address without having to tell everyone about the address change. Just keep the DNS server updated with your new IP address. If DNS fails, you will not be able to access the target or you will resort to typing the IP address (if known).

Figure 4.28 shows the process of DNS looking at the company name and responding to your request.

Dynamic Host Configuration Protocol

For years, the job of a network administrator entailed the tedious task of configuring IP addresses on each computer. Manual settings are still the best choice for network servers; however, the user workstation is another matter.

FIGURE 4.28   DNS name service (address lookup)

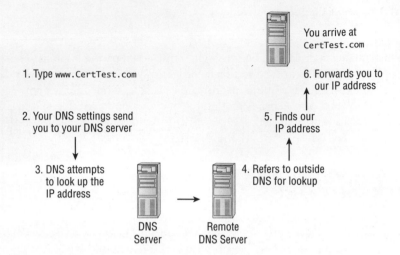

Dynamic Host Configuration Protocol (DHCP) can automatically configure the IP address, subnet mask, and DNS settings on a computer. DHCP is an improved version of the original BOOTP protocol. Both DHCP and BOOTP have the same operational design.

The theory of operation is simple. Figure 4.29 shows how DHCP works. Here are the steps:

1. A computer on your network is set up as the DHCP server. For remote dial-up, the better access servers will have this ability built in to support the modems. The DHCP server will be configured by your network administrator with a pool of IP addresses eligible for dynamic allocation.

2. The DHCP server listens on the network for an IP packet containing a type 67 code in the header. (Don't worry, that level of detail is not on your exam.)

3. A computer is booted on your network without an IP address. During the boot process, the computer recognizes that an IP is needed. The computer sends out a type 67 request asking for any DHCP server to assign it an IP address. The request contains the MAC address of the computer asking for an IP.

4. The requesting computer waits several seconds for a response.

5. Your DHCP server recognizes the type 67 request and responds with a type 68 reply addressed to the MAC address of the sender.

6. If the reply is received in time, the computer will accept the IP address and configuration settings. Then it will finish boot up and begin talking on the network.

Every idea in the world has its Achilles heel. DHCP is no different. DHCP is implemented on OSI layer 2. This means that the mechanism is depending on the ability to make a broadcast with its MAC address. Routers will not pass broadcasts because the resulting traffic is undesired on all other occasions. Remember, the router has two jobs: one is routing, and the second is to provide insulation from unnecessary traffic. The DHCP server would need to be located on the same subnet in order to hear the computer making a DHCP request.

Figure 4.30 shows how DHCP is blocked by the router.

FIGURE 4.29   How DCHP works

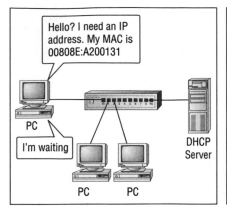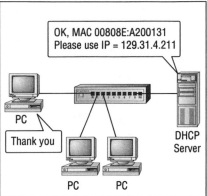

FIGURE 4.30   DHCP and the router issue

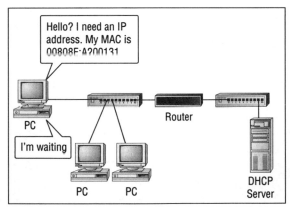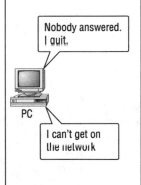

The DHCP Router Solution

Rather than building a bunch of DHCP servers, you can make a simple change to the router configuration. The router will still perform its normal functions; however, it can be set to forward DHCP requests to another subnet. The router command setting is called a bootp-helper-address or DHCP-helper-address.

This helper address setting will forward both the initial request and the associated DHCP server reply. The process is simple, as shown in Figure 4.31.

FIGURE 4.31   Router with DHCP helper address

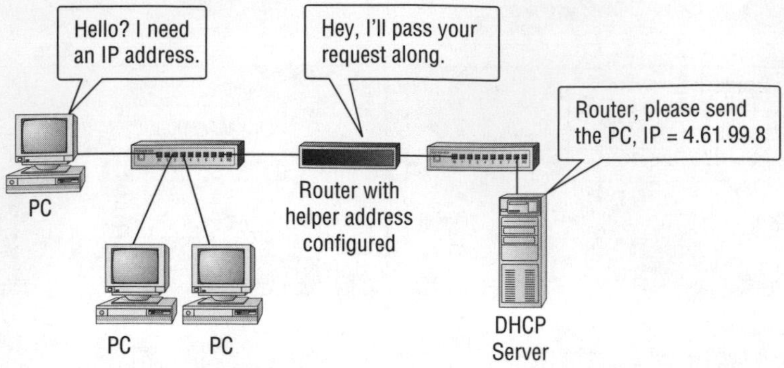

Dynamic IP addressing under DHCP is quite convenient for users. However, unsecured implementations of DHCP could grant an intruder easier access into the network. We will discuss this security issue further in Chapter 7.

Expanding the Network

Modern routers can connect high-speed LANs to remote places for the purpose of creating a wide area network (WAN). Figure 4.32 shows what a WAN might look like.

Remote access is a popular feature. WANs are similar to a LAN; however, the implementation is different. Special equipment is necessary to adapt the transmission signal to telephone and radio equipment. Figure 4.32 shows the basics of expanding a network.

Setting up a WAN requires planning. Let's start with the most important component, which is information. The first thing you need is the customer requirements. What do they intend to connect to the network? Questions should be asked about who will be connecting to the network. Will the users be employees, business partners, or clients? Once again, you ask questions about their intended usage while on the network. What controls are planned? Hopefully, the client will be able to impress the auditor with answers that are well thought out.

Your client might want to have dial-in access to the network for their users. This can be accomplished in two ways:

Individual modems   An individual modem can be connected to a computer on the network. This is a simple method that is adored by every hacker in the world. Individual modem connections bypass the majority of network security controls. Your monitoring tools may think this is just an ordinary internal computer with free rein over the attached subnet—or worse, the whole network. A hacker can easily find modems by using automated dialing tools or checking a list of known modems posted at hacker sites. Insecure modems are still a threat to security. A sharp auditor will investigate the compliance of dial-in modems to their security policy.

FIGURE 4.32   Expanding the network

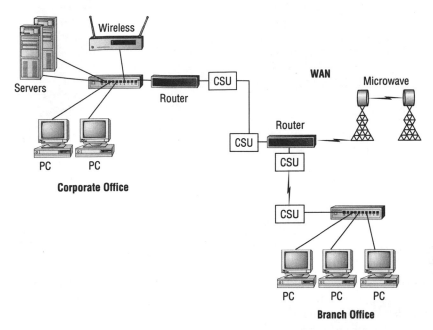

Network access server   An access server can be used with a modem pool. It can be a slick product from Cisco or a PC configured with special software such as Microsoft Remote Access Server (RAS). The access server should have special monitoring and security controls.

It is safe to assume that the remote connection will be attached to one of the routers. You should encourage the practice of separating remote connections into their own subnet. This promotes separation of duties with the benefit of simplifying the implementation of security controls. Remote router connections will probably need a firewall if the connection is wireless or could involve someone besides the organization's employees.

High-speed telephone circuits such as T-1 (1.54Mbps) and T-3 (44.5Mbps) use a central service unit (CSU) instead of a regular modem. The CSU is a special device used by the telephone company and designed for connection to their equipment. Telephone circuits like this can be divided or combined by using a *multiplexor*. A multiplexor converts one high-speed telephone port into many lower-speed ports, or combines several lower-speed lines to appear as one high-speed line. Multiplexors are invisible to the user.

Table 4.4 summarizes the various types of equipment you might use when connecting to a WAN.

The telephone company will provide whatever service the client is able to afford. In some areas, the services may be limited. High-speed services such as DSL are available in only limited areas. The limitation is based on cost: Your telephone company will invest in areas that have enough demand to warrant the business cost. In rural areas, people have few choices. These are known as last-mile service areas, where the phone company will lose money.

TABLE 4.4   Networking Equipment

Device	Purpose
Router with WAN port	Connect LAN to remote WAN connections over telephone circuits.
Modem	Low-speed telephone dial-up connection to the access server for users, or attached to the router for remote administration.
Channel Service Unit (CSU)	Similar to a very special modem. Designed to connect router port to a high-speed telephone company circuit. Fast transmission speeds from 1MB to 44MB per line. Common in WANs.
Multiplexor	Can combine multiple lower-speed telephone circuits to appear as a single fast circuit, or split a fast circuit into multiple lower-speed connections. It has a function similar to that of a splitter or combiner.

The world of telephone circuits is based on several generations of telephone company equipment. The older generation is based on the Integrated Services Digital Network (ISDN). The newest generation is built by using Dense Wave Multiplexing (DWM) with multiple lasers over fiber optics with Asynchronous Transfer Mode (ATM). Each generation of technology has intrinsic advantages and disadvantages. Let's run down the list. We suggest you pay attention because these details may be of value.

The following are various ways you can connect to your network via a wired route:

Plain Old Telephone Service (POTS)   POTS is available almost everywhere. This is the regular telephone line capable of data transmission up to 56Kbs. POTS is based on using half of an ISDN circuit. POTS is the only circuit that is considered to be "off" when not in use. All the other telephone circuits we discuss are always live and transmitting.

Integrated Services Digital Network (ISDN)   ISDN is the foundation of POTS. Therefore, you should be able to get ISDN almost anywhere. The bandwidth starts at 128K per line. It can be used at 128K or divided into two 56K circuits. Optional ISDN speeds can go up to 1.544Mbps. You can run data, voice, and video over ISDN. Most video conference sets use ISDN. (The ISDN circuit is always on and live.)

International Telecommunication Standard X.25 (X.25)   X.25 was an early digital packet-switching protocol. It was considered the foundation of modern switched networks. X.25 contained a field for handling parameters called the facility code. This would allow you to specify a quality of service. X.25 is now used only as a reference model, except for a few old customers.

Asynchronous Transfer Mode (ATM)   ATM is the new backbone of the telecommunications industry. The transmission speeds are very high, from 155Mbps to more than 1GBps. That is more bandwidth than most companies could ever use. The design implements cell switching and multiplexing to ensure solid delivery. Data is sent down multiple concurrent paths to the same destination. The first data cell to arrive will be used, while later duplicates will be discarded. ATM can use 132 paths during transmission. It is very reliable. The ATM circuit is always on and live.

Frame-relay   Frame-relay is an inexpensive packet-switching system. The data packets may arrive out of sequence. Therefore, it is important to have equipment capable of caching enough data to allow reassembly before use by the user. Frame-relay works great for data/voice applications, but some video transmissions may appear choppy to the viewer. Frame-relay speeds range from less than 1.544Mbps up to 44.5Mbps. (The frame-relay circuit is always on and live.)

Digital Subscriber Line (DSL)   DSL is a least-expensive higher-speed circuit running at a high transmission frequency over a standard telephone line. This allows your standard voice telephone line to simultaneously carry DSL higher-speed traffic without conflict. DSL is substantially limited by distance. It is available in only high-density areas where the phone company can make a profit. Speeds range from 368Kpbs to 1.544Mbps. The DSL circuit is always on and live.

WARNING   We have discussed several communication circuits that are always on and live. This can allow a hacker to attack you 24 hours a day, every day. High-speed circuits can support high-speed attacks or high-speed theft of your data. Think firewalls!

Wireless Access Solutions

The basic network concepts are identical for developing a wireless network solution sans wire. Wireless is used when the wiring costs are prohibitive or the wires would defeat the intended purpose.

Each wireless system requires a minimum of two antenna systems. The antenna stations have transmit and receive capabilities.

The following are various ways you can connect to your network via wireless access.

Wi-Fi radio   This is the most common type of wireless access. The design uses a layer 1 transmitter/receiver to support a signal range of up to 1,500 feet. It uses digital spread spectrum or frequency hopping over a private radio channel. It is commonly used by the military and private companies operating mobile fleets. Largescale Wi-Fi may use cellular service. Smaller scale use includes Wi-Fi hot spots.

Satellite radio   This is the next most common method. The signal is bounced off a low-orbit satellite in space. Obviously, the service area is huge. Very popular for remote communications or linking to numerous field locations, satellite is heavily used in trucking fleets, ships, and retail chain operations. The transmission speeds are lower, and cost is an issue unless you buy a large volume of air time. Private uplinks are available for telephone, data, fax, and video applications. Satellite data-phones are common in emergency response. Transmission speeds are 9.6bps to 4MBps. A primary issue is transmission cost with specialized hardware required. Satellite has a 2- to 5-second transmission delay due to signal propagation.

Microwave   Microwaves are used in short-distance runs—1 to 30 miles— across cities and over mountain ranges. The service has been around for 50 years. The only drawbacks are a clear line of sight for transmission and the construction cost. Connection speeds range from 1MBps to 100MBps. The primary advantage is no recurring transmission costs aside from equipment purchase and regular maintenance. Severe weather and fog can disrupt signals.

Laser   Lasers are being used as an alternative to microwaves. Lasers also work to connect two offices by using the unobstructed aerial space to cross above public roads. It is similar to fiber optics without the fiber cable. Transmission speeds from are from 1MBps to 100MBps. Severe weather and fog can disrupt signals.

It is strongly recommended that every land-based wireless connection have a firewall installed between the wired network and the wireless equipment. Many implementations of wireless encryption still contain holes in security. Motivated hackers can access radio connections by using technology available in the amateur radio community. Laser access may be more difficult, but possible.

It is important that we address the subject of short-range wireless networking for use with Radio Frequency Identification tags. This is an area that will increase as more organizations attempt to implement automated tracking.

Wireless RFID Systems

Radio Frequency Identification (RFID) is a hot topic. RFID uses a tiny tag, which contains silicon chips and antennas that enable the tag to be detected by scanners. The original purpose was to protect inventory from department store shoplifters. Later RFID was expanded to include planting tags in boxes for better warehouse control.

The security and privacy issues regarding RFID are increasing every day. As an IS auditor, you are expected to have a basic understanding of RFID. You will encounter an increasing number of issues regarding RFID implementations.

Passive RFID tags are regularly used in inventory control and for implant in live animals. These tags may be covertly read at a distance. Newer tags are built into the product and are not detectable. The user could be scanned as they walk through a building. RFID tags in adult products or medical prescription packages could lead to interesting conversations about privacy.

The US Food and Drug Administration and other government agencies have approved the use of RFID tags for human implant. There are multiple human implant vendors on the market today. The ads for human implant claim RFID tags are safe and nonremovable. One vendor claims that the intended purpose is to protect newborn infants by tracking your baby in the hospital. Other advertised uses include prisoner identification or the identification of elderly individuals unable to provide information for themselves. This new RFID situation poses an increasing variety of privacy concerns.

Another type of RFID uses a transponder to transmit a signal. The RFID transponder uses an internal power source to respond to queries by an antenna in the area. A common example would be the toll tag used by a toll road authority for the electronic collection of usage fees.

A variety of organizations including law enforcement collect surveillance data on common citizens by using active RFID toll tags along with automobile satellite services and cell phone records. The implications may be either good or evil depending on the desire of individuals.

Summarizing the Various Area Networks

The IT management may choose to maintain a network administration staff at each site or use remote access. Either choice has its advantages and disadvantages.

Routers can use a modem for individual low-speed telephone connections of 56K. This would be intended for remote support of the router itself. (Turn off the modem when not in use to keep out the hackers.)

We have discussed both LAN and WAN networks. The discussion would not be complete without mentioning the multitude of variations. In the beginning, the LAN was the focus. Then we discussed the need to connect to remote users. Supporting remote connections became rather involved, and the whole idea was termed a WAN. Since that time, the world has continued to generate new products with a combination of need, politics, and marketing. The LAN-WAN naming convention has brought us new terminology for other types of area networks, including personal area networks (PANs), campus area networks (CANs), metropolitan area networks (MANs), and storage area networks (SANs).

Table 4.5 introduces you to the assorted types of area networks that the CISA is expected to encounter. You need to know the descriptive features of each one.

TABLE 4.5   Common Networking Acronyms

Network Acronyms	Description
Local area network (LAN)	Connecting computers within the building by using hubs, switches, and routers. Usually very fast connection speed of 100/1000 MB.
Virtual local area network (VLAN)	Artificial grouping of disparate workstation ports across various LAN switches to appear as if all were connected to a common subnet. Similar to a PBX conference calling group. Primitive VLANs use fixed ports. Advanced VLANs use dynamic rules to automatically assign ports without user/administrator intervention. User can plug in anywhere, and the switch reconfigures the port within fractions of a second. Moves are automatic using IP address rule, protocol rule, or MAC address rule.
Storage area network (SAN)	A cluster solution for interconnecting different kinds of file storage for server farms. Often use Ethernet, SCSI, ATM, or fiber-optic connections.
Personal area network (PAN)	Coverage is within 10 feet of the immediate area. Used for connecting PDA and handheld personal devices to synchronize with your computer.

TABLE 4.5 Common Networking Acronyms *(continued)*

Network Acronyms	Description
Campus area network (CAN)	Connecting computers between buildings in a school or corporate campus by using cable, fiber optics, or wireless transmitters.
Metropolitan area network (MAN)	Connecting computers between different buildings located in the same city.
Wide area network (WAN)	Multi-city connection over longer distances. Connection speeds range from under 1MB on cheap telephone circuits to over 1GB on optical carrier circuits (OCx)

Political battles over authority will exist regarding the control over most networks. The basic operation of local and wide area networks is quite similar. The principal difference is the area of coverage and who is in charge of that area.

Managing Your Network

Networks are constantly increasing in complexity. A network outage can cause significant impact to the organization's business activities. It would be naïve to assume that the systems could run without supervision. The network administrator holds the duty of monitoring network performance and is the first line of defense for detecting security violations. This is possible only with specialized tools designed to manage network assets. Let's take a look at the basic tools used to manage the network.

Syslog

Today almost all computers and network devices have the capability for centralized system logging, known as *Syslog*. The design sends audit log messages to a centralized server for aggregation of event logs and alerts. Syslog is a common and simple utility that requires little processing power.

It is an excellent tool to aid the monitoring efforts of system administrators. This form of centralized logging is excellent for security monitoring and audit log retention. Syslog can be enabled on an individual system within a few minutes.

Syslog has some disadvantages. Unfortunately, it does not contain message authentication. There is still no mechanism for providing message integrity. The Syslog design also lacks the mechanism to verify delivery of a message.

The principal advantage of Syslog is that audit logs can be automatically transmitted to another server for safe storage. This assists in providing evidence for the auditor. It can also be a compensating control in environments where the logs may be deleted.

Automated Cable Tester

Cable industry studies report that 97 percent of all network problems are related to faults in the physical cable plant (layer 1). Advanced handheld cable testers are used to certify the quality of network wire runs. These handheld scanners test individual data cables by automatically running a series of electrical tests and transmission tests. The tests check a variety of conditions, including compliance to recommended length, signal strength, transmission cross talk, electrical noise interference, and electrical pin connections. Cables that pass these tests are certified as compliant. Once certified, the cable is ready for production use.

Protocol Analyzer

A computer can be configured with special software designed to record and analyze network transmissions. This software is often referred to as a *packet sniffer*. Network administrators use this as a tool for troubleshooting network performance problems. The sniffer operates in promiscuous mode and records transmissions of every packet transversing the segment. The sniffer can see only traffic within the segment to which it is attached. It cannot see traffic across the routers or switches unless the traffic is passing down the segment where the computer is attached. The sniffer will show you communication between systems and the passwords used.

Hackers can use a sniffer to capture user IDs, passwords in clear text, and mapping of the network. This is why sniffers are considered a tremendous threat.

Simple Network Management Protocol

Networks can be monitored and controlled by using the Simple Network Management Protocol (SNMP). The network administrator usually runs an SNMP network management program such as HP OpenView to monitor servers and routers. A Network Management System (NMS) gives you the capability to check the up/down status of individual network devices.

You can use SNMP to monitor almost any network device, including servers, routers, gateways, hubs, and workstations. By default, the SNMP protocol provides the capability to do the following:

- Monitor a device with notification of possible error conditions.
- Reconfigure limited system parameters.
- Use SNMP to reboot or shut down the network device.

The SNMP security mechanism is extremely weak and relies on simple passwords transmitted in clear text that are easy to read. As an auditor, you should be concerned about SNMP being allowed to travel unregulated across the network. All SNMP managed devices need to use unique passwords rather than the default passwords *public* and *private*.

Vendor documentation will refer to the passwords of *public* and *private* by using the term *community strings*. A community string is actually a simple passwords used to gain control of the target system. All that is needed is the target system IP address and matching SNMP password (community string). Many organizations are not properly educated about the *public* and *private* password risk. It is the network administrator's job to define SNMP access control lists and to manage the implementation of unique SNMP passwords for each device. Failure to do so would grant anyone control of any system using the same SNMP password (community string). Otherwise, SNMP is a good internal monitoring tool.

Remote Monitoring Protocol Version 2

The Remote Monitoring Protocol version 2 (RMON2) is a major improvement over version 1, offering data beyond basic network health via up/down status. RMON2 gives you the ability to monitor all seven layers of the OSI model, including application performance. You can view the performance of a single application running across the network or select a stratified view of the combined bandwidth allocation.

Twenty-one layers of RMON performance data are available. By comparison, a network packet sniffer can record only a snapshot containing a few minutes or hours of layer 1, 2, and 3 data. RMON2 can provide a broader range of nonstop performance while recording tremendous levels of detail covering a time span of hours, days, months, and even years. Most RMON2 implementations write the records to a SQL database for reporting and long-term retention. This is a true enterprise-class monitoring system.

It is important to remember that useful administration tools also make good hacker tools. Every administrative tool needs to be governed by the organization's internal controls.

Summary

The information systems auditor is expected to understand common networking technology. You should know the name of each piece of equipment and its role in the computer network. Occasionally, you may encounter systems that are filling an all-in-one role. In that event, you should remember computer architecture limitations: It is not possible for single-processor systems to perform all functions without a momentary interruption of the security software. Both single-user systems and multiuser systems have design vulnerabilities that can be exploited.

It is the job of the CISA to evaluate the auditee's technology implementation. Despite advancements in technology, common problems will usually be rooted in fundamental errors of design or implementation. Security is best implemented in multiple layers for compensating control for design vulnerabilities. The purpose of this chapter has been to familiarize you with the basic concepts. The world depends on the CISA to review the client's design for the purpose of identifying vulnerabilities or failure points. You should always ask yourself whether the technology truly fulfills the objectives of the business and the objectives of security controls. If not, it might just be a superfluous investment in way-cool technical junk. Technology without proper internal controls is a bomb waiting to explode.

Exam Essentials

Understand the basics of computer architecture.   Computer architecture comprises a central processor unit with high-speed cache memory and solid-state RAM memory. All the computer's components communicate by using a shared data bus, constructed of electrical wires. Interfaces connect the data bus to the electronic components such as the video display or the hard disk drive. There are different classes of computers based on size and capability including the personal computer, minicomputer, mainframe, and supercomputer.

Remember that computers may use single CPUs or multiple CPUs.   In either case, the system can be running in time-sharing mode to support multiple users (multiuser mode). With multiple CPUs, it is possible to assign each processor to a particular task. Multiple CPU architecture provides a way for security software to run completely uninterrupted. Otherwise, the computer security software will be interrupted in the normal course of servicing processing requests.

Know that the computer operating system manages communications between the hardware and user programs.   The operating system provides services for scheduling, dispatching, security, and input and output functions. All operating systems are not equal in their implementation of internal controls. The mainframe represents a role model for the highest level of system controls. Security controls are lacking while the system is in supervisory state during maintenance or initial program load (IPL).

Understand that system ports must be protected from physical access and logical access.   Examples of system ports include interface ports, the console or master terminal, and all network communication ports.

Know that computer networking is accomplished by using a variety of devices.   Network cables are joined together by hubs or network switches to form a network. Smaller networks are known as subnets. Multiple subnets can be joined together by using a router. The purpose of the router is to direct traffic between different networks. A firewall is a specially configured device that selectively routes traffic between two networks. The firewall's method depends on its internal architecture. A proxy firewall prevents direct access into the network. Proxies relay the request on behalf of the user.

Remember that wide area networks are created by using wired telephone circuits or wireless transmitters to connect LANs.   Network security at external access points is always a concern. Every network access point presents an opportunity to motivated hackers. High-speed communications circuits allow for high-speed attacks. Modern telephone circuits, except for POTS, are always on and present a 24-hour attack opportunity. The first wide area networks were created by using circuit-switched telephone lines that were billed by distance traveled. Newer packet-switching technology charges for the data sent, not the distance traveled.

Understand that the OSI model provides a simple reference for explaining the functions occurring in computer networking.   Nobody actually runs the OSI protocol; in the real world, most communication is performed over the Internet Protocol (IP). A CISA must demonstrate an understanding of how OSI relates to IP.

Remember that computer networks can be complex and require constant monitoring. Typical monitoring tools include the packet sniffer to analyze communications, Syslog to transmit system logs to a safe location for review, and Simple Network Management Protocol (SNMP) to alert administrators about conditions impacting network operations. SNMP can feed a network management system, such as HP OpenView or Remote Monitoring Protocol (RMON).

Review Questions

1. Which RAID level does not improve fault tolerance?

   A. RAID level 0

   B. RAID level 1

   C. RAID level 2

   D. RAID level 5

2. Which type network device directs packets through the Internet?

   A. Hubs

   B. Routers

   C. Repeaters

   D. Modems

3. This type of data transmission is often used to transmit video signals across the network.

   A. Unicasting

   B. Broadcasting

   C. Multicasting

   D. Pinging

4. This address is manufactured or burned into network equipment and is totally unique.

   A. Domain name

   B. IP

   C. Media Access Control

   D. Street address

5. This network is often used to provide vendors and customers limited access to corporate network services.

   A. Internet

   B. Extranet

   C. Intranet

   D. Access net

6. Which of the following is a list of OSI model levels from the top down?

   A. Application, Physical, Session, Transport, Network, Data-Link, Presentation.

   B. Presentation, Data-Link, Network, Transport, Session, Physical, Application

   C. Application, Presentation, Session, Transport, Network, Data-Link, Physical

   D. Presentation, Data-Link, Network, Transport, Session, Physical, Application

7. Which of the following is the most popular media for connecting workstations in a corporate environment?

    A. Coaxial

    B. Shielded twisted-pair

    C. Unshielded twisted-pair

    D. Fiber optics

8. This protocol is layer 3 routable and is the backbone of the Internet.

    A. IP

    B. OSI

    C. TCP

    D. NetBIOS

9. What type of network firewall is often the simplest to implement but has the worst logging capabilities?

    A. Proxy

    B. Application

    C. Packet-filtering

    D. Adaptive

10. What does the third layer of the OSI model equate to in the TCP/IP model?

    A. Network

    B. Data-Link

    C. Transport

    D. Internet

11. At which layer of the OSI model does a gateway operate?

    A. Layer 3

    B. Layer 5

    C. Layer 6

    D. Layer 7

12. Which of the following network topologies provides a redundant path for communication?

    A. Fiber-optic

    B. Star

    C. Ring

    D. Bus

13. What is the purpose of the Address Resolution Protocol (ARP)?

   A. Find the IP address.

   B. Find the mailing address.

   C. Find the MAC address.

   D. Find the domain name.

14. What is the security issue regarding packet analyzers?

   A. Viewing passwords

   B. Special training

   C. Purchase cost

   D. Only for auditor's use

15. Which of the following is an implementation of the demilitarized zone concept?

   A. Dedicated processor and a multiprocessor system

   B. Screened subnet

   C. Bastion host on the network

   D. Dedicated subnet for internal users

16. Which of the following protocols is likely to be used for monitoring the health of the network?

   A. OSI

   B. SNMP

   C. SMTP

   D. RIP

17. What does the designation of N-1 best represent?

   A. Need for additional equipment

   B. Number of routers

   C. Meshed network

   D. Number of links

18. What is the difference between a router and a switch?

   A. Both operate at layer 2; the router routes traffic, and the switch connects various users to the network.

   B. Both operate at layer 3; the router routes traffic, and the switch connects various users to the network.

   C. They operate at OSI layer 3 and layer 2, respectively.

   D. They operate at OSI layer 2 and layer 3, respectively.

19. Which type of network cabling is relatively immune to interference, difficult to tap, and can run extended distances?

    A. Coaxial

    B. Shielded twisted-pair

    C. Unshielded twisted-pair

    D. Fiber-optic

20. Which type of memory is used to permanently record programs on solid-state chips and retains the data even after power is turned off?

    A. Random access memory

    B. Read-only memory

    C. Flash memory

    D. Optical memory

Answers to Review Questions

1. A. RAID level 0 improves performance and can provide large logical drives but it does not increase redundancy. It is often used in combination with other levels to improve performance and redundancy. The purpose of RAID 0 is to combine multiple disks into one giant virtual disk.

2. B. The function of network routers is to route IP packets throughout the network or the Internet. The router does not know the entire route to the destination. The router holds a routing table that simply provides the address of the next point down the path to the destination. Network routing is like a game of connect-the-dots. The data must travel sequentially from one router to the next router until it reaches the intended destination.

3. C. Multicasting is used to transmit packets to multiple systems simultaneously but does not transmit to all systems. It is often used to transmit video across the network. Broadcasting is used when transmitting to all systems. Unicasting is transmitting packets to a single destination system only.

4. C. The 48-bit MAC address is manufactured into network equipment. Often, it is possible to override by using configuration tools. In a local area network, a 32-bit IP address is used for routing.

5. B. An extranet allows certain people limited access to corporate network services. An intranet is an internal corporate network. Access net is made up.

6. B. It helps to remember the memory tool, "Please Do Not Throw Sausage Pizza Away."

7. C. The most popular media is UTP, or unshielded twisted-pair. STP, or shielded twisted-pair, is more resistant to electronic noise and may be used in a shop environment. Coaxial cable is no longer used for connecting workstations. Fiber-optic cable is often used for interconnecting servers.

8. A. Internet Protocol (IP) is the major routable protocol. Transmission Control Protocol (TCP) is used on top of IP to provide reliable sessions. User Datagram Protocol (UDP) is connectionless without delivery confirmation. NetBIOS is not a routable protocol. The OSI model is used to explain network communications.

9. C. A router can be configured as a simple packet-filtering firewall by using an access control list. Packets are filtered based on the source address, destination address, and type of service. The problem is that packet filters have poor logging and the filter rules may be too broad to be effective. Packet filters do not support complex rules using if-then statements.

10. D. The third layer of the OSI model is the Network layer. Use the memory tool of "Nor Do I Throw Apples" to remember the layers of the TCP/IP model. The third layer of the TCP/IP model is the Internet layer.

11. D. According to ISACA, the gateway operates at application layer 7 in the OSI model. The function of the gateway is to convert data contained in one protocol into data used by a different protocol. An example is an SNA PC-to-mainframe gateway converting ASCII to mainframe Extended Binary Coded Decimal Interchange Code (EBCDIC).

12. C. The ring topology provides two paths for communication. If the ring is damaged, the data can be transmitted in the other direction through the undamaged segment. The most common implementation of a ring topology is IBM token ring and looped fiber-optic rings used by the telephone company to connect the central office wiring centers.

13. C. The Address Resolution Protocol (ARP) is used when you have an IP address and need to find the MAC address. Reverse ARP (RARP) is used going in the other direction, when you have a MAC address that needs the IP.

14. A. Network protocol analyzers, also known as sniffers, can view clear text passwords being transmitted across the network. The sniffer can decode packets being transmitted and is useful for troubleshooting network protocol problems.

15. B. The screened subnet off of a firewall is also known as the demilitarized zone (DMZ). The DMZ concept is based on a military concept of providing a semiprotected transfer area. Data is relayed from the DMZ to external users. Data is also transferred from the DMZ to internal users by some method to ensure data integrity.

16. B. The Simple Network Management Protocol (SNMP) is frequently used to monitor the health of the network in conjunction with a Network Management System (NMS) such as HP Open-View. The security of the SNMP configuration on each device can be a concern for the auditor. SNMP can be used in a malicious fashion to paint a picture of the network's design.

17. C. The N-1 designation is frequently used to represent a fully meshed network.

18. C. The network router operates at layer 3 for the purpose of directing traffic across the network to other subnets. The network switch operates at layer 2 to provide Data-Link services between the computers in the same subnet. A router connects different subnets.

19. D. Fiber-optic cable can transmit signals for several miles. The primary issue regarding fiber optics is the cost and special handling to prevent damage. Fiber-optic cable can be tapped by using special tools and skills; however, the process is relatively difficult for most individuals.

20. B. Solid-state integrated circuits implementing read-only memory (ROM) will provide permanent storage of data, regardless of electrical power. ROM is programmed by burning electrical connections inside the intgrated cicuit (IC) chip. Optical memory is not a solid-state process. Flash memory can be erased and reprogrammed. Random access memory (RAM) is volatile and will be erased when power is turned off.

Chapter 5

Life Cycle Management

THE OBJECTIVE OF THIS CHAPTER IS TO ACQUAINT THE READER WITH THE FOLLOWING CONCEPTS:

- ✓ Understanding how to evaluate the business case for proposed system and feasibility to ensure alignment to business strategy

- ✓ Understanding the process of conducting the proper system feasibility and design analysis

- ✓ Understanding the process for developing systems and infrastructure requirements, acquisition, and development and testing to ensure it meets business objectives

- ✓ Understanding how to evaluate the readiness of systems for production use

- ✓ Understanding the purpose of post-implementation system reviews to relating to anticipated return on investment and proper implementation of controls

- ✓ Evaluating system retirement and disposal methods to ensure compliance with legal policies and procedures

In this chapter, you will study the methodology of best practices for software development. You will learn an overview of the preferred management techniques for designing, building, and maintaining custom computer software. This is referred to as the *System Development Life Cycle*.

When auditing software development, you will assess whether the prescribed project management, System Development Life Cycle, and change-management processes were followed. You are expected to evaluate the processes used in developing or acquiring software to ensure that the program deliverables meet organizational objectives.

We will discuss software design concepts and terminology that every CISA is expected to know for the CISA.

Governance in Software Development

Every organization strives to balance expenditures against revenue. The objective is to increase revenue and reduce operating costs. One of the most effective methods for reducing operating costs is to improve software automation.

Computer programs may be custom-built or purchased in an effort to improve automation. All business applications undergo a common process of needs analysis, functional design, software development, implementation, production use, and ongoing maintenance. In the end, every program will be replaced by a newer version, and the old version will be retired. This is what is referred to as the *life cycle*.

It is said that 80 percent of a business's functions are related to common clerical office administration tasks. The clerical functions are usually automated with commercial off-the-shelf software. Each organization does not need to custom-write software for word processing and spreadsheets, for example. These basic functions can be addressed through traditional software that is easily purchased on the open market. This type of commodity software requires little customization. The overall financial advantages will be small but useful. When purchasing prewritten software, an organization follows a slightly different model that focuses on selection rather than software design and development. Prewritten software follows a life cycle of needs analysis and selection, followed by implementation, which leads to production use and ongoing maintenance.

The remaining 20 percent of the business functions may be unique or require highly customized computer programs. This is the area of need addressed by custom-written computer software. The challenge is to ensure that the software actually fulfills the organization's strategic objectives.

Let's make sure that you understand the difference between a strategic system and a traditional system.

A *strategic system* fundamentally changes the way the organization conducts business or competes in the marketplace. A strategic system significantly improves overall business performance with results that can be measured by multiple indicators. These multiple indicators include measured performance increases and noticeable improvement on the organization's financial statement. An organization might, for example, successfully attain a dramatic increase in sales volume as a direct result of implementing a strategic system. The strategic system may create an entirely new sales channel to reach customers.

Auction software implemented and marketed by eBay is an example of a strategic system. The strategic software fundamentally changes the way an organization will be run. For a strategic system to be successfully implemented, management and users must be fully involved. Anything less than significant fundamental change with dramatic, measurable results would indicate that the software is a traditional system.

You should be aware that some software vendors will use claims of strategic value with obscure results to try to sell lesser products at higher profit margins. Your job is to determine whether the organizational objectives have been properly identified and met. Claims of improvement should be verifiable.

More *traditional systems* provide support functions aligned to fulfill the needs of an individual or department. Examples of traditional systems include general office productivity and departmental databases. The traditional system might provide 10 percent return on investment, whereas a strategic system might have a return of more than 10 times the investment.

Managing Software Quality

Controlling quality is an ongoing process of improving the yield of any effort. True quality is designed into a system from the beginning. In contrast, inspected quality is no more than a test after the fact. In this section, we will discuss models designed to promote software quality:

- Capacity Maturity Model (CMM)
- International Standards Model (Spice)

Let's review the Capability Maturity Model and introduce the related international standards.

Capability Maturity Model

As you may recall from Chapter 3, "IT Governance," the Software Engineering Institute's Capability Maturity Model (CMM) was developed to provide a strategy for determining the maturity of current processes and to identify the next steps required for improvement. Let's quickly review the five levels contained in this model:

Level 0 This level is implied but not always recognized. Zero indicates that nothing is getting done.

Level 1 = Initial Processes at this level are ad hoc and performed by individuals.

Level 2 = Repeatable These processes are documented and can be repeated.

Level 3 = Defined These are lessons learned and integrated into institutional processes.

Level 4 = Managed This level equates to quantitative management.

Level 5 = Optimized This is the highest level of control with continuous improvement.

International Organization for Standardization

A significant number of the best practices for quality in American manufacturing have been adopted by the International Organization for Standardization (ISO). The original works of Philip Crosby, W. Edwards Deming, and Joseph Juran focused on reducing manufacturing defects. Their original concepts have been expanded over the last 50 years to include almost all business processes. One of the functions of the ISO is to identify regional best practices and promote acceptance worldwide. The CMM is no different. ISO has modified the five levels of the CMM for international acceptance.

As a CISA, you should be interested in three of the ISO standards relating to software development.

ISO 15504: Variation of CMM

The ISO 15504 standard is a modified version of CMM. The changes were intended to clarify the different maturity levels. Notice that level zero is labeled as incomplete. Level 1 is renamed to indicate the process has been successfully performed. Level 2 is to indicate the process is managed. Level 3 shows the process is well established in the organization. Level 4 indicates the process output will be very predictable. Level 5 shows the process is under a continuous improvement program using statistical process control. Table 5.1 illustrates the minor variations between the CMM and the ISO 15504 standard, also known as *Spice*.

TABLE 5.1 CMM Compared to ISO 15504 (Spice)

CMM Levels	ISO 15504 Levels
0 = process did not occur yet	ISO level 0 = Incomplete
CMM level 1 = Initial	ISO level 1 = *Performed*
CMM level 2 = Repeatable	ISO level 2 = *Managed*

TABLE 5.1   CMM Compared to ISO 15504 (Spice) *(continued)*

CMM Levels	ISO 15504 Levels
CMM level 3 = Defined	ISO level 3 = *Established*
CMM level 4 = Managed	ISO level 4 = *Predictable*
CMM level 5 = Optimized	ISO level 5 = Optimized

The purpose of ISO 15504 is very similar to the purpose of the CMM. Notice how the terminology is different in the ISO version. Let's move on to a quick overview of two ISO quality-management standards.

ISO 9001: Quality Management

The ISO has promoted a series of quality practices that were previously known as ISO 9000, 9001, and 9002 for design, manufacturing, and service, respectively. These have now been combined into the single ISO 9001 reference. Many organizations have adopted this ISO standard to facilitate worldwide acceptance of their products in the marketplace. ISO compliance also brings the benefits of a better perception by investors. Compliance does not guarantee a better product, but it does provide additional assurances that an organization should be able to deliver a better product.

Within the ISO 9001 reference, you will find that a formally adopted quality manual is required by the ISO 9001:2000. The ISO 9001:2000 quality manual specifies detailed procedures for quality management by an organization. The same quality manual provides procedures for strong internal controls when working with vendors, including a formal vendor evaluation and selection process. To ensure quality, the ISO 9001:2000 mandates that personnel performing work shall be properly trained and managed to improve competency. Because an organization claiming ISO compliance is required to have a thoroughly written quality manual in place, an IS audit may request evidence demonstrating that the quality processes are actively used.

It's important to understand the naming convention of ISO standards. Names of ISO standards begin with the letters ISO, which are then followed by the standard's numeric number, a colon (:), and the year of implementation. You would read ISO 9001:2000 as ISO standard 9001 adopted in year 2000 (or updated in year 2000).

ISO 9126: Software Quality

ISO 9126 is a variation of ISO 9001. The ISO standard 9126-2:2003 explains how to apply international software quality metrics. This standard also defines requirements for evaluating software products and measuring specific quality aspects.

The six quality attributes are as follows:

- Functionality of the software processes

- Ease of use

- Reliability with consistent performance

- Efficiency of resources

- Portability between environments

- Maintainability with regard to making modifications

 You need to know the six major attributes contained in the ISO 9126 standard.

Once again, organizations claiming ISO compliance should be able to demonstrate active use of software metrics and supporting evidence for ISO 9126-2 compliance. You need to remember that no evidence equals no credit.

As a CISA, you should be prepared to identify the terminology used by the CMM and various ISO quality standards. Now that we've reviewed these standards, it is time to discuss the leadership role of management. We will begin with an overview of the steering committee.

Overview of Steering Committees

The steering committee should be involved in software decisions to provide guidance toward fulfillment of the organizational objectives. We have already discussed the basic design of a steering committee in Chapter 3.

As you may recall, the *steering committee* comprises executives and business unit managers. Their goal is to provide direction for aligning IT functions with current business objectives. Steering committees provide the advantage of increasing the attention of top management on IT. The most-effective committees hold regular meetings focusing on agenda items from the business objectives rather than IT objectives. Most effective decisions are obtained by mutual agreement of the committee rather than by directive. The steering committee increases awareness of IT functions, while providing an avenue for users to become more involved. In this chapter, we are focusing on the identification of business requirements as they relate to the choices made for computer software.

As a CISA, you should understand how the steering committee has developed the vision for software to fulfill the organization's business objectives. What was the thought process that led the steering committee to its decision? Two common methods are the use of critical success factors (CSFs) and a scenario approach to planning.

Identifying Critical Success Factors

A *critical success factor (CSF)* is something that must go right every time. To fail a CSF would be a showstopper. The process for identifying CSFs begins with each manager focusing on their current information needs. This thought process by the managers will help develop a current list of CSFs.

Some of the factors may be found in the specific industry or chosen business market. External influences—such as customer perception, current economy, pressure on profit margin, and the posturing of competitors—could be another source of factors. The organization's internal challenges can provide yet another useful source. These can include internal activities that require attention or are currently unacceptable.

As an IS auditor, you should remain aware that critical success factors are highly dependent on timing. Each CSF should be reexamined on a regular basis to determine whether it is still applicable or has changed.

Using the Scenario Approach

The *scenario approach* is driven by a series of "what if" questions. This technique challenges the planning assumptions by creating scenarios that combine events, trends, operational relationships, and environmental factors. A series of scenarios are created and discussed by the steering committee. The most likely scenario is selected for a planning exercise.

The major benefit of this approach is the discovery of assumptions that are no longer relevant. Rules based on old assumptions and past situations may no longer apply. The scenario approach also provides an opportunity to uncover the mindset of key decision-makers.

The role of the scenario is to identify the most important business objectives and CSFs. After some discussion, the scenario should reveal valuable information to be used in long-term plans. Remember, the goal is to align computer software with the strategic objectives of the organization, which we will look at next.

Aligning Software to Business Needs

As a CISA, you should understand the alignment of computer software to business needs. Information systems provide benefits by alignment and by impact. *Alignment* is the support of ongoing business operations. Changes created in the work methods and cost structure are referred to as *impact*.

Each organizational project will undergo a justification planning exercise. Management will need to determine if the project will generate a measurable return on investment. The purpose of this exercise is to ensure that the time, money, and resources are well spent. The basic business justification entails the following four items:

Establish the need   Business needs can be determined from internal and external sources. Internal needs can be developed by the steering committee and by interviewing division managers. Internal performance metrics are an excellent source of information. External sources include regulations, business contracts, and competitors.

Identify the work effort   The next step is to identify the people who can provide the desired results. Management's needs are explained to the different levels of personnel who perform the work. The end-to-end work process is diagrammed in a flowchart. Critical success factors are identified in the process flow. A project plan is created that estimates the scope of the work.

This may use traditional project management techniques in combination with the System Development Life Cycle.

Summarize the impact   The anticipated business impact can be presented by using quantitative and qualitative methods. It is more effective to convert qualitative statements into semi-quantitative measurements. Semi-quantitative measurements can be converted into a range scale of increased revenue by implementing the system or by cost savings. The CISA candidate should recall the discussion in Chapter 2 regarding the use of semi-quantitative measurement with a range scale similar to A, B, C and D school report card grades.

Present the benefits   Management will need to be sold on the value of the system. The benefits will typically entail promises of eliminating an existing problem, improving competitive position, reducing turnaround time, or improving customer relations.

In this chapter, we are focusing our discussions on computer software. The steering committee should be involved in decisions concerning software priorities and necessary functions. Each software objective should be tied to a specific business goal. The combined input will help facilitate a *buy* vs. *build* decision about computer software. Should the organization buy commercial software or have a custom program written? Let's consider the questions to ask in regard to making this decision. The list presented here is for illustration purposes; however, it is similar to the standard line of questions an auditor will ask:

- What are the specific business objectives to be attained by the software? Does a printed report exist?

- Is there a defined list of objectives?

- What are the quantitative and qualitative measurements to prove that the software actually fulfills the stated objectives?

- What internal controls will be necessary in the software?

- Is commercial software available to perform the desired function?

- What level of customization would be required?

- What mechanisms will be used to ensure the accuracy, confidentiality, timely processing, and proper authorization for transactions?

- What is the time frame for implementation?

- Should building the software be considered because of a high level of customization needed or the lack of available software?

- Are the resources available to build custom software?

- How will funding be obtained to pay for the proposed cost?

The steering committee should be prepared to answer each of these questions and use the information to select the best available option. Effective committees will participate in brainstorming workshops with representation from their respective functional areas. The goal is to solicit enough information to reach an intelligent decision. The final decision may be to buy software, build software, or create a hybrid of both.

Organizations may use the answers from the questions asked in conjunction with a written request to solicit offers from vendors. The process of inviting offers incorporates a statement of the current situation with a request for proposal (RFP). The term *RFP* is also related to an invitation to tender (ITT) or request for information (RFI).

RFI/RFP Process

The steering committee charters a project team to perform the administrative tasks necessary for an information request (RFI) or proposal request (RFP). The request is sent to a small number of prospective vendors or posted to the public, depending on the client's administrative operating procedure. An internal software development staff may provide their own proposal in accordance with the RFP or participate on the review team. A typical RFP will contain at least the following elements:

- Cover letter explaining the specific interest and instructions for responding to the RFP

- Overview of the objectives and time line for the review process

- Background information about the organization

- Detailed list of requirements including the organization's desired service level

- Questions to the vendor about their organization, expertise, support services, implementation services, training, and current clients

- Request of a cost estimate for the proposed configuration with details about the initial cost and all ongoing costs

- Request for a schedule of demonstrations and visit to the installation site of existing customers

The RFP project team works with the steering committee to formulate a fair and objective review process. The organization may consult ISO 9001:2000 and ISO 9126-2:2003 standards for guidance. The proposed software might be evaluated by using the CMM. In addition, the ISACA's control objectives for IT (CoBIT) provides valuable information to be considered when reviewing a vendor and their products.

As an IS auditor, you should remember that your goal is to be thorough, fair, and objective. Care should be given to ensure that the requirements and review do not grant favor toward a particular vendor. The reviews are actually a form of audit and should include the services of an internal or external IS auditor. It is essential that vendor claims are investigated to ensure that the software will fulfill the desired business objectives.

Reviewing Vendor Proposals

The systematic process of reviewing vendor proposals is a project unto itself. Each proposal has to be scrutinized to ensure compliance requirements identified in the original RFP documents provided to the vendor. You need to ask the following questions:

- Does the proposed system meet the organization's defined business requirements?

- Does the proposed system provide an advantage that our competitors will not have, or does the proposed system provide a commodity function similar to that of our competitors?

- What is the estimated implementation cost measured in total time and total resources?

- How can the proposed benefits be financially calculated? The cost of the system and the revenue it generates should be noticeable in the organization's financial statement. To calculate return on investment, the total cost of the system including manpower is divided by the cost savings (or revenue generated) identified as a line item in the profit and loss statement.

- What enhancements are required to meet the organization's objectives? Will major modifications be required?

- What is the level of support available from the vendor? Support includes implementation assistance, training, software update, system upgrade, emergency support, and maintenance support.

- Has a risk analysis been performed with consideration of the ability of the organization and/or vendor to achieve the intended goal?

- Can the vendor provide evidence of financial stability?

- Software escrow. Will the organization be able to obtain rights to the program source code if the vendor goes out of business? Escrow refers to placing original software programs and design documentation into the trust of a third party (similar to financial escrow). The original software is expected to remain in confidential storage. If the vendor ceases operation, the client may obtain full rights to the software and receive it from the escrow agent. A small number of vendors may agree to escrow the source code, whereas most would regard the original programs as an intellectual asset that can be resold to another vendor. Modern software licenses provide only for the right to benefit from the software's use, not software ownership.

One of the major problems in reviewing a vendor is the inability to get a firm commitment in writing for all issues that have been raised. There are major vendors that will respond to the RFP with a lowball offer that undercuts the minimum requirements. Their motive is to win by low bid and then overcharge the customer with expensive change orders to bring the implementation up to the customer's stated objective.

A CISA reviews the documentation of business needs and that of the proposed system. The objective is to ensure that the system is properly aligned to business requirements and contains the necessary internal controls.

Change Management

The accepted method of controlling changes to software is to use a Change Control Board (CCB). Members of the change control board include IT managers, quality control, user liaisons from the business units and internal auditors. A vice president, director, or senior manager will preside as the chairperson. The purpose of the board is to review all change requests before determining whether authorization should be granted. This fulfills the desired separation of duties. Change control review must include input from business users. Every request should be weighed to determine business need, required scope, level of risk, and preparations necessary to prevent failure.

You can refer to the client organization's policies concerning change control. You should be able to determine whether separation of duties is properly enforced. Every meeting should include a complete tracking of current activities and the minutes of the meetings. Approval should be a formal process. The ultimate goal is to prevent business interruption. This is performed by following the principles of version control, configuration management, and testing. We will discuss separation of duties will additional detail in Chapter 6, "IT Service Delivery."

Managing the Software Project

Let's move on to a discussion of the challenges in managing a software development project. In this section, you'll learn about the two main viewpoints for managing software development. You'll then take a closer look at the role of traditional project management in software development.

Choosing an Approach

There are two opposing viewpoints on managing software development: evolutionary and revolutionary.

The traditional viewpoint promotes *evolutionary* development. The evolutionary view is that the effort for writing software code and creating prototypes is only a small portion of software development. The most significant work effort occurs during the planning and design phase. The evolutionary approach works on the premise that the number one source of failures is a result of errors in planning and design. Evolutionary software may be released in *incremental stages* beginning with a selected module used in the architecture of the first release. Subsequent modules will be added to expand features and improve functionality. The program is not finished until all the increments are completed and assembled. The evolutionary development approach is designed to be integrated into traditional software life cycle management.

The opposing view is that a revolution is required for software development. The invention of advanced fourth-generation programming languages (4GL) empowers business users to develop their own software without the aid of a trained programmer. This approach is in stark contrast to the traditional view of developing specific requirements with detailed specifications before writing software. The *revolutionary* approach is based on the premise that business users should be allowed to experiment in an effort to generate software programs for their specific needs. The end user holds all the power of success or failure under this approach. The right person might produce useful results; however, the level of risk is substantially greater. The revolutionary approach is difficult to manage because it does not fit into traditional management techniques. Lack of internal controls and failure to obtain objectives are major concerns in the revolutionary development approach.

Real World Scenario

An Example of Evolutionary Development

The creation of this Study Guide began with the evolution of study objectives. A prototype outline was created. The outline was refined and later divided into chapters. Each chapter was written as a separate increment. Our technical editor and developmental editor provided independent review of every page. The results of the review were compared to the objectives. Deficiencies were identified for correction and then rechecked. Finally, the finished chapters were assembled to create a working draft. The draft was edited in two more iterations until the final edition was obtained. Each version of this Study Guide will be updated following a similar process until retirement.

The analogy to revolutionary development would be to tell a person to go write their own software. A tiny number of individuals would have the competence necessary to be successful.

Using Traditional Project Management

Evolutionary software development is managed through a combination of the *System Development Life Cycle (SDLC)* and traditional project management. We covered the basics of project management using the Project Management Institute (PMI) methodology in Chapter 1, "Secrets of a Successful IS Auditor." The SDLC methodology—which is discussed in detail in the following section—addresses the specific needs of software development, but still requires project management for the nondevelopment business management functions.

When using traditional project management, the advantages include Program Evaluation Review Technique (PERT) with a Critical Path Methodology (CPM). You will need to be aware of the two most common models used to illustrate a software development life cycle: the waterfall model and the spiral model.

Waterfall Model

Evolutionary software development is an iterative process of requirements, prototypes, and improvement. In the 1970s, Barry Boehm developed the famous waterfall diagram to illustrate the software development life cycle. A simplified version of the *waterfall model* used by ISACA is shown in Figure 5.1.

Based on the SDLC phases, this simplified model assumes that development in each phase will be completed before moving into the next phase. That assumption is not very realistic in the real world. Changes are discovered that regularly require portions of software to undergo redevelopment.

Boehm's original software life cycle model contained seven phases of development. Each of the original phases included validation testing with a backward loop returning to the previous phase. The backward loop provides for changes in requirements during development. Changes are cycled back to the appropriate phase and then regression-tested to ensure that the changes do not produce a negative consequence. Figure 5.2 shows Boehm's unadulterated model as it appeared in 1975 from the Institute of Electrical and Electronic Engineers (IEEE).

FIGURE 5.1   Simplified waterfall model

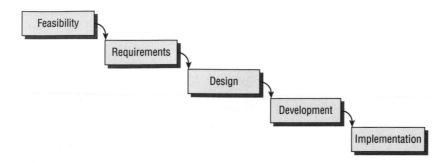

FIGURE 5.2   Original waterfall model

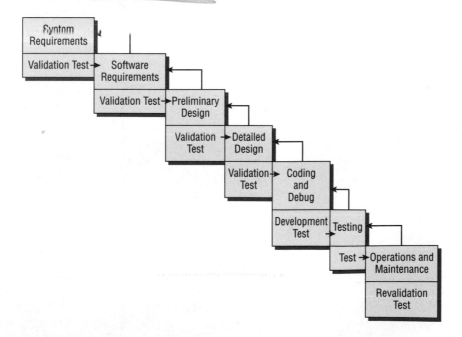

Spiral Model

About 12 years later, Boehm developed the *spiral model* to demonstrate the software life cycle including evolutionary versions of software. The original waterfall model implied management of one version of software from start to finish. This new spiral model provided a simple illustration of the life cycle that software will take in the development of subsequent versions. Each version of software will repeat the cycle of the previous version while adding enhancements. Figure 5.3 shows the cycle of software versions in the spiral model.

Notice how the first version starts in the planning quadrant of the lower left and proceeds through requirements into risk analysis and then to software development. After the software is written, we have our first version of the program. The planning cycle will commence for the second version, following the same path through requirements, risk analysis, and development. The circular process will continue for as long as the program is maintained.

Overview of the System Development Life Cycle

All computer software programs undergo a life cycle of transformation during the journey from inception to retirement. The System Development Life Cycle (SDLC) used by ISACA is designed as a general blueprint for the entire life cycle. A client organization may insert additional steps in their methodology This SDLC model comprises six unique phases (see Figure 5.4).

FIGURE 5.3   Spiral model for software life cycle

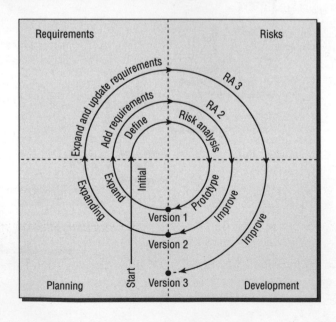

FIGURE 5.4   Six phases of SDLC

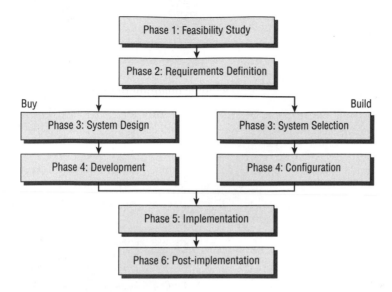

Let's start with a simple overview of SDLC:

Phase 1: Feasibility Study   This phase focuses on determining the strategic benefits that the new system would generate. Benefits can be financial or operational. A cost estimate is compared to the anticipated payback schedule. Maturity of the business process and personnel capabilities should be factored into the decision.

Phase 2: Requirements Definition   The steering committee creates a detailed definition of needs. We discussed this topic a few pages ago. The objective is to define inputs, outputs, current environment, and proposed interaction. The system user should participate in the discussion of requirements.

Phase 3: System Design or Selection   The client moves in one of two possible directions based on whether the decision is to build or to buy:

> **Build (Design)**   It was decided that the best option is to build a custom software program. This decision is usually reached when a high degree of customization is required. Efforts focus on creating detailed specifications of internal system design. Program interfaces are identified. Database specifications are created by using entity-relationship diagrams (ERDs). Flowcharts are developed to document the business logic portion of design.

> **Buy (Selection)**   The decision is to buy a commercial software program. The RFP process is used to select the best vendor and product available.

Phase 4: Development or Configuration   The client continues down one of two possible directions based on the earlier decision of build vs. buy:

Build (Development)   The design specifications, ERD, and flowcharts from phase 3 will become the master plan for writing the software. Programmers are busy writing the individual lines of program code. Component modules of software will be written, tested, and submitted for user approval.

Buy (Configuration)   Customization is typically limited to program configuration settings with a limited number of customized reports. The selection process for customization choices should be a formal project.

Phase 5: Implementation   This phase is common to both buy and build decisions. The new software is installed using the proposed production configuration. Final user acceptance testing begins. The system undergoes a process of certification and accreditation prior to approval for production use. The approved implementation begins production use.

Phase 6: Post-implementation   After the system has been in production use, it is reviewed for its effectiveness to fulfill the original objectives. The implementation of internal controls is also reviewed. System deficiencies are identified. The last step is to perform a return on investment (ROI) calculation comparing cost to the actual benefits received.

Do not confuse the SDLC with the Capability Maturity Model (CMM). A system life cycle covers the aspects of selecting requirements, designing, and installing software. The CMM focuses on metrics of maturity for software and for increasing maturity of IT governance controls.

Now that you have a general understanding of the SDLC model, we will discuss the specific methods used in each phase. These methods are designed to accomplish the stated SDLC objectives.

Phase 1: Feasibility Study

The *Feasibility Study phase* begins with the initial concept of engineering. In this phase, an attempt is made to determine a clearly defined need and the strategic benefits of the proposed system. A business case is developed based on initial estimates of time, cost, and resources. To be successful, the feasibility study will combine traditional project management with software development cost estimates. The most common model for estimating software development cost is the constructive cost model, which uses an estimated count of lines of program code and Function Point Analysis. Let's begin with the constructive cost model.

Software Cost Estimation

The *Constructive Cost Model (COCOMO)* was developed by Barry Boehm in 1981. This forecasting model provides a method for estimating the effort, schedule, and cost of developing a new software application. The original version is obsolete because of evolution changes in software development. COCOMO was replaced with COCOMO II in 1995.

The COCOMO II model provides a solid method for performing "what if" calculations that will show the effect of changes on the resources, schedule, staffing, and predicted cost.

The COCOMO II model deals specifically with software programming activities but does not provide a definition of requirements. You must compile your requirements before you can use either COCOMO model. COCOMO II templates are available on the Internet to run in Microsoft Excel.

The COCOMO II model permits the use of three internal submodels for the estimations: Application Composition, Early Design, or Post Architecture. Within the three internal submodels, the estimator can base their forecast on a count of Source Lines of Code or Function Point Analysis.

Source Lines Of Code (SLOC) forecasts estimates by counting the individual lines of program source code regardless of the embedded design quality. This method has been widely used for more than 40 years and is still used despite advances with 4GL programming tools. It is important for you to understand that counting lines of code will not measure efficiency. The most efficient program could have fewer lines of code, and less-efficient software could have more lines. Having a program with few lines of program code typically indicates that the finished software will run faster. Smaller programs also have the advantage of being easier to debug.

Function Point Analysis (FPA) is a structured method for classifying the required components of a software program. FPA was designed to overcome shortfalls in the SLOC method of counting lines in programs. The FPA method (see Figure 5.5) divides all program functions into five classes:

- External input data from users and other applications
- External output to users, reports, and other applications
- External inquiries from users and other applications
- Internal file structure defining where data is stored inside the database
- External interface files defining how and where data can be logically accessed

FIGURE 5.5   Concept overview of Function Point Analysis

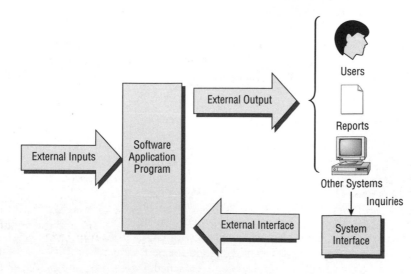

The five classes of data are assigned a complexity ranking of low, average, or high. The ranking is multiplied by a numerical factor and tallied to achieve an estimate of work required (see Figure 5.6).

FIGURE 5.6   Calculating function points

Function Class	Complexity Ranking						
	LOW		MEDIUM		HIGH		Adjusted Weight
Counts per	Count	Multiplier	Count	Multiplier	Count	Multiplier	
External inputs	____	X 3 =____	____	X 4 =____	____	X 5 =____	
External outputs	____	X 4 =____	____	X 5 =____	____	X 6 =____	
External inquiries	____	X 3 =____	____	X 4 =____	____	X 5 =____	
Internal files	____	X 7 =____	____	X 9 =____	____	X 12 =____	
External interfaces	____	X 5 =____	____	X 7 =____	____	X 9 =____	
						Total Adjusted Value =	

FPA is designed for an experienced and well-educated person who possesses a strong understanding of functional perspectives. Typically this is a senior-level programmer. An inexperienced person will get a false estimate. This model is intended for counting features that are specified in the early design. It will not create the initial definition of requirements. Progress can be monitored against the function point estimate to assess the level of completion. Changes can be recorded to monitor scope creep. Scope creep refers to the constant changes and additions that can occur during the project. Scope creep may indicate a lack of focus, poor communication, lack of discipline, or an attempt to distract the user from the project team's inability to deliver to the original project requirements.

You should acquire formal training and consult a Functional Point Analysis training manual if you are ever asked to perform FPA.

The overall cost budget should include an analysis of the estimated personnel hours by function. The functions include clerical duties, administrative processes, analysis time, software development, equipment, testing, data conversion, training, implementation, and ongoing support.

Phase 1 Review and Approval

Best practices in software development require a review meeting at the end of each phase to determine whether the project should continue to the next phase. The review is attended by an executive chairperson, project sponsor, project manager, and the suppliers of key deliverables.

The meeting is opened by the chairperson. The project manager provides an overview of the business case and presents the initial assessment reports. Presentations are made to convey the results of risk management analysis for the project. Project plans and the initial budget are presented for approval. Meeting attendees review the phase 1 plans to ensure that the skills and resource requirements are clearly understood.

Real World Scenario

Getting a Fair Estimate with SLOC and FPA

Estimation of software projects by using either the SLOC or FPA method will render an incorrect estimate if you are using multiple levels of programming languages such as 3GL and 4GL. It is important to mention that programmers refer to each programming language generation as a unique level (third generation equals third level, fourth generation equals fourth level, and so on). We will discuss the different levels of programming languages later in this chapter, in the subsection "Writing Program Code." As an auditor, you should simply be aware that the issue does exist and will have a negative effect on the accuracy of an estimate. Each generation level of programming language used will have to be estimated separately to achieve reasonable accuracy.

At the end of the phase review meeting, the chairperson determines whether the review has passed or failed based on the evidence presented. In the real world, a third option may exist: deciding that the project should be placed on temporary hold and reassessed at a future date. All outstanding issues must be resolved before granting approval to pass the phase review.

Auditor Interests in the Feasibility Phase

In the Feasibility Study phase, you should review the documentation related to the initial needs analysis. As an auditor, you would review the risk mitigation strategy. You would ask whether an existing system could have provided an alternative solution. The organization's business case and cost justifications would be verified to determine whether their chosen solution was a reasonable decision. You would also verify that the project received formal management before proceeding into the next phase.

Phase 2: Requirements Definition

The *Requirements Definition phase* is a documentation process focused on discovering the proposed system's business requirements. Defining the requirements requires a broader approach than the initial feasibility study. It is necessary to develop a list of specific conditions in which the system is expected to operate. Criteria need to be developed to specify the input and output requirements along with the system boundaries.

In this phase of gathering detailed requirements, the entity-relationship diagram (ERD) technique is often used. The ERD helps define high-level relationships corresponding to a person, data element, or concept that the organization is interested in implementing. ERDs contain two basic components: the entity and the relationship between entities.

An *entity* can be visualized as a database comprising reports, index cards, or anything that contains the data to be used in the design. Each entity has specific attributes that relate to another entity. Figure 5.7 shows the basic design of an ERD.

FIGURE 5.7   Entity-relationship diagram

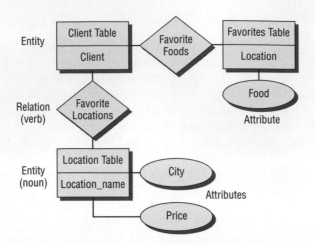

It is a common practice to focus first on defining the data that will be used in the program. This is because the data requirement is relatively stable. The purpose of the ERD exercise is to design the data dictionary. The *data dictionary* provides a standardized term of reference for each piece of data in the database. After the data dictionary is developed, it will be possible to design a database schema. The *database schema* represents an orderly structure of all data stored in the database.

After the ERD is complete, it is time to begin construction of transformation procedures used to manipulate the data. The transformation procedures detail how data will be acquired and logically transformed by the application into usable information. High-level flowcharts define portions of the required business logic. A low-level flowchart illustrates the details of the transformation process from beginning to end. The flowchart concept will map each program process, decision choice, and handling of the desired result. The flowchart is a true blueprint of the business logic used in the program. Figure 5.8 shows a simple program flowchart.

The ERD and flowcharts from phase 2 provide the foundation for the system design in SDLC phase 3. Security controls are added into the design requirement during phase 2. You should understand that internal controls are necessary in all software designs.

The internal controls for user account management functions are included in this phase to provide for separation of duties. *Preventative controls* such as data encryption and unique user logins are specified. *Detective controls* for audit trails and embedded audit modules are added. *Corrective controls* for data integrity are included. Features that are not listed in the requirements phase will most likely be left out of the design.

It is important that the requirements are properly verified and supported by a genuine need. Each requirement should be traced back to a source document detailing the actions necessary for performance of work or legal compliance.

A gap analysis is used to determine the difference between the current environment and the proposed system. Plans need to be created to address the deficiencies that are identified in the gap analysis. The deficiencies may include personnel, resources, equipment, or training.

FIGURE 5.8   Program flowchart

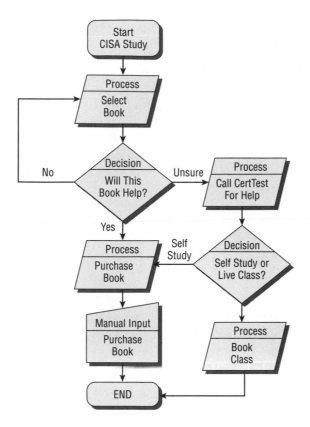

Phase 2 Review and Approval

At the end of phase 2, a phase 2 review meeting is held. This meeting is similar in purpose to the previous phase 1 review. This time, the second phase review focuses on success criteria in the definition of software deliverables and include a timeline forecast with date commitments. The proposed system users need to submit their final feedback assessment and comments before approval is granted to proceed into phase 3. The purpose of the phase 2 review meeting is to gain the authority to proceed with preliminary software design (phase 3). Once again, all outstanding issues need to be resolved before approval can be granted to proceed to the next phase.

Auditor Interests in the Requirements Definition Phase

You should obtain a list of detailed requirements. The accuracy of the requirements can be verified by a combination of desktop review of documentation and interviews with appropriate personnel. Conceptual ERD and flowchart diagrams should be reviewed to ensure that they address the needs of the user.

The Requirements Definition phase creates an output of detailed success factors to be incorporated in the acceptance test specifications. As an auditor, you will verify that the project and estimated costs have received proper management approval.

Phase 3: System Design

The System Design phase expands on the ERD and initial concept flowcharts. Users of the system provided a great deal of input during phase 2, which is then used in this phase for in-depth flowcharting of the logic for the entire system. The general system blueprint is decompiled into smaller program modules.

Internal software controls are included in the design to ensure a separation of duties within the application. The work breakdown structure is created for effective allocation of resources during development. The initial plans for developing a prototype in phase 4 are created during the System Design phase.

Reverse Engineering and Reengineering

In certain situations, *reverse engineering* may be used to accelerate the creation of a working system design.

> The 2003 movie *Paycheck* starring Ben Affleck was themed around reverse engineering a competitor's product to jumpstart employer's development of their own product.

Reverse engineering is a touchy subject. A software decompiler will convert programs from machine language to a human readable format. The majority of software license agreements prohibit the decompiling of software in an effort to protect the vendor's intellectual design secrets.

An existing system may loop back into phase 3 for the purpose of *reengineering*. The intention would be to update the software by reusing as many of the components as is feasible. Depending on the situation, reengineering may support major changes to upgrade the software for newer requirements.

Software Design Baseline

At the end of the System Design phase, a *software baseline* is created from the design documents. The baseline incorporates all the agreed-upon features that will be implemented in the initial version of software (or next version in the case of reengineering). This baseline is used to gain approval for a design freeze. The design freeze is intended to lock out any additional changes that could lead to scope creep.

Phase 3 Review and Approval

The phase 3 review meeting starts with a review of the detailed design for the proposed system. Engineering plans and project management plans are reviewed. Cost estimates are compared to the assumptions made in the business case. A comparison is made between the intended features and final design. Final system specifications, user interface, operational support plan, and test and verification plans are checked for completeness. Data from the risk analysis undergoes a review based on evidence. Approval is requested to proceed to the next phase. Once again, all outstanding issues must be resolved before proceeding to the next phase.

Auditor Interests in the System Design Phase

You need to review the software baseline and design flowcharts. The design integrity of each data transaction should be verified. During the design review, you verify that processing and output controls are incorporated into the system. Input from the system's intended power users may provide insight into the effectiveness of the design.

It is important that the needs of the power users are implemented during the design phase. This may include special functions, screen layout, and report layout. You should have a particular interest in the logging of system transactions for traceability to a particular user. You look for evidence that a quality control process is in use during the software design activities. It is important to verify that formal management approval was granted to proceed to the next phase.

Phase 4: Development

Now the time has come to start writing actual software in the *Development phase*. This process is commonly referred to as *coding* a program. Design planning from previous phases serves as the blueprint for software coding. The systems analysts support programmers with ideas and observations. The bulk of the work is the responsibility of the programmer who is tasked with writing software code.

Implementing Programming Standards and Quality Control

Standards and quality control are extremely important during the Development phase. A talented programmer can resolve minor discrepancies in the naming conventions, data dictionary, and program logic. Computer software programs will become highly convoluted unless the programmer imposes a well-organized structure during code writing. Unstructured software coding is referred to as *spaghetti bowl programming*, making reference to a disorganized tangle of instructions.

The preferred method of organizing software is to implement a top-down structure. *Top-down structured programming* divides the software design into distinct modules. If top-down program structures were diagrammed, the result would look like an inverted tree. Within the tree, individual program modules (or subroutines) perform a unique function. Modules are logically chained together to form the finished software program. The modular design exponentially improves maintainability of the finished program. Individual modules can be updated and replaced with relative ease. By comparison, an unstructured spaghetti bowl program would be a nightmare to modify. Modular design also permits the delegation of modules to different teams of programmers. Each module can be individually tested prior to final assembly of the finished program.

Adhering to the Development Schedule

The software project needs to be managed to ensure adherence to the planned schedule. Scope creep with unforeseen changes can have a devastating impact on any project. It is common practice to allow up to a 10 percent variance in project cost and time estimates.

The development project will be required to undergo *management oversight review* if major changes occur in assumptions, requirements, or methodology. Management oversight review would also be warranted if the total program benefits or cost are anticipated to deviate by more than 10 percent. The project schedule needs to be tightly managed to be successful. The change control process should be implemented to ensure that necessary changes are properly incorporated into the software development phase.

A *version control* system is required to track progress with all of the minor changes that naturally occur daily during development.

Writing Program Code

The effort to write program code depends on the programming language and development tool selected. Examples of languages include Common Business Oriented Language (COBOL), C language, Java, and the Beginner's All-purpose Symbolic Instruction Code (BASIC). The choice of programming languages is often predetermined by the organization. If the last 20 years' worth of software was developed using COBOL, it might make sense to continue using COBOL.

Understanding Generations of Programming Languages

Computer programming languages have evolved dramatically over the last 50 years. The early programming languages were cryptic and cumbersome write. This is where the term *software coding* originated. Each generation of software became easier for a human being to use. Let's walk through a quick overview of the five generations of computer programming languages:

First-generation programming language   The first-generation computer programming language is machine language. *Machine language* is written as hardware instructions that are easily read by a computer, but illegible to most human beings. First-generation programming is very time-consuming but was useful enough to give the computer industry a starting point. The first generation is also known as 1GL. In the early 1950s, 1GL programming was the standard.

Second-generation programming language   The second generation of computer programming is known as *assembly language*, or 2GL. Programming in assembly language can be tedious but is a dramatic improvement over 1GL programming. In the late 1950s, 2GL programming was the standard.

Third-generation programming language   During the 1960s, the third generation (3GL) of programming languages began to make an impact. The third generation uses English-like statements as commands within the program, for example, IF THEN and GOTO. Examples of third-generation program languages include COBOL, Fortran, BASIC. Another example is the C programming language written by Ken Thompson and Dennis Ritchie. Most 3GL programs were used with manually written databases.

Fourth-generation programming language   During the late 1970s, the fourth-generation programming languages (4GL) began to emerge. The fourth-generation programming languages included prewritten database utilities. This advancement allowed for rapid development due to an embedded database or database interface. The fourth-generation design is a true revolution in computer programming. An untrained user could write a program that merely formats reports on a screen and allows a software generation utility to write the software automatically.

A 4GL is designed to automate reports and the storage of data in a database. Unfortunately, it will not create the necessary business logic without the aid of a skilled programmer. An amateur using a 4GL can generate nice-looking form screens and databases. But the amateur's program will be no more than a series of buckets holding data files. The skilled programmer will be required to write transformation procedures (program logic) that turn those buckets of data into useful information. Examples of commercial 4GL development tools include Sybase's PowerBuilder, computer-aided software engineering (CASE) tools, and YesSoftware's Code-Charge. 4GL is the current standard for software development.

Fifth-generation programming language   The fifth-generation programming languages (5GLs) are designed for artificial intelligence applications. The 5GL is characterized as a learning system that uses fuzzy logic or neural weighing algorithms to render a decision based on likelihood. Google searches on the Internet use a similar design to assess the relevance of search results.

Figure 5.9 shows the hierarchy of the different generations of programming languages.

FIGURE 5.9   Generation levels of programming languages

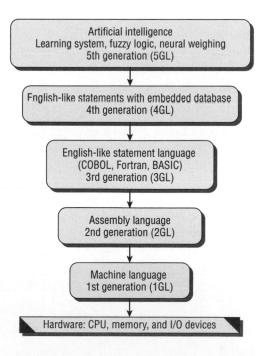

Using Integrated Development Environment Tools

After the programming language has been selected, the next step is to choose the development tool. There are still some programmers able to sit down and write code manually by using the knowledge contained in their head. This type of old-school approach will usually create very efficient programs with the smallest number of program lines.

The majority of programmers will use an advanced fourth-generation software code program to write the actual program instructions. This advanced software enables the programmer to focus on drawing higher-level logic while the computer program creates the lower-level set of instructions similar to what a manual programmer would have done. Simply put, a computer program will write the computer program.

The better development tools will provide an integrated environment of design, code creation, and debugging. This type of development tool is referred to as an *integrated development environment (IDE)*.

One of the best examples of an IDE is the commercial CASE tool software. You need to understand the basic principles behind CASE tools. CASE tools are divided into three functional categories that support the SDLC phases of 2, 3, and 4, respectively:

Upper CASE tools   Business and application requirements can be documented by using upper CASE tools. This provides support for the SDLC phase 2 requirements definition. Upper CASE tools permit the creation of ERD relationships and logical flowcharts.

Middle CASE tools   The middle CASE tools support detailed design from the SDLC phase 3. These tools aid the programmer in designing data objects, logical process flows, database structure, and screen and report layouts.

Lower CASE tools   The lower CASE tools are software code generators that use information from upper and middle CASE to write the actual program code.

Using Alternative Development Techniques

As a CISA, you should be aware of two alternative software development methods: Agile and Rapid Application Development (RAD). Each offers the opportunity to accelerate software creation during the Development phase. The client may want to use either of these methods in place of more traditional development. Both offer distinct advantages for particular situations. Both also contain drawbacks that should be considered.

Agile Development Method

Agile uses a fourth-generation development environment to quickly develop prototypes within a specific time window. The Agile method uses time-box management techniques to force individual iterations of a prototype within a very short time span. Agile allows the programmer to just start writing a program without spending much time on preplanning documentation. The drawback of Agile is that it does not promote management of the requirements baseline. Agile does not enforce preplanning. Some programmers prefer Agile simply because they do not want to be involved in tedious planning exercises.

When properly combined with traditional planning techniques, Agile development can accelerate software creation. Agile is designed exclusively for use by small teams of talented programmers. Larger groups of programmers can be broken into smaller teams dedicated to individual program modules.

> The primary concept in Agile programming is to place greater reliance on the undocumented knowledge contained in a person's head. This is in direct opposition to capturing knowledge through project documentation.

Rapid Application Development Method

A newer integrated software development methodology is *Rapid Application Development (RAD),* which uses a fourth-generation programming language. RAD has been in existence for almost 20 years. It automates major portions of the software programmer's responsibilities within the SDLC.

RAD supports the analysis portion of SDLC phase 2, phase 3, phase 4, and phase 5. Unfortunately, RAD does not support aspects of phase 1 or phase 2 that are necessary for the needs of a major enterprise business application. RAD is a powerful development tool when coupled with traditional project management in the SDLC.

Building Prototypes

During the Development phase, it is customary to create system prototypes. A *prototype* is a small-scale working system used to test assumptions. These assumptions may be about user requirements, program design, or the internal logic used in critical functions. Prototypes usually are inexpensive to build and are created over a few days or weeks. The principal advantage of a prototype is that it permits change to occur before the major development effort begins. However, there is always a concern that a working prototype may be rushed into production before it is ready for a production environment.

Prototypes seldom have any internal control mechanisms. Each prototype is created as an iterative process, and the lessons learned are used for the next version. A successful prototype will fulfill its mission objective and validate the program logic. All development efforts will focus on the production version of the program after the prototype has proven successful.

Compiling Software Programs

A computer program can be written as either a program script or a compiled program. *Program scripts* are written like movie scripts and contain instructions for the computer to follow. The programmer uses a scripting language such as Perl, JavaScript, or Microsoft's Visual Basic. The advantage of scripts is that they are easy to maintain. The program script is stored in human-readable form. The disadvantage is that program scripts run by using a script interpreter. The script interpreter is slow to execute. A script interpreter compiles a temporary version of the scripted program as it is running on the computer. The scripted program is considered a crystal box, or white box, because a trained human being could read the program script and decipher the structural design of the program.

Compiling programs is a process of converting human-readable instructions into machine-language instructions for execution. The human-readable version of software is referred to as *source code.* A computer programmer will compile programs to increase the execution speed of the software. A simple way to remember the definition is that source code is what the compiler started with. The compiled program is unreadable to humans. This unreadable version of the program is referred to as the *object code.*

Think of object code as the output object created by the compiler. Compiling software provides rudimentary protection of the program's internal logic from inquisitive people. The disadvantage of compiled programs is that reviewing the internal structural design would be practically impossible. The compiled program is essentially a black box. Figure 5.10 shows the different creation paths for compiled programs and program scripts.

FIGURE 5.10 Compiled programs vs. scripts

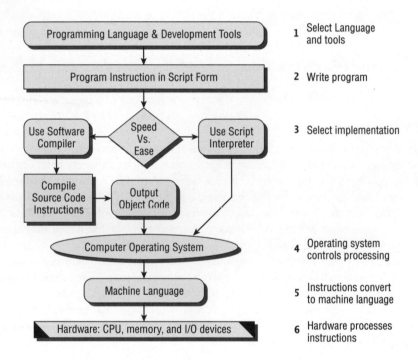

Computer programmers will usually compile multiple versions of a program during development and debug testing. Without proper management, this scenario could become a nightmare. How do you ensure that the latest copy is in use? It is the job of configuration and version management to provide a traceable history of multiple versions of computer software.

Implementing Configuration and Version Management

Managing a changing environment is a significant challenge. Constant changes make it difficult to remain organized and coordinated, no matter what you're trying to accomplish. But suppose, for example, that a company wants to release a new software product.

During software development, multiple programmers may be working on different modules of the same program. For this example, let's name the program *Report Whiz*. The programming used in the individual modules for Report Whiz may have different levels of maturity to consider. For example, the screen printing utility might be in version 1.1, while the report writer module may be in version 6.0. By combining these two modules into Report Whiz, the result will become our finished configuration for Report Whiz version 1.0. Does it sound like this could get confusing?

Well, it can. That is the challenge. How will the company manage and track all these different components with the correct versions?

Version control is the tracking of all the tiny details inside of both major and minor version changes. By tracking these tiny details, we can understand the internal construction of our finished software configuration. Detailed version control is the foundation of *configuration*. With version control, we have a detailed configuration that is ready to be managed.

Configuration management is focused on management exercising control over the finished software version. You should understand how the client manages and records changes to a configuration. After obtaining this understanding, you need to ask who authorizes the changes. Finally, you need to ask how the changes are tested and accepted for production use.

Fortunately, there are software tools to assist software developers in managing version control. One of the most common commercial applications for tracking version changes is known as a Poly Version Control System (PVCS). PVCS software contains a database that manages the tracking of programming changes and revisions of software code. In industry slang, we may refer to the PVCS function as a *Top Copy* or *Latest Copy* system. The purpose of PVCS is to ensure that each programmer is working with the latest version of the software program code. During the day, the programmer checks out the latest copy of the program code from the PVCS database. The check out process is similar to the checkout of books from your local library. The PVCS database is designed to synchronize the work of every programmer. A programmer checks out the latest software version and then uses that version to start writing program code. Each day the programmer returns their finished work to the PVCS controlled library by using a check-in process. During check-in, the PVCS database informs the programmer with a list of any related changes made by the other programmers. This provides coordination for the team of programmers.

 Real World Scenario

Automated Version Control Tools

Version control software is available from multiple vendors. In addition to the commercial Poly Version Control System (PVCS), other common software options include the Source Code Control System (SCCS), the Concurrent Version System (CVS), and the Revision Control System (RCS). There are license versions that are free for noncommercial use. Version control software was written to track revision changes in lines of programming code. The usage has grown to include tracking for changes in server configuration, web pages, legal contracts, and complex printed documents.

Debugging Software

A vast assortment of errors naturally occur during the development process. These errors may include syntax errors, inconsistent naming structures, logic errors, and other common mistakes. Most online development tools will assist the programmer by debugging some of the errors. Using top-down structured programming techniques makes it easier to troubleshoot problems.

Testing the Software

During the Development phase, it is imperative that tests and verification plans are created to debug the software programs. Tests should be performed to validate processing accuracy. Test plans are created to uncover program flaws, manage defects, and search for unintended results. A *logic path monitor* can be used to provide programmers with information about errors in program logic.

During development, software testing occurs at multiple levels. Any deficiencies or errors need to be discovered before the finished program is implemented. There are four basic types of test methods:

White-box testing   Also known as *crystal-box testing* because it allows the user to view and test the logic of procedures and data calculations. The intention is to verify each transformation process as data passes through the system. This can be an expensive and time-consuming process. This testing is commonly used for unit and integrity testing of self-developed software. Legal obstacles concerning ownership and proprietary rights may be encountered when attempting to use this type of testing on commercial software.

Black-box testing   Intended to test the basic integrity of system processing. This is the most common type of test. The process is to put data through the system to see whether the results came out as expected. You do not get to see the internal logic structures; all you get is the output. Black-box testing is often used for user acceptance tests. This is the standard test process run when you buy commercial software.

Functional, or validation, testing   Compares the system against the desired functional requirements. We want to see whether the product has met our objectives for its intended use.

Regression testing   Tests changes against all the existing software models to detect any conflicts. The purpose of regression testing is to ensure that modifications do not damage existing processes. During regression testing, internal controls are retested for integrity.

All tests should follow a formal procedure in a separate testing environment. The following types of structured technical tests occur during the Development phase:

- Program module tests (unit test)
- Program interface tests (integration test)
- Internal security control tests
- Processing volume tests (stress test of maximum workload)
- Performance tests
- Integrity tests (processing accuracy)

- Recovery tests (verify data integrity after failures)
- Sociability tests (to determine whether the program will have conflicts with another program on the system)

The test plan and results of each test need to be carefully documented. In environments where strong controls are desired, archiving test records for future reference is necessary. After all the technical tests have been completed to satisfaction, it is time for the most important test of all. The last test in the Development phase is user acceptance testing. This is when the project sponsor makes the determination of whether to accept the system. If accepted, the system moves into the Implementation phase.

Phase 4 Review and Approval

Once again, a phase review meeting is held. The phase 4 review focuses on the software being delivered by the programmers for the users. The Development phase has now concluded. The finished software is compared for compliance against the original objectives, requirements list, and design specifications. Evidence is presented from test results, which should indicate that the software is performing as expected. Plans for ongoing operation are compared to the previous gap analysis to uncover any remaining deficiencies. After all outstanding issues have been resolved, the plan is put before the chairperson for approval to proceed to the Implementation phase.

Auditor Interests in the Development Phase

As an auditor, your prime interest in the Development phase is to verify that a quality control process has been utilized to develop an effective computer program. All internal control mechanisms should be present in the finished program. The programs have undergone debugging with formal testing. Evidence from test results is expected to provide assurance of system integrity. Support documentation has been created in conjunction with an operational support plan for production use. The finished software capabilities have been verified for compliance to the original objectives. The user has accepted the finished computer program. And finally, management has granted formal approval for the software to be implemented.

Phase 5: Implementation

The computer program is fully functional by the time it reaches phase 5. This phase focuses on final preparations for actual production use. The computer program is now a finished version ready for final acceptance testing and user training. The first step for implementation is to load the client's current data.

Data Conversion

A data conversion plan is developed to migrate existing data into the new system. Great care needs be taken to prevent loading garbage data into the new system. A successful technique to prevent loading garbage is to reload selected portions of shared data directly from the latest source file. An example is reloading a manufacturing kit list directly from the latest engineering design. This would eliminate the migration of outdated information into the new system.

A list of data files eligible for migration is developed. Each file is verified against the system design requirements. If the file is required, procedures would be created to scrub (remove) outdated entries from each file. It is a common practice to hire a data entry service to assist in data conversion. Sometimes it is easier to re-create a file with minimal data, as opposed to the tedious job of grooming existing files. The programmers may write a data conversion utility to reformat existing files, such as a customer list, into the new system. A comprehensive data conversion plan is always required.

System Certification

Certification is a technical process of testing against a known reference. The system is tested to ensure that all internal controls are present and functioning correctly. The system certification is based on measuring compliance to a particular requirement. Systems used in the government are required to undergo a certification process before being placed in production use. Internal control standards require business systems to undergo a similar certification process. Every computer system and application should undergo a certification process prior to use in a production environment.

You can find more information on system certification procedures in the US Federal Information Security Management Act (FISMA) guide available through www.nist.gov, in the ISACA control objectives for IT CoBIT, and by researching various regulations.

As a CISA, you will be required to undergo update and renewal training to keep your certification current. Existing information systems should also go through a recertification process to remain up-to-date. You should be concerned about systems that the customer has not certified for production, or systems for which the certification was not maintained and is now out of date.

System Accreditation

The next step after certification is *accreditation*. After passing the certification test, management determines how or where the system may be used. Accreditation is an administrative process based on management's comfort level with demonstrated performance or fitness of use (management acceptance). Management is responsible for accreditation of systems during the system's useful life cycle.

User Training

Now it is time to train the users and system operators. Hopefully, the organization had some of its power users actively involved in prior phases. The new system's power users were usually involved in the phase 2 design. If so, these power users can serve as instructors and mentors to the new system users. A user training plan is necessary to ensure that everyone receives appropriate training for their role. During the training process, each user should receive specific instructions on the new functions of the system. Care should be taken to explain which of the old procedures will no longer be used. The training plan needs to provide for ongoing training of new users.

Special training is required for the system custodians (system administrator, database administrator, and computer console operator). The custodians need to be trained for normal operations and emergency procedures unique to the system. After the people are trained, it is time to move the system into production use.

Go Live and Changeover

The new system has been running separately from production up to this point. A plan is necessary for switching production processing from the old system to the new system. This process is commonly described by the term *changeover*, *cut over*, or *go live*. The changeover can be a substantial challenge depending on the complexity of the environment. A comprehensive migration plan is required in order to be successful. It is imperative that risk management is used to select and sequence changeover plans.

You need to be aware of the following changeover techniques:

Parallel operation   The old and new systems are run in parallel, usually for an extended period of time. Dual operation allows time to compare the operational differences between the two systems. During parallel operation, software developers can fine-tune any software discrepancies. The primary advantage of parallel operation is the ability to validate the results obtained from the new system against the accuracy of the old system. With parallel operation comes the added burden of simultaneously supporting two major systems. At a future date, the old system will be brought to an idle state while the new system takes over all production processing. Depending on data retention requirements, the field system may still need to be operational for a number of years. The switch from parallel operation to single operation may be performed by using a phase changeover or hard changeover.

> Overall parallel operation is an excellent technique with the lowest level of risk. Making changes in small doses is always advisable. Major failures during changeover can be a real career killer.

Phased changeover   In larger systems, converting to the new system in small steps or phases may be possible. This may take an extended period of time. The concept is best suited to either an upgrade of an existing system, or to the conversion of one department at a time. The phased approach creates a support burden similar to that of parallel operation. A well-managed phased changeover presents a moderate level of risk.

Hard changeover   In certain environments, executing an abrupt change to the new system may be necessary. This is known as a hard changeover, a full change occurring at a particular cutoff date and time. The purpose is to force migration of all the users at once. A hard changeover may be used after successful parallel operation or in times of emergency. One of the biggest concerns about a hard changeover is that it can cause major disruption of normal operations. For this reason, the hard changeover presents the highest level of risk. Risk mitigation activities are of the highest priority whenever the hard changeover technique is chosen.

Phase 5 Review and Approval

This is the last review meeting, and it is concerned with the implementation of a new system. The chairperson opens the meeting with the project sponsor present. The project manager makes a presentation of project updates and achievements. Progress is reported against the plan objectives. Attention then focuses on a review of outstanding engineering issues, system performance as realized in production use, and ongoing service and support plans. The final risk analysis is presented for management approval. After approval is obtained, the system is authorized for production use.

Auditor Interests in the Implementation Phase

The system should be installed and fully operational by the Implementation phase. Support documentation must be in place prior to the system entering production use. All of the appropriate personnel will have been trained to fulfill their roles. The system has completed a final user acceptance test. A production operating schedule should now be in use. The completed system will have undergone a technical certification process. Management reviews the system's fitness of use for a particular task or environment. Management accredits the system for a specified use, based on fitness of use for a particular task or by site location.

You need to verify that appropriate quality control procedures have been executed in support of these objectives. You also need to verify that formal management approval was obtained before the system entered production use. Any deficiencies in management approval should be reported to the audit committee or project oversight.

Phase 6: Post-implementation

The last SDLC phase deals with project closure and the administrative process of verifying that the system meets the organizational objectives. A complete project management review is performed. Evidence is checked to verify that the system was implemented as originally designed, with all necessary internal controls present.

The results of actual use are compared to the anticipated benefits cited in phase 1. The objective is to ensure that these benefits were actually realized by the finished system implementation. Performance measurements are reviewed. A celebration may be in order if the performance exceeded original expectations. Otherwise, a remediation plan may be created to improve current performance.

Phase 6 Review Meetings

Periodic reviews are necessary to verify that the system is maintained in a manner that supports the original objectives and controls. The review should occur at least annually or following a significant change in the business, regulatory climate, or application itself. You may need to utilize the services of a professional expert to conduct the post-implementation review.

You need to remain aware of the conditions necessary to safely rely on using the work of others. The client will frequently request the auditor to use reports from internal staff in order to reduce audit costs. We discussed this issue in Chapter 1 and Chapter 2, "Audit Process."

Auditor Interests in the Post-implementation Phase

As an auditor, you review evidence indicating that the system objective and requirements were achieved. You should pay attention to users' overall satisfaction with the system. You should review evidence indicating that a diligent process of support and maintenance is in use. In this phase, you review system audit logs and compare them to operational reports.

You want to know whether support personnel are actively monitoring for error conditions. A process of incident response and change control should be in use. Management must demonstrate that they are aware of system limitations with regard to the changing requirements of the organization. Management needs to be cognizant of any deficiencies requiring remediation.

In addition, management and the audit committee should remain aware of any external issues that may dictate system modification or removing the application from service. Examples include changes in regulatory law governing minimum acceptable internal controls. A perfect example is the current trend for strong data encryption to be implemented to protect the privacy of individuals. Previously the concerns were focused on using encryption during external data transmission. The latest requirement is for data in databases and on backup tapes to be stored in encrypted form. The loss of unencrypted data will soon carry harsh penalties.

Overview of Data Architecture

A chapter on software development would not be complete without a discussion of the different types of data architecture. The selection of data architecture depends on multiple influences, often including the desires and objectives of the system designer. In this section, we will focus on the fundamentals of data architecture.

Databases

A *database* is simply an organized method for storing information. Early databases were composed of index cards. Some of you may recall using the manual card catalog at the local library to look up the location of a particular book. Later, the library's manual card catalog system was automated with a computer database. Data may be organized into a table rows and columns similar to an Excel spreadsheet.

Databases are designed by using one of two common architectures:

DODB A data-oriented database (DODB) contains data entries of a fixed length and format. The information entered into a data-oriented database is predictable.

OODB An object-oriented database (OODB) does not require a fixed length, nor a fixed format. In fact, the object-oriented database was designed for data of an unpredictable nature.

 You may find that some people refer to the two common database architectures as a data-oriented structured database (DOSD) and an object-oriented structured database (OOSD).

Let's start the discussion with an overview of the data-oriented database.

Data-Oriented Database

The first type of database is designed around data in a predefined format, that is, numbers or characters of a particular length. A perfect example is the typical web form or Excel spreadsheet. This DODB the simplest type of database to create.

For this example, we would like to start with a simple database for client entertainment. Say that you have a few key clients to entertain. Your firm wants to ensure that you build rapport by inviting the client to join you in their favorite activities whenever possible.

The first step is to define the data to be recorded in the database. In the SDLC model, this would be part of phase 2, the Requirements Definition phase. Follow along by using Figure 5.11 as we explain the key points.

Let's start by defining a database table of rows and columns to hold the clients' contact information. The first table is named `client_table`. This will hold the name, address, phone number, and email address of every client.

Next, build a table for each location where you may take the client to be entertained. This is called the `locations_table`. We have added a space to record the average price for this location and a space to record the specialty of the house.

A third table is created to keep track of all of the favorites. The `favorites_table` could be used to record favorite food, a game such as billiards, sporting events, and so forth. One of the objectives in the DODB is to divide information into multiple tables that are relatively static. This allows the system to perform a basic search very fast and not have to process all the data at once. The standardization and removal of duplicates is referred to as *database normalization*.

FIGURE 5.11   Example of client entertainment database

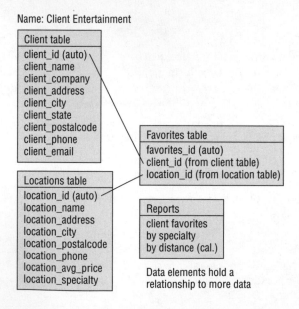

Now you have your tables ready to store information. The next step is to link tables together with a referential link or relation. This is where the term *relational* enters into the description of the database. An item of data in one table relates to data contained in a separate table. Every entry in the database must have at least one required item to show that the entry actually exists. For example, an account number or a person's name would be required for each entry in the database, even if you don't have all the information. This single required entry is referred to as the *primary key*. Data items used to link to tables are referred to as *foreign keys*. The idea is that other data is foreign to the first table. Data that you can search is called a *candidate key* to the search. The purpose of using the term *key* is to illustrate that it would be impossible to unlock the information unless we know what to use as the key.

To be usable, a database must also have *referential integrity*. This means that data is valid across the linked entries (keys) in two tables. Take a look at Figure 5.12 and you will notice the reference lines drawn between client ID and location ID. This diagram is a primitive ERD.

Another way to view the database is to consider a box of index cards. Each entry is the equivalent of a separate index card. The box of index cards is referred to as the table. A table is made up of rows and columns, like an Excel spreadsheet. Computer programmers may use the term *tuple* in place of the word *row*. Figure 5.13 shows the database row, or tuple, as it would appear on index cards.

The actual database displays its contents as rows and columns. It is also common to hear the term *attribute* as a synonym for a database column.

Figure 5.14 shows the columns, or attributes, as they would appear on the computer screen.

FIGURE 5.12   Example database showing data relationships

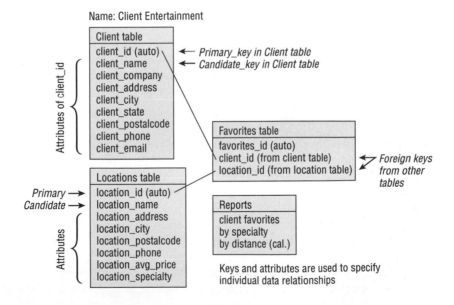

FIGURE 5.13   Database row, also known as a tuple

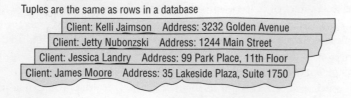

Tuples are the same as rows in a database

Client: Kelli Jaimson   Address: 3232 Golden Avenue
Client: Jetty Nubonzski   Address: 1244 Main Street
Client: Jessica Landry   Address: 99 Park Place, 11th Floor
Client: James Moore   Address: 35 Lakeside Plaza, Suite 1750

FIGURE 5.14   Database columns, also known as attributes

Database columns are also known as attributes

ID	Name	Address	City
003691	CertTest Training Center	1340 S. Main Street	Grapevine
004212	CertTest Training Center	5030 Paradise Road, Bldg C	Las Vegas

Unique identifier (primary key)   Attributes of primary key

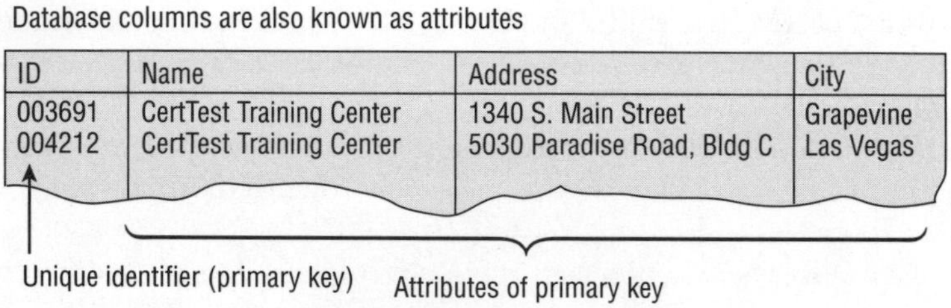

In the illustration, you can see that the ID number is used as a unique identifier (primary key) for each entry. Using a unique ID number allows duplicate names to appear within the database. This is valuable if you have the same company listed with multiple shipping addresses. The unique ID number also permits a name to be updated without any headaches. A common example is to change a maiden name to a married name, or vice versa as the case may be.

In summary, the DODB is designed to be used when the structure and format of your data is well known and predictable. What about data whose structure and format is unpredictable? What about a database that stores documents, graphics, and music files simultaneously? Well, that is the very challenge that led programmers to develop the object-oriented database.

Object-Oriented Database

In a data-oriented database, the program procedures and data are separate. An object-oriented database (OODB) is the opposite. In an OODB, the data and program method are combined into an object. Think of programmed objects as tiny little people or animals with their own way of doing things. Each programmed object has its own data for reference and its own method of accomplishing a required task. Figure 5.15 shows the basic internal design of program objects.

The number one advantage of using programmed objects is that you can delegate work to another object without having to know the specific procedure or characteristics in advance. An example is the computer display settings in the Microsoft operating system. Microsoft XP and Office are examples of object-oriented programs. When Microsoft Word was written, for example, the program did not need to know the details of the display screen. The Word program would simply delegate screen output to an object specified by the screen display setting. A configuration file would exist that contains the setting of "*SET DISPLAY=vendors_ device_driver*". The hardware manufacturer for the display would write an object or driver to paint the image on the screen. The whole object-oriented design lends a great deal of flexibility for modular change.

FIGURE 5.15   Concept overview of program objects

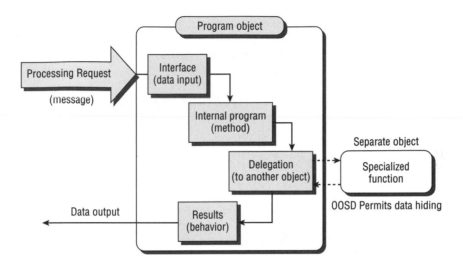

FIGURE 5.16   Illustration of object classes

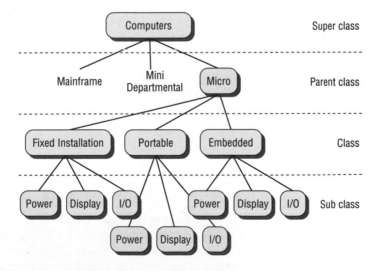

Object-oriented programming is extremely powerful, and the functional design can be confusing to a novice. Objects are grouped together in an *object class*. An object class is quite similar to a particular class of economy automobiles or a class of luxury automobiles, for example. The reference to class indicates the object's position in the hierarchy of the universe. Figure 5.16 shows an example of object classes.

Database Transaction Integrity

Transaction management refers to the computer program's capability to deal with any failure in the logical data update operations used for a particular transaction. Integrity could be damaged if an incomplete transaction was permanently recorded into the database. On the failure of a transaction, the change is backed out of the database, and the data is restored to its original state of consistency.

This capability is based on a transaction log used with a *before-image* journal and *after-image* journal. The journals act as a temporary record of work in progress. A version of the database entry before the update is recorded is the before-image. Changes made are held in the after-image. The transaction can be reversed (undone) until the transaction is actually committed (written) to the master file. Once committed, the transaction is then deleted from the journals. A real-world example can be found in the redo and backout capabilities of the MySQL Max database.

Decision Support Systems

Advancements in computer programming technology and databases have led to the creation of decision support systems (DSS). A *decision support system* is a database that can render timely information to aid the user in making a decision. There are three basic types of decision support systems:

Reference by context   This type of primitive decision-support system supplies the user with answers based on an estimated level of relevance. The overall value is low to moderate.

Colleague, or associate, level   The colleague level provides support for the more tedious calculations but leaves the real decisions to the user.

Expert level   It has been reported in graduate studies that the mind of an average expert contains over 50,000 points of data. By comparison, a colleague or associate might possess only 10,000 points of data. The expert system is usually written by capturing specialized data from a person who has been performing the desired work for 20 or 30 years. This type of information would take a human a significant amount of time to acquire. It is also possible that the events are so far apart that it would be difficult to obtain proficiency without the aid of a computer.

Every decision support system is built on a database. The data in the database is retrieved for use by the program rules, also known as heuristics, to sort through the knowledge base in search of possible answers. The heuristic program rules may be based on a fuzzy logic using estimation, mean, and averages to calculate a likely outcome. The programmers refer to the process as *fuzzification* and *defuzzification* depending on if we are sharpening the average with a stratified mean or derating the average. The meaning of information in the knowledge base can be recorded into a linkage of objects and symbols known as semantic networks. Another technique is to use weight averages in program logic designed to simulate the path of synapses in the human brain.

Let's look at the common terminology used with decision support systems.

Data mining   After the database and rules are created, the next step in the operation of a decision support system is to drill down through the data for correlations that may represent answers. The drilling for correlations is referred to as *data mining*. To be successful, it would be necessary to mine data from multiple areas of the organization. It is the job of the *data warehouse* to accomplish the feat of combining data from different systems.

Data warehouse   Data is captured from multiple databases by using image snapshots triggered by a timer. The timer may be set to capture data daily, weekly, or monthly depending on the needs of the system architect.

Data mart   The data mart is a repository of the results from data mining of the warehouse. You can consider a data mart the equivalent of a convenience store. All of the most common requests are ready for the user to grab. A decision support system retrieves prepackaged results of data mining and displays them for the user in a presentation program, typically a graphical user interface (GUI).

Figure 5.17 shows the basic hierarchy of the databases loading the data warehouse, which is mined to create a data mart.

FIGURE 5.17   Design of data warehouse and data mart

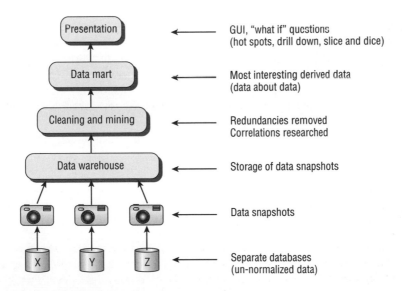

Presenting DSS Data

The information presented from the data mart could indicate correlations of significance for the system user. Senior executives may find this information extremely useful in detecting upcoming trends or areas of concern throughout the organization. Keep in mind, the primary purpose of the decision support system is to give the senior level manager timely information that will aid in making effective decisions.

The next step up from decision support systems is artificial intelligence.

Using Artificial Intelligence

Artificial intelligence (AI) is the subject of many technology dreams and some horror movies. The concept is that the computer has evolved to the level of being able to render its own decisions. Depending on your point of view, this may be good or bad. Artificial intelligence is useful for machines in a hostile environment. The Mars planetary rover requires a degree of artificial intelligence to ensure that it could respond to a hazard, without waiting for a human to issue instructions.

Now that the database has been developed, the next concern is to ensure that the transactions are processed correctly. Let's move along into a discussion of program architecture.

Program Architecture

Computer programs may be written with an open architecture or proprietary, also known as closed, design. The software architect makes this decision.

The open system architecture is founded on well-known standards and definitions. The primary advantage of open architecture is flexibility. Computer software can be updated and modified by using components from multiple sources. Fortunately, the design promotes the ability to use best-of-breed programs. The disadvantages include having a potential hodgepodge of unstructured programs. For a client, the open system architecture reduces dependence on a particular vendor.

A closed system contains methods and proprietary programming that remain the property of the software creator. Most of the program logic is hidden from view or stored in encrypted format to prevent the user from deciphering internal mechanisms. Most commercial software products are a closed, proprietary system with industry standardized program interfaces for data sharing with other programs—in essence, closed architecture with open architecture interfaces. The advantage is that the user can still share data between programs. Another advantage is that the vendor can lock in the customer to their product. The disadvantage is that the customer may be locked in to the vendor's product.

Centralization vs. Decentralization

Every organization will face the challenge of determining whether to use a centralized database or a distributed database application. The centralized database is easier to manage than a distributed system. However, the distributed system offers more flexibility and redundancy. The additional flexibility and redundancy of a distributed system carries higher implementation and support costs.

The decision of centralization vs. decentralization would have been addressed by the steering committee and requirements gathered in the SDLC Requirements Definition phase (phase 1). Let's consider the requirements for electronic commerce.

Electronic E-commerce

Electronic commerce is also known worldwide as *e-commerce*, which is the conducting of business and financial transactions electronically across the globe. This concept introduces the challenges of maintaining confidentiality, integrity, and availability for every second of the entire year. An additional challenge is to ensure regulatory compliance for each type of transaction that may occur over the e-commerce system.

Let's look at a few transactions, for example:

Business-to-business (B-to-B)   Regular transactions between a business and its vendors. This could include purchasing, accounts payable, payroll, and outsourcing services. This type of transaction will be governed by business contracts in accordance with federal law.

Business-to-government (B-to-G)   The online filing of legal documents and reports. In addition, this includes purchasing and vendor management for the products and services used by the government. This type of transaction is governed by a variety of government regulations. An example is the U.S Central Contractor Registration system (CCR). Vendors doing business with the US Government are required to maintain their company profiles in the CCR database.

Business-to-consumer (B-to-C)   Direct sales of products and services to a consumer. B-to-C also includes providing customer support and product information to the consumer. The payment transaction in this type of environment may be governed by banking, privacy, and credit authorization laws.

Business-to-employee (B-to-E)   The online administration of employee services, including payroll and job benefits. This type of transaction is governed by federal employment regulations and privacy regulations.

Figure 5.18 shows the common e-commerce avenues in use today. Each of these should be the subject of an IS audit.

FIGURE 5.18 E-commerce programs

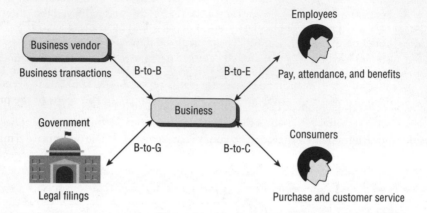

E-commerce poses a number of challenges to security. Because of the level of risk, security should weigh heavily in any considerations of reducing security for convenience. Strong internal controls are mandatory for e-commerce systems.

 We will discuss data security in Chapter 7, "Information Asset Protection."

Summary

In this chapter, we covered IT governance in the System Development Life Cycle. The primary objective of this governance is to ensure that systems are developed via a methodical process that aligns business requirements to business objectives. During this chapter, we touched on standards used in the development of computer software. This chapter included an introduction to the design of databases, program architecture, and e-commerce.

Throughout the entire System Development Life Cycle are a series of processes to ensure control and promote quality. It is the IS auditor's job to determine whether the organization has fulfilled its duties of leadership and control. The purpose of this chapter was to provide you with a basic understanding of the concepts and terminology used in software development.

Exam Essentials

Evaluate the business case for new systems. You need to evaluate the requirements for a new system to ensure that it will meet the organization's business goals. You should understand how critical success factors are developed and risks are identified.

Evaluate risk management and project management practices.   You need to review the evidence of the organization's project management practices and risk mitigation practices. The objective is to determine whether the solution was cost-effective and achieved the stated business objectives. A formal selection process should be in use and clearly documented.

Conduct regular performance reviews.   Each project should undergo a regular performance review to verify that it is conforming to planned expectations. The review process should be supported by formal documentation and accurate status reporting. Management oversight review should be in use when plans deviate, assumptions change, or the scope of the project substantially changes.

Understand the practices used to gather and verify requirements.   The organization may use a steering committee with the assistance of various managers to identify critical success factors. Scenario exercises can be used to assist in developing requirements for planning. Additional requirements may be obtained from the business internal operation, specific business market, customer commitments, and other sources of information.

Know the system development methodology being used.   You need to review the thoroughness and maturity of processes by which all systems (including infrastructure) are developed or acquired.

Know the system development tools, including their strengths and weaknesses.   You need to understand the advantages and disadvantages of traditional programming, Agile, and RAD methodologies. You are expected to understand that 4GL programming languages do not build the necessary business logic without the involvement of a skilled programmer. You are expected to have a basic understanding of the differences between data-oriented programming and object-oriented programming.

Understand quality control and the development of a test plan.   A quality control process should be in use throughout the entire project and system life cycle. Formal testing should occur in accordance with a structured test plan designed to verify software logic, defects, transaction integrity, efficiency, controls, and validation against requirements.

Be familiar with the internal control mechanisms in place and working.   All systems are required to have functioning internal control mechanisms. You need to evaluate the effectiveness of the selected safeguards. Evidence should exist that each control was planned during the system specification phase and that the controls were implemented during development and tested for effectiveness.

Understand the difference between certification and accreditation.   Every system should undergo acceptance testing, followed by formal technical certification testing for production use. After completing technical certification, the system should be reviewed by management for accreditation based on fitness of use. Systems should be recertified on a regular basis to ensure that they meet new demands of evolving requirements.

Be familiar with ongoing maintenance and support plans in use.   You need to evaluate the process of ongoing support and maintenance plans. The intention is to ensure that the plans fulfill the organizational objectives. You verify that the internal control process is in use for authorizing and implementing changes. System changes should undergo a regression test to ensure that no negative effects were created as a result of the change.

Know how to conduct post-implementation reviews.   Every system should undergo a post-implementation review. The purpose is to compare actual deliverables against the original objectives, and to compare performance to the project plan. Regular reviews should occur throughout the system's usable life cycle, preferably on an annual basis.

Know the various programming terms and concepts.   You need to have a working knowledge of the terminology and concepts used in the development of computer software.

Review Questions

1. The advantages of using 4GL software applications include which of the following?

   A. Automatically generates the application screens and business logic

   B. Includes artificial intelligence fuzzy logic

   C. Reduces application planning time and coding effort

   D. Reduces development effort for primitive functions but does not provide business logic

2. The best definition of database normalization is to

   A. Increase system performance by creating duplicate copies of the most accessed data, allowing faster caching.

   B. Increase the amount (capacity) of valuable data.

   C. Minimize duplication of data and reduce the size of data tables.

   D. Minimize response time through faster processing of information.

3. Which of the following statements is true concerning the inerference engine used in expert systems?

   A. Makes decisions using heuristics

   B. Contains nodes linked via an arc

   C. Used when a knowledge base is unavailable

   D. Records objects in a climactic network

4. An IT steering committee would most likely perform which of the following functions?

   A. Explain to the users how IT is steering the business objectives.

   B. Issue directives for regulatory compliance and provide authorization for ongoing IT audits.

   C. Facilitate cooperation between the users and IT to ensure that business objectives are met.

   D. Ensure that the business is aligned to fulfill the IT objectives.

5. Software Engineering Institute's Capability Maturity Model (CMM) would best relate to which of the following statements?

   A. Measurement of resources necessary to ensure a reduction in coding defects

   B. Documentation of accomplishments achieved during program development

   C. Relationship of application performance to the user's stated requirement

   D. Baseline of the current progress or regression

6. Which of the following best describes a data mart?

   A. Contains raw data to be processed

   B. Used in place of a data warehouse

   C. Provides a graphical GUI presentation

   D. Stores results from data mining

7. Object-oriented databases (OODBs) are designed for data that is _____.

    A. predictable

    B. consistent in structure

    C. variable

    D. fixed-length

8. What does the term *referential integrity* mean?

    A. Transactions are recorded in before-images and after-images.

    B. It's a valid link between a data entry contained in two tables.

    C. It's a completed tuple in the database.

    D. Candidate keys are used to perform a search.

9. Which of the following statements best explains a program object in object-oriented programming?

    A. It contains methods and data.

    B. Methods are stored separate from data.

    C. It contains 100 percent of all methods necessary for every task.

    D. It does not provide methods.

10. What is the primary objective of post-implementation review?

    A. Recognition for forcing an installation to be successful.

    B. Authorize vendor's final payment from escrow.

    C. Conduct remedial actions.

    D. Determine that its organizational objectives have been fulfilled.

11. What is the most important concern regarding the RFP process?

    A. Vendor proposals undergo an objective review to determine alignment with organizational objectives.

    B. The vendor must agree to escrow the program code to protect the buyer in case the vendor organization ceases operation.

    C. The RFP process requires a substantial commitment as opposed to a request for information (RFI).

    D. The RFP planning process is not necessary for organizations with internal programming capability.

12. Which SDLC phase uses the Function Point Analysis (FPA)?

    A. SDLC phase 3: System Design

    B. SDLC phase 4: Development

    C. SDLC phase 1: Feasibility Study

    D. SDLC phase 5: Implementation

13. Which of the following statements is true concerning regression testing?

    A. Used to observe internal program logic

    B. Verifies that a change did not create a new problem

    C. Provides testing of black box functions

    D. Compares test results against a knowledge base

14. Which of the following migration methods provides the lowest risk to the organization?

    A. Phased

    B. Hard

    C. Parallel

    D. Date specified

15. When is management oversight of a project required?

    A. If time, scope, or cost vary more than 5 percent from the estimate

    B. When the feasibility study is inconclusive

    C. To verify that total program benefits met anticipated projection

    D. When major changes occur in assumptions, requirements, or methodology

16. What are the advantages of the integrated development environment (IDE)?

    A. Generates and debugs program code

    B. Eliminates the majority of processes in SDLC phase 2

    C. Prevents design errors in SDLC phase 3

    D. Eliminates the testing requirement in SDLC phase 4

17. What is the difference between certification and accreditation?

    A. Certification is a management process, and accreditation is a technical process.

    B. No difference; both include technical testing.

    C. Certification is a technical test, and accreditation is management's view of fitness for use.

    D. Certification is about fitness of use, and accreditation is a technical testing process.

18. Which of the following development methodologies is based on knowledge in someone's head, as opposed to traditional documentation of requirements?

    A. System Development Life Cycle (SDLC)

    B. Program Evaluation Review Technique (PERT)

    C. Rapid Application Development (RAD)

    D. Agile

19. What is the IS auditor's primary purpose in regard to life cycle management?

    A. To verify that evidence supports the organizational objective and that each decision is properly authorized by management

    B. To verify that all business contracts are properly signed and executed by management

    C. To verify that internal controls are tested prior to implementation by a third-party review laboratory

    D. To verify that a sufficient budget was allocated to pay for software development within the allotted time period

20. Which of the following design techniques will document internal logic functions used for data transformation?

    A. Entity-relationship diagram

    B. Flowchart

    C. Database schema

    D. Function Point Analysis

Answers to Review Questions

1. D. The 4GL provides screen authoring and report writing utilities that automate database access. The 4GL tools do not create the business logic necessary for data transformation.

2. C. Database normalization minimizes duplication of data through standardization of the database table layout. Increased speed is obtained by reducing the size of individual tables to allow a faster search.

3. A. The inerference engine uses rules, also known as heuristics, to sort through the knowledge base in search of possible answers. The meaning of information in the knowledge base can be recorded in objects and symbols known as semantic networks.

4. C. The IT steering committee provides open communication of business objectives for IT to support. The steering committee builds awareness and facilitates user cooperation. Focus is placed on fulfillment of the business objectives.

5. D. The Capability Maturity Model creates a baseline reference to chart current progress or regression. It provides a guideline for developing the maturity of systems and management procedures.

6. D. Data mining uses rules to drill down through the data in the data warehouse for correlations. The results of data mining are stored in the data mart. The DSS presentation program may display data from the data mart in a graphical format.

7. D. Data-oriented databases (DODBs) are designed for predictable data that has a consistent structure and a known or fixed length. Object-oriented databases (OODBs) are designed for data of a variable length in a variety of possible data formats.

8. B. Referential integrity refers to a valid link between an entry in two tables. Lack of referential integrity would prevent the database from running correctly. The reference link ties together related information.

9. A. Objects contain both methods and data to perform a desired task. The object can delegate to another object.

10. D. Post-implementation review collects evidence to determine whether the organizational objectives have been fulfilled. The review would include verification that internal controls are present and in use.

11. A. Each proposal must undergo an objective review to determine whether the offer is properly aligned with organizational objectives. RFP review is a formal process that should be managed as a project.

12. C. Function Point Analysis (FPA) is used to estimate the effort required to develop software. FPA is used during SDLC phase 1, the Feasibility Study phase, to create estimates by multiplying the number of inputs and outputs against a mathematical factor.

13. B. The purpose of regression testing is to ensure that a change does not create a new problem with other functions in the program. After a change is made, all of the validation tests are run from beginning to end to discover any conflicts or failures. Regression testing is part of the quality control process.

14. C. Parallel migration increases support requirements but lowers the overall risk. The old and new systems are run in parallel to verify integrity while building user familiarity with the new system.

15. D. Management oversight review is necessary when it is anticipated that the estimates are incorrect by more than 10 percent. Management oversight is also necessary if major changes occur in assumptions, requirements, or methodology used.

16. A. The integrated development environment automates program code generation and provides online debugging for certain types of errors. It does not replace the traditional planning process. IDE does not alter the testing requirements in SDLC phase 4. Full testing must still occur.

17. C. Certification is a technical testing process. Accreditation is a management process of granting approval based on fitness of use.

18. D. The Agile method places greater reliance on the undocumented knowledge contained in a person's head. Agile is the direct opposite of capturing knowledge through project documentation.

19. A. Evidence must support the stated objectives of the organization. Software that is built or purchased should be carefully researched to ensure that it fulfills the organization's objectives. Each phase of the life cycle should be reviewed and approved by management before progressing to the next phase.

20. B. A flowchart is used to document internal program logic. An entity-relationship diagram (ERD) is used to help define the database schema. Function Point Analysis is used for estimation of work during the feasibility study.

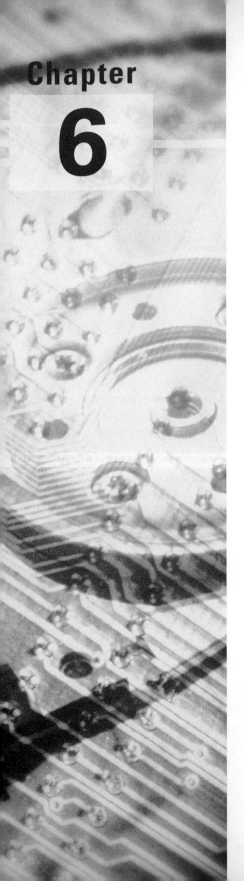

Chapter

6

IT Service Delivery

THE OBJECTIVE OF THIS CHAPTER IS TO ACQUAINT THE READER WITH THE FOLLOWING CONCEPTS:

- ✓ Knowledge of service level management practices including operations workload, scheduling, services management, and preventive maintenance

- ✓ Data administration for integrity and optimization Databases

- ✓ Passing performance monitoring using analyzers, system utilization, and load balancing

- ✓ Understanding of change management, configuration release management, and emergency changes

- ✓ Knowledge of techniques for problem reporting and incidence management

- ✓ Knowledge of control functionality in the IT infrastructure

In this chapter, you will focus on the management of IT operations designed to support the organization. You will learn about the recommended practices for monitoring service levels and controlling change in the organization. The best practices of incident management and problem resolution will also be discussed.

ISACA expects every IS auditor to understand how to evaluate the techniques and best practices used in IT support.

IT Operations

Information technology (IT) provides a service to business users. Technology is so pervasive that no organization can exist without computers and telephones. IT service represents a commitment to manage technology as efficiently and effectively as possible within the organization. As business needs change, IT services should adapt accordingly. This constant adaptation can be a significant challenge. There's always the possibility of a gap occurring between the IT services delivered and user expectations.

In previous chapters, we discussed the requirement for IT services to be aligned with business objectives. Many of the topics we discussed are practically transparent to business users. IT service delivery is different. In this chapter, we will discuss the daily activities necessary to support information technology.

Let's begin with a basic review of the functions in IT operations:

Management of the IT department   The Information Technology department contains managers and staff workers focused on system availability, system integrity, and data confidentiality.

Systems life cycle   All IT systems are to be maintained in a systems life cycle by using the concepts of the System Development Life Cycle (SDLC) and Capability Maturity Model (CMM).

IT policies   Executive management and IT management are responsible for developing and issuing policies that support agreed-upon information technology objectives. Examples include a corporate acceptable use policy (AUP), antivirus protection policy, and the designation of information technology as the official custodian for corporate data.

IT standards   Operating standards are developed by managers and approved by executive management. One such standard is the separation of duties. Other examples include the hours of system availability and system certification prior to production use.

IT procedures   Operating procedures are developed by staff workers with the assistance of their manager. Operating procedures include the handling of software licenses and escalation procedures for user reported trouble tickets.

IT job descriptions and responsibilities   To support the operating procedures, the IT department must have job descriptions that reflect the current requirements and responsibilities for each position.

IT risk management process   Risk management is required in all areas of an organization. The IT department is subject to a high level of inherent risk. Failures that occur in information technology have wide-reaching impact. The IT department is required to exercise risk mitigation on a daily basis. The process of change control is one technique used to help mitigate risk.

IT asset management   Every Information Technology department maintains control over numerous capital assets, including data, software licenses, computing hardware, networking equipment, and facility space. We view data as a capital asset because of the capital investment necessary to create and maintain current data. Creating a customer list requires substantial investment of capital through marketing campaigns. A list of customers and hot prospects can easily be valued at five to ten times annual gross sales. The organization's total investment in technology, inclusive of all departments, is usually in excess of 4.5 percent of annual gross sales. This makes IT the second-largest custodian of capital assets, following facilities.

IT service to the user   Information technology exists to support business users. The number one representation of value is IT user satisfaction. Attaining high user satisfaction results from a significant effort in back-office systems coupled with a prompt, helpful, and friendly help desk. The typical business user is interested only in how IT solves their individual problem. Customer satisfaction is earned by individual problem-by-problem solutions.

 Real World Scenario

Lights-Out Operations

Based on business requirements and risks, an organization may adopt a policy of running a *lights-out operation*. This term refers to an unmanned facility—although personnel may be in other areas of the building, the control room or data center remains unmanned. Operations are either fully automated or run by remote control. Removing personnel from the data center significantly reduces the risk of environmental contaminants (liquids, debris, food), malicious actions, and human error.

We visited one data center that had so many cables under the raised floor that the floor tiles were bulging under our feet. This was not only unsafe, but also led to communication failures as some brittle cables broke when people walked across the tiles. Service personnel would occupy the room only for maintenance.

Now is a good time to discuss how IT results are demonstrated and customer satisfaction is obtained. We will start with the IT balanced scorecard.

Using the IT Balanced Scorecard

 The *balanced scorecard* is a strategic methodology implemented by senior executives. The scorecard approach converts organizational objectives of growth and learning, business process, customers, and financial goals into a series of defined metrics.

When properly implemented, the scorecard concept enforces better alignment with strategic business objectives. Use of the scorecard should eliminate activities of little or no strategic value.

The scorecard methodology is common outside of the IT environment. Information technology can benefit from using the balanced scorecard if it is implemented by the CEO or CFO. To be effective, the scorecard must be driven from the top down. Table 6.1 illustrates the four scorecard perspectives and matching emphasis area of the balanced scorecard methodology. For example, the finance perspective will place emphasis on cost control and company profits.

TABLE 6.1 Balanced Scorecard Methodology

Perspective	Emphasis
Growth and learning	What are the organization's growth plans? How will we keep or obtain the knowledge and workers necessary to support the organization's plans?
Financial	What are the financial goals? What are the shareholder goals?
Business process	What is our mission? What are our critical success factors? What are the key performance indicators?
Customer	What is our market image? How should the organization appear to the customer?

The balanced scorecard approach is shown in Figure 6.1. Some organizations are successful at using the balanced scorecard approach, and some fail. Let's look at why this occurs. The advantages and disadvantages of using the scorecard methodology are as follows:

Scorecard advantages   Promotes focus on specific metrics in direct support of organizational objectives. When fully implemented, each employee works from a personal scorecard. The combined effect of the personal scorecards will achieve their department's objective. Achievement of the departmental objectives will help fulfill the organizational objectives.

Scorecard disadvantages   The scorecard requires a careful selection of metrics by the CEO or CFO. It is reported in executive trade journals that metrics derived from a committee will fail. The balanced scorecard fundamentally changes how employees prioritize and report their work. Activities and projects will be selected on the basis of the value created under established metrics. This also results in a change of how the employee is evaluated. It is essential that management and staff receive proper training prior to implementation. Without full buy-in at all levels, the balanced scorecard is likely to fail.

The IT balanced scorecard should be a subset of the organization's overall balanced scorecard. When properly implemented, the scorecard methodology supports the highest-level business objectives.

FIGURE 6.1   Balanced scorecard

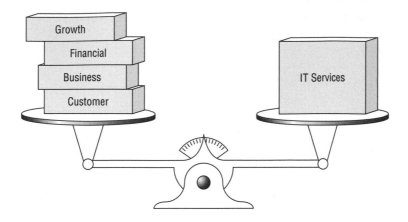

As a CISA, you need to understand how the balanced scorecard can be applied specifically to information technology. ISACA implements the scorecard by using three layers that incorporate all four perspectives (growth and learning, financial, business process, and customer). The three layers for IT scoring according to ISACA are as follows: mission, strategy, and metrics.

Mission   Develop opportunities for future needs. Become the preferred supplier of IT systems to the organization. Obtain funding from the business for IT investments. Deliver effective and cost-efficient IT services.

Strategy   Attain IT control objectives. Obtain control over IT expenses. Deliver business value through IT projects. Provide ongoing IT training and education. Support R&D to develop superior IT applications.

Metrics   Develop and implement meaningful IT metrics based on critical success factors and key performance indicators.

In the next section we will discuss using metrics, the help desk, and service-level management.

Using Metrics

Using metrics to measure IT service is required. These service metrics are tools designed to demonstrate the effectiveness of IT operations. Many regulations require the use of IT metrics in general. Each metric should provide a quantifiable measurement corresponding to the organization's internal controls. The IT metrics therefore also aid in the evaluation of an organization's performance.

Metrics must be developed for each organization. Each metric should be developed by using the following four principles:

- Data for calculating metrics must be readily obtainable.

- Each process under consideration needs to be repeating and measurable. It must represent a value to the business.

- Each metric must demonstrate a level of performance by using quantifiable information in the form of a numeric total, average, or percentage.

- A metric can be derived by automated or manual means.

The success of IT metrics depends on finding useful measurements that are of value to the organization's stakeholders. Data can be obtained from automated system reports. Data can also be collected manually through self-assessment tools, questionnaires, and user surveys. The metrics may change as new processes and projects are developed in the organization. It is important that each metric selected is realistic and can be used for measuring performance improvement.

Types of Metrics

The goal of every metric is to establish a performance target. Performance targets are combined to establish a baseline. Four basic types of metrics can be used to measure IT performance:

Implementation metric   An implementation metric provides a percentage or comparative count for the quantity of conforming installations—for example, the number of systems with antivirus software installed, or the number of users who have attended IT security orientation training.

Efficiency metric   The efficiency metric measures the timeliness of service delivery. Examples include resolution time from the help desk or elapsed time for response to an incident.

Effectiveness metric   This metric evaluates the quantifiable effectiveness of IT service activities. An example is the number of user reported trouble tickets opened and closed by the help desk with a resolution that was satisfactory to the user. Another example is the number of systems currently maintained in a life-cycle program by IT staff.

Impact metric   The impact metric provides a quantitative measure of incidents by their type—for example, the number of help desk tickets opened and closed for the month. Another example is the number of systems compromised by a virus attack. This metric can be presented as a numeric value, a percentage of the total population, or a dollar figure.

Figure 6.2 illustrates the nature of the four basic types of measurement metrics.

The IT department and each major stakeholder need to agree on which metrics to use. It is important to limit the number of metrics to a sustainable quantity. It is recommended that no more than five to ten metrics be collected for each major stakeholder. The metrics are not free; an organization must allocate resources to gather and create meaningful metrics. The data collection and subsequent reporting process must be standardized.

FIGURE 6.2   Basic types of measurement metrics

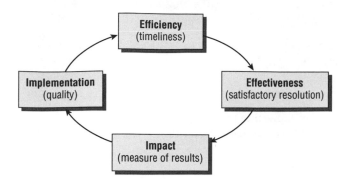

Developing and Selecting a Metric

Every metric developed will contain nine elements of information. ISACA does not expect you to recite each of these points in detail. The objective is to understand how a valid metric is created and managed. Let's look at the nine elements:

Purpose   Describe the overall functional value of this metric. Is this metric for customer measurement, compliance with a regulatory requirement, or internal performance?

Performance goal   State the desired results of implementation, or the question to be answered by this metric. For example, the goal may be orientation training for new hires or separation of duties on IT servers.

Performance objective   State the actions that are required to obtain the performance goal. This may be posed as one or multiple questions. For example, are participant training materials in place for the orientation of new hires? What is the training schedule?

Type of measurement   Define the quantitative measurement to be used. The measurement is expressed as a percentage, average, number, or frequency—for example, the numeric count and percentage based on attendance.

Data source   Indicate where the data was captured from. List the specific tools, databases, and personnel that provided the data used in this metric—for example, a Human Resources (HR) employee count, and class attendance records signed upon entry and exit from training.

Available evidence   List the sources of proof that can document the success or failure represented by this particular metric—for example, an HR roster, invitation list, attendance sheet, or attendee exit examination.

Frequency   State the time period used for data collection. Is this information based on hours, days, weeks, months, or years? For example, data collection may be reported monthly.

Formula used   State the formula used in the calculation. One example is the number of incidents divided by the total number of systems. Another example is the formula ratio = (attendees ÷ total number of employees).

Indicators   Explain the goal of this metric and how it should be interpreted by the reader. For example, if the target for a metric on system certification is 100 percent, a low percentage would indicate a high risk exposure. A higher percentage would indicate a risk reduction by educating users about basic IS security safeguards and high-level notification procedures.

Help Desk

The purpose of a *help desk* is to provide ad hoc assistance to business users. The help desk is the point of origination for new support requests. A help desk may support specific applications or general computer needs. In service delivery, the objective is to provide high quality and prompt service to the user during the appropriate work hours.

People may call in for help with a variety of computing problems. It is the help desk's responsibility to escalate trouble tickets in a timely manner. Some trouble tickets might be escalated to the system administrator or application support programmer. Other trouble tickets might be escalated to a third party. The help desk provides a single point of contact for the user. Each trouble ticket should be tracked by the help desk until closed or resolved to the user's satisfaction.

The help desk tracks call metrics so that trends can be analyzed. As an IS auditor, you should understand the help desk function. It would be beneficial to conduct a review of the staff on the help desk to determine their level of competency. An audit trail should exist, documenting the process for logging and tracking service requests. You should evaluate the level of documentation for help desk activities and troubleshooting procedures.

Service-Level Management

A *service-level agreement (SLA)* represents an understanding between users and the service provider. The purpose of this agreement is to define performance criteria by specifying the quantity and quality of service desired by the customer.

Let's look at some of the components of the service-level agreement:

System availability   What are the scheduled hours of system uptime and system downtime for maintenance? How is the processing workload scheduled to prevent conflict? What is the nature and extent of continuity plans?

Service definition   What are the specific services expected by the user?

Personnel qualifications   What are the qualifications of the IT support personnel? Will these same personnel be supporting business users? Will the support personnel be trained in the unique requirements of the business?

Security requirements   What access controls will be implemented? How will physical and logical access controls be implemented? How will the program libraries be protected? How will the data be protected? Will separation of duties be fully implemented?

Data integrity   What are the data storage and retention requirements? What is the method and frequency of data backup? How will data be protected during transportation?

SLA performance reporting   Are all metrics reported against a quantifiable service level? What metrics will be reported? How will the content and format of the metrics be reported? Do the report metrics fulfill actual business objectives? What is the frequency of reporting?

Right to audit   What level of cooperation and access will a customer have to audit the service provider? Define any schedule or access restrictions in regard to auditing. This was discussed in Chapter 3 "IT Governance."

SLA change procedures   What is the process for making changes to the service? What is the cancellation process and how much would it cost?

Cost of service   What is the cost of the service offered? How are the charges calculated? How will the service be billed? Are the charges realistic for the level of service provided?

This list is provided as an overview of the components in a service-level agreement. Every service-level agreement should be a formal contract between the vendor and customer. This contract should include the effective period of coverage and renewal options. It is understood that internal service-level agreements will take the form of an agreement of mutual understanding. Either type of agreement must be formally approved by appropriate management, representing both the provider's interests and the user's interests.

Monitoring Controls

Your job as a CISA is to evaluate an organization's internal controls. Internal controls are required during the normal processing at every computer terminal or computer workstations Without proper controls, a minor error could become a major outage.

We have discussed a series of controls in this Study Guide. In Chapter 7, "Information Asset Protection," we will discuss specific security controls for protecting information assets. Let's recap the controls that apply to IT service delivery:

- System access controls
- Data file controls
- Application processing controls
- Maintenance controls

System Access Controls

Access to computing resources needs to be controlled. It is imperative that the concept of *least privilege* be implemented with regard to user access of IT computing resources. No individual should be able to log in to the system by using a level of authority higher than their job requires. There are three types of login accounts you need to consider: user login, privileged administrator login, and maintenance login.

User Login and Account Management

New user login IDs are created after Human Resources notifies the IT department of an employee being hired. A similar process should exist when a contractor begins work. Some type of authorization mechanism must exist to control the creation of new accounts.

Each system user is required to have a unique login ID and password. The user login accounts should be given the minimum access rights necessary to perform their job (least privilege). Biometrics or electronic tokens may be implemented on systems with higher levels of security. Every user login should contain the following control attributes:

- A warning banner is displayed prior to login to inform the user that inappropriate access may result in prosecution.

- A minimum password length of six to eight characters is required. The password should be a mix of numbers and letters. The password should not be a printed word found in any dictionary regardless of language. (we discuss the details behind this in chapter 7)

- Unique passwords are forced. The computer system will not allow a password to be reused.

- Passwords are required to be changed at a frequency of 30 to 60 days, depending on the organization's policy.

- User login ID is suspended after three to five unsuccessful login attempts.

- Unauthorized attempts to access the system are recorded in audit logs.

- The date and time of the last successful login will be displayed to the user upon login. This is to inform the user of when their login ID was last used.

A user login account is suspended or disabled when a notice is received from HR that a particular user is no longer employed by the organization. The disabled account needs to undergo administrative review prior to deletion of the user ID. This review seeks to discover whether the user engaged in any attempts of unauthorized access. If not, the user's data files are archived and forwarded to the appropriate department manager.

Privileged Login Accounts

Logical access to system administration functions needs to be protected by a separation of duties. Privileged login accounts should not be used for any function other than administration and maintenance. System administrators should possess two separate login accounts. The first login account should be used exclusively for system administration duties. The second login account should have no privileges other than the basic rights of the common user.

The system administrator should perform office administration functions while logged in as a regular user. This reduces the potential impact of errors. In addition, it improves security by reducing the time duration of privileged access. If the administrator walks down the hall to the restroom, the risk of another individual gaining physical access to the computer has been reduced. The logical separation of duties can be verified by reading system logs.

All privileged login accounts contain control attributes of a normal user plus the following additional controls:

- Passwords must be changed every 30 days.

- Retired passwords must be written down and stored with backup tapes. Those passwords may be necessary again when older files are restored. Both the tapes and the password lists shall be stored in a fireproof rated media safe, and also in a secure controlled environment designed for off-site media storage.

- The current passwords should be written down and stored in a safe in case something unforeseen happens to the system administrator. Current passwords will be required for disaster recovery. A second copy of the passwords should be kept in a safe off-site location separate from the data files.

Maintenance Login Accounts

All computer systems have default user accounts for system setup and maintenance. The login IDs of these maintenance accounts are often well known and commercially published. Hackers love to use maintenance accounts that have been left open by careless administrators. Default login accounts should be disabled in a production system. Any valid maintenance accounts should utilize nontypical login names with strong passwords or station restrictions. A station restriction allows login to occur only from a particular system, based on the machine's serial number or address.

Data File Controls

Access to data files should be controlled to ensure that unauthorized access is effectively impossible. Data access can occur through a perimeter control, direct file access, and middleware. *Middleware* is software that handles data traveling from the user interface to its destination in the database. Each of these types of access requires special controls. It is naïve to think that a perimeter control will be completely effective.

Four basic types of data protection controls are required:

Standing data controls   *Standing data* refers to information contained in a file or database table. The information should possess controls commensurate with the data value or regulatory requirement. Standing data can be found on disk drives and tape backups. Standing data may require additional controls such as storage in encrypted format within the database.

 A significant portion of credit-card number theft on the Internet is due to unauthorized copying of standing data in shopping cart databases. The US Fair and Accurate Credit Transactions Act of 2003 mandates increased security with truncation of account numbers on receipts and destruction of account numbers after the transaction is processed.

System control parameters   Data files should be protected from system control parameters that would change the way the files are processed. System control parameters are used to customize the configuration settings and software applications. These settings can alter performance, logging, or file security. Improper implementation can lead to the loss of data, unauthorized access, or undetected errors.

Logical access controls   All access to data files should be forced through authentication in a user rights management program (access control program). Direct access to data files through Open Database Connectivity (ODBC) should be prohibited unless controlled by a rights management program with user authentication. It is common for a user to request direct access to the database for the purpose of reading data from another program. This type of uncontrolled direct access should be discouraged.

Transaction processing controls   All transactions involving data files should be controlled with authentication and validation checks. The data transformation procedure must be officially approved and managed as part of the system application life cycle. Transaction processing monitors (TP monitors) are frequently used to ensure that database activity does not overload the processing capacity of the available hardware.

Application Processing Controls

System security and integrity is assured through the use of *application processing controls*. Logical access controls require the user to log in with a unique ID and password. The user can begin processing after a successful login. Each application should provide at least three internal processing controls: input, authorization, and output.

Input Controls

An *input control* ensures that only valid and authorized information is entered into a transaction. Input controls operate by using a combination of user authorization rights, edit checking, and data entry validation. Sequence checks are used to ensure that each transaction is processed only once. For an excellent analogy, consider how checks and ATM transactions are authorized at a bank.

Input authorization controls include the following:

- Unique login and password
- Signatures on source documents
- Identification of client workstation or terminal

Processing Controls

The purpose of *processing controls* is to ensure that the data and transactions are valid. Production software programs reside in the production program library. Access to the production program library should be restricted to read-only. There is no reason for the computer programmer or the user to have write access into a production program library.

Allowing a programmer to have write access to a production program library would be a violation of change control. The computer operator will move authorized software from the development library to the production library when instructed and authorized by the change control manager.

Most data processing occurs by using a batch processing mode. The data batch may be small or large. The frequency of processing may be seconds or hours. Regardless of the method, it is necessary to ensure data integrity by using data validation and edit procedures. Without operational processing controls, the database would be no more effective than a garbage can.

Processing controls include the following:

Batch totals   To compare input against actual processing.

Total number of items   To verify that each item was processed.

Transaction logs   To record activity.

Run-to-run totals   To provide verification of the data values during the different stages of processing. This helps ensure the completeness of all transactions.

Limit checks   To prevent processing of any amount in excess of the expected average. Overly large transactions will not be processed. For example, no employee should receive a paycheck for $50,000. That amount would obviously be excessive.

Exception reporting   To identify errors. The exception may hold the batch and suspension until the errors are corrected, or reject individual transactions containing errors, or reject the entire batch of transactions.

Job cost accounting   The operating cost of computer processing may be billed to a particular department, project, or application. It is important to observe the effectiveness of job cost accounting when it is used.

Output Controls

Data generated by the system should be protected to ensure confidentiality until it is delivered to the designated user. *Output controls* are just as important for paychecks as confidentiality is for business plans or HR records.

Let's review a few basic output controls:

Report generation and distribution   Confidential reports should be output on a printer with restricted access. The report title should indicate that the report is confidential. Exception reports should always generate a page to indicate the exceptions that occurred, or a page to indicate that no exceptions occurred.

Negotiable instruments   Checks, bonds, and stock certificates are frequently printed on computers. These items should be protected by a combination of logical and physical controls.

Report retention   Certain types of reports may be required to be controlled under a document retention policy. This applies to records used for regulatory or legal compliance.

Event logs   Processing logs and audit trails should be protected for integrity and confidentiality at all times. These logs need to be placed under record retention controls.

Maintenance Controls

Maintenance controls exist to ensure that hardware and software changes will have a minimum impact on processing schedules and system availability. All maintenance should be approved by the change control process before it occurs. It is not uncommon for an organization to issue blanket approval for small changes with low risk. Let's look at some of the issues that should be addressed prior to performing maintenance.

Backup and Recovery

System programs and data should be backed up before maintenance occurs. The backup tapes (or media) should be read/write verified. Verifying a backup ensures that the data copy matches the original. The backup provides a second copy of current data if something goes horribly wrong.

Project Management

Project management with a risk analysis should be performed prior to starting maintenance. Most maintenance is a mini project. As the scope of the maintenance increases, so should the project planning. Each project plan should include a provision for workarounds and fallback procedures. A fallback procedure will be executed if the change fails to deliver the desired result.

Change Management

We discussed change management in Chapter 3, "IT Governance," and Chapter 5, "Life Cycle Management." In terms of IT service delivery, change management concerns relate to hardware and software maintenance. The introduction of any change constitutes a risk to system integrity and availability. However, change is inevitable.

A flowchart of the change management process appears in Figure 6.3.

ISACA wants every CISA to be aware of four concepts that apply to change management in IT service delivery.

FIGURE 6.3   Change management process

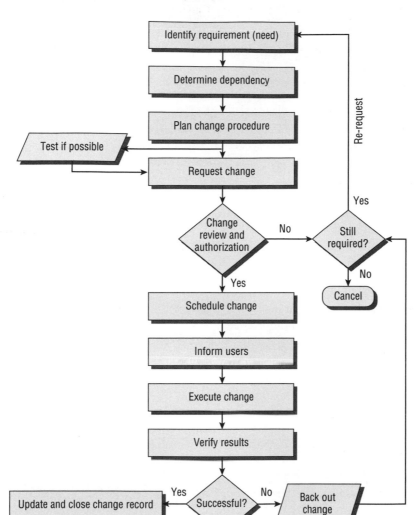

Software Release and Patch Management

Computer software is authorized for distribution via a release process. Software is released from development and authorized to be installed for production use. Each vendor has their own release schedule.

Computer software releases fit one of the following profiles:

Major release   A significant change in the design or generation of software is known as a *major release*. Major releases tend to occur in the interval of 12 to 24 months.

Minor release, or update   *Updates* are also known as *minor releases*. Their purpose is to correct small problems after the major release has been issued.

Emergency software fixes   These are known as *program patches* or *hot fixes*. Emergency fixes should be tested prior to implementation. Every fix should undergo a pretest, even if the test is informal. Emergency software fixes may introduce new problems that are unexpected.

Configuration Control

The configuration of production systems must be controlled. The method of configuration control is similar to the one we discussed in Chapter 5 concerning software development. Changes should not be made to a production system unless the change has undergone formal testing under the control of the change management process.

Change Authorization

No change should occur without management authorization, and any changes must remain within the authorized scope. It is unfortunate that some technicians will attempt to implement additional changes at the first opportunity. These changes have consistently proven to be the source of a related failure. The objective of change authorization is to ensure that nobody bypasses the life-cycle management process.

Emergency Changes

At times emergency changes are necessary to minimize system interruption. A senior individual should be consulted for review and approval prior to implementing an emergency change. If the emergency change works, it may remain in production. If it fails, the change should be withdrawn (backed out) immediately. After an emergency change is implemented, the standard change control process will be invoked after the fact. The change should undergo formal testing and analysis to determine whether it may have created additional problems.

Management Controls

Administrative management controls are used to provide written policy and procedure guidance for people. These management controls help overcome shortfalls from the limited implementation of technical controls. You need to be aware of the common administrative controls used in IT service delivery. We will begin with software licensing.

Software Licensing

Software licenses are an asset of the corporation and need to be controlled and managed. All computer systems are required to have a valid, lawfully obtained software license for the operating system along with a license for each application and each utility installed. A violation of software copyright laws carries substantial penalties and the possibility of public embarrassment. You should observe the client's attitude toward software licenses. Most organizations purchase licenses by a per user count. There should be evidence to indicate that the licenses are managed for copyright compliance.

Asset and Media Tracking

Technology assets should be inventoried and tracked. Proper ownership labels or property tags should be in use. Tagging and labeling are preventive controls. The audit of inventory tags is a detective control. Media containing software and data should be managed under a physical asset program. All media should be properly labeled. The media librarian is responsible for tracking the location of media. Evidence should exist to indicate that assets and media are properly controlled.

Asset Disposal

A proper asset disposal process contains procedures to ensure that data is purged (erased) from all equipment prior to disposal so that the data can never be recovered. Physical assets should be formally discharged from inventory. These assets can be destroyed, sold, or donated depending on the organization's desire. As an IS auditor, you need to determine whether the organization is following an acceptable asset disposal process. Employees should not profit from asset disposal. All devices leaving the controlled environment must be purged of data using disk wiping utilities or degaussing methods. Disk reformatting is not an effective method since it will not destroy raw data that is accessible using special utilities that bypass the operating system.

User Training

Proper training of system users can reduce the occurrence of problems. User training may include new hire orientation, security awareness training, software application training, and refresher programs for existing users. Well-educated users can provide valuable assistance to IT objectives. The educated user will understand when to bring potential concerns to the attention of IT management.

Ineffective and Inefficient Controls

A management review process should exist to deal with ineffective and inefficient controls. Failing controls should be reviewed for merit and potential impact. A compensating control may be implemented to overcome an ineffective control.

Procedures vs. Actual Work

The procedures used in the operation of information technology systems should reflect the actual work performed. The purpose of a procedure is to ensure consistency with the desired result. Actual work that does not match the procedure would indicate a management control failure.

System Monitoring

Technology systems require continuous monitoring to uncover operational inconsistencies, errors, and processing failures. Managing a system would be impossible if you did not know its present condition.

Let's discuss a few types of monitoring that should be implemented by IT:

Hardware   Electronic hardware should be monitored for workload utilization, errors, and availability. Utilization and errors could indicate an upcoming condition that will affect system availability. The goal of every system is to be usable. The system administrator should always be aware of hardware conditions observed, problems reported, and alerts recorded in system logs.

Software   Most computer software provides event logging. Event logs and audit logs should be enabled and configured to capture information of interest—for example, error conditions, successful logins, unsuccessful login attempts, and configuration changes.

Centralized system logging (syslog)   It is a recommended practice for centralized system logging to be installed. This process forwards a copy of each system log to a centralized console for review. The configuration process is relatively simple. A log-reading tool is necessary to convert raw data into meaningful information. System logs contain a lot of duplicate entries. Without a log-reading tool, understanding the priorities would be difficult because of the volume of log entries.

Network Management

Servers and routers on the network can be managed by using the Simple Network Management Protocol (SNMP) discussed in Chapter 4, "Networking Technology." One of the most common SNMP platforms is HP OpenView, although less-expensive management platforms are also available. Network-management software provides insight into the overall condition of the networked environment. System alarms are generated before a user calls in to complain. The network-management system is useful only if someone is available to view the alert.

Capacity Management

Capacity management focuses on the monitoring of computing resources and planning for future availability. By using system monitoring tools, the IT administrator should be able to reasonably estimate the system capacity needed. System utilization reports provide insight into the current processing workload. This workload can be prorated against the operating schedule to forecast future shortfalls.

External changes in the service-level agreements or number of users will have a direct impact on available capacity. During capacity management planning, it is important to assess single points of failure. There will always be a few single points of failure in a system because of the technology selected or the cost of redundancy.

Two Different Outcomes in redundancy

When available, hardware redundancy may increase or decrease the normal operating capacity. For example, a duplicate disk drive system will never exceed 50 percent of combined total gross capacity. A 100 gigabyte (GB) drive array would split into two separate sets of disks with a total capacity of less than 50GB each. In fact, the usable capacity may be reduced to only 40GB each after allowing for minimum necessary free space. So only 40 would be usable from a total capacity of 100.

Duplicate firewalls, on the other hand, may double available capacity if they shared the workload in parallel. The firewalls would provide two independent communication paths, thereby doubling normal capacity.

Problem Management

The IT operations staff should have a problem management process in place. Effective problem management provides a timely response by using predefined procedures that include a method for problem escalation.

Situations requiring problem management include the following:

Incident handling   Incidents reported to IT may be either accidental or malicious. An established procedure is required to ensure a thorough investigation. Care must be taken to prevent damage to the evidence in case it is later determined that the location is a technology crime scene. Members of the incident response team should be identified and trained in advance. The reporting of certain types of incidents may be required by law. The organization's incident response plans should contain a provision for legal reporting. Incident handling is a corrective control.

 There are still organizations that do not have a published incident-handling guide. A good start would be to purchase the incident-handling kit available from the SANS Institute (www.sans.org). The SANS kit uses a fill-in-the-blank template, complete with job descriptions and procedures. The cost is under $150.

Acceptable use policy (AUP) violation Violation of the acceptable use policy could include the misuse of corporate resources or the presence of nonbusiness materials The discovery of an AUP violation should trigger the incident-handling process and notification to Human Resources.

Job accounting Computer processing is always subject to problems. Conditions of concern include abnormal job terminations and exception handling. Other problems can include jobs that run too fast or excessively slow for the volume of work. Jobs that end too fast may indicate that a portion of the processing was skipped. Consider, for example, a tape backup that appears to complete in record time. An investigation may find that the data written to tape is incomplete or nonexistent. Either condition would indicate a substantial problem.

Training The training of users and staff is a good response to prevent the recurrence of a problem. Training plans should exist for new hire orientation, basic user training, and additional awareness training. Test exercises for business continuity also serve to train individuals about their job role during a crisis.

All incidents, problems, and errors are to be recorded. The event should be analyzed by a competent individual with the proper training. The problem should be escalated as necessary to ensure it receives the correct level of attention. All instances of problems are expected to be resolved in a timely manner. For example, computer security problems should be dealt with immediately. Printing problems may be a lower priority.

IT Performance Indicators

The performance of information technology is ultimately interpreted by three fundamental business performance indicators: the IT budget, user satisfaction, and technical indicators. Technical indicators could include a combination of automated and manual metrics. You can gain a reasonable understanding of IT performance by reviewing these indicators.

IT management should conduct regular performance reviews of all the items discussed in this chapter. Management and staff should make provisions for an independent audit to review their work. The auditor's focus in IT service delivery will be to determine the effectiveness and efficiency of IT.

Summary

When reviewing IT service delivery, the paramount concern is that action items are identified, properly tracked, assigned to a competent individual, and resolved in a timely manner. IT's performance can be measured by a combination of metrics, budget performance, and user satisfaction.

The IT auditor evaluates the client's performance and effectiveness of their management techniques.

Exam Essentials

Know how to evaluate service-level management practices from internal and external providers. Service-level management is based on an understanding between the provider and the user as to system availability, service definition, personnel qualifications, security requirements, data integrity requirements, SLA performance reporting, right to audit, SLA change procedures, and the cost of service.

Understand the principles of IT operations management to ensure that the service meets the business requirements. IT operations management can be aligned to business requirements by using the traditional processes of mission, strategy, and metrics supported by policies, standards, and procedures. Alternatively, the alignment can occur by using the balanced scorecard methodology.

Understand how the IT organization implements functional controls for service delivery. Controls are established for system access, data files, input, application processing, output, maintenance, change management, asset control, capacity management, and problem management.

Know the issues in problem and incident management. Problem and incident management requires a timely response via predefined procedures and a method for escalating problems. The purpose of problem response is to correct a condition. Incident response determines the impact and the steps necessary for resolution. A concern is that the location of an incident may be a potential technology crime scene.

Understand the issues surrounding software licensing. Software licenses are assets that need to be controlled, inventoried, tracked, and managed. Unauthorized installation of computer software is a violation of copyright law, which carries stiff penalties.

Understand production change control, release management, and configuration control. Changes need to be carefully managed in a production environment to prevent an interruption or outage. Software may be released as a major release, an update, or an emergency fix. Emergency changes should undergo the standard change management process after implementation.

Understand the demands of ensuring processing integrity. Data files must be protected from unauthorized access. Standing data is vulnerable to unauthorized copying. Application processing uses input controls, processing controls to ensure the completeness of processing, and output controls to ensure the confidentiality of the output.

Understand the purpose of valid backups and project management in maintenance controls. Data backups are used to ensure that two copies of the data exist in case a failure occurs during maintenance. Project management is used with risk analysis to manage maintenance changes. The goal is to ensure that the maintenance occurs with the least possible impact to the system's availability and integrity.

Review Questions

1. Performance of a third party should be compared to the agreed service-level metrics and must be
   A. Supplied by an independent employee of the service provider.
   B. Accepted at face value by the customer.
   C. Reviewed by management.
   D. Review is not necessary because it is a third party and outside of customer's control.

2. What is the most important responsibility of the IT security person?
   A. Controlling and monitoring compliance to data security policies
   B. Promoting security awareness within the organization
   C. Establishing procedures for IT and reviewing for legal accuracy
   D. Assisting in system administration of the servers and database

3. Segregation of duties may not be practical in a small environment. A single employee may be performing the combined functions of server operator and application programmer, for example. The IS auditor should recommend controls for which of the following?
   A. Automated logging of changes made to development libraries
   B. The hiring of additional technical staff to force segregation of duties
   C. Preventing the operator login ID from making program modifications
   D. Procedures that verify that only approved program changes are implemented

4. What are the four basic types of metrics that can be used to measure IT performance?
   A. Efficiency, implementation, impact, effectiveness
   B. Cost, quantifiable, qualitative, historical
   C. Process control, compliance, efficiency, cost
   D. Service definition, performance goal, cost, effectiveness

5. What type of control is representative of exception reporting?
   A. Processing
   B. Output
   C. Database integrity
   D. Service level

6. How should management act to best deal with emergency changes?
   A. Emergency changes cannot be made without advance testing.
   B. All changes should still undergo review.
   C. The change control process does not apply to emergency conditions.
   D. Emergency changes are not allowed under any condition.

7. What is one of the bigger concerns regarding asset disposal?

    A. Residual asset value

    B. Employees taking disposed property home

    C. Standing data

    D. Environmental regulations

8. Why is ongoing system monitoring important?

    A. For preventative control

    B. For historical logging and trend analysis

    C. To collect metrics for SLA reports

    D. To find inconsistencies and errors

9. What is the primary objective in problem escalation?

    A. Improve customer satisfaction.

    B. Optimize the number of skilled personnel.

    C. Ensure the correct response.

    D. Prove that the IT staff is competent.

10. Which of the following is a major issue facing incident response?

    A. The location may be a technology crime scene.

    B. Scheduling of personnel.

    C. Developing appropriate procedures.

    D. Compliance with IT policies.

11. Which of the following functions should be separated from the others if segregation of duties cannot be achieved in an automated system?

    A. Origination

    B. Authorization

    C. Correction

    D. Reprocessing

12. What is the primary concern regarding maintenance login accounts?

    A. Computer systems have default user accounts for system setup.

    B. Access to maintenance accounts must be restricted to a particular station address.

    C. Maintenance accounts must be configured to use the hardware that was selected by the organization.

    D. The default login ID used by maintenance accounts is often well known.

13. An IS auditor is auditing controls related to an employee termination. Which of the following is the *most* important aspect to be reviewed?

    A. Company staff are notified about the termination.

    B. All login accounts of the employee are terminated.

    C. The details of the employee have been removed from active payroll files.

    D. Company property provided to the employee has been returned.

14. What are the three layers for scoring IT performance according to ISACA?

    A. Policy, standards, established procedures

    B. Budget, service-level agreement, problem management

    C. Mission, strategy, metrics

    D. Definition of service, internal controls, change management

15. What is one of the first concerns that the IS auditor should have when reviewing service-level agreements?

    A. The vendor can provide evidence that security controls are present.

    B. The services in the agreement are aligned to actual business needs.

    C. The client received the absolute best price for services offered.

    D. The contract guaranteed the right to audit the outsource vendor.

16. Which of the following statements is *not* true concerning SLA performance reporting?

    A. Metrics are reported against qualitative measurement.

    B. Both parties need to agree on the content of metrics.

    C. Metrics are reported against quantitative measurement.

    D. Metrics must be developed to fill actual business objectives.

17. Which of the following statements about standing data is true?

    A. Standing data improves database performance. The data is standing ready for processing.

    B. Standing data is an operational requirement.

    C. Standing data is a security concern.

    D. Standing data is a normal occurrence in the database.

18. Which of the following is *not* an input authorization control?

    A. Signatures on source documents

    B. Sequence numbers

    C. Management review

    D. Separation of duties

19. What are three of the four key perspectives on the IT balanced scorecard?

    A. Cost reduction, business process, growth

    B. Business justification, service-level agreements, budget

    C. Organizational staffing, cost reduction, employee training

    D. Service level, critical success factors, vendor selection

20. What is biggest advantage of using a lights-out operation?

    A. Reduced operating expense.

    B. The ability to run systems by remote control.

    C. Removing personnel from the data center reduces risk.

    D. Service personnel will occupy the room only during times of maintenance.

Answers to Review Questions

1. Answer C. All performance by a third party under the servic-level agreement should be compared to the service levels that the provider and the user of the service agreed on.

2. A. The primary responsibility of the IT information security person is to ensure the proper implementation of data security policies and to monitor the level of compliance.

3. D. Compensating controls may be used when segregation of duties is not practical for a small staff. Procedures must exist to verify that only approved program changes are implemented.

4. A. The four basic types of metrics are efficiency (which indicates timeliness), implementation (which demonstrates a comparative count or percentage attained), impact (shown as a qualitative measure of incidents sorted by type or represented as a dollar figure), and effectiveness (measured as a quantifiable number demonstrating satisfactory resolution).

5. A. Exception reporting is a processing control used to capture input errors before processing occurs. The exception may be held in suspension until the errors are corrected or rejected.

6. B. All emergency changes should still undergo the formal change management process after the fact.

7. C. Any standing data should be purged from the equipment prior to disposal.

8. D. Proper IT management focuses on proactive discovery of inconsistencies, errors, and processing failures. The results can be used for secondary value in trend analysis and SLA reporting.

9. C. Problem escalation is used to ensure that the problem is analyzed by a competent individual with the proper training.

10. A. The incident location may be a technical crime scene. The response should be preplanned and structured to ensure that the value of evidence is not diminished and confidentiality is maintained. The other points may be contributing circumstances but are not major issues.

11. B. Authorization for changes should be separated from other work if separation of duties cannot be achieved. Additional compensating controls would be required.

12. D. The default login ID used for maintenance accounts is frequently well known and commercially published. Login may be restricted to a particular station address. However, that is not the primary concern.

13. B. Employee access to information systems should be promptly terminated. The accounts for contractors no longer employed by the organization should be suspended.
All accounts should be reviewed before the account is deleted.

14. C. ISACA defines the three layers for IT scoring as mission, strategy, and meaningful metrics for performance measurement.

15. B. The services provided should fulfill the organization's business objectives. The second concern would be the presence of security controls, followed by the right to audit. The last concern should be the absolute best price. Price would not matter if the services provided did not fulfill an actual business requirement.

16. A. Service-level performance metrics should be quantitative measurements rather than qualitative. Qualitative measurements are too subjective. All other statements are true.

17. C. Standing data is a security concern that requires additional controls such as storage in an encrypted format.

18. D. Separation of duties does not grant input authorization. The other three answers represent valid input authorization.

19. A. The four perspectives on the IT balanced scorecard are the customer perspective, business process perspective, financial perspective, and growth perspective. Each of these seek to define the highest return by IT.

20. C. Removing personnel from the data center reduces the risk to systems by reducing the risk of error, malicious attacks, and environmental contaminants.

Chapter 7

Information Asset Protection

THE OBJECTIVE OF THIS CHAPTER IS TO ACQUAINT THE READER WITH THE FOLLOWING CONCEPTS:

- ✓ Implementing data classification schemes to specify appropriate controls
- ✓ Logical access controls for identification, authentication, and restriction of users
- ✓ Perimeter security designs, firewalls, and intrusion detection
- ✓ Encryption systems using symmetric and asymmetric public keys
- ✓ Dealing with malicious software, viruses, worms, and other attacks
- ✓ Security testing, monitoring and assessment tools
- ✓ Physical security protection methods
- ✓ Storage, retrieval, transport, and disposition of confidential information
- ✓ Controls and risks with the use of portable devices

In this chapter, you will study the implementation of access controls. These controls are implemented by using administrative, physical, and technical methods. The IS auditor is required to evaluate the implementation, processes, and procedures used by the client.

The goal of information asset protection is to ensure that adequate safeguards are in use to store, access, transport, and ultimately dispose of confidential information. The auditor must understand how controls promote confidentiality, integrity, and availability.

We will discuss a variety of technical topics related to network security, data encryption, design of physical protection, biometrics, and user authentication. This chapter represents the most significant area of the CISA exam.

Understanding the Threat

Protecting information assets is a significant challenge. The very subject of security conjures up a myriad of responses. This chapter provides you with a solid overview of practical information about security. The unfortunate reality is that concepts of security have not evolved significantly over the last 2,000 years. Let us explain.

The medieval design of security is still pervasive. Most of your customers will view security as primarily a perimeter defense. History is riddled with failed monuments attesting to the folly of over-reliance on perimeter defenses. Consider the castle walls to be equivalent to the office walls of the client's organization. Fresh water from the creek would be analogous to our modern-day utilities. The castle observation towers provide visibility for internal affairs and awareness of outside threats. The observation tower is functionally equal to network management and intrusion detection. A fortress drawbridge provides an equivalent function of the network firewall, allowing persons we trust to enter our organization. The castle courtyard serves as the marketplace or intranet. This is where our vendors, staff, and clients interact. During medieval times, it is necessary for our emissaries to enter and exit the castle fortress in secret. Confidential access is accomplished via a secret tunnel. Our modern-day equivalent to the secret tunnel is a virtual private network (VPN). Consider these thoughts for a moment while you look at Figure 7.1, concerning the medieval defensive design.

It is possible that security has actually regressed. In medieval times, royalty would use armed guards as an escort when visiting trading partners. In the modern world, the princess is given a laptop, PDA, cell phone, and airline ticket with instructions to check in later. Where is the security now?

FIGURE 7.1   Medieval defensive design

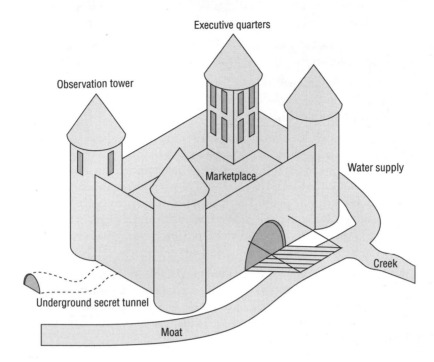

Medieval castles fell as a result of infiltration, betrayal, loss of utilities such as fresh water, and brute force attacks against the fortress walls. This example should make it perfectly clear why internal controls need improvement. The only possible defensive strategy utilizes multiple layers of security with a constant vigil by management. Anything less is just another castle waiting to fall.

Let's take a quick look at some examples of computer crime and threats to the information assets.

Examples of Threats and Computer Crimes

There is nothing new about the threats facing organizations. History shows that these threats and crimes date back almost 4,000 years (over 130 generations). Therefore, none of these should be a surprise. We need to take a quick review of the threats and crimes that shall be mitigated with administrative, physical, and technical controls:

Theft   The *theft* of information, designs, plans, and customer lists could be catastrophic to an organization. Consider the controls in place to prevent theft of money or embezzlement. Have equivalent controls in place to prevent the theft of valuable information?

Fraud   Misrepresentation to gain an advantage is the definition of *fraud*. Electronic records may be subject to remote manipulation for the purpose of deceit, suppression, or unfair profit. Fraud may occur with or without the computer.

Sabotage   *Sabotage* is defined as willful and malicious destruction of an employer's property, often during a labor dispute or to cause malicious interference with normal operations.

Blackmail   *Blackmail* is the unlawful demand of money or property under threat to do harm. Examples are to injure property, make an accusation of a crime, or to expose disgraceful defects. This is commonly referred to as *extortion*.

Industrial espionage   The world is full of competitors and spies. *Espionage* is a crime of spying by individuals and governments with the intent to gather, transmit, or release information to the advantage of any foreign organization. It's not uncommon for governments to eavesdrop on the communications of foreign companies. The purpose is to uncover business secrets to share with companies in their country. The intention is to steal any perceived advancements in position or technology. Telecommunications traveling through each country are subject to legal eavesdropping by governments. Additional care must be taken to keep secrets out of the hands of a competitor.

Unauthorized disclosure   *Unauthorized disclosure* is the release of information without permission. The purpose may be fraud or sabotage. For example, unauthorized disclosure of trade secrets or product defects may cause substantial damage that is irreversible. The unauthorized disclosure of client records would cause a violation of privacy laws, not to mention details that would be valuable for a competitor.

Loss of credibility   *Loss of credibility* is the damage to an organization's image, brand, or executive management. This can severely impact revenue and the organization's ability to continue. Fraud, sabotage, blackmail, and unauthorized disclosure may be used to destroy credibility.

Loss of proprietary information   The mishandling of information can result in the loss of trade secrets. Valuable information concerning system designs, future marketing plans, and corporate formulas could be released without any method of recovering the data. Once a secret is out, there is no way to make the information secret again.

Legal repercussions   The breach of control or loss of an asset can create a situation of undesirable attention. Privacy concerns have created new requirements for public disclosure following a breach. Without a doubt, the last thing an organization needs is increased interest from a government regulator. Stockholders and customers may have grounds for subsequent legal action in alleging negligence or misconduct, depending on the situation.

According to the US Federal Bureau of Investigation (FBI), the top three losses in 2005 were due to virus attack, unauthorized access, and theft of proprietary information. There is a trend of dramatic increase in unauthorized access and theft of proprietary information. So the auditor may ask, who is doing this?

Identifying the Perpetrators

There is one fundamental difference between a victim and a perpetrator. The victim did not act with malice. The perpetrators of crime may be casual or sophisticated. Their motive may be financial, political, thrill seeking, or a biased grudge against the organization. The damage impact is usually the same regardless of the perpetrator's background or motive. A common trait is that a perpetrator will have time, access, or skills necessary to execute the offense.

Today's computer criminal does not require advanced skills, although they would help. A person with mal-intent needs little more than access to launch their attack. For this reason, strong access controls are mandatory. The FBI reported the number of internal attacks vs. external attacks were approximately equal in 2005. So, who is the attacker?

Hackers

The term *hacker* contains a double meaning. The honorable interpretation of hacker refers to a computer programmer who is able to create usable computer programs where none previously existed. In this Study Guide, we refer to the dishonorable interpretation of a hacker— an undesirable criminal. The criminal hacker focuses on a desire to break in, take over, and damage or discredit legitimate computer processing. The first goal of hacking is to exceed the authorized level of system privileges. This is why it is necessary to monitor systems and take swift action against any individual who attempts to gain a higher level of access. Hackers may be internal or external to the organization. Attempts to gain unauthorized access within the organization should be dealt with by using the highest level of severity, including immediate termination of employment.

Crackers

The term *cracker* is a variation of *hacker*, with the analogy equal to a safe cracker. Some individuals use the term cracker in an attempt to differentiate from the honorable computer programmer definition of hacker. The criminal cracker and criminal hacker terms are used interchangeably. Crackers attempt to illegally or unethically break into a system without authorization.

Script Kiddies

A number of specialized programs exist for the purpose of bypassing security controls. Many hacker tools began as well-intentioned tools for system administration. The argument would be the same if we were discussing a carpenter's hammer. A carpenter's hammer used for the right purpose is a constructive tool. The same tool is a weapon if used for a nefarious purpose. A *script kiddie* is an individual who executes computer scripts and programs written by others. Their motive is to hack a computer by using someone else's software. Examples include password decryption programs and automated access utilities. Several years ago, a login utility was created for Microsoft users to get push-button access into a Novell server. This nifty utility was released worldwide before it was recognized that the utility bypassed Novell security. The utility was nicknamed Red Button and became immensely popular with script kiddies. Internal controls must be put in place to restrict the possession or use of administration utilities. Violations should be considered severe and dealt with in the same manner as hacker violations.

Employee Betrayal

There is a reason why the FBI report cited the high volume of internal crimes. A person within the organization has more access and opportunity than anyone else. Few persons would have a better understanding of the security posture and weaknesses. In fact, an employee may be in a position of influence to socially engineer coworkers into ignoring safeguards and alert conditions. This is why it is important to monitor internal employee satisfaction. The great medieval fortresses fell by the betrayal of trusted allies.

Ethical Hacker Gone Bad

The term *ethical hacker* or *white hat* is a new definition in computer security. An ethical hacker is one who conducts computer hacks and attacks with the goal of identifying an organization's weaknesses Some individuals participate in special training to learn about penetrating computer defenses. This will usually result in one of two outcomes. In the first outcome, a few of the ethical white hat technicians will exercise extraordinary restraint and control. The objective of ethical hacking is to exercise hacker techniques only in a highly regimented, totally supervised environment. The white hat technician will operate from a prewritten test plan, reviewed by internal audit or management oversight. The slightest deviation is grounds for termination. This additional level of control is to protect the organization from error or personal agenda by the white hat technician.

The second outcome is that a white hat technician will direct their own efforts. Some individuals will demonstrate great pride in their ability to circumvent required controls. These self-directed hacking techniques create an unacceptable level of risk for multiple reasons including organizational liability.

As a professional auditors, we've been engaged on several occasions to determine whether the internal staff has been using hacker techniques and tools without explicit test plans and approval. In each event except one, the technician was fired for violating internal controls. Additional controls are necessary when a white hat technician is employed by the organization. Honest people may be kept honest with proper supervision.

Third Parties

External persons are referred to as a third parties. *Third parties* include visitors, vendors, consultants, maintenance personnel, and the cleaning crew. These individuals may gain access and knowledge of the internal organization.

You would be surprised by how many times we auditors have been invited to join the client in a meeting room with internal plans still visible on the whiteboards. The client's careless disregard is obvious by the words *important do not erase* emblazoned across the board. You can bet this same organization allows their vendors to work unsupervised. In the evening, the cleaning crew will unlock and open every door on the floor for several hours while vacuuming and emptying waste baskets. We seriously doubt the cleaning crew would challenge a stranger entering the office. In fact, a low-paid cleaning crew may be exercising their own agenda.

Ignorance

The term *ignorance* is simply defined as the lack of knowledge. An ignorant person may be a party to a crime and not even know it. Even worse, the individual may be committing an offense without realizing the impact of their actions. Fortunately, ignorance can be cured by training. This is the objective of user training for internal controls. By teaching the purpose of internal security controls, the organization can reduce their overall risk.

Overview of Attack Methods

Your clients will expect you to have knowledge about the different methods of attacking computers. We will try to take the boredom out of the subject by injecting practical examples. Computer attacks can be implemented with the computer or against a computer. There are basically two types of attacks: passive and active. Let's start with passive attacks.

Passive Attacks

Passive attacks are characterized by techniques of observation. The intention of a passive attack is to gain additional information before launching an active attack. Three examples of passive attacks are network analysis, traffic analysis, and eavesdropping:

Network analysis   The computer traffic across a network can be analyzed to create a map of the hosts and routers. Common tools such as HP OpenView or OpenNMS are useful for creating network maps. The objective of network analysis is to create a complete profile of the network infrastructure prior to launching an active attack. Computers transmit large numbers of requests that other computers on the network will observe. Simple maps can be created with no more than the observed traffic or responses from a series of ping commands. The network *ping* command provides a simple communications test between two devices by sending a single request, aka a ping. The concept of creating maps by using network analysis is commonly referred to as *painting* or *footprinting*.

Host traffic analysis   *Traffic analysis* is used to identify systems of particular interest. The communication between host computers can be monitored by the activity level and number of service requests. Host traffic analysis is an easy method used to identify servers on the network.

Specific details on the host computer can be determined by using a *fingerprinting* tool such as Nmap. The Nmap utility is active software that sends a series of special commands, each command unique to a particular operating system type and version. For example, a Unix system will not respond to a NetBIOS type 137 request. However, a computer running Microsoft Windows will answer. The exact operating system of the computer can usually be identified with only seven or eight simple service requests. Host traffic analysis will provide clues to a system even if all other communication traffic is encrypted. This is an excellent tool for tracking down a rogue IP address. The Nmap utility provides information as to whether the destination address is a Unix computer, Macintosh computer, computer running Windows, or something else like an HP printer. This fingerprinting technique is also popular with hackers for the same reason.

Eavesdropping   *Eavesdropping* is the traditional method of spying with the intent to gather information. The term originated from a person spying on others while listening under the roof eaves of a house. Computer network analysis is a type of eavesdropping. Other methods include capturing a hidden copy of files or copying messages as they traverse the network. Email messages and instant messaging are notoriously vulnerable to eavesdropping because of their insecure design. Computer login IDs, passwords, and user keystrokes can be captured by using eavesdropping tools. Encrypted messages can be captured by eavesdropping with the intention of breaking the encryption at a later date. The message can be read later, after the encryption is compromised. Eavesdropping helped the Allies crack the secret code of radio messages sent using the German Enigma machine in World War II. Network sniffers are excellent tools for capturing communications traveling across the network.

Now let's move on to discuss the active attacks.

Active Attacks

Passive attacks tend to be relatively invisible, whereas active attacks are easier to detect. The attacker will proceed to execute an active attack after obtaining sufficient background information. The *active attack* is designed to execute an act of theft or to cause a disruption in normal computer processing. Following is a list of active attacks:

Social engineering   Criminals can trick an individual into cooperating by using a technique known as *social engineering*. The social engineer will fraudulently present themselves as a person of authority or someone in need of assistance. The social engineer's story will be woven with tiny bits of truth. All social engineers are opportunists who gain access by asking for it. For example, the social engineer may pretend to be a contractor or employee sent to work on a problem. The social engineer will play upon the victim's natural desire to help.

Phishing   A new social engineering technique called *phishing* (pronounced *fishing*) is now in use. The scheme utilizes fake emails sent to unsuspecting victims, which contain a link to the criminal's counterfeit website. Anyone can copy the images and format of a legitimate website by using their Internet browser. A phishing criminal copies legitimate web pages into a fake email or to a fake website. The message tells the unsuspecting victim that it is necessary to enter personal details such as US social security number, credit card number, bank account information, or online user ID and password. Phishing attacks can also be used to implement spyware on unprotected computers. Many phishing attacks can be avoided through user education.

Real World Scenario

Real-Life Social Engineering

There is a wonderful movie about social engineering titled *Catch Me If You Can* (released in 2002), starring Leonardo DiCaprio with Tom Hanks and Christopher Walken. It is the story of teenager Frank Abagnale who successfully masqueraded for years as a doctor who actually practiced in a hospital, a commercial airline pilot who actually flew in the cockpit, and a lawyer with a genuine appointment to assistant district attorney. Abagnale at 19 was the youngest person to be on the FBI's most wanted list for forging over $6 million in fake checks passed worldwide.

Dumpster diving   Attackers will frequently resort to rummaging through the trash for discarded information. The practice is also known as *dumpster diving*. Dumpster diving is perfectly legal under the condition that the individuals are not trespassing. This is the primary reason why proper destruction is mandatory. Most paper records and optical disks are destroyed by shredding.

Virus   Computer *viruses* are a type of malicious program designed to self-replicate and spread across multiple computers. The purpose of the computer virus is to disrupt normal processing. A computer virus may commence damage immediately or lie dormant, awaiting a particular circumstance, such as the date of April Fools' Day. Viruses will automatically attach themselves to the out-going files. The first malicious computer virus came about in the 1980s during prototype testing for self-replicating software. Antivirus software will stop known attacks by detecting the behavior demonstrated by the virus program (*signature detection*) or by appending an antivirus flag to the end of a file (*inoculation*, aka *immunization*). New virus attacks can be detected if any program tries to append data to the antivirus flag. Not all antivirus works by signature scanning, it can also be by heuristic scanning, integrity checking, or activity blocking. These are all valid virus detection methods.

Worm   Computer *worms* are very destructive and able to travel freely across the computer network by exploiting known system vulnerabilities. Worms are independent and will actively seek new systems on their own.

Logic bomb   The concept of the *logic bomb* is designed around dormant program code that is waiting for a trigger event to cause detonation. Unlike a virus or worm, logic bombs do not travel. The logic bomb remains in one location, awaiting detonation. Logic bombs are difficult to detect. Some logic bombs are intentional, and others are the unintentional result of poor programming. Intentional logic bombs can be set to detonate after the perpetrator is gone.

Trapdoor   Computer programmers frequently install a shortcut, also known as a *trapdoor*, for use during software testing. The trapdoor is a hidden access point within the computer software. A competent programmer will remove the majority of trapdoors before releasing a production version of the program. However, several vendors routinely leave a trapdoor in a computer program to facilitate user support. The commercial version of PGP encryption software contained a trapdoor designed to recover lost encryption keys and to allow the government to read the encrypted files, if necessary. Trapdoors compromise access controls and are considered dangerous.

Brute force attack   *Brute force* is the use of extreme effort to overcome an obstacle. For example, an amateur could discover the combination to a safe by dialing all of the 63,000 possible combinations. There is a mathematical likelihood that the actual combination will be determined after trying less than one-third of the possible combinations. *Brute force attacks* are frequently used against user logon IDs and passwords. In one particular attack, all of the encrypted computer passwords are compared against a list of all the words encrypted from a language dictionary. After the match is identified, the attacker will use the unencrypted word that created the password match. This is why it is important to use passwords that do not appear in any language dictionary.

Denial of service (DoS)   Attackers can disable the computer by rendering legitimate use impossible. The objective is to remotely shut down service by overloading the system and thereby prevent the normal user from processing anything on the computer.

IP fragmentation attack   One of the common Internet attack techniques is to send a series of fragmented service requests to a computer through a firewall. The technique is successful if the firewall fails to examine each packet. For this reason, firewalls are configured to discard IP fragments.

Crash-restart   A variation of attack techniques is crash-restart. An attacker loads malicious software onto a computer or reconfigures security settings to the attacker's advantage. Then the attacker crashes the system, allowing the computer to automatically restart (reboot). The attacker can take control of the system after it restarts with the new configuration. The purpose is to install a backdoor for the attacker.

Maintenance accounts   Most computer systems are configured with special maintenance accounts. These maintenance accounts may be part of the default settings or created for system support. An example is the user account named *DBA* for database administrator, or *tape* for a tape backup device. All maintenance accounts should be carefully controlled. It is advisable to disable the default maintenance accounts on a system. The security manager may find an advantage in monitoring access attempts against the default accounts. Any attempted access may indicate the beginnings of an attack.

Remote access attacks   Most attackers will attempt to exploit remote access. The goal of the attack is often based on personal satisfaction for political gain. There is less personal risk involved in gaining remote access. The common types of remote access attacks are referred to as follows:

War dialing   The attacker uses an automated modem-dialing utility to launch a brute force attack against a list of phone numbers. The attack generates a list of telephone numbers that were answered by a computer modem. The next step of the attack is to break in through an unsecured modem. This is why it's necessary for modems to reject inbound calls or to be protected by a telephone firewall such as Telewall by SecureLogix.

War driving/walking   Wireless access is known to be insecure. Wireless manufacturers have seriously compromised security in an effort to improve Plug and Play capabilities for users. The trade-off of fewer user support issues for less security permits casual attackers the opportunity to gain remote access by walking or driving past wireless network transmitters. Previous attackers use symbols to mark the unsuspecting organization's property, to show other attackers that wireless access is available at that location. This marking technique is referred to as *war chalking*. War chalk maps of insecure access points are available for download on the Internet.

Cross-network connectivity   Interconnected networks are effective in business. The connectivity across networks provides an avenue for more-efficient processing by the user. Computer networks are cross-connected internally, and even across the Internet. It is not uncommon for a business partner to have special access. All of these connections can be exploited by an attacker. Business partner connections can provide an opportunity for the attacker to remotely compromise the systems of a partner organization with little chance of detection. The purpose of internal and external firewalls is to block attacks. The implementation of internal firewalls is an excellent practice that dates back to the Great Wall of China. Unfortunately, few organizations recognize the need.

Source routing   As stated earlier, useful system administration tools can be implemented as weapons. In the early days of networking, it was necessary to send data across a network without any reliance on the network configuration itself. Therefore, a special network protocol known as *source routing* was developed. Source routing is designed to ignore the configuration of the network routers and follow the instructions designated by the sender (the source). Source routing is a magnificent diagnostic tool for reaching remote networks. As you can imagine, source routing also is popular with hackers, because it allows a hacker to bypass routing configurations used for firewall security. For this reason, every firewall and most routers must be configured to disable source routing.

Salami technique   The *salami technique* is used for the commission of financial crimes. The key here is to make the alteration so insignificant that in a single case it would go completely unnoticed, e.g., a bank employee inserts a program into the bank's servers that deducts a small amount of money from the account of every customer. No single account holder will probably notice this unauthorized debit, but the bank employee will make a sizable amount of money every month.

Packet replay   Network communications are sent by transmitting a series of small messages known as packets. The attacker captures a series of legitimate packets by using a capture tool similar to a network sniffer. The packets are retransmitted (replayed) within a short time window to trick a computer system into believing that the sender is a legitimate user. This technique can be combined with a denial of service technique to compromise the system. The legitimate user is knocked off the network by using denial of service, and the attacker attempts to take over communications. This can be effective for hijacking sessions in single sign-on systems such as Kerberos. We will discuss Kerberos single sign-on later in this chapter.

Message modification   Message modification can be used to intercept and alter communications. The legitimate message is captured before receipt by the destination. The contents of the message, address, or other information is modified. The modified message is then sent to the destination in a fraudulent attempt to appear genuine.

This technique is commonly used for a man-in-the-middle attack: A third party places themselves between the bona fide sender and receiver. The person in the middle pretends to be the other party. If encryption is used, the middle person tricks the sender into using an encryption key known by the middle person. After reading, the message will be re-encrypted using the key of the true recipient. The message will be retransmitted to be received by the intended recipient. The man-in-the-middle is able to eavesdrop without detection. Neither the sender nor the receiver is aware of the security compromise.

Email spamming and spoofing   You are probably aware of email spamming. *Spamming* refers to sending a mass mailing of identical messages to a large number of users. The current laws governing email allow a business to send mass emails as long as the recipient is informed of the sender's legitimate address and the recipient is provided a mechanism to stop the receipt of any future emails.

Email spamming is a common mechanism used in phishing attacks. The term *spoofing* refers to fraudulently altering the information concerning the sender of email. An example of email spoofing is when an attacker sends a fake notice concerning your eBay auction account. The spoofed email address appears as if it were sent by eBay. Email spamming is illegal in some countries, and email spoofing is prosecuted as criminal fraud and/or electronic wire fraud.

A variety of other technical attacks may be launched against the computer. A common attack is to send to the computer an impossible request or series of requests that cannot be serviced. These cause the system to overload its CPU, memory, or communication buffers. As a result, the computer crashes. An example is the old Ping of Death command (`ping -l 65510`), which exceeded the computer's maximum input size for a communication buffer.

The first step in preventing the loss of information assets is to establish administrative controls. Let's begin the discussion on implementing administrative safeguards.

Using Administrative Protection

Throughout this Study Guide, we have discussed the importance of IT governance over internal controls. The first step for a protection strategy is to establish administrative operating rules. Information security management is the foundation of information asset protection. Let's discuss some of the administrative methods used to protect data: information security management, IT security governance, data retention, documenting access paths, and other techniques. We will begin with Information security management.

Information Security Management

The objective of *information security management* is to ensure confidentiality, integrity, and availability of computing resources. To accomplish this goal, it is necessary to implement organizational design in support of these objectives. Let's discuss some of the job roles in information security management:

Chief security officer   The chief security officer (CSO) is a role developed to grant the highest level of authority to the senior information systems security officer. Unfortunately, this tends to be a position of title more than a position of real corporate influence. The purpose of the CSO position is to define and enforce security policies for the organization.

Chief privacy officer   New demands for client privacy have created the requirement for a chief privacy officer (CPO). This position is equal to or directly below the chief security officer. The CPO is commonly a position of title rather than genuine corporate authority. The CPO is responsible for protecting confidential information of clients and employees.

Information systems security manager   The information systems security manager (ISSM) is responsible for the day-to-day process of ensuring compliance for system security. The ISSM follows the directives of the CSO and CPO for policy compliance. The ISSM is supported by a staff of information systems security analysts (ISSAs) who work on the individual projects and security problems. An ISSM supervises the information system security analysts and sets the daily priorities.

IT Security Governance

The concept of IT governance for security is based on security policies, standards, and procedures. For these administrative controls to be effective, it is necessary to define specific roles, responsibilities, and requirements. Let's imagine that an information security policy and matching standard have been adopted. The next step would be to determine the specific level of controls necessary for each piece of data. Data can be classified into groups based on its value or sensitivity. The data classification process will define the information controls necessary to ensure appropriate confidentiality.

The federal government uses an information classification program to specify controls over the use of data. High-risk data is classified top secret, and the classifications cascade down to data available for public consumption. Every organization should utilize an information classification program for their data. Let's take a look at the typical classifications:

Public   Information for public consumption. It is important to understand that data classified as public needs to be reviewed and edited to ensure that the correct message is conveyed. Examples of public information include websites, sales brochures, marketing advertisements, press releases, and legal filings. Most information filed at the courthouse is a public record, viewable by anyone.

Sensitive   There is a particular type of data that needs to be disclosed to certain parties but not to everyone. We refer to this data as *sensitive*. This data may be a matter of record or legal fact. However, the organization would not want to go about advertising the details. Examples of sensitive information include client lists, product pricing structure, contract terms, vendor lists, and details of outstanding litigation.

Private, internal use only   The classification of data for internal use only is commonly applied to operating procedures and employment records. The details of operating procedures are usually provided on a need-to-know basis to prevent a person from designing a method for defeating the procedure. Examples of private records include salary data, health-care information, results of background checks, and employee performance reviews.

<u>Confidential</u>   This is the highest category of general security classification outside of the government. It may be subdivided into confidential and highly confidential trade secrets. Confidential data is anything that must not be shared outside of the organization. Examples include buyout negotiations, secret recipes, and specific details about the inner workings of the organization. Confidential data may be exempt from certain types of legal disclosure.

The overall purpose of using an information classification scheme is to ensure proper handling based on the information content and context. *Context* refers to the usage of information.

Two major risks are present in the absence of an information classification scheme. The first major risk is that information will be mishandled. The second major risk is that without an information classification scheme, all of the organization's data may be subject to scrutiny during legal proceedings. The information classification scheme safeguards knowledge.

Authority Roles over Data

To implement policies, standards, and procedures, it is necessary to identify persons by their authority. Three levels of authority exist in regard to computers and data. The three levels of authority are owner, custodian, and user.

Data Owner

The *data owner* refers to executives or managers responsible for the data content. The role of the data owner is to do the following:

- Assume responsibility for the data content.
- Specify the information classification level.
- Specify appropriate controls.
- Specify acceptable use of the data.
- Identify users.
- Appoint the data custodian.

As an IS auditor, you will review the decisions made by the data owner to evaluate whether the actions were appropriate.

Data User

The *data user* is the business person who benefits from the computerized data. Data users may be internal or external to the organization. For example, some data is delivered for use across the Internet. The role of the data user includes the following tasks:

- Follow standards of acceptable use.
- Comply with the owner's controls.
- Maintain confidentiality of the data.
- Report unauthorized activity.

You will evaluate the effectiveness of management to communicate their controls to the user. The auditor investigates the effectiveness and integration of policies and procedures with the user community. In addition, the auditor determines whether user training has been effectively implemented.

Data Custodian

The *data custodian* is responsible for implementing data storage safeguards and ensuring availability of the data. The custodian's role is to support the business user. If something goes wrong, it is the responsibility of the custodian to deal with this promptly. Sometimes the custodian's role is equivalent to a person holding the bag of snakes at a rattlesnake roundup or the role of a plumber when fixing a clogged drain. The duties of the data custodian include the following:

- Implement controls matching information classification.
- Monitor data security for violations.
- Administer user access controls.
- Ensure data integrity through processing controls.
- Back up data to protect from loss.
- Be available to resolve any problems.

Now we have identified the information classification and the job roles of owner, user, and custodian. The next step is to identify data retention requirements.

Identify Data Retention Requirements

Data retention specifies the procedures for storing data, including how long to keep particular data and how the data will be disposed of. The requirements for data retention can be based on the value of data, its useful life, and legal requirements. For example, financial records must be accessible for seven years. Medical records are required to be available indefinitely or at least as long as the patient remains alive. Records regarding the sale or transfer of real property are to be maintained indefinitely, as are many government records.

The purpose of data retention is to specify how long a data record must be preserved. At the end of the preservation period, the data is archived or disposed of. The disposal process frequently involves destruction. We will discuss storage and destruction toward the end of this chapter.

Now the authority roles and data retention requirements have been identified. So, the next administrative step is to document the access routes (paths) to reach the data.

Document Access Paths

It would be extremely difficult to ensure system security without recognizing common access routes. One of the requirements of internal controls is to document all of the known access paths. A physical map is useful. The network administrator or security manager should have a floor plan of the building. The locations of computer systems, wiring closet, and computer room should be marked on the map. Map symbols should indicate the location of every network jack, telephone jack, and modem. The location of physical access doors and locking doors should also be marked on the map. This process would continue until all the access paths have been marked. Even the network firewall and its Internet communication line should appear on the map.

Next, a risk assessment should be performed by using the map of access paths. Hackers can injure the facility via the Internet or from within an unsupervised conference room. Special attention should be given to areas with modem access. Modems provide direct connections, which bypass the majority of IT security. Computer firewalls are effective only if the data traffic passes directly through the firewall. A computer firewall cannot protect any system with an independent, direct Internet connection.

The purpose of documenting access paths and performing a risk assessment is to ensure accountability. Management is held responsible for the integrity of record keeping. Guaranteeing integrity of a computer system would be difficult if nobody could guarantee that access restrictions were in place.

The change control process should include oversight for changes affecting the access paths. For example, a change in physical access security may introduce another route to the computer room. Persons entering and leaving through the side door, for example, would have a better opportunity to reach the computer room without detection.

The next step to ensure security is to provide constant monitoring. Physical security systems can be monitored with a combination of video cameras, guards, and alarm systems. Badge access through locked doorways provides physical access control with an audit log. A badge access system can generate a list of every identification badge granted access or denied access through the doorway. Unfortunately, a badge access system will have difficulty ensuring that only one person passed through the doorway at a particular time. A mantrap system of two doorways may be used to prevent multiple persons from entering and exiting at the same time. A *mantrap* allows one person to enter and requires the door to be closed behind the person. After the first door is closed, a second door can be opened. The mantrap allows only one person to enter and exit at a time.

To support the increased security, it will be necessary to train the personnel.

Personnel Management

Everyone in the organization should undergo a process of security awareness training. Education is the best defense. Computer training and job training are commonplace. The organization should introduce a training program promoting IT governance in security to generate awareness. Let's consider the possible training programs:

- New hire orientation, should include IT security orientation
- Physical security safeguards and asset protection
- Reeducating existing staff about IT security requirements
- Introducing new security and safety considerations
- Email security mechanisms
- Virus protection
- Business continuity

Every organization should have a general IT security training program to communicate management's commitment for internal controls.

A good training program can run in 20 minutes or less. The intention is to improve awareness and understanding. This objective does not require a marathon event. Training can occur in combination with normal activities. A favorite technique of ours is to place a 20-minute video presentation on the back end of HR benefits and orientation sessions. This ensures that the audience will be present. HR will provide time and attendance reporting for the participants. Each person on staff will be tracked through a series of presentations, leading to cumulative awareness training. Other methods include a brown-bag lunch event, followed by a contest giveaway to promote attendance.

Physical Access

Physical access is a major concern to IT security. As an IS auditor, you need to investigate how access is granted for employees, visitors, vendors, and service personnel. Which of these individuals are escorted and which are left unattended? What is the nature of physical controls and locking doors? Are there any internal barriers to prevent unauthorized access?

The following is a list of the three top concerns regarding physical access:

Sensitive areas   Every IS auditor is concerned about physical access to sensitive areas such as the computer room. The computer room and network wiring closets are an attractive target. Physical access to electronic equipment will permit the intruder to bypass a number of logical controls. Servers and network routers can be compromised through their keyboard or service ports. Every device can be disabled by physical damage. It is also possible for the intruder to install eavesdropping access by using wiretaps or special devices.

Service ports   Network equipment, routers, and servers have communication ports that can be used by maintenance personnel. A serial port provides direct access for a skilled intruder. Shorting out the hardware can create a denial of service situation. Special commands issued through a serial port may bypass the system's password security. When security is bypassed, the contents in memory can be displayed to reveal the running configuration, user IDs, and passwords.

As an auditors, we have observed maintenance personnel from the two largest router manufacturers. During one particular crisis, the skilled technicians successfully bypassed security and reconfigured a major set of changes to routers without halting network service and without knowing the actual administrator passwords.

Computer consoles   The keyboard of the server is referred to as the *console*. Direct access to servers and the console should be tightly controlled. A person with direct access can start and stop the system. The processes stopping the system may be crude and cumbersome, but the outcome will be the same. Direct access also provides physical access to disk drives and special communication ports. It would be impossible to ensure server security without restricting physical access.

Real World Scenario

Ensuring That Personnel Are Honest

Personnel in the organization are expected to be honest. Before access is granted, each person should undergo a formal hiring process complete with background checks. Some individuals in sensitive positions may be bonded to protect the company. The bonding process is a type of insurance that will pay the company for losses caused by the employee. *Fidelity bonding* protects the organization from employee theft. Unfortunately, most fidelity bonds will require the organization to successfully prosecute the accused before any money will be paid out.

Terminating Access

Administrative procedures are necessary to ensure that access is terminated when an employee leaves the organization. The access of existing employees should also be reviewed on a regular basis. In a poorly managed organization, the employee will be given access to one area and then to additional areas as their jobs change. Unfortunately, this results in a person with more access than their job requires. Access to sensitive areas should be limited to persons who perform a required job function in the same area. If the person is moved out of the area, that access should be terminated. The IS auditor should investigate how the organization terminates access and whether it reviews existing access levels. The concept of least privilege should be enforced. The minimum level of access is granted to perform the required job role.

Incident Handling

Incident handling is an administrative process. Physical damage or an unlocked door at the wrong time should initiate the incident handling process. You will need to investigate how the organization deals with incident handling.

You need to ask the following questions:

- What are the events necessary to trigger incident response?

- What is the process for activating the incident response team?

- Does the incident response team have an established procedure to ensure a proper investigation and protect evidence?

- Are members of the incident response team formally appointed and trained?

Violation Reporting

Policies and procedures in security plans are ineffective unless management is monitoring compliance. An effective process of monitoring will detect violations. The IS auditor needs to investigate how violations are reported to management. Does a formal process exist to report possible violations?

The next question is whether a violation report will trigger the incident response team to investigate.

The role of the IS auditor in personnel management is to determine whether appropriate controls are in place to manage the activities of people inside the organization. Now we will move on to physical protection.

Implementing Physical Protection

Physical barriers are frequently used to protect assets. A few pages ago, we discussed the creation of a map displaying access routes and locked doors. After risk assessment, the next step is to improve physical protection.

Let's review a few of the common techniques for increasing physical protection:

Closed-circuit television   Closed-circuit television can provide real-time monitoring or audit logs of past activity. Access routes are frequently monitored by using closed-circuit television. The auditor may be interested in the image quality and retention capabilities of the equipment. Some intrusions may not be detected for several weeks. Does the organization have the ability to check for events that occurred days or weeks ago?

Guards   Security guards are an excellent defensive tool. Guards can observe details that the computerized security system would ignore. Security guards can deal with exceptions and special events. In an emergency, security guards can provide crowd control and direction. Closed-circuit television can extend the effective area of the security guard. The monitoring of remote areas should reduce the potential for loss.

Special locks   Physical locks come in a variety of shapes and sizes. Let's look at three of the more common types of locks:

Traditional tumbler lock   An inexpensive type of lock is the tumbler lock, which uses a standard key. This is identical to the brass key lock used for your home and automobile. The lock is relatively inexpensive and easy to install. It has one major drawback: Everyone uses the same key to open the lock. It is practically impossible to identify who has opened the lock.

Electronic lock   Electronic locks can be used by security systems. The electronic line is frequently coupled with a badge reader. Each user is given a unique ID badge, which will unlock the door. This provides an audit trail of who has unlocked the door for each event. Electronic locks are usually managed by a centralized security system. Unfortunately, electronic locks will not tell us how many people went through the door when it was open. To solve that problem, it would be necessary to combine the electronic lock with closed-circuit television recording.

Cipher lock   Cipher locks may be electronic or mechanical. The purpose of the cipher lock is to eliminate the brass key requirement. Access is granted by entering a particular combination on the keypad. Low-security cipher locks use a shared unlock code. Higher-security cipher locks issue a unique code for each individual. The FBI office in Dallas has a really slick electronic cipher lock using an LCD touchpad. The user touches a combination of keys in sequence on the LCD keypad. Between each physical touch, the key display changes to prevent an observer from detecting the actual code used. This is an example of a higher-security cipher lock.

Biometrics   The next level of access control for locked doors is biometrics. Biometrics use a combination of human characteristics as the key to the door. We will discuss this in a few pages under "Technical Protection."

Burglar alarm   The oldest method of detecting a physical breach is a burglar alarm. Alarm systems are considered the absolute minimum for physical security. An alarm system may be installed for the purpose of signaling that a particular door has been opened. Remote or unmanned facilities frequently implement a burglar alarm to notify personnel of a potential breach. Burglar alarm systems should be monitored to ensure appropriate response in a timely manner.

Data Processing Locations

We have discussed the need for security to restrict physical access. The data processing facility requires special consideration in its design. Data processing equipment is a valuable asset that needs to be protected from environmental contamination, malicious personnel, theft, and physical damage.

The data center location should not draw any attention to its true contents. This will alleviate malicious interest by persons motivated to commit theft or vandalism. The facility should be constructed according to national fire-protection codes with a 2-hour fire protection rating for floors, ceilings, doors, and walls.

Access to the data center should be monitored and restricted. The same level of protection should be given to wiring closets because they contain related support equipment. Physical protection should be designed by using a 3D space consideration: Intruders should not be able to gain access from above, below, or through the side of the facility.

The physical space inside of the data processing facility should be environmentally controlled.

Environmental Controls

The first concern in the data center is electrical power. Electrical power is the lifeblood of computer systems. Unstable power is the number one threat to consistent operations. At a minimum, the data center should have power conditioners and an uninterruptible power supply.

   You are expected to understand a few of the terms used to describe conditions that create problems for electrical power.

Figure 7.2 illustrates the different types of electrical power conditions.

FIGURE 7.2   Electrical power conditions

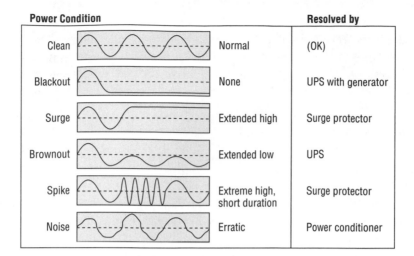

Power Condition		Resolved by
Clean	Normal	(OK)
Blackout	None	UPS with generator
Surge	Extended high	Surge protector
Brownout	Extended low	UPS
Spike	Extreme high, short duration	Surge protector
Noise	Erratic	Power conditioner

Emergency Power Shutoff

Electricity is both an advantage and a hazard. The national fire-protection code requires an emergency power off (EPO) switch to be located near the exit door. The purpose of this switch is to kill power to prevent an individual from being electrocuted. The EPO switch is a red button, which should have a plastic cover to prevent accidental activation. The switch can be wired into the fire-control system for automatic power shutoff if the fire-control system releases water or chemicals to disable a fire.

Uninterruptible Power Supply

The uninterruptible power supply (UPS) is an intelligent power monitor coupled with a string of electrical batteries. The UPS constantly monitors electrical power. A UPS can supplement low-voltage conditions by using power stored in the batteries. During a power outage, the UPS will provide a limited amount of battery power to keep the systems running. The duration of this battery power depends on the electrical consumption of the attached equipment. Most UPS units are capable of signaling the computer to automatically shut down before the batteries are completely drained. Larger commercial UPS systems have the ability to signal the electrical standby generator to start.

Standby Generator

The standby generator provides auxiliary whenever commercial power is disrupted. The standby generator can be connected to the UPS for automated start. The UPS will signal the generator that power is required, and the generator will start warming up. After the generator is warmed up, a transfer circuit will switch the electrical feed from commercial power to the generator power. The UPS will filter the generator power and begin recharging batteries. The standby generator can run for as long as it has fuel. Most standby generators run on diesel fuel or natural gas:

Diesel generator   A diesel generator requires a large fuel storage tank with at least 12 hours of fuel. Better-prepared organizations will store at least 3 days worth of fuel and as much as 30 days of fuel.

Natural gas generator   Natural gas–powered generators have the advantage of tapping a gas utility pipeline directly or using a connection through a storage tank. The natural gas generator does not require a fuel truck to refill its fuel tank. The natural gas pipeline provides a steady supply of fuel for an extended period of time. The natural gas supply is a good idea in areas that are geologically stable.

Dual Power Leads

The best way to prevent power outages is to install power leads from two different power substations. It would be extremely expensive to just pay someone to run special power cables. Instead, the location of the building housing the computer room should be selected according to area power grids. Power grids are usually divided along highways. Careful location selection will place your building within a quarter-mile of two power grids. This makes the cost of the dual connection affordable. Dual power leads should approach the building from different directions without sharing the same underground trench. A construction backhoe is extremely effective in destroying underground connections.

Power Transfer System

The power transfer system, known as a transfer switch, provides the connection between commercial power and UPS battery power in the generator. The transfer switch may be manual or computerized. It is not uncommon for the power transfer switch to fail during a power outage. Therefore, manual power transfer procedures should be in place. Automated power transfer switches may not be able to react to a pair of short power failures occurring within the same 30-minute window. After the first power failure, the generator will come online to produce electrical current. After commercial electrical power is restored, the power switch will transfer back to commercial electricity. At the same time, the generator will receive a signal to begin cooling down and finally shut off. If another power outage occurs during the generator cooling period, the power transfer switch will cycle to generator power while the generator is not producing electrical current. This condition may be resolved by increasing the battery capability of the UPS and adjusting generator start and stop times.

Figure 7.3 illustrates the basic electrical power system used for computer installations.

Heating, Ventilation, and Air-Conditioning

The computer installation requires heating, ventilation, and air-conditioning. Electronic equipment performs well in cold conditions; however, magnetic media should not be allowed to freeze. Ventilation is necessary for cooling computer equipment. Physical damage occurs if the computer circuitry sustains extended use at temperatures of 104 degrees or higher. Physical damage will also occur if the internal electronic circuitry exceeds 115 degrees during operation.

Air-conditioning is also used to control humidity. Humidity will control static electricity that could damage electrical circuits. The ideal humidity for a computer room is between 35 percent and 45 percent at 72 degrees. This will reduce the atmospheric conditions that would otherwise create high levels of static electricity.

FIGURE 7.3   Power system overview

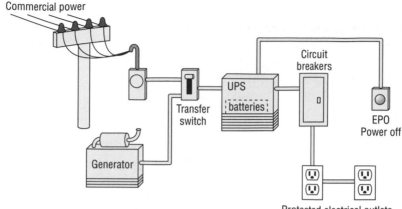

Fire, Smoke, and Heat Detection

The data center and records storage area should be equipped for fire, smoke, and heat detection. Unheated areas may need to be monitored for freezing conditions. There are three basic types of fire detectors, using smoke detection, heat detection, or flame detection:

Smoke detection   Uses optical smoke detectors or radioactive smoke detection

Heat detection   Uses a fixed temperature thermostat (which activates above 200 degrees), or rapid-rise detection (which activates the alarm if the temperature increases dramatically within a matter of minutes)

Flame detection   Relies on ultraviolet radiation from a flame or the pulsation rate of a flame

A fire detection system activates an alarm to initiate human response. A fire detection system may also activate fire suppression with or without the discharge of water or chemicals.

Fire Suppression

Fire suppression is the next step after fire detection. A fire suppression system may be fully automated or mechanical. There are three basic types of fire suppression systems:

Wet pipe system   The wet pipe system derives its name from the concept of water remaining inside the pipe. Most sprinkler heads in a ceiling-based system are mechanical. Each sprinkler head is an individual valve held closed by a meltable pin. A fire near the sprinkler head will melt the pin, and the valve will open to discharge whatever is in the pipe. This type of system can burst due to freeze or leak due to corrosion, which would create an unscheduled discharge. Figure 7.4 shows a wet pipe system.

FIGURE 7.4 Wet pipe system

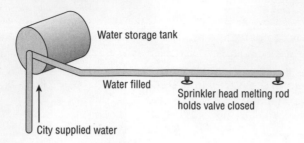

Water storage tank

Water filled

Sprinkler head melting rod
holds valve closed

City supplied water

Dry pipe system The dry pipe system is an improvement over the wet pipe for two reasons. First, the pipe is full of compressed air rather than water prior to discharge. When the valve opens, there is a delay of a few seconds as the air clears from the line. The water will discharge after the air is purged. This leads us to the second advantage. The flow of rushing air can trigger a flow switch to activate the EPO switch to kill electrical power. Equipment will shut off during the few seconds before the water is discharged. This will reduce the amount of damage to computer equipment. Special computer cabinets are made to shed water away from electronic hardware mounted inside. Figure 7.5 shows a dry pipe system.

Dry chemical system Dry chemical systems are frequently used in computer installations because dry chemicals avoid the hazards created by water. The dry chemical system uses a gas such as FM-200 or NAF-S-3 to extinguish fire.

Gaseous halon is no longer used because it is a CFC that destroys the Earth's ozone layer. The only exception is aircraft since an inflight fire would be devastating. All of the former halon installations should have been converted to FM-200 dry chemical.

FIGURE 7.5 Dry pipe system

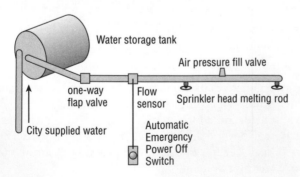

Water storage tank

Air pressure fill valve

one-way
flap valve

Flow
sensor

Sprinkler head melting rod

City supplied water

Automatic
Emergency
Power Off
Switch

When electronic sensors detect a fire condition, the dry chemical system will discharge into the room. Figure 7.6 shows the basic design of a dry chemical system.

Special administrative controls are necessary with dry chemical systems. Maintenance personnel must never lift floor tiles or move ceiling tiles while the dry chemical system is armed. Floating particles of dust can activate a discharge of dry chemicals. Humans should not inhale the gas used in dry chemical systems because it may be lethal. A dry chemical discharge introduces a great deal of air pressure into the room within seconds. Fragile glass windows may shatter during discharge, creating a temporary airborne glass hazard.

 You need to be aware that a water pipe system may be required even if a dry chemical system is installed. Fire safety codes can require wet pipe systems throughout the building, without exception. Some building owners will not allow the tenant to alter existing fire control systems. The dry chemical system would then have to be installed in parallel to the existing water-based system.

Water Detection

Water is discharged from air-conditioning or cooling systems and usually runs to a drain located under the raised floor. Water detection systems are necessary under the floor to alert personnel of a clogged drain or plumbing backup. Water detection sensors also may be placed in the ceiling to detect leakage from pipes in the roof above. It is common for water pipes to be located over a computer room directly above the ceiling tiles or higher floors. Water can even cascade down inside the building from the roof.

Figure 7.7 provides a simple overview of a data processing center and the various environmental control systems.

FIGURE 7.6   Dry chemical system

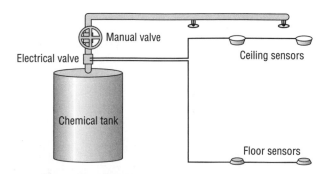

FIGURE 7.7 Typical computer room

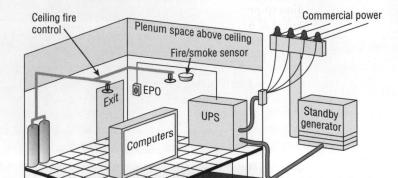

To minimize risk, the organization should have a policy prohibiting food, liquids, and smoking in the computer facility. Now it is time to discuss safe storage of assets and media records.

Safe Storage

Vital business records and computer media require protection from the environment, fire, theft, and malicious damage. Safe on-site storage is required. The best practice is to use fireproof file cabinets and a fireproof media safe. Normal business records are kept in the fireproof file cabinet. Computer tapes and disk media are stored in a special fire safe. The fire safe provides physical protection and ensures that the internal temperature of the safe will not exceed 130 degrees. Copies of files and archived records are transferred to off-site storage.

Off-Site Storage

The off-site storage facility provides storage for a second copy of vital records and data backup files. The off-site storage facility should be used for safe long-term retention of records. The normal practice is to send backup tapes off-site every day or every other day. The off-site storage location should be a well designed, secure, bonded facility with 24-hour security. This site must be designed for protection from flood, fire, and theft. The off-site vendor should maintain a low profile without visible markings identifying the contents of the facility to a casual passerby. Most off-site storage facilities provide safe media transport.

Media Transport

Business records and magnetic media should be properly boxed for transit. The contents in the box must be properly labeled. An inventory should be recorded prior to shipping media off-site for any reason. The tape librarian is usually responsible for tracking data media in transit.

Backup tapes contain the utmost secrets of any organization. All media leaving the primary facility must be kept in secure storage at all times and tracked during transit. New regulations are mandating the use of encryption to protect the standing data on backup tapes. The tape librarian should verify the safe arrival of media at the off-site storage facility. Random media audits at the off-site facility are a good idea. The custodian must track the location and status of all data files outside of the primary facility.

Disposal Procedures

Information and media will be disposed of at the end of its life cycle. A formal authorization process is required to dispose of physical and data assets. Improper controls can lead to the untimely loss of valuable assets. Let's review the common disposal procedures for media:

Paper, plastic, and photographic data   Nondurable media may be disposed of by using physical destruction such as shredding or burning.

Durable and magnetic media   Durable media may be disposed of by using data destruction techniques of overwriting and degaussing:

Overwriting   Data files are not actually deleted by a Delete command. The only change is that the first character of the file is set to zero. Setting the first character to zero indicates that the remaining contents can be overwritten whenever the computer system needs more storage space. Undelete utilities operate by changing the first character back to a numeric value of one. This makes the file contents readable again. To destroy files without recovery, it is necessary to overwrite the contents of the disc. A file overwrite utility is used to replace every single data bit with a random value such as E6X, BBB, or other meaningless value.

Degaussing   Degaussing is a bulk erase process using a strong electromagnet. Degaussing equipment is relatively inexpensive. To operate, the degaussing unit is turned on and placed next to a box of magnetic media. The electromagnet erases magnetic media by changing its electrical alignment. Erasure occurs within minutes or hours, depending on the strength of the device.

As a CISA, you are required to understand the fundamental issues of physical protection. Advanced study in physical security is available from the American Society for Industrial Security, for the Certified Protection Professional (CPP) credential.

You're now ready to begin the last major of the section of this chapter, which covers technical methods of protection.

Using Technical Protection

Technical protection is also referred to as *logical protection*. A simple way to recognize technical protection is that technical controls typically involve a hardware or software process to operate. Let's start with technical controls, which are also know as automated controls.

Technical Control Classification

Technical protection may be implemented by using a combination of mandatory controls, discretionary controls, or role-based controls. Let's discuss each:

Mandatory access controls   Mandatory access controls (MACs) use labels to identify the security classification of data. A set of rules determines which person (subject) will be allowed to access the data (object). The security label is compared to the user access level. The comparison process requires an absolute match to permit access. Here is an example:

```
(User label "subject" = Data label "object") = ALLOW
Label does not match = DENY
```

The process is explicit. Absolutely no exceptions are made when MACs are in use. Under MACs, control is centralized and all access is forbidden unless explicit permission is specified for that user. The only way to gain access is to change the user's formal authorization level. The military uses MACs.

Discretionary access controls   Discretionary access controls (DACs) allow a designated individual to decide the level of user access. The data owner determines access control at their discretion. The IS auditor needs to investigate how the decisions concerning DAC access controls are authorized, managed, and regularly reviewed. Most businesses use discretionary access control.

Role-based access controls   Certain jobs require a particular level of access to fulfill the job duties. Access that is granted on the basis of the job requirement is referred to as role-based access control (RBAC). A user is given the level of access necessary to complete work for their job. The system administrator position is an example of role-based access control.

The type of access control used is based on risk, data value, and available control mechanisms. Now we need to discuss application software control mechanisms.

Application Software Controls

Application software controls provide security by using a combination of user identity, authentication, authorization, and accountability. As you will recall, *user identity* is a claim that must be *authenticated* (verified). *Authorization* refers to the right to perform a particular function. *Accountability* refers to holding a person responsible for their actions. Most application software uses access control lists to assign rights or permissions. The access control list contains the user's identity and permissions assigned.

Database Views

Data within the database can be protected by using database views. The database view is a read restriction placed on particular columns (attributes) in the database. For example, Figure 7.8 illustrates using a personnel file to create a telephone list. Data that is not to be read for the telephone list has been hidden by using the database view.

FIGURE 7.8   Database views for security

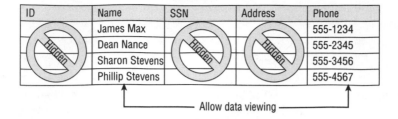

— Allow data viewing —

Restricted User Interface

Another method of limiting access is to use a restricted user interface. The restricted interface may be a menu with particular options grayed out, or not displayed at all. Menu access is preferred to prevent the user from having the power of command-line arguments. The command line is difficult to restrict.

Security Labels

A major concern in security is the ability for users to bypass the security label. The security label is a control that specifies who may access the file and how the file may be used. The IS auditor should work with security managers to identify ways in which labels and security settings may be bypassed. Additional compensating controls are necessary to protect against the bypassing of labels and security.

Authentication Methods

The first step of granting access is identification of the user: A user presents a claim of identity. The second step is to authenticate the user identity claim against a known reference. The purpose of this authentication is to ensure that the correct person is granted access. Table 7.1 illustrates the difference between identification and authentication.

TABLE 7.1   Identification vs. Authentication

Concept	Function
Identification	Claim of identity -OR- Search process of comparing all known entries until either a match is found or the data list is exhausted. Identification is known as a one-to-many search process.
Authentication	A single match of the identity claim against reference information. If a single attempt fails, the authentication failed. Authentication is a single-try process, also known as a one-to-one process (compare only, no search).

Three types of authentication are possible using discreet information. The most common type of authentication is the user password. The user password is expected to be a secret known only to the user. Unfortunately, many user passwords are poorly constructed or suffer from ineffective protection. When a user logs in with a password, the only information known is that someone has logged in with the password. That is no guarantee of who that person is. Let's take a look at the three types of information, or factors, that can be used to authenticate the user:

Type 1: something a person knows   The login ID and password should be unique to each user. Unfortunately, the password may be discovered by observation or insufficient security by the user. Passwords should be considered weak authentication. Passwords can be forgotten, shared, discovered by observation, and broken by technical means.

Type 2: something a person has in possession   An improvement above the password is to authenticate the user based on a unique item in their possession. This requires the user to have a login ID with a password and the unique item at the time of login. Banks use type 2 authentication with your ATM card and PIN. Another example of type 2 authentication is the smart card. A smart card contains a microchip with unique information read by a card scanner. Figure 7.9 shows a drawing of a smart card.

It is possible to use type 2 authentication without specialized hardware. Two common techniques are to use a hard token or USB token. The hard token is a card or key fob read by the user during login. The user types a username and password combined with the number that appears on the token display screen. The number displayed by the token changes every 1 to 2 minutes, thereby making each password unique. The illustration below shows a sample login and the password containing the code from the token.

```
Login ID = jmorris  Password = ******94328
```

Another method is to use a USB token. Authentication information is recorded in a microchip on a USB token device. The user plugs the USB token into the USB port when logging in to the computer. This type is popular in hospitals for use by doctors and nurse practitioners. A software-only token is a digital certificate, aka soft token. Figure 7.10 shows a drawing of the two common types of hard tokens.

FIGURE 7.9   Smart card with embedded microchip

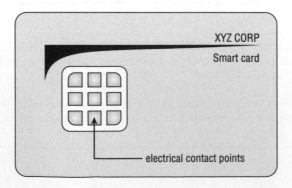

FIGURE 7.10   Hard authentication token

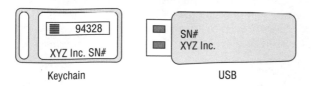

Keychain   USB

Unfortunately, hardware and software tokens can be stolen or lost, and some can be secretly duplicated. These problems are what bring us to the third type of authentication.

Type 3: physical characteristic   The third type of authentication is based on a unique physical characteristic. The recording of physical characteristics and the matching process is known as biometrics. Let's investigate biometrics further.

Biometrics

Biometrics uses unique physical characteristics to authenticate the identity claimed by the user. You are expected to understand the different types of biometric data used for authentication:

Fingerprint   Fingerprints have been used for many years to identify people, especially criminal offenders. In biometrics, the fingerprint is used to authenticate (not identify) the user. Information about the user's fingerprint is recorded into a biometrics database. Rather than the actual image, only a summary list of unique feature characteristics are recorded about the fingerprint. These features include curvature, position, ridge patterns, delta (separation), combined ridges (crossover), islands, and burification (ridge join). The feature data recorded in the database is called *minutiae*. When the user logs in, the minutiae are identified by the acquisition hardware and compared to the database. Authentication occurs when the acquired minutiae data from the biometrics scanner matches the minutiae from the database. Using fingerprint minutiae instead of capturing the image allows a smaller file size to be stored. Minutiae file size is usually 250 bytes to more than 1,000 bytes. Figure 7.11 illustrates fingerprint minutiae.

FIGURE 7.11   Using fingerprint data (minutiae)

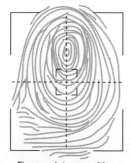

Finger print recognition

Palm print   A person's palm print is as unique as a fingerprint. Like a fingerprint, the palm of the hand contains a significant number of unique minutiae plus additional wrinkle lines and scars. The palm offers a larger volume of data. Figure 7.12 illustrates the palm data.

FIGURE 7.12   Using palm print data

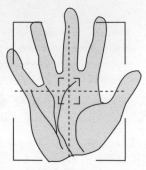

Palm of hand

Hand geometry   The concept of hand geometry is to measure the details of a person's hand in a three-dimensional image. The usual technique is to put your hand into a machine with your fingers spread between metal pegs. Hand geometry is quite effective and inexpensive.

Retina scan   The retina, located at the rear of the eyeball, contains a unique pattern of tiny veins and arteries that reflect light. The red-eye in photographs is the reflection of the retina. Changes in the retina occur during a person's life. Some of these changes may signal the onset of a new medical condition, such as stroke or diabetes. Users may be concerned about physiological issues or the possible invasion of privacy. Overall, retina scanning is very reliable. Figure 7.13 illustrates retina scanning.

FIGURE 7.13   Retina scanning

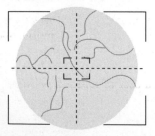

Retina

Iris scan   Iris-scanning technology is based on visible features of freckles, rings, and furrows in the color ring surrounding the eye's pupil. The iris provides stable data from one year of age through a person's entire life. The visible features and their location are combined to form an iris-code digital template. To use an iris scanner, a person is asked to look into an eyepiece and focus on a displayed image. A camera records a picture of the iris and compares it to the biometric database to ensure the viewer is a living person. Fake color contacts would fail the iris scan. Iris scanning is very dependable.

Face scan   New face-scanning technology uses a series of still images captured by video camera. The technology uses three-dimensional measurements of facial features, including the position of eye sockets, nose, and mouth openings. The feature data is extracted from the image to form a digital facial template of 1,000 to 1,500 bytes. Major advances are occurring in facial recognition that are reducing former problems of speed and accuracy. Figure 7.14 illustrates face recognition.

FIGURE 7.14   Face recognition

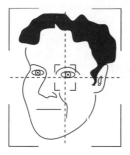

Signature dynamics   Signature dynamics is a behavioral form of biometric data. The user's signature is monitored for time duration, pressure, and technique. The advantage is the low cost of implementation. The disadvantage is that many individuals do not write their signature consistently. Some individuals, such as the authors of this Study Guide, refuse to allow their signature to be digitally recorded because it is still used as the primary means of authenticating legal documents.

Voice pattern   Voice pattern recognition is an inexpensive method of identifying a person by the way they talk. Voice pattern recognition is not the same as speech recognition. Speech recognition assembles sounds into words. Voice pattern analysis checks for characteristics of pitch, tone, and sound duration. A person's voice is analyzed for unique sound characteristics, tone, inflection, and speed. The typical method is to ask a user to repeat a particular passphrase. The characteristics of the passphrase are converted into a digital template. Voice pattern recognition is less expensive and less accurate than other types of biometrics. Voice authentication can be fooled by recorded audio playback of a person's voice. Figure 7.15 illustrates voice recognition.

FIGURE 7.15   Voice pattern analysis in biometrics

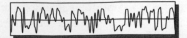

 As a CISA candidate, you are expected to understand the older biometric techniques of signature dynamics and voice pattern analysis.

Biometric systems have several technical advantages that must be balanced against the known problems. Let's discuss some of the known problems with biometrics.

Problems with Biometrics

Using biometric systems has some drawbacks. One of the first questions is, how will the biometric results be used? Is the biometric system expected to provide identification or authentication?

Biometric systems face issues of social acceptability. The users may have concerns about sanitary health issues regarding physical contact or about invasion of privacy. Biometric data must be managed to ensure the security of initial data collection, data distribution, and processing. A biometric data policy is required to specify the data life cycle and control procedures. Biometric data must always be protected for confidentiality and integrity.

Error rates exist in all automated systems, and biometric systems are no different. It is possible for an error to occur during data collection or data processing. The following are various types of errors that can occur in a biometric system:

Enrollment   Every user provides a sample for the biometric system during the enrollment process. The sample may fail to be accepted by the system. The typical enrollment process should take only 2 to 5 minutes; any longer could lead to user dissatisfaction.

False reject   A legitimate person could be rejected and fail authentication; the correct user fails to authenticate. This failure to accept a legitimate user is known as the false rejection rate (FRR) or type 1 error. The biometric systems rejects a legitimate user. This is considered a type 1 error since it is the most common type of error.

False accept   It is possible for the system to permit access to an individual who should have been rejected; the wrong person is authenticated. This is referred to as the false acceptance rate (FAR) or type 2 error. The biometric system accepts an unauthorized user.

Equal error/crossover error rate   Every system has a delicate balance of speed over efficiency. In biometrics, this balance is referred to as the equal error rate (ERR) or the crossover error rate (CER). The biometric system is not perfect. An acceptable error rate will always exist.

We have discussed the methods for authenticating a user. Now it is time to discuss the types of access that could be granted on the network.

Network Access Protection

All computer networks are prone to access control problems. It is an ongoing challenge to provide access to legitimate users while blocking access from all others. Several methods have been developed to accomplish this goal. Computer users demand ease of use, while computer custodians strive for tighter controls. Unfortunately, network access is predominantly a perimeter defense. Better controls are sorely needed at the application level.

In this section we will discuss several technologies including firewall. We will start with single sign-on. The CISA is expected to understand the concept of single sign-on. The purpose of single sign-on is to improve network access controls by implementing a higher-security system that is easier for the user. One of the most common examples is Kerberos, developed by the Massachusetts Institute of Technology.

Kerberos Single Sign-On

The Kerberos single sign-on (SSO) system was developed to improve both security and user satisfaction. The name *Kerberos* refers to the mythical three-headed dog guarding the gates to the underworld. Kerberos provides security when the end points of the network are safe but the transmission path cannot be trusted—for example, when the servers and workstations are trusted but the network is not.

The concept of operation is for the user to log in once to Kerberos. After login, the Kerberos system authenticates the user and grants access to all resources. The process works as follows:

1. The user authenticates to the Kerberos workstation software.

2. The workstation software authenticates to the Kerberos server.

3. Shared encryption keys are used. A network access ticket is created by Kerberos.

4. A Kerberos access ticket is sent to the workstation, signed in the workstation's shared encryption key. All other network servers receive a similar ticket granting the workstation access to shared servers.

5. The user is automatically signed in to all servers.

The belief is that a user with a strong password and strong encryption will improve overall security. Unfortunately, Kerberos works only with specially modified versions of software designed for use with Kerberos. Merely installing Kerberos will not improve security. There are compatibility problems with different versions of implementation.

Special skills and experience are required to make a Kerberos installation successful. First, a knowledgeable installer will understand how to divide Kerberos access by using separate domains to partition access for better security. Second, restoring data from tape backup is quite involved. The Kerberos system must be shut down and the date rolled back to the timestamp of the file being restored. As soon as the file is restored, the time clocks must be rolled forward again with the system resynchronized for the users. Any compromise of the Key Distribution Center (KDC) means the entire system is compromised and must be shut down. Using Kerberos requires highly experienced system administrators. Figure 7.16 illustrates the design of a Kerberos single sign-on.

FIGURE 7.16   Kerberos single sign-on

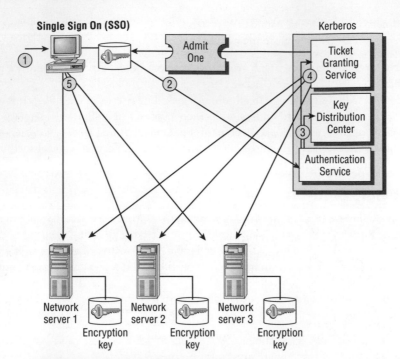

1. User authenticates to workstation.
2. Workstation authenticates to Kerberos.
3. Encryption keys are used, ticket granted,
4. Ticket sent to workstation and every server.
   Tickets encrypted with each computer's own key.
5. User is automatically logged in to all servers.

Network Firewalls

Computer networks can be protected from internal and external threats by using firewalls (FW). The concept is that a specially configured firewall on the network will block unwanted access. However, this is a grossly misunderstood concept, and many organizations do not understand firewall capabilities and limitations. As a result, there can be a false sense of security. Let's consider the advantages and disadvantages of network firewalls:

Firewall advantages   Reduces external access to the network.

Firewall disadvantages   There is always a hole for traffic to pass through—either good traffic or bad traffic or both. A firewall can control only the traffic that passes directly through it. It does not protect modems or other access points. A firewall can be misconfigured or technically circumvented. There is no such thing as a completely safe firewall. The firewall concept creates a false sense of security.

Network firewalls have undergone several generations of improvement. The first generation was simply a router with a primitive access list specifying the "to" destination and the sender's "from" network addresses. Attackers became more sophisticated, and so did the need for a better firewalls. The following are the different generations of firewall technology:

First generation: packet filter   The first generation was a packet filter. Filtering is based on the sending and receiving address combined with the service port (a packet). The advantage of this design is its low cost.

The first-generation packet filter design was prone to problems. The design was plagued with poor logging and granular rules that were difficult to implement effectively. Hackers were still able to get in.

Second generation: application proxy filter   A firewall application program was added to the first-generation design of packet filtering. The second generation uses an application proxy to relay requests through the firewall. The proxy checks the inbound requests to ensure that it complies with safe computing in both format and type of requests. Application proxies perform user requests without granting direct access to the target software. The application proxy is also referred to as a *circuit-level* firewall. This is because the application proxy is required to complete the circuit; otherwise, no connection exists. This design improved event logging; however, hackers were still able to get in.

Third generation: stateful inspection   Hackers were able to trick second-generation firewalls by sending a request that was formatted to bypass the proxy design. Application proxy firewalls relied on open connections maintained with the user. Connectionless sessions such as the user datagram (UDP) protocol in IP were not protected. In the third generation, UDP connectionless requests are recorded into a history table. The historic "state" of connectionless requests is now controlled by the firewall for better protection. This is referred to as *stateful inspection*. Stateful inspection is the de facto minimum standard for network firewall technology. However, there's still room for improvement.

Fourth generation: adaptive response   Improvements in technology allow the firewall to communicate with an intrusion detection system. This provides an adaptive response to network attacks. The firewall administrator can configure stored procedures designed to rebut many types of firewall attack. The firewall can reconfigure itself to block ports or reset connections. One drawback is that a skilled attacker may masquerade as a critical device such as a necessary server. The fourth-generation firewall could accidentally disable the critical device, which would create a denial of service problem.

Fifth generation: kernel process   The fifth-generation firewall is actually an internal control mechanism designed into the operating system kernel. Individual processing requests are verified against an internal access control list. Those not on the list are rejected. Special military systems have been using fifth-generation firewalls for many years. Microsoft Windows XP has implemented a basic fifth-generation firewall.

The network firewall is the best defense for protecting a network. Each generation provides different levels of cost and protection. Figure 7.17 illustrates the firewalls by generation in relation to the OSI model. We covered the OSI model in Chapter 4.

FIGURE 7.17   Firewall generations compared to OSI model

	Packet Filtering	Application Proxy w/ packet filter	Stateful Inspection w/ proxy	Adaptive Response OS	Kernel
Application OSI layer 7	None	Varies	Varies	Varies	÷
Presentation OSI layer 6	None	None	Varies	Varies	Varies
Session OSI layer 5	None	÷	÷	÷	÷
Transport OSI layer 4	None	Varies	÷	÷	÷
Networking OSI layer 3	÷	÷	÷	÷	÷
Data-Link OSI layer 2	÷	÷	÷	÷	÷
Physical OSI layer 1	None	None	None	None	None

Network firewalls can be implemented by using one of three basic designs. The first method is the screened host implementation. The screened host protects a single host through the firewall. The host computer is strongly defended. Figure 7.18 illustrates the screened host implementation.

The next method of firewall implementation is to install two interface cards in the same host. This method is referred to as to dual-homed. The host computer is configured with the routing disabled. A special software application such as an application proxy relays appropriate communication between the two interface cards. This is the configuration of many Internet firewalls. Figure 7.19 illustrates the dual-homed host.

FIGURE 7.18   Firewall screened host

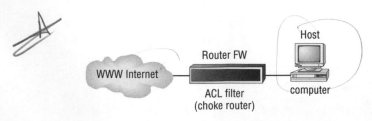

FIGURE 7.19   Dual-homed host

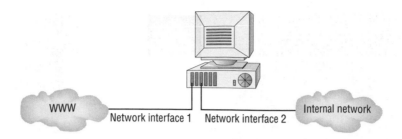

The third method of firewall implementation is known as the screened subnet, or DMZ design. *DMZ* is a term that refers to the demilitarized zone between enemy forces on a battlefield. The DMZ design allows for several computers to be placed in a protected subnet that is accessible from the outside and by systems inside the network. Figure 7.20 illustrates the DMZ concept.

Firewall systems should be implemented to support a separation of duties. Separation of duties is just as important for machines as for personnel. The intention is to provide additional layers of control. Separate firewalls allow tighter access control rules. Selected data is mirrored from internal production servers to a DMZ server for access by business partners or clients. This eliminates the dangers of direct access to an internal server. In addition, the redundancy improves overall availability. An outage would affect a smaller audience. Figure 7.21 illustrates the separation of duties using a firewall.

FIGURE 7.20   Screened subnet, aka DMZ subnet

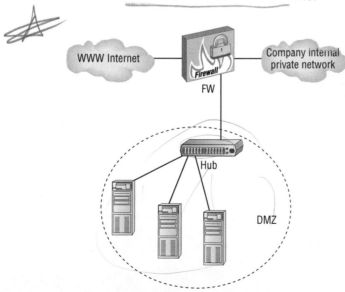

FIGURE 7.21   Separation of duties with firewalls

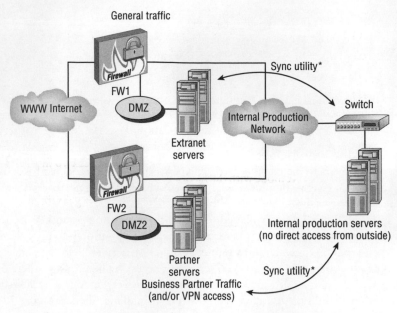

Remote Dial-Up Access

Remote users can often access the network over standard telephone lines with modems. This method completely bypasses security mechanisms provided by the network firewall. The dial-up user may access the network through an access server modem bank or an individual modem on a networked computer. As an IS auditor, you need to determine whether the client has adequate safeguards to prevent this method of circumvention. Are the phone connections to modems properly managed considering the higher level of risk?

Remote VPN Access

Virtual private networks (VPN) connect remote users over an insecure public network such as the Internet. The connection is virtual because it is temporary with no physical presence. VPN technology is cost-effective and highly flexible. A VPN creates an encrypted tunnel to securely pass data as follows:

- Between two machines

- From a machine to a network

- From one network to another network

There are four types of VPN technology and protocol in use today. ISACA wants you to be familiar with the basic terms for each of the four types of VPNs:

- Point-to-Point Tunneling Protocol, or PPTP
- Layer 2 Tunneling Protocol, or L2TP (OSI layer 2, Data-Link)
- Secure Sockets Layer, or SSL (OSI layer 5, Session)
- IP Security, or IPSec, Internet protocol (OSI layer 3, Networking)

Secure Sockets Layer (SSL) and Transaction Layer Security (TLS) are commonly used for confidentiality and integrity in the session between the user and the server. The design uses a digital certificate on the server to generate one-way authentication. A secure login to the server can be generated by using Secure Shell (SSH). SSH provides confidentiality and integrity in a terminal session with the host server. The IPSec design is the newest. IPSec uses two modes of creating a VPN. The first type is transport mode with the payload encrypted. The second type of IPSec VPN is tunnel mode with the payload and network addresses both encrypted. Figure 7.22 illustrates the IPSec design.

The goal of every VPN is to grant remote access to authorized users. Data can be shared across the Internet at a very low cost with relative safety if the proper internal controls are implemented. A VPN can be combined with a firewall DMZ by using a separation of duties between internal production servers and the external accessible server. Figure 7.23 illustrates a VPN with a separation of duties between servers.

Wireless Access

User demands for wireless access to network resources increase every day. When you read the vendor ads, it appears that wireless can provide security equal to wired access. However, wireless access to networks represents an additional level of threat. Wireless security has been completely compromised by vendors to improve Plug and Play capabilities.

All wireless access points should traverse a network firewall for security reasons. New regulations like the joint Credit card Information Security Policy (CISP) of Visa, Mastercard, Discover, and American Express have mandated firewalls be used when merchant organizations process credit transaction on the network. The firewall itself should be separate from the existing Internet firewall. It would be difficult or impossible to successfully combine the two functions into a single firewall. Figure 7.24 provides an overview of using a firewall with wireless access points.

We've spent quite a bit of time discussing firewalls and access controls. It is time to discuss methods for detecting intrusion to the network. Intrusion detection systems have been in the marketplace for more than 10 years. Every organization should have intrusion detection systems in place.

Intrusion Detection

Network intrusion detection systems (IDSs) function in a manner similar to virus detection or a burglar alarm. The objective is to inform the administrator of a suspected intrusion or attack occurring. Constant monitoring is necessary in order to receive the benefit of intrusion detection; otherwise, intrusion detection is no more valuable than an audit log of past history. An improved version of intrusion detection is the Intrusion Prevention System (IPS). The IPS concept is to ensure the attck is blocked immediately upon detection.

FIGURE 7.22 VPN using IPSec

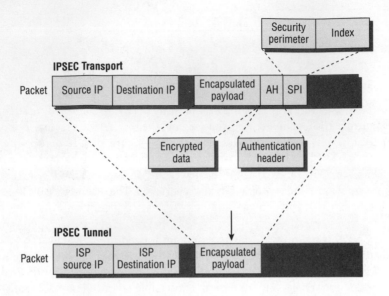

FIGURE 7.23 VPN with separation of duties

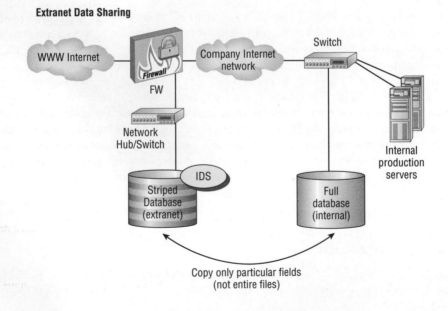

FIGURE 7.24   Firewall protecting wireless access points

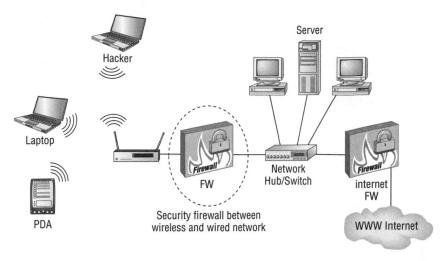

There are two types of intrusion detection systems:

Host based   The host-based system monitors activity on a particular computer host or device such as a router. Attacks on other devices will not be seen by the host-based IDS.

Network based   Network IDS systems observe traffic in a manner similar to a packet sniffer. The network IDS monitors activity across a network link. The IDS can see attacks on promiscuous connections, but not across discreet switched network connections. The design of a network switch can prevent an IDS system from detecting attacks occurring on systems connected to the other switch ports.

There are three technical methods of detecting a network intrusion:

Statistical   The statistical system uses a calculation of network traffic, CPU, and memory loading to determine whether an attack is occurring. Statistical systems are prone to false alarms because the traffic patterns of most networks are sporadic. The statistical system offers the advantage of being able to detect new attacks that might otherwise go unnoticed if a signature-based system were in use.

Signature   Signature-based IDS relies on a database of attack techniques. The signature-based IDS is similar in design to a signature-based virus scanner. The IDS is looking for behaviors that indicate a particular type of known attack. Unfortunately, the signature-based IDS cannot detect attacks that are not listed in its database.

Neural   Neural-based learning networks are being implemented on intrusion detection systems. The objective is to create a learning system that is a hybrid between statistical- and signature-based methods.

Figure 7.25 illustrates an IDS on the network.

FIGURE 7.25 Intrusion detection system

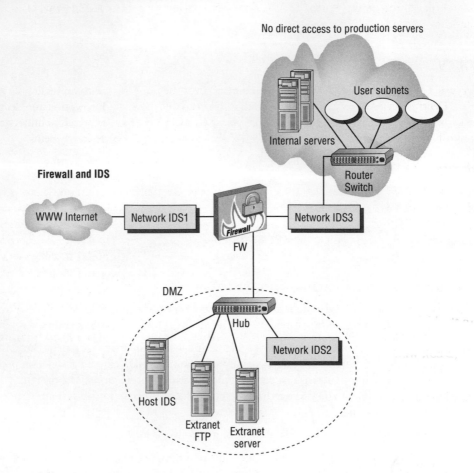

Intrusion detection systems are helpful for identifying network attacks in progress. Some of the more successful techniques are to make a server or subnet appear as an enticing target for the attacker. The purpose of the systems is to be a decoy target. An attack of the decoy provides early warning to the appropriate personnel. The decoy can be high interaction in a simulated production environment or low interaction of a static host. There are two basic styles of decoys:

Honey pot The honey pot is a sacrificial server placed in such a manner as to attract the interest of the attacker. The honey pot server has no legitimate business value other than alerting the organization of an attack. The honey pot utilizes host-based IDS or network-based IDS.

Honey net A honey net is a sacrificial subnet with a few machines designed to attract the interest of the attacker. All traffic from the honey net is considered suspicious because no real production activity is taking place. The purpose of this design is to allow security personnel the opportunity for advance notice of a potential attack against real production.

We have discussed firewalls, remote access, and intrusion detection. Now it is time to discuss the encryption methods used to hide data from prying eyes. Encryption provides a method of hiding data from other people.

Encryption Methods

Encryption systems provide a method of converting clear, readable text into unintelligible gibberish. Decryption converts the gibberish back into a readable message. Encryption and decryption systems have been in use for thousands of years. As a CISA, you are expected to understand the two basic types of encryption systems: public-key systems and private-key systems.

Private Key

Private-key encryption systems use a secret key, which is shared between the authorized sender and the intended receiver. Private-key systems contain two basic components. The first component is the mathematical algorithm for scrambling and unscrambling the message (encrypting and decrypting). The second component is the mathematical key used as a randomizer in the encryption algorithm. The longer the key length, the higher the security it will generate.

A single secret key is carefully shared between the sender and receiver. This is referred to as *symmetric-key* cryptography (see Figure 7.26). Symmetric-key cryptography is very fast, because the same key is used on both ends. The drawback is that the key must be protected with the highest possible diligence. Anybody who has a copy of the secret key can read the message. Examples of symmetric-key (secret key) cryptography include Data Encryption Standard (DES), which is now obsolete, and the new Advanced Encryption Standard (AES) designed by two Belgian researchers, Joan Daemen and Vincent Rijmen.

FIGURE 7.26   Symmetric-key cryptography

Sender

Receiver

Clear text message

Secret key

Encryption

Send (transmit)

Unreadable ciphertext

Decryption

Secret key

Clear text message

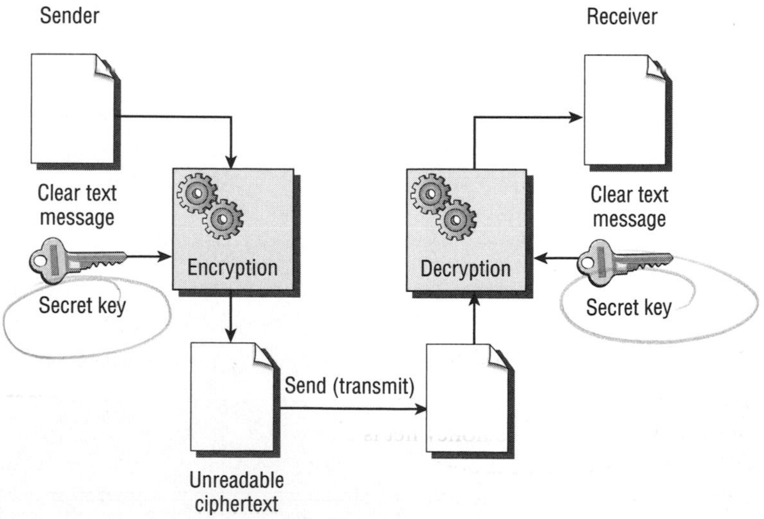

Because of the secret-key design of symmetric cryptography, encryption and decryption is very fast and efficient. The drawback is that the secret-key design cannot be used for digital signatures. To do so would expose the key to outsiders. Exchanging the secret key in symmetric cryptography is a major problem.

Public Key

Asymmetrical cryptography is referred to as public-key cryptography. This design utilizes a separate pair of keys for encryption and decryption. The key pair is composed of a secret key protected by the owner and a second public key that is freely distributed. These two keys are mathematically related to each other. The secret key and public key are generated from a supersized prime number. It is practically impossible for a cryptographic hacker to derive the super prime number or related keys in use.

The strength of public-key cryptography depends on the algorithm used and the encryption key length. To encrypt a message, the sender would use their own secret key and public key, plus the public key of the intended recipient. Figure 7.27 shows the process of encrypting by using public-key (asymmetrical) cryptography.

The process of decrypting the message returns it to readable text. To decrypt, the recipient uses their secret key and public key, plus the public key of the sender. The basic concept is that you can solve for one missing value in an algebraic formula (A + B + C = ___). If two values were missing, decrypting the file would be impossible. Figure 7.28 shows the process of decrypting by using public-key cryptography.

The design of public-key cryptography eliminates the need to exchange a secret key between the sender and receiver. Public-key cryptography is designed to allow digital signing of files.

FIGURE 7.27 Encryption using public-key system

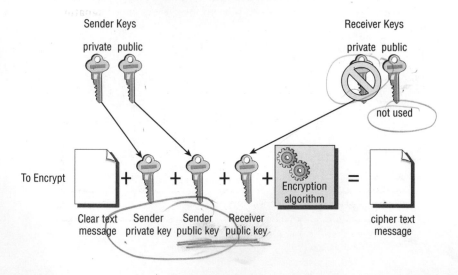

FIGURE 7.28 Decryption using public-key system

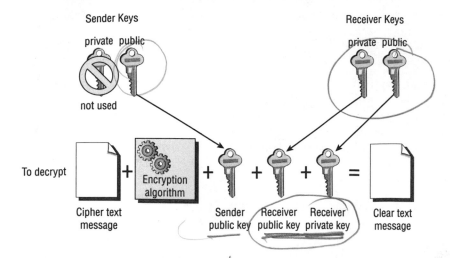

Digital Signatures

A digital signature is intended to be an electronic version of a personal signature. The purpose is to indicate that the message was sent by a uniquely identified individual. A digital signature created by running a hash utility against any size of file will generate a 120-bit or 160-bit output. Figure 7.29 illustrates the process of generating a hash file and digital signature.

The digital signature is attached to the message file, and both are sent to the recipient. The receiver must use the message file, digital signature file, and the sender's public key to test the validity of the signature. Without testing the digital signature, there is no indication of its authenticity. Figure 7.30 illustrates the process of verifying a digital signature.

FIGURE 7.29 Generating a digital signature

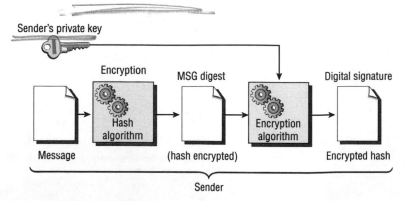

FIGURE 7.30 Verifying a digital signature

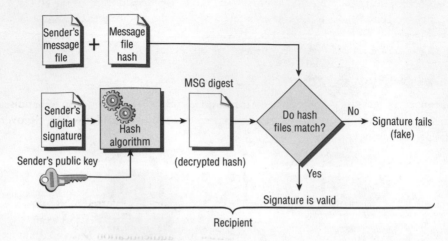

There is a new method for sending an encrypted message and the key along with it. The process uses digital envelope. A message is encrypted along with a session key. The session key is encrypted a second time, using the recipient's public key. After transmission, the recipient can decrypt by using their private key, and then decrypt again by using the sender's public key. The double-step encryption ensures that no one else is able to decrypt the key in transit. Figure 7.31 illustrates the process of using a digital envelope.

Elliptic-Curve Cryptography

The newest method for encryption algorithms is the elliptic curve. The concept of an elliptic curve is to generate a three-dimensional space. The encryption key refers to a reference point within those dimensions. It would be extremely difficult to calculate keys generated from an elliptic curve. A small elliptic curve key is exponentially stronger than one generated by linear math.

FIGURE 7.31 Using a digital envelope

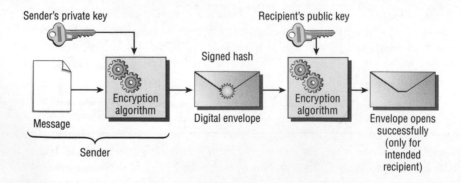

Elliptic-curve cryptography is used with wireless encryption. The implementation within wireless encryption is completely compromised; however, the concept of the elliptic-curve algorithm is essentially strong. Unfortunately a 97-bit elliptic-curve encryption has been cracked from the Web by the same people who cracked the RSA 512-bit encryption key. It took twice as long, but the cracking attack was successful.

Quantum Cryptography

Quantum cryptography is based on polarization metrics of random photon light pulses. This promising technology is not available as a commercial product yet. However, the overall design appears to be quite strong.

Public-Key Infrastructure

The process of sharing encrypted files between various parties is referred to as *public-key infrastructure (PKI)*, which you should have a basic understanding of for the CISA exam. Public-key infrastructure is designed to provide a level of trust and authentication between different users. This infrastructure is built by using the public-key encryption system we discussed earlier in this chapter. Public-key infrastructure comprises four basic components:

Certificate authority (CA)   A user contacts a certificate authority to procure a digital certificate. The digital certificate contains the user's contact information along with unique identifying characteristics. The certificate authority will vouch for the authenticity of the user after the certificate is issued. Certificate authorities typically follow the X.509 exchange standard.

Registration authority (RA)   Some big customers such as IBM, Novell, and Microsoft issue certificates from a block of certificates acquired through a certificate authority such as VeriSign or Entrust. The registration authority (RA) is delegated bookkeeping and issuing functions from the CA. The certificate authority maintains the certificates that have been issued and verifies their authenticity.

Certificate revocation list (CRL)   Digital certificates are checked to ensure that they are valid at the time of use. A certificate revocation list is maintained by the certificate authority to indicate that certificates have expired or are revoked. This process allows invalid certificates to be cancelled.

Certification practice statement (CPS)   A certification practice statement (CPS) is a disclosure document that specifies how a certificate authority will issue certificates. The CPS specifically states how PKI participants will issue, manage, use, renew, and revoke digital certificates. It does not facilitate interoperation between certificate authorities, but rather the practices (procedures) of a single certificate authority.

Figure 7.32 shows the concept of registering and acquiring a PKI digital certificate from the certificate authority.

After acquiring a digital certificate, the user will present it during a transaction. The receiver will check the certificate against the certificate authority's database. If the certificate is valid, the transaction will continue. Certificates can be checked against other authorities, using a cross-verification process. Figure 7.33 shows the concept of presenting and using a PKI digital certificate.

FIGURE 7.32 Getting PKI digital certificate

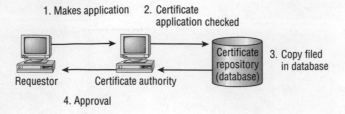

1. Makes application   2. Certificate
                          application checked

Requestor   Certificate authority   Certificate repository (database)   3. Copy filed in database

4. Approval

FIGURE 7.33 Using PKI certificate

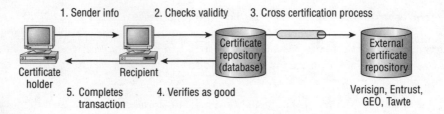

1. Sender info   2. Checks validity   3. Cross certification process

Certificate holder   Recipient   Certificate repository (database)   External certificate repository

5. Completes transaction   4. Verifies as good   Verisign, Entrust, GEO, Tawte

Secure Multipurpose Internet Mail Extension

Secure Multipurpose Internet Mail Extension (S/MIME) was developed so that people could send email across the Internet without having to worry about whether the recipient could read it. The original design was Privacy Enhanced Mail (PEM), developed in 1993. S/MIME was created in 1999 and incorporated several enhancements including support for the newer SHA-1 hash and MD5 hash. Additional support was added for the RSA encryption system and signing time attributes. S/MIME provides authentication of the sender and receiver and also verifies message integrity. S/MIME is the current standard for secure email and attachments. Figure 7.34 illustrates the reason why email security is so important.

FIGURE 7.34 Email security issues

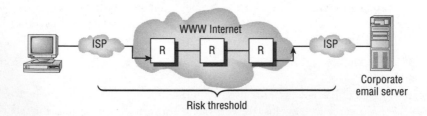

WWW Internet

ISP   R   R   R   ISP

Corporate email server

Risk threshold

Encryption-Key Management

Encryption-key management is critical to ensure confidentiality and integrity of encrypted data. There are several risks with regard to encryption keys. First, the key itself must be protected from theft or illegal copying. Second is a requirement to use several different keys, with one for each purpose. This is to ensure integrity of the encrypted files. Unfortunately, this multitude of keys also creates a significant administrative burden, which if mishandled can turn into a catastrophe.

Encryption keys must be stored with a great deal of care. The keys will need to be managed throughout their life cycle. At a future date, a key will be marked for destruction. Creating, managing, storing, and destroying the keys is of particular concern to the auditor. Few organizations do a good job.

Network Security Protocols

The world of safe e-commerce is built on a handful of network security protocols. These security protocols include:

- PGP — pretty good privacy for personal file encryption
- SSL — SecureSocketsLayer, which is used by most InternetWeb sites for HTTPS sessions
- HTTPS — secure hyper text protocol (uses SSL)
- TLS — Transport layer security
- IPSec — IP security protocol using the authentication header (AH) and encapsulated security payload (ESP)

Without these protocols, it would be impossible for businesses, individuals, and the government to conduct confidential transactions. Figure 7.35 shows where these protocols fall within the OSI model.

E-commerce is becoming more important in today's IT landscape. Figure 7.36 illustrates several types of e-commerce in use today.

There is one special type of payment protocol that has been developed to protect credit card accounts. The Secure Electronic Transaction protocol (SET) provides a method for purchasing over the Internet without disclosing the credit card number to the merchant.

FIGURE 7.35   Security protocols and where they fall within the OSI model

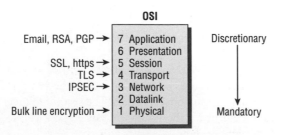

The merchant opens an account with a payment system such as VeriSign's Payflow. A customer makes a purchase using the merchant's shopping cart. At the appropriate time, the shopping cart passes the transaction to the SET payment gateway. The customer enters their credit card number on the SET gateway, completely out of sight from the merchant. The SET payment gateway sends to the merchant a transaction authorization to complete the purchase. The merchant uses the transaction authorization as authorization to ship the product. The SET gateway system deposits the funds into the merchant's bank account. This prevents a questionable merchant from being able to view a customer's credit card number. It also prevents credit card numbers from being retained in insecure shopping cart databases.

FIGURE 7.36   Types of e-commerce

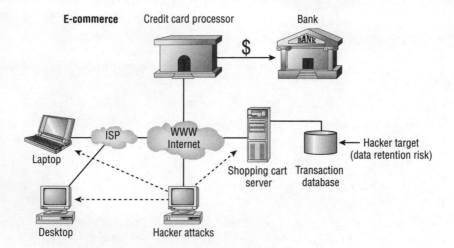

Design for Redundancy

There is more to protecting information assets than just encryption. Communication networks must be designed for redundancy. One method of improving redundancy is to use alternate telecommunications routing. We discussed meshed networks in Chapter 4, "Networking Technology." Alternate routing provides multiple communication paths in case the normal path fails. Alternate routing can be used in a local area network or a wide area network.

Another technique to ensure availability and integrity of information assets is the use of mirrored, or high-availability, servers.

Two servers acting as one are said to be *mirrored*. Mirrored servers are also known as high-availability servers. One of the servers acts as a primary server. The second server is the failover server, which runs in the background until the primary server dies. The second failover server assumes all processing responsibilities if the primary should fail for any reason. Figure 7.37 shows the basic design of a mirrored, or high-availability, server pair.

Computer disk systems are known to experience failures. The loss of a disk system could result in the loss of valuable data. A tape backup system can restore the data at the cost of additional downtime. A solution to this problem is the implementation of redundant hard drives. A Redundant Array of Independent—or Inexpensive—Disks (RAID) provides an excellent method of protecting information assets. Special software drivers copy the data files onto different hard disk controllers on two separate sets of hard drives. Either set of hard drives is capable of running the system without data loss. Figure 7.38 shows the basic layout of a RAID system.

FIGURE 7.37   Mirrored, or high-availability, servers

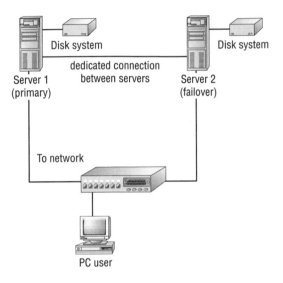

FIGURE 7.38   RAID system

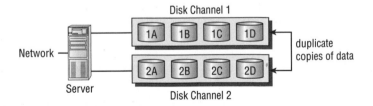

Telephone Security

The security of the telephone system is a major concern. Telephone hackers, known as *phreakers*, are notorious for attempting to steal telephone service.

The telephone PBX—which stands for private branch exchange—needs to be protected by using the same techniques as those used to protect a network server or router. Care must be given to the life-cycle controls of the PBX. Maintenance accounts and unauthorized access are major concerns.

Newer phone systems use voice-over-IP networks to save money. This introduces the problems of network security controls to telephone systems. As an auditor, you should be aware of the issues regarding IP networks for both data and voice.

Technical Self-Assessment

Clients should undergo a regular schedule of vulnerability assessment by using the control self-assessment (CSA) and technical tools such as port scanners. Management needs to promote the discovery and resolution of vulnerabilities.

Penetration tests are commonly used to uncover vulnerabilities that may be discovered by an attacker. The US National Security Agency has created a certification program for the level 1 information systems assessment methodology (IAM) to be used for federal systems. Use in private industry is recommended but not required. The NSA level 2 information evaluation methodology (IEM) provides the planning details for running a penetration test and reporting the results against the government-approved NSA baseline.

The NSA IAM and IEM techniques will be of significant interest to auditors specializing in regulatory compliance. The NSA certification is the only technical assessment method approved and endorsed by the US government.

Summary

As an IS auditor, you should be extremely interested in the implementation of information asset protection mechanisms by the client. There are numerous threats that could compromise administrative, physical, and technical controls.

You should understand how these controls have been implemented by the customer and what level of monitoring is occurring. Implementing controls without constant monitoring would be a waste of effort. Without effective monitoring processes, the client would be negligent.

This chapter has covered several technical methods that the CISA will be expected to know. Be sure to read this chapter at least twice and study the definitions carefully.

Exam Essentials'

Be able to evaluate the effectiveness of technical (logical) access controls. Technical controls include access control mechanisms, encryption, firewalls, and intrusion detection capabilities. Technical access control mechanisms include passwords, access control lists, and biometrics for authentication.

Understand the perimeter defense mechanisms. The network security infrastructure must provide sufficient perimeter defenses along with mechanisms to minimize loss from hackers, viruses, and worms. But the network is susceptible to attack by hacking, spoofing, spamming, and denial of service, along with other threats such as social engineering.

Know the purpose of the environmental controls used in the IT environment.   Environmental controls are necessary to prevent an interruption to the system's availability and to protect assets from loss. Environmental systems include power, water detection, heating and air-conditioning, fire detection, fire control, and humidity to prevent the buildup of static electricity.

Recognize the different types of technical attacks.   Passive attacks collect information to be used later in an active attack. Active attacks are designed to break down the defenses and execute the will of the attacker.

Understand the different motives of the malicious attacker.   Internal controls are used to prevent or detect most crimes committed by strangers and internal personnel. Remain aware that most theft is committed by someone that is known within the organization, due to access, motive, and time. The police refer to this concept as MOM: motive, opportunity, and means.

Understand how biometrics are used to judge the authenticity of a user.   Physical access controls are used to prevent loss of assets during safe storage, retrieval, operations, transport, and disposal.

Understand the need to implement physical access controls.   The goal of all perimeter controls is to insure only trusted and honest individuals are allowed access. The weakest method of authentication is using a password (type 1 authentication). A better method is to test unique physical characteristics such as the possession of a device (ATM card, Smart card, Hard token) and combine possession with a password (secret). Type 2 authentication uses a password with proof of a physical item in your possession (ATM card plus password). It is possible for the legitimate users to be denied access by the system (type 1 error, aka False rejection). Accordingly the illegitimate users may get access by mistake (type 2 error, aka False acceptance).

Understand the differences between public-key and private-key encryption systems.   PThe public key interchange (PKI) provides authentication, integrity and confidentiality between parties. A public key system uses asymmetric cryptography with a public key that is shared and a secret private key that must be protected for disclosure. Secret key systems use symmetric cryptography with a single shared secret key. The symmetric system is faster but fails to provide authentication. A compromised secret key will destroy confidentiality.

Recognize technical mechanisms.   Technical mechanisms like server mirroring and RAID disk systems can be used to increase redundancy to promote better system availability. The redundant hardware will increase fault tolerance for conditions involving hardware failure and possibly intruder attacks.

Understand intrusion detection systems.   Intrusion detection systems are designed to function as a computer-based hacker alarm. The intrusion detection system can be implemented using either a host-based method or network-based method. An IDS will only react to perceived attacks that occur on the system with host-based IDS installed or to attack traffic transmitted down a network link that is actively monitored by a network-based IDS. Attacks on all other systems are invisible to the IDS. The IDS identifies attacks by using one of three methods: comparing a database of known attack signatures, changes to a statistical baseline, or using a neural network with knowledge-based rules.

Review Questions

1. What is the best method for an organization to allow its business partners to access the company intranet across the Internet?

    A. Shared virtual private network

    B. Shared lease line

    C. Internet firewall

    D. Network router with MLSP

2. Digital signatures are primarily designed to provide additional protection with electronic messages in order to ensure which of the following?

    A. Message deletion

    B. Message read by unauthorized party

    C. Sender verification

    D. Message modification

3. Internet communication requires more security. To audit Internet security and access control, the IS auditor will first need to examine what?

    A. Validity of password changes

    B. Architecture of the client/server application

    C. Network architecture and design

    D. Virus protection and firewall servers

4. Which of the following is the most appropriate method to ensure confidentiality in data communications?

    A. Secure hash algorithm (SHA-1)

    B. Virtual private network (VPN)

    C. Digital signatures

    D. Digital certificates with public-key encryption

5. What is the most effective method for preventing or limiting the damage caused by a software virus attack?

    A. Access control software configured for restricted setting

    B. Updated virus signatures

    C. Antivirus policies and standards

    D. Data download standards with administrative review

6. What is the primary purpose of a network firewall?

    A. Protect company systems from attack by external systems.

    B. Protect downstream systems from all the internal attacks.

    C. Protect all modem-connected systems from Internet attacks.

    D. Protect attached systems from attacks running through the firewall.

7. Which of the following is the least dependable form of biometrics?

    A. Hand geometry

    B. Facial recognition

    C. Signature analysis

    D. Iris scanning

8. The IS auditor has just completed a review of an organization. Which of the following weaknesses would be considered the most serious?

    A. Lack of separation of duties for critical functions.

    B. Weak password controls without effective policy enforcement.

    C. Business continuity plans include noncritical applications.

    D. Network server is not backed up regularly.

9. What is the purpose of the DMZ (demilitarized zone) concept for Internet communications?

    A. *Demilitarized* refers to a safe zone that is protected from all Internet attacks.

    B. Subnet that is semiprotected and allows external access.

    C. Protected subnet implemented using a fifth-generation firewall.

    D. Safeguard control for communication allowing access to internal production servers.

10. An e-commerce website needs to be monitored to detect possible hacker activity. What would be the best security component to perform this function?

    A. Third-generation firewall

    B. Honey net ACL router with built in sniffer software

    C. Elliptic data encryption for privileged files

    D. Statistical or signature-based detection software

11. The auditee organization decided to implement single sign-on (SSO) for all their users. Their implementation will be using logon ID and passwords for access control. What situation should they be concerned about?

    A. Password aging must be set to force unique password changes every 30 to 60 days using alphanumeric characters.

    B. The user's system access will have protection; however, password changes will be more difficult because of synchronization issues between servers.

    C. Unauthorized login would have access to the maximum resources available on the network.

    D. The servers will need memory and CPU upgrades to handle the extra workload generated by SSO.

12. What is the primary purpose of intrusion detection systems (IDSs) compared to firewall systems?

    A. A firewall blocks all attacks; IDS informs us if the firewall was successful.

    B. IDS will notify the system administrator at every possible attack that has occurred, whether successful or unsuccessful.

    C. A firewall reports all attacks to the IDS.

    D. IDS logs and notifies the system administrator of any suspected attacks but may not recognize every attack.

13. Which of the following statements is true concerning asymmetric-key cryptography?

    A. The sender and receiver have different keys.

    B. The sender and receiver use the same key.

    C. The sender encrypts the files by using the recipient's private key.

    D. Asymmetric keys cannot be used for digital signatures.

14. The IS auditor is auditing the controls related to employee termination. Which of the following is the most important aspect to be reviewed?

    A. Company staff is notified about the termination.

    B. All login accounts of the employee are terminated.

    C. Details of the employee have been removed from active payroll files.

    D. Company property provided to the employee has been returned.

15. Which is the most important responsibility of the IS security person?

    A. Controlling and monitoring data security policies

    B. Promoting security awareness within the organization

    C. Establishing new procedures for IT and reviewing their legal accuracy

    D. System administration of the servers and database

16. What method provides the *best* level of access control to confidential data being processed on a local server?

    A. Writing a history of all transaction activity to the system log for auditing.

    B. Processing of sensitive transactions requires a separate login and password.

    C. Application software uses internal access control rules to implement least privilege.

    D. System login access is restricted to particular stations or hours of operation.

17. What is the primary purpose for using database views?

    A. Allow the user access into the database.

    B. Provide a method for generating reports.

    C. Allow the system administrator access to maintain the database.

    D. Restrict the viewing of selected data.

18. Which of the following statements is true concerning an Internet worm?

   A. Able to travel independently through the systems

   B. Self-replicates and attaches itself to files during execution

   C. Uses a backdoor to access system resources

   D. Can be dormant until triggered by particular date or time

19. What is the issue with regard to the use of source routing?

   A. Source routing is a diagnostic tool used with firewalls.

   B. No issue with compensating controls.

   C. Source routing can bypass network defenses.

   D. Is a desired feature for network monitoring.

20. The equal error rate (ERR) or crossover error rate (CER) refers to which of the following?

   A. Firewalls

   B. Biometrics

   C. Encryption

   D. Separation of duties

Answers to Review Questions

1. A. The virtual private network (VPN) is the most flexible and least expensive solution for accessing company resources across the Internet.

2. C. Digital signatures provide authentication assurance of the email sender. Digital signatures use the private key of the sender to verify identity.

3. C. The IS auditor will need to understand the network architecture and design before being able to evaluate the security and access controls. Later, the architecture of the client/server application and virus protection will be of interest.

4. B. The virtual private network (VPN) would ensure data confidentiality. A secure hash algorithm would identify that a file has been changed but will not provide confidentiality. Digital signatures are used to assess the identity of the sender but do not provide confidentiality.

5. B. Maintaining updated virus signature files. Access control software is not directly responsible for limiting the virus attack. Antivirus policies and standards should require updated virus signature files in order to be effective. Data download standards will help; however, virus signatures is the best choice.

6. D. The network firewall can protect only those systems that route communication through the firewall. The firewall can not protect systems attached via modem. Unsecure wirless networks are also a major threat.

7. C. Signature analysis is the most undependable form of biometrics. Hand geometry and iris scanning are very dependable. Facial recognition is improving.

8. D. The network server not being backed up regularly is the most significant threat to data integrity and availability. Weak passwords would be a lesser concern. The lack of separation of duties may be offset by compensating controls.

9. B. The DMZ is a subnet that is semiprotected by the firewall and allows for external access.

10. D. An intrusion detection system (IDS) with statistical or signature-based detection software would be the best choice.

11. C. Any unauthorized logon would have access to all the server resources on the network. Password aging with unique passwords is a good idea anyway.

12. D. The IDS keeps the transaction log and alerts the system administrator of any suspected attacks. The IDS can use statistical behavior or signature files to determine whether an attack has occurred.

13. A. The sender and receiver each have their own public and private (secret) key pair. All the other statements are false. Asymmetric keys are definitely used for creating digital signatures. The sender would never use the recipient's private key, only the recipient's public key.

14. B. The system access and login accounts of the employee should be terminated immediately. Company property is important, but a lesser concern than system access.

15. A. Controlling and monitoring data security policies is the highest priority of the IS security person.

16. C. Application controls should use internal access control lists to implement least privilege. System login restrictions are of less importance by comparison.

17. D. Database views are used to implement least privilege and restrict the data that can be viewed by the user.

18. A. An Internet worm is able to travel independently through systems, unlike a virus. The virus self-replicates and attaches itself to files during execution.

19. C. Source routing should not be allowed to operate on network firewalls. It presents a significant risk by allowing a hacker to bypass router security settings.

20. B. In biometrics, the trade-off between the false acceptance rate (FAR) and the false rejection rate (FRR) is known as the equal error rate (ERR) or crossover error rate (CER).

Chapter 8

Disaster Recovery and Business Continuity

THE OBJECTIVE OF THIS CHAPTER IS TO ACQUAINT THE READER WITH THE FOLLOWING CONCEPTS:

- ✓ Business process resumption
- ✓ Continuous essential processes
- ✓ Business impact analysis
- ✓ Plan development
- ✓ Human resource management
- ✓ Invocation processes
- ✓ Alternate sites

This chapter focuses on an organization's ability to recover from a disaster and to continue minimum acceptable operations. Your CISA exam maintains a very narrow focus of disaster recovery as it relates to an organization's ability to restore services to a predefined service-level agreement. However, we feel that to be a successful IS auditor, you should be taught a broader reference. Therefore, we're going to provide a brief introduction to the expanded scope of business continuity as well as the principles of disaster recovery.

We will compare the CISA exam's ISACA material to business continuity best practices. We will also introduce some of the terminology ISACA wants every CISA to know as it relates to disaster recovery and business continuity.

Defining Disaster Recovery

During the 1980s, the term *disaster recovery* became popular as a definition for rebuilding and recovery following a natural disaster. The entire focus of disaster recovery could be summed up with a one-word definition: *rebuilding*.

In 1988, the Disaster Recovery Institute International (DRII) was founded and set forth to produce a list of professional practices for disaster recovery planning. Its objective was to help organizations with their planning efforts to ensure that they could rebuild and recover their facilities and equipment following a natural disaster.

In 1992, Hurricane Andrew proved that disaster recovery lacked a critical element for survival. We could survive the storm, protect the people, and rebuild the facilities. However, without a steady stream of incoming revenue, organizations might recover only to find they were forced out of business by bankruptcy, or a lack of money. Granted, facilities and IT systems are important for an organization to conduct business. Unfortunately, those elements alone are not enough for any organization's existence to continue. The scope of disaster recovery needed to be expanded to include revenue and customers.

Let's discuss the financial challenges that lead into defining business continuity.

Surviving Financial Challenges

The greatest threats to the survival of any organization center on financial concerns of continued existence. One needs to be sure that under all conditions special measures have been taken to ensure the following:

- The organization does not breach any significant contractual commitments.
- The banker does not call business loans due, rerate available credit lines, or increase the interest rate.

- Investors do not back out or dump their stock in a rapid sell-off.
- Clients continue to do business without hesitating, or canceling their orders.
- Business partners continue to perform under the original terms of contract without placing new demands or suspending services.

The loss of any of these items can structurally weaken the organization and management's ability to continue operation. In fact, the loss of any these items would probably be a show-stopper. The organization would grind to a halt and cease to function.

Valuing Brand Names

Let's consider for a moment the subject of brand names. Brand names include well-known corporate names such as Gulf Oil, Frontier Airlines, and Holiday Inn. Brand names represent the recognition of goodwill established after years of successful advertising. If the advertising was successful, the brand name alone brings about recognition in the consumer's mind and a perception of value. Successful advertising generates revenue from 5 times to 30 times the cost of the advertisements. In fact, the established brand name may be one of the most viable assets of the organization.

You may ask, "What does this have to do with disaster recovery?" The answer is simple. Business continuity planning focuses on maintaining the public image of the corporate entity—in order to ensure survival of the organization.

In 1994, a new airline was started by former Frontier Airline executives. The Frontier brand name had reverted to public domain during eight years of disuse and was available again. Many consumers never realized that the original airline had ceased operation. The brand's value had continued to survive.

Rebuilding after a Disaster

Even the mightiest of organizations can be brought down by a variety of events. Every day in the *Financial Times* or The *Wall Street Journal,* you can find an example of operational failure, leadership failure, or a mishandled incident that became a man-made disaster.

If you recall, a simple definition of *disaster recovery (DR)* is *rebuilding.* Almost all activities under disaster recovery focus on rebuilding to match a particular historical configuration. This leads us to the evolution from disaster recovery to business continuity.

Defining the Purpose of Business Continuity

Unlike DR, *business continuity (BC)* focuses on *revenue.* As long as the organization has time and money at its disposal, the organization can continue to function. Money can take the form of capital, credit lines, investors, and payments from customers. Business continuity focuses on putting more money in the bank, even if the business is not delivering a product. A perfect example is the age-old "fire sale." The objective of a fire sale is to increase the amount of capital on hand in order to allow the business time to continue operation and possibly fund their rebuilding activities.

 Real World Scenario

AOL Tries to Rebuild after an Internal Disaster

Organizations can be affected by events that disrupt the daily operation of their business. Consider, for example, America Online (AOL), which suffered a change management crisis in which the configuration of the routers and servers was lost. The result was an operational disaster in 1994 with a complete blackout of AOL's Internet services for more than three days. As a result, AOL suffered a negative public perception and negative publicity. This operational mistake ultimately led to the sale of the business. In 2003, while AOL was owned by Time Warner, AOL was again the subject of much controversy and rapidly falling stock prices. The issue this time centered on the management team refusing to sign for the integrity of the company financial statement. Their failure to sign created a legal requirement for the organization to notify the entire world that their record keeping was questionable and that there was no assurance of integrity in any statements made. AOL management was aware of the consequences but did not want to accept personal liability for signing a potentially false integrity statement. The resulting news stories led many investors to dump stock at a fraction of its previous value.

The purpose of business continuity is to ensure that core business functions will continue with minimal or no interruption. When focusing on business continuity, you may choose not to return to the past and to instead focus all endeavors toward new opportunities. The objective is to ensure that the organization will survive and continue to deposit revenue. Uninterrupted revenue equals money that provides the luxury of time and opportunity.

An organization can use the principles of business continuity to accomplish the following:

Survive man-made or natural disaster   Survival means sustaining control while ensuring that enough money is flowing to the bank to keep the organization running during and after the event.

Acquire or divest business units   The business continuity planning process creates an incredibly valuable set of documents, including a current risk analysis and a low-level blueprint of business processes currently in use. This information would be invaluable for outsourcing or insourcing.

Change to a different market   Some markets are no longer profitable because of changes in consumer attitude, cost/competition, or increasing regulatory law. Management may find a more profitable market for their efforts. As an example, consider Daisytek International. Daisytek started business as a distributor of office supplies, later to become a hardware manufacturer for Hewlett-Packard. After several years, the management team decided to quit manufacturing hardware and refocus on the more-profitable market of distributing office supplies. Recently the supplies portion of the business was sold because of low profit margin, and the remaining organization was renamed PFSweb. Now PFSweb operates as a contract fulfillment and distribution vendor, providing fulfillment services for other organizations. Many of the original executives and staff remain.

Improve market position by demonstrating a potential for surviving or profiting   One of the reasons an organization participates in business continuity planning is to attract better financial terms from investors and to attract more clients. A good business continuity plan could attract new contracts and revenue opportunities by demonstrating an organizational plan to fulfill contractual commitments.

Gain advantage over a competitor in the marketplace   An organization might gain advantage by demonstrating an ability to help their customers in spite of whatever may occur. We can use the example of Federal Express and their "Absolutely positively overnight" reputation to demonstrate this point. Customers pay a premium for this level of commitment.

Other examples of gaining an advantage are as follows:

- To execute business continuity plans in order to undertake a higher than normal business volume, shedding low-profit tasks to make resources available for the increased volume.

- To lead an aggressive campaign against a faltering competitor. The competitor may be facing temporary delivery problems, an unfavorable media image, labor issues, or a man-made or natural disaster. Our client would unleash a marketing campaign with compelling offers to entice clients to abandon the competition. Customer swings have been recorded of 20 percent to 55 percent of market share during a 16-hour period.

- To be available for customer needs. Consider the story of the Bank of Italy during the California earthquake of 1906. The earthquake lasted only 30 seconds but destroyed the city of San Francisco. All the banks were ordered closed to prevent a run on the banks. The little tiny Bank of Italy set up temporary operation in a wooden horse cart at the wharf. While the other banks were closed, the Bank of Italy was making small loans to help people rebuild. Many individuals wanted to make deposits to this little bank in a horse cart. The customers wanted their money from coffee cans and from under mattresses to be protected. Serving $10 depositors, the little Bank of Italy took in over $800,000 during the next few years. This was an incredible sum of money during that period. Multiple divisions were formed under other names, and ultimately these were combined under one new name: Bank of America.

Survive a runaway marketing campaign   Do you remember the fabulously successful "Where's the beef?" campaign by Wendy's hamburgers? It is a marketing legend. It also illustrates how a runaway marketing campaign can place excessive strain on an organization's resources. Dave Thomas, the founder of Wendy's told the story as follows:

Wendy's had run a series of advertising campaigns which never really seemed to catch on. Other competitors were able to attract customers using lower-priced products with less meat. Wendy's "Where's the beef?" marketing campaign was based upon a common sense observation

and was well timed to the marketplace. Wendy's advertisement caught on like wildfire and was even used in coattail publicity by political candidates during campaign rallies. The campaign was enormously successful beyond everyone's expectations. This one campaign created so much attention, new customers were lining up at their door. The ad also brought the attention of Wendy's larger competitors. Wendy's was forced into a rapid national expansion or face losing their marketplace. Wendy's opened over 500 new stores during a one-year period at the rate of two or more stores per workday. (Source: Discovery channel)
Could your organization have done the same?

Uniting Other Plans with Business Continuity

As we have said, business continuity is the next level beyond disaster recovery. Business continuity is double-sided. One side protects what a business already has while the other offers the opportunity to generate more money than ever before.

A good continuity plan defines a strategy and details for supporting a business with fewer resources. After the business has learned how to make more money, there is no need to wait for a disaster. The business can begin to execute the revenue-enhancement plans immediately, and will be prepared for both disaster and market opportunity.

Business continuity planning integrates and coordinates the narrow scope of smaller plans. Figure 8.1 shows this integration.

FIGURE 8.1   Business continuity integrates other plans.

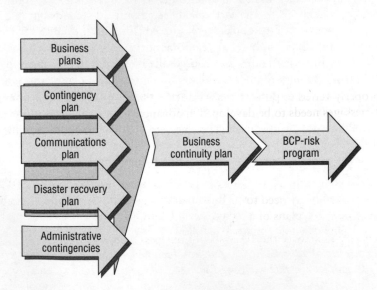

Identifying the Business Continuity Planning Phases

There are 10 phases in the business continuity model, according to DRII and the Business Continuity Institute (BCI). It is the job of the business continuity/disaster recovery planner to determine whether the focus will be disaster recovery for rebuilding, or business continuity for revenue. This type of planning uses a very specialized version of project management. Each of these areas is a project unto itself.

The phases are as follows:

Initiation   Get a sponsor, authority, scope, and funding.

Risk analysis   Document and prioritize current risks. Risks include natural disasters and man-made events.

Business impact analysis   Develop a low-level business process blueprint; determine what is needed to sustain the business.

Create strategy   Use the risk analysis and business impact analysis to formulate a possible strategy based on facts and assumptions in evidence.

Emergency response   Integrate the planned strategy with the first responder by using the Incident Command System (ICS).

Plan creation   Create and organize the plan, including personnel assignments and detailed procedures.

Training and awareness   Teach individuals the necessary roles and skills to perform the required functions of the BC/DR plan. Educate the organization about the plan's existence and anticipated areas of coverage.

Maintain and test   Nothing is out of date faster than a big book of plans. People have to practice their roles to gain proficiency, and a change control system will be needed to improve the documentation. It is impossible to keep plans current without structured exercises to improve skills and identify deficiencies.

Communications   Clients, investors, partners, employees, and stakeholders need to be kept informed and feel comfortable with the information they receive. Internal and external messages need to be properly vetted to portray the intended message; a schedule of communications and scripted messages needs to be developed in advance. Poor communications can be more damaging than the actual disaster itself. Plans need to include an uninterruptible communication system.

Integrate with other organizations   No organization can exist by itself. A good plan will integrate with plans of business partners, suppliers, clients, and government agencies. You may need to rely on them, or they may need to rely on us during critical functions. Often a prime contractor will incorporate the plans of a subcontractor into their own.

Figure 8.2 shows an overview of the 10 phases of business continuity planning.

FIGURE 8.2   The 10 phases of best practices in business continuity planning

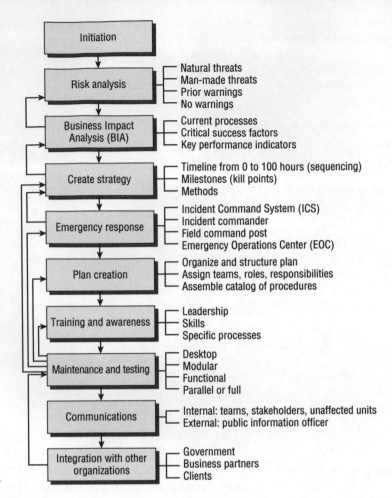

Some individuals are of the opinion that IT technology and facilities are the most important functions in business continuity. Although they have a significant role, it is important to remember that the priority is the customer and the customer interface. Without the customer, there is no revenue. Without revenue, business continuity would be difficult or impossible.

Now let's explore the 10 phases of business continuity with a little more depth. Our goal is to provide you with a basic understanding that you can use in your audit work.

Real World Scenario

Best Practices Compared to the CISA Exam

The CISA exam and ISACA have a narrower view of business continuity and disaster recovery. The best practices for business continuity presented in this chapter are endorsed by the DRII and the BCI.

You are expected to know the terminology used by ISACA for the exam. Each organization uses similar terms of reference. You should also be introduced to an overview of best practices in business continuity to increase understanding of real-life situations. We have reduced the content to remain focused on the CISA exam. Each of the examples presented should help increase your value as an IS auditor.

The following shows the differences between business continuity best practices and the ISACA knowledge areas.

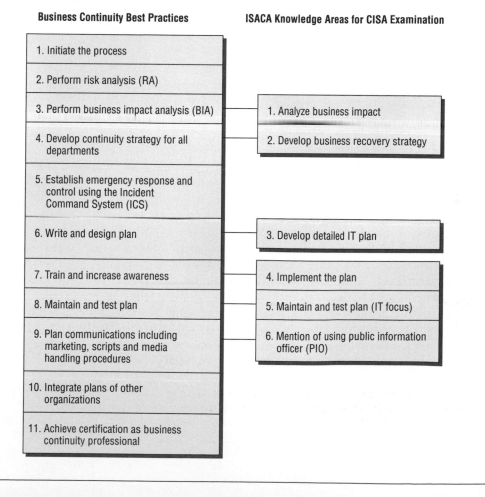

Business Continuity Best Practices

1. Initiate the process
2. Perform risk analysis (RA)
3. Perform business impact analysis (BIA)
4. Develop continuity strategy for all departments
5. Establish emergency response and control using the Incident Command System (ICS)
6. Write and design plan
7. Train and increase awareness
8. Maintain and test plan
9. Plan communications including marketing, scripts and media handling procedures
10. Integrate plans of other organizations
11. Achieve certification as business continuity professional

ISACA Knowledge Areas for CISA Examination

1. Analyze business impact
2. Develop business recovery strategy
3. Develop detailed IT plan
4. Implement the plan
5. Maintain and test plan (IT focus)
6. Mention of using public information officer (PIO)

Phase 1—Initiation

Every project undergoes an initiation phase with the objective to secure the following:

- A sponsor to pay for the project
- A charter to grant responsibility and authority
- A defined scope (for a particular geographic site, division, product, or client)
- Specific business objectives (critical success factors, management direction)

We need to introduce the simple definition of two important terms:

Critical success factor (CSF) Something that must function correctly every single time. The failure of a CSF would be a showstopper.

Key performance indicator (KPI) May not indicate a problem until it's too late. Similar to report-card grades in school.

During the initiation phase, specific discussions are held between the business continuity/disaster recovery planner and executive management. The planner may use the technique of doom and gloom to threaten a variety of negative consequences. This technique is intended to intimidate executives with liability if they fail to cooperate. A more favorable technique would be to provide clippings of related news articles to generate awareness. A person could ask, "If this happened to us, would we have a similar outcome?"

The majority of business continuity/disaster recovery planners will use a shortsighted approach that business continuity or disaster coverage is similar to insurance. Their goal is to protect the business from a future loss. The problem is that many executives are more worried about generating revenue than they are about maintaining comprehensive insurance.

The business continuity/disaster recovery planner should develop a list of benefits that the enterprise would derive by developing and implementing a business continuity plan.

Brands and goodwill affiliated with a company name contain significant "real" value. Most marketing campaigns are built up year after year using anywhere from 15 percent to 25 percent of product gross revenue to pay for advertising. It is common to expect strong ad campaigns to earn returns that are 5 times to 30 times the cost of the campaign itself. Years of happy customers create brand loyalty. A hard-earned image can be destroyed by adverse publicity or disaster. Approach value by calculating the amount of money invested in advertising and public relations over the past years.

The business continuity/disaster recovery planner needs to communicate the multiple categories of risk that face the organization. Consider this to be the short and broad list in discussions with management. Each of these situations could rapidly surface and get out of control during a crisis or even cause a disaster.

The threat categories include the following:

Strategic (plans) Poor marketing strategy, changes in laws, consumer attitudes

Financial (controls) Fraud, poor record keeping, failed reconciliation, poor cash/credit management, treasury problems, Securities and Exchange Commission (SEC) reports, Gramm-Leach-Bliley bank performance rules.

Operational (human)   Human error, apathy, wrong procedures, poor judgment, communications conflict, politics, lack of up-to-date training

Commercial (relationships)   Loss of key supplier/customer; supply-chain failure; scandal involving partner, supplier, or significant customer

Technical (assets)   Equipment breakdown, natural disaster, destruction, loss of use, other perils

Figure 8.3 shows that business continuity can be focused on protecting a variety of business processes.

An incredibly effective technique is to tie business continuity objectives into plans for revenue and market share. Earlier, we touched on a few examples of using business continuity planning to generate revenue. Funding is less of an issue when you include marketing plans in the objectives. This lends itself to acquiring a significant amount of funding from the advertising budget—far less money than advertising would miss, and far more money than most DR plans would ever acquire.

FIGURE 8.3   Selecting the business process to protect

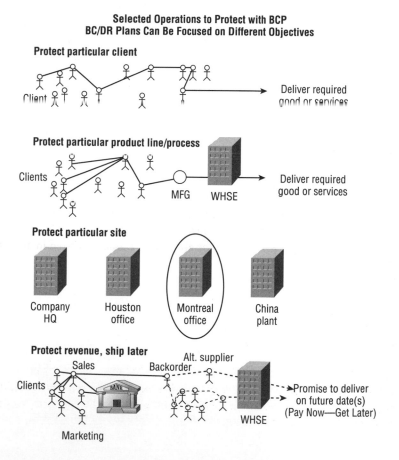

Some of the possible deliverables from the business continuity/disaster recovery planning process include the following:

- Verification of capabilities (efficiency, inefficiency, deficiency, over reliance, unused capacity)

- Identification of new revenue opportunities

- Functional blueprint of current business processes with mapping of interrelationships and sequence

- Definition of risk and performance strategy

- Documentation of specific required tasks for business survival

- Strategy to increase revenue

- Fulfillment of a business interest or executive business desire

> **NOTE**   People agree to fund and support projects for a variety of reasons. The goal of the initiation phase is to determine what the sponsor will pay for and why, and to document the desired result.

As an IT auditor, you will focus on whether the IT functions will be able to support the business objectives. Planning for business continuity/disaster recovery will be successful only when sponsored from the top down. It is the responsibility of senior executive management to ensure that this planning occurs. A business continuity/disaster recovery steering committee will be necessary to create an effective of plan.

Phase 2—Risk Analysis

The next phase is to conduct a risk analysis. The business continuity/disaster recovery planner creates a list of all the threats known to face the organization—including both man-made and natural, those with prior warning, and those without. Many people see this phase as a well-known requirement but then to proceed to skip right past without any regard. In Chapter 2, "Audit Process," we provided a flowchart detailing the methods for performing risk analysis.

The starting point in risk analysis entails listing the threats and assigning a potential score. Risk managers are similar to gamblers: They want to calculate the present odds and see what can be done to improve them. Your goal at this stage of the planning process is to accurately document the present state of each threat. After you have identified all of the risks, the planner will focus their efforts on the threats of the highest priority. Priority may be determined by frequency, consequence, or dependency.

A sense of order is necessary to manage the list of potential threats. Your sponsor and executive management team will have little interest in wading through volumes of spreadsheets. The easy way to deal with this is to create a summary sheet and related detail sheets. Each item on the summary sheet will relate to an entire page or pages of detail sheets.

Figure 8.4 illustrates risk assessment worksheets. Shown are the summary and related detail reports.

FIGURE 8.4   Risk assessment worksheets for summary and detail

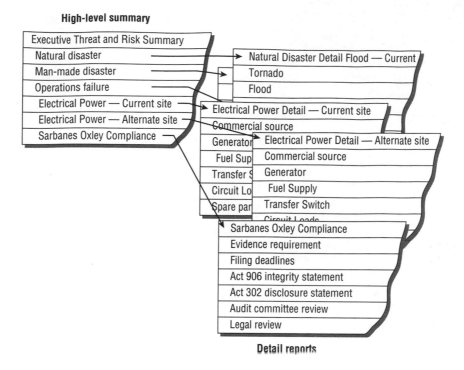

The higher-level summary sheet will include a list of threats related to the following:

- Various natural disasters
- Man-made disasters
- Operational and technology failures
- Vendor failures
- Current site failures
- Alternate site failures
- Relocation threats

Each of these line items will be broken down into individual components listed on a detail sheet. From the detail sheet, the planner will create a composite score that will appear on the summary sheet. Figure 8.5 shows the detailed ranking for each threat.

A well-documented threat listing will note where the evidence was acquired from, or where the evidence can be found. All risk analysis worksheets represent a tremendous value in time, effort, and informational detail. These worksheets should be preserved and protected. Every intelligent risk manager will review them on a regular basis. Finished worksheets may contain hundreds or thousands of line items.

FIGURE 8.5   A risk assessment worksheet

Threat	Likelihood (frequency)	Human Impact	Property Impact	Business Impact	Internal Resources	External Resources	Threat Score	Related Notes Archive (files)
Labor Strike	1	3	1	4	4	3	16	strike.doc
WTO Protest	0.3	2	1	2	4	3	11.3	wto.doc
Workplace Violence	0.7	4	1	2	5	2	14.7	wrkviol.rpt

Let's take a moment to discuss the often neglected area of selecting an alternate site and potential threats to relocation. All too often the alternate site is selected by the service company providing the facility. In some cases, this could prove to be an absolute killer.

Suppose you were looking for an alternate site. What would be the geographic location requirements? Hopefully, the geographic selection process would include consideration of the following:

- General area hazards. Ask questions about the neighbors, crime rate, and previous events in the area.

- Downwind hazards from military targets and nuclear power plants.

- Known storm tracks for severe weather, including hurricanes and tornadoes.

- Potential flood areas.

- Geophysical data concerning potential earth movement.

- Access to telecommunications.

- Nearby airports, helpful for regular visits and necessary for rapid relocation.

- Roadway access. Remember September 11, 2001. Who says airplanes will be flying the day you need to fly? Some major city airports may be closed.

- Proximity. You need to be close enough to drive, yet not so close that you are affected by the same regional disaster.

- Railway access for shipping heavy loads or volume goods.

- Municipal services, including fire, police, and hospital.

- Expedited services and mail services.

- Safe accommodations.

All this data is readily available, including maps of military targets and nuclear materials. Contrary to myth, worldwide military targets and nuclear materials maps are still available on the Internet at the time of this writing.

Figure 8.6 shows a simple map illustrating basic geographic threats for the state of Texas. Any country or state could have been used for this demonstration; however, the Texas map does a nice job of illustrating our objective. The northeastern United States is considered a more likely terrorist target; however, we still need to consider technical failure no matter where the business is located.

FIGURE 8.6   Geographic threat map for Texas

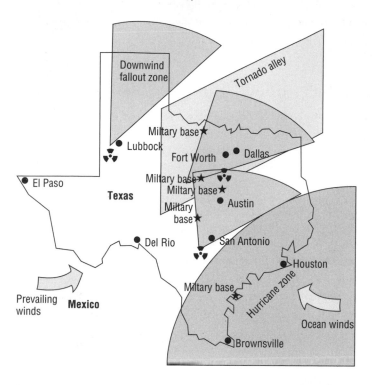

Notice how each of the elements of the selection process overlay the state. The major cities of Dallas, Fort Worth, Houston, Austin, and San Antonio contain multiple area threats. An upwind biological or nuclear hazard could affect each of the cities by carrying contaminates downwind.

Now take a look on the left side of the state. The Rio Grande River is the western border between Texas and Mexico. Notice the town of Del Rio, Texas, along the Rio Grande River. Del Rio is outside of most of the severe weather zones. It has no significant upwind biological or nuclear hazard. The town is located within 175 to 300 miles of the major Texas cities. The highway to Del Rio could fulfill the minimum access requirement. An organization could transport their staff by car, bus, or truck within 8 hours of normal driving time. Del Rio is a switching point along Union Pacific railroad's main line. Rail access is good for heavy shipments but could represent a concern regarding possible transportation of hazardous materials. Amtrak provides regular passenger rail service. The Del Rio airport offers regularly scheduled flights and supports private aircraft operations. The organization can charter a full-sized commercial jet for about $8,500 an hour to move a large group of people in a hurry. The jet's cargo bay can be loaded with the freight needed for recovery. It is usually cheaper to charter rather than buy a handful of last-minute airline tickets. All major air freight carriers operate from this airport, including DHL, UPS, and FedEx. There are practically no geophysical concerns regarding earth movement. Reasonable fiber-optic communication access is available. Land is relatively cheap. The crime rate is low. Based on this information, Del Rio, Texas, scores well as an alternate site location.

Successful planners will go to this level of detail when selecting an alternate site.

Phase 3—Business Impact Analysis (BIA)

The *business impact analysis (BIA)* is the singular most important component of every business continuity plan. It is impossible to have a business continuity plan without performing a current BIA. Without the BIA, the best you could hope for would be basic disaster recovery.

The BIA process offers substantial benefits to an organization. The resulting information is invaluable for business process reengineering, outsourcing activities, resizing plans, acquisition or divestiture activities, and business continuity planning.

In Figure 8.7, you can see the relationships among business processes.

FIGURE 8.7 Relationships among business processes

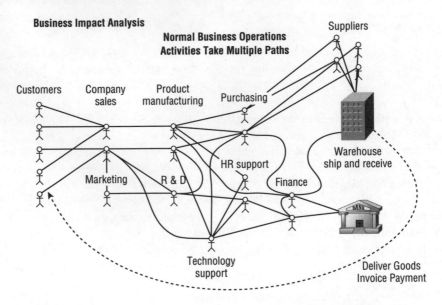

A BIA documents current low-level process dependencies and discovers new opportunities.

A BIA is a specialized project designed to uncover the inner workings of an organization. The value of this phase cannot be overstated. In Chapter 2, we discussed using both qualitative and quantitative assessment for planning. The same qualitative and quantitative technique can be used in the BIA. Proper execution of the BIA process entails a series of discovery exercises, including the following:

- Asking a series of questions similar to those used in business process reengineering (BPR). These questions would focus on identifying trigger events and the current sequence of the organization's workflow.

- Interviewing key personnel.

- Reviewing existing documentation.

- Collecting data by observing actual processes.

- Possibly surveying personnel performing actual tasks. The auditor should recall that using surveys can raise issues of accuracy and consistency.

- Looking for existing workarounds and alternate procedures. Many times, the client's personnel may be aware of workarounds that could prove valuable during a business continuity situation.

- Verifying critical success factors (CSFs).

- Identifying vital materials and records necessary for recovery. This would include numerous items: data backups, vendor list, inventory records, customer lists, employee records with contact data, bill of materials, procedure documents, BC plan, banking information, copies of all contracts, and legal documents.

Collecting and organizing this information is a formidable task. All the disciplines of project management are invoked during the execution of the BIA. Later, during the business continuity planning process, the BC planners use the risk analysis and BIA information to guide the formulation of the BC strategy. Almost every organization would be unable to properly sequence business continuity activities if they failed to collect the correct information during the BIA phase.

All the data collected from the BIA and risk analysis should be properly archived and protected with the highest level of security available. This archive creates a central repository of all the organization's plans, secrets, and capabilities—hence effective security controls are paramount. The contents of this archive will be reused in subsequent planning sessions that should occur at the following times:

- At least annually

- Whenever the organizational structure changes

- Upon addition or loss of key customers

- Upon change of current business processes

- Upon change in the management direction

The business users must always be involved in the planning of business continuity. Without their input, it would be impossible to align the plans with real world-requirements.

Keeping users involved is the secret to attaining buy-in.

Phase 4—Strategy Selection

In using information from the first three phases, you can begin the process of selecting a business survival strategy. This strategy may be one of protection, growth, or change. It is unfortunate, but a number of uninformed individuals in all job roles may immediately jump ahead into technology solutions without having exercised a proper strategy selection process.

Strategy selection should take into account the management directives from initiation as well as the identified risks and documented process dependencies. Your risk analysis will allow the determination of the worst-case scenario. The BIA process will furnish a blueprint that can provide a critical path sequence.

The next step in planning is to create a timeline sequence of activities necessary to support the critical path. A great deal of discussion and politics may enter into this otherwise simple process. Effective business continuity planners will categorize everything into one of three areas of interest:

Core process   Those activities that are specifically required in the critical path and related directly to production of revenue.

Supporting process   Those activities necessary for the minimum support to fulfill revenue activities. This may include an alternate mechanism for delivering invoices to the customer for prompt payment.

Discretionary process   Everything else that is not part of core or supporting processes. These activities are not used in critical business functions, and do not feed or process data for critical or supporting systems. These activities would cost more to protect than the value of work the system produces.

With this information, the planner creates a working timeline for all business continuity/ disaster recovery activities. This timeline would reference multiple levels of time and service delivery. We will identify these as follows:

Recovery time objective (RTO)   The point in time at which a particular level of recovery should be obtained. Multiple RTOs will exist (RTO1, RTO2, RTO3, and so on).

Maximum acceptable outage (MAO)   The maximum time the systems can be off-line before breaching a deadline or causing damage to the organization. The MAO is factored into creating recovery time objectives (RTOs). This may also be referred to as *maximum tolerable downtime (MTD)*. Both terms are similar in purpose.

Recovery point objective (RPO)   The defined level of recovery for a particular item. Processing that occurs between the RPO and the incident will be lost work. An example is recovery of last night's backup tape or recovery to completed database transactions that occurred 5 minutes ago (based on a redundant high-availability system). Multiple RPOs may exist.

Work in progress will be lost at the time of disruption. The business continuity/disaster recovery planner should review the risk and plan according to the criticality. Each RPO should take into consideration the following:

Critical function   These must occur to fulfill the minimum requirements to accomplish *core processes* (mission). These functions will be very time-sensitive and might not be recoverable by manual operation.

Vital function   These are less critical, with somewhat more time before recovery is necessary. Vital functions may be able to run manually depending on volume and duration of work.

Sensitive function   These can be delayed for several days, and might be performed manually or outsourced to another vendor.

Non-critical (everything else)   These may be discontinued for extended periods of time, and may or may not be restarted in the future. The recovery point (RPO) may be none.

Service delivery objective (SDO)   The level of service available at a particular point in time. In the banking industry, an example of the first SDO (SDO1) may allow customers to deposit money, withdraw money, and check balances. The next SDO (SDO2) might allow the execution of financial trades. However, the customer may not be able to open or close new accounts until the account management SDO (SDO3) is reached. We use this reference to indicate the level of reduced or suspended service. Our final SDO (SDOx) would be full-service in normal operation.

NOTE   At CertTest, we teach business continuity planners to organize and illustrate these objectives by using a visual timeline. Our timeline begins at 100 hours in the past and proceeds to 100 hours in the future. This will cover approximately four calendar days before and after the event. It is well documented that an organization that does not recover by the fourth day will likely fail during the coming year. Unfortunately, some organizations may fail in fewer than four days. Either way, our timeline will accomplish its purpose.

One of the most important objectives of business continuity planning efforts is to identify what constitutes the zero hour. In most organizations, nobody wants to be the person who cried wolf, nor the person who activated the plan before its designated time. Management holds the responsibility of identifying situations that would mandate activating the continuity plan. The senior manager on duty would be under orders to execute the plan whenever the predetermined conditions were met. Otherwise, the plan may be executed too early or too late to save the organization. The zero hour may be defined based on the level of physical damage, marketing failure, degraded media image, loss of production capability, or the runaway success of a marketing campaign.

By using this information, a variety of strategies may be selected. The IT strategy selection is based on the unique needs of individual departments, available personnel, facilities, capital management, technology, and business processes. An effective strategy will fit within the requirements of each RTO, RPO, and SDO. In highly regulated industries, the target objectives may be clearly defined by regulatory law.

After you identify the proper sequence of objectives, you need to decide the best method of implementation. Available options include the following:

Do nothing   This is often unacceptable and creates the potential for catastrophic liability.

Redundant hardware   A redundant hardware strategy may be used for equipment within the facility. The concept of redundancy could be to have spare systems online, or to stock an in-house supply of replacement parts.

Mirrored servers   Mirrored high-availability servers are an example of redundant online systems. Two servers operate as one machine. If functioning correctly, a secondary server takes over processing when the primary server fails.

Mirrored disk drives   Using RAID technology, the date on disk drives can be mirrored. We discussed mirrored servers and RAID in Chapter 7, "Information Asset Protection."

Redundant communication   Network routers can be set up in a redundant configuration to ensure maximum uptime. This effective design utilizes communication services from more than one communication provider—for example, Internet connections from both AT&T and MCI.

Alternate processing location   Alternate sites are used for processing in the event the organization is unable to use a regular location. The alternate sites are usually one of the following types:

Redundant site   This location contains either duplicate mirror facilities that are online at all times, or computing facilities of a reduced capacity that can process at the acceptable SDO requirement. The data is live—no delays waiting for files to be restored. All necessary personnel are already present and on the job. The redundant site is in full operation and able to take over processing within seconds or minutes. A redundant site can offer a competitive marketing and operational advantage. Redundant sites can be located in the same geographic region or across the country. A location should be selected that is not subject to disasters in the same proximity as the primary site. The two sites should be geographically separated. The dominant issue of operating a redundant site is the cost.

Hot site   This is similar to a redundant site except that it is off-line when not in use. Hot sites can be obtained by subscription (rented) or by capital investment (owned). All necessary facilities, equipment, and communication lines are ready to go without delay or setup time. Basically, a hot site is fully operational and gathering dust until it is ready to be used. Data files will need several hours to load from backup tapes before the systems can go live. A hot site is fully equipped and capable of being in operation within hours. A delay may occur as personnel are traveling to the site. Hot sites may be elaborate for use in executive marketing to attract key investors and clients. Hot sites are ideal for supporting IT functions and live customer communication.

Warm site   This location offers significantly less opportunity for success. Warm sites are typically shell buildings with basic utility services and require extra time to make ready. Computer equipment may not be on-site yet, or may require configuration before it is ready to use. After several hours of system configuration, additional delays will occur as data files are loaded. Communication lines will need to be activated and traffic rerouted before the voice and data can go online. This type of site will be operational in a matter of days or weeks. The location may be a branch office of the same organization.

🌐 Real World Scenario

A Lesson in Hot Site Declaration Criteria

During the fall of 2005, several hurricanes impacted the southeastern United States. A handful of business continuity/disaster recovery planners complained that they were placed in a dangerous situation of being denied access to a hot site that they had paid to use by subscription. The vendor gave excuses that other customers from prior hurricanes were still using the facility. Another customer was told by the hot site vendor that they would not be allowed to declare hot site activation because their city had not been hit by the hurricane nor was it designated a disaster area. Their vendor allocated hot site space based on a *first to declare* criteria rather than guaranteed access. Stories verifying the situation appeared in newspapers and on the Internet.

Cold site   This option offers the lowest possibility of success. Cold sites are typically building shells without any computing equipment, and offer no more than a street address and basic shelter. Examples include a hotel conference room. A cold site is the cheapest of all alternate site options and is unacceptable for IT functions. A cold site may be acceptable for recovery of noncritical systems as time permits.

Mobile site   Very popular with vendors selling alternate site solutions, the mobile site is usually a trailer configured so that it is equivalent to the level of a hot site or warm site. These are popular for extended use on-site while buildings and facilities are reconstructed. Unfortunately, mobile sites may be restricted by building permit delays, mandatory evacuations, or inaccessible regions due to roadway damage or roadblocks. A handful of customers affected by hurricanes Charlie, Katrina, and Wilma reported that their mobile sites did not arrive as promptly as promised because of travel restrictions and fuel shortages. Many professionals consider the mobile site to be a derivative of the cold site, with no guarantee of timely service. If a mobile site can be reliably obtained, a practical application may be to use the site as an interim facility for the months after leaving a hot site, but before reoccupying a permanent site.

Table 8.1 shows the basic differences between the types of alternate sites.

TABLE 8.1   Comparison of Recovery Site Types

Type	Recovery time	Basic Advantage
Redundant	Seconds	Always online and processing. Staff is in place and working. Prefect for high-priority processing that cannot be interrupted.
Hot site	Hours	Preconfigured, just restore data files. Designed for rapid 4- to 24-hour recovery of applications.

TABLE 8.1 Comparison of Recovery Site Types *(continued)*

Type	Recovery time	Basic Advantage
Warm site	Days	Cheaper. Will need to assemble equipment and activate communication lines.
Cold site	Weeks	Cheapest. Provides a building shell without equipment. Used for noncritical recovery or staging of salvaged assets.
Mobile site	8+ hours to days	Can supplement damaged facilities at original site. Can be configured with equipment equal to hot, warm, or cold site depending on customer's interest.

Fortification in place   It may be determined that an acceptable option is to create a fortress out of an existing facility. Fortifications can be made to compensate for minor natural disasters and varying degrees of man-made disasters. The fortification process requires a significant investment in structural reinforcement. Unfortunately, the fortification may not survive acts of terrorism, airborne contaminants of chemical or biological nature, flood, or mandatory evacuation. History is riddled with thousands of years' worth of failed fortifications.

Reciprocal agreements   This option is based on the belief that two organizations could render mutual aid to each other to save money. Unfortunately, often neither organization has the free space or excess capacity to support the other. Two organizations in the same geographic area could also be affected by the same event. Issues of security and noncompetition will also exist. Traditionally, reciprocal agreements are both unenforceable and unrealistic.

Cooperative recovery sites in banking are an exception for reciprocal agreements. Small banks in the financial industry frequently operate a shared hot site as a cooperative venture. Banking laws require even the smallest of bank to prove its continuity strategy on a quarterly basis. Several smaller banks will form a cooperative to rent or purchase the necessary recovery site facilities. If a smaller bank fails to prove an effective recovery capability, federal regulators will reassign all of the small bank's accounts to a larger bank.

Data backup strategy   Every recovery strategy requires data to be kept on backup tapes. The tapes need to be managed by a librarian, as discussed in Chapter 3, "IT Governance," and Chapter 6, "IT Service Delivery." The typical data backup strategy implements one of the following methods:

Full backup   Creates an entire copy of each file on the system. This is the most effective backup method and requires a significant amount of time.

Incremental method   Copies only the files that have changed since the last backup. The incremental method is commonly used for backups on weekdays. This method requires less time than a full backup. Unfortunately, the file restoration process takes longer because it is necessary to restore the full backup and each version of incremental backup. An incremental backup resets the archive bit (backup flag) to indicate that a file needs to be backed up.

Differential method   Copies every file that has changed between full backup runs. Differential is the preferred method for business continuity. This method ensures that multiple copies of daily files should exist on multiple tapes. A differential backup is very fast on the first day after a full backup, and then takes longer each day as more files are copied. A differential backup does not change the archive bit (backup flag).

When selecting the data backup strategy, it is important to consider the time necessary for data restoration. Care should be given to ensure the RTO and RPO are met.

Insurance   Most business continuity/disaster recovery planners review insurance during the risk assessment phase. Insurance carries several risks, including significant delays in receiving payments, likelihood of claims being denied, and difficulties proving financial loss within the policy limitations. Insurance is commonly used for durable goods, property, and life or casualty. Most policies pay for only a percentage of loss and do not include lost income, increased operating expenses, or consequential loss. Businesses at the World Trade Center at the time of the bombing in 1993 have yet to receive any financial settlements for damages or the extended utility service outages. Insurance is available for a variety of situations. Let's look at a few of the types of insurance available:

Property insurance   Property insurance provides financial protection against the loss of or damage to physical property—for example, burglary, plate glass damage, and fire. It may include coverage for the loss of income-producing ability.

Casualty insurance   Casualty insurance revolves around legal liability for losses caused by injury to other people. Examples include robbery and workers compensation insurance.

Fidelity insurance or bonding   This protects the employer from theft caused by a dishonest employee. This type of insurance also covers embezzlement and fraudulent acts. To collect on this policy, the employer may need to prosecute the employee and win each court trial.

Omissions and errors insurance   A special policy covering administrative omissions and errors by corporate executives. This is commonly referred to as O&E insurance.

Machinery insurance (aka boiler insurance)   Covers accidental loss to machinery and equipment. It is called boiler insurance for the historic reasons from 100 years ago. This type of insurance can cover almost any mechanical or electrical device.

Business interruption insurance (BI)   A policy that covers consequential losses of earnings due to property loss. Business interruption insurance typically pays a historical average of earnings during the coverage period. This type of insurance typically covers the fixed operating cost while business operations are suspended. The cost of premiums may be high.

The number one concern with insurance is that potential loss decisions have been transferred to the insurance company. The insurance company may decide that salvage is inevitable. The cost of salvage is usually less than 15 percent of the cost of replacement. Salvage operations may take weeks and place the organization in a bind. Costs of salvage may be reimbursed for only a particular amount of services from a preauthorized vendor.

Stockpile of supplies   It is a common practice to stockpile supplies in preparation for recovery. These include common office supplies, items with long lead time, and spare parts. Stockpiling supplies is in direct conflict with just-in-time (JIT) inventory practices. A rule is to stockpile 30 days' worth of consumable supplies at the off-site or alternate storage facility.

Figure 8.8 shows the various recovery strategies compared to the amount of time it would take to resume processing.

FIGURE 8.8   Recovery options compared to time

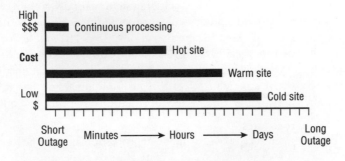

Phase 5—Emergency Response

The emergency response phase is considered part of the "foundation" information that the business continuity/disaster recovery professional needs to know early in planning for the project.

An *incident* is defined as a negative or harmful event that involves people, property, or assets. After the event occurs, regaining control over the situation is a challenge. Advance planning is necessary to ensure that personnel are properly trained. Each response activity needs to be coordinated to ensure timeliness and the safety of personnel. The number one priority in an emergency response is the safety of life. Nothing has a higher priority.

To develop emergency response procedures and document them as part of the plan, the business continuity/disaster recovery planner needs to understand how to fulfill the following objectives:

- Set activation criteria. Management needs to create a set of criteria for declaring a business continuity emergency. The criteria should clearly state a set of conditions that would dictate activation of the plan. Nobody wants to be the one who is accused of crying wolf and activating the plan too early. As a result, management will likely activate the plan later than desired—for example, upon major injury to persons, or if it appears that the business operation will be interrupted for more than four hours. Management needs to respond to the activation criteria. A rule should be instituted that if the criteria are met, the senior manager is required to declare plan activation. This removes uncertainty from the process.

- Identify potential types of emergencies and the responses necessary (for example, fire, hazardous materials leak, collapse, terrorism, medical). Each event contains unique response requirements; however, all events will include the following:

  - Reporting procedures for communicating information during the emergency. This information will be necessary after the event to justify actions taken and to provide evidence for legal challenges, insurance claims, and personnel training.

  - Pre-incident preparation, making plans for responding to the crisis situation with equipment, planning, and training.

  - Emergency actions to be taken to protect life, provide safety, minimize loss, and contain the situation.

- Identify the existence of, or develop, appropriate emergency response procedures. Most organizations have varying degrees of plans under different departments. Plans would include the following:

  - Personnel protection procedures

  - Emergency declaration process with procedures designed to contain the incident

  - Procedures to assess the situation

  - Procedures for providing emergency response and triage

  - Salvage and restoration procedures

- Establish invocation procedures to activate the alternate site. The decision to activate the alternate site will cascade into a variety of tasks necessary for recovery or relocation. The hot site vendor will accept an activation request from only a list of preauthorized individuals. The activation process will cost the organization a significant sum of money for exercising the declaration. This is how the hot site vendor ensures that the client is serious.

- Establish written procedures with decision trees to lead management and others in determining the best actions to take in response to a specific situation. A decision tree is a logical process of questions and answers, often in the format of a flowchart. As you ask the question, the answer will lead you through the decision tree until a final decision is reached. If you can't agree before the stress induced by the emergency, you can bet that decisions during the emergency will be questionable. Now is the time to work out the decision criteria—before you need it.

- Integrate disaster recovery/business continuity procedures with emergency response procedures, creating one comprehensive plan. Everyone must be executing the same objectives and agreed-upon procedures in order to combat conflicting efforts and time delay in recovery. The last thing you need is someone attempting to push their own agenda ahead of predefined priorities. Changing sequence or emphasis is a sure sign of a pending failure by interrupting the recovery sequence.

- Identify the command and control requirements for managing the emergency. Learn the Incident Command System (ICS), the international command and control system used by first responders. The expanded version is called the Unified Command System (UCS). It would be unrealistic to expect public authorities to conform to your leadership method; therefore, you need to conform to theirs. ICS outlines roles and duties regarding the following:

- Incident commander (IC), the person in charge leading on-scene activities in the field during emergency response. Response teams report to the incident commander. A field command post is established to offload logistical tasks from the IC. Incident commanders direct emergency teams and communicate to the field command post. Field command provides support services and coordination for the IC. Field command keeps the Emergency Operations Center (EOC) updated with the current status of the crisis control efforts. Figure 8.9 shows the roles and reporting structure of the Incident Command System.

- Creating the Emergency Operations Center (EOC), which serves as command headquarters for the emergency management team (EMT). This team of executives makes decisions and takes actions based on reports from the IC. The EMT uses procedures outlined in the business continuity plan to provide crisis communication with stakeholders regarding support recovery plans. The EOC handles all communications with the undamaged portions of the business still in operation. A designated public information officer (PIO) handles all media communications. Some key investors may want to see the EOC in operation, and a degree of caution is urged before you agree to allow financially interested observers in a crisis. Negative observations could rattle investor confidence.

FIGURE 8.9   Roles in the Incident Command System

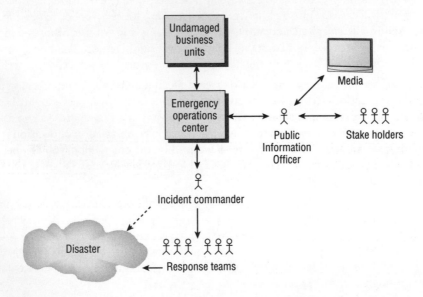

- Documenting command and decision authorities. Multiple authorities may respond to your emergency, and each will carry the full authority of their position. You can gain their trust and cooperation by demonstrating your ability to provide leadership. This can buy you time and grace to extend your business continuity efforts. You will be pushed aside if you fail to attain or maintain their confidence. This can get confusing, and the time to work out conflicts is before the crisis.

- Creating procedures for opening the EOC and providing extra security. The media and competitors will likely have great interest in your situation. Details could make an interesting news story or competitive battle. To survive the situation, you must remain in control.

- Recommend and develop command and control procedures to define roles, authority, and communications processes for managing an emergency. These will become the structure of your plan in the next phase, developing and writing a usable plan.

Phase 6—Plan Creation

Nothing goes out of date faster than a big book of plans. The written plan must be clear, intuitively organized, and easy to read. The business continuity plan is usually a multivolume set. The best practice is to use a modular design to enhance security and updating. Full sets are kept at off-site storage and at the EOC. Security and version control are paramount concerns. This set of plans contains all the organization's secrets, process blueprints, and documented priorities.

Figure 8.10 shows the content outline for creating the plan.

The plan should be organized for quick and easy location of personnel duties and specific procedures. A suggest layout includes sections for the following:

- Executive summary to provide a brief overview of the plan's purpose, scope, and assumptions.

- Command and control instructions to identify who is actually in charge.

- Life safety procedures. Protection of life is the highest priority.

- Emergency response activities, including incident containment procedures and environmental protection plans.

FIGURE 8.10   Creating the plan structure and content

LOCATION	CUSTOMER SERVICE	SALES & MARKETING	FINANCE	HUMAN RESOURCES	MANUFACTURING	INFORMATION TECHNOLOGY	SHIPPING
Corporate HQ	√	√	√	√	√	√	√
Atlanta Office	√	√			√		√
Dallas Office	√	√					
Montreal Office	√	√				√	√
Tokyo Office	√	√				√	√

- Asset protection strategy and procedures. A copy of inventory and vital materials will be useful.

- Recovery plans to support restoration and resumption efforts. What are some alternate site provisions? Did you include a copy of the risk analysis?

- Administration and logistics designed to keep appropriate records of the event, maintain the emergency budget, and provide support to the recovery effort. Logistics include transportation requirements, relocation housing, meals, and sanitation needs.

The plan is intended to provide everyone with clear instructions on where each person is to report for work and what they will be working on at various time intervals. The business will not be running business as usual. All efforts need to focus on the predetermined priorities in assigned sequence.

Alternate personnel may be necessary to accomplish all the tasks within the RTO and SDO requirements. The plans should account for the additional personnel. Procedures should contain easy-to-follow diagrams, photographs, maps, flowcharts, and step-by-step checklists. A significant number of concurrent activities will need to be coordinated.

The common practice is to divide into teams. The number of personnel is not as important as ensuring that all job duties are fulfilled. A risk management approach needs to be used. The following teams may be needed:

Emergency response team   The first responders internal to the organization. This team has the responsibility of accounting for personnel and rendering aid. The emergency response team includes fire wardens for each floor and those persons trained in administering first aid. The team may provide initial aid to victims and route injured personnel to the hospital. During a crisis, the injured will likely need to be routed to a hospital with available capacity, not necessarily the nearest hospital. The emergence response team needs to keep track of the location of injured personnel.

Emergency management team   Executives and line managers able to make tough decisions at the Emergency Operations Center. This team coordinates the managers still operating undamaged areas of the business. The EMT makes decisions about the allocation of personnel necessary to support the response and recovery effort. The leaders of each team report to the emergency management team.

Damage assessment team   Works with structural engineers to assess damage to the facility. This team is trained to provide accurate analysis and estimates of the impact. This team works with the safety team for matters of safe reentry to the facility.

Physical security team   This team addresses crowd control and security and operates 24 hours a day to protect individuals and organizational assets. This function may be provided by existing security staff and supplemental personnel. Physical security is needed at the original site and the alternate site. During a major disaster, a higher level of security is required.

IT recovery teams   May be deployed on-site at the incident and/or the alternate site depending on the situation. The IT recovery teams typically comprise several smaller teams, each with a unique specialty. Each of these functions would be operating in parallel to save time. The smaller teams include the following:

IT hardware recovery   The hardware recovery team focuses on getting the hardware up and running as rapidly as possible in accordance with the RTO and SDO. Hardware recovery may be split into two categories: server hardware and user workstations.

Software loading   As hardware is recovered, a software loading process begins. This may be from a tape backup, disk image, or program CDs.

Server applications   Application programs and data from tape are loaded onto servers as the hardware becomes available. This process may be dependent on the IT hardware recovery function. After software loading is complete, the systems administrator or database administrator verifies that the application is functioning correctly. After the application is up and running, users may log in and begin using it. Complex databases may require the dedicated attention of several technical personnel.

Network communications   This group ensures that computer and telephone communication are back online. The process may entail verifying that redundant circuits are functioning correctly, installing new connections as needed, or working with a recommendations vendor to expedite changes in order to restore service.

Data entry   The data entry personnel focuses on reloading the most recent transactions and executing manual procedures during recovery. This may be an in-house or outsourced function.

User support   This team assists users in restoring individual workstations. It provides special assistance for workarounds to help persons with greatest impact on the recovery effort. Normal user support may be suspended during the recovery effort. The help desk focuses on finding user support necessary to achieve the stated RTO and SDO.

Marketing and customer support team   It is imperative to maintain communication with customers. The customer support team provides communication and reassurance to customers. Key customers will want to know that their needs will be met by the organization. Some customers may be impacted by the same event and may require the assistance of the organization—for example, customers may need to reschedule airline tickets due to a hurricane, while the airline is evacuating its own headquarters to a safer location. The customer support team may be a combination of in-house personnel and services contracted through an external vendor. The business does not want customers to switch vendors or cancel orders. The goal is to ensure that the organization continues to receive revenue even if they are not shipping a product.

Salvage team   The salvage team is responsible for on-site cleanup and recovery of assets. This team inventories, stages, and coordinates the salvage of assets. This team also is responsible for creating documentation to be used for insurance filings, legal actions (lawsuits), and future training exercises. The team will need provisions for site security during the salvage effort.

Communications and media relations team   This team provides communication via radio, phone, fax, and TV. The team uses preapproved scripts for communication to employees, stockholders, clients, and the media. Provisions are made for both inbound and outbound communication. All outbound communication to the media is handled by a designated PIO.

Media relations involves issuing news releases, scheduling press conferences, and providing a controlled release of information to the news. News reporters will get the story one way or another, so stories should be released in a manner that demonstrates the organization's care, concern, and control of the situation. The media team needs to be aware of local and national broadcast deadlines. The plan will be needed to communicate with the appropriate personnel and each of the news agencies.

Logistics team   This team handles administrative support activities necessary to relocate personnel and equipment. The team facilitates resumption efforts by providing meals and rest locations for workers. The team also is responsible for transportation, mail rerouting, and a thousand other administrative details necessary to support the recovery effort.

Safe operations team (safety team)   The safety team supervises activities to ensure that nobody is placed in a hazardous work situation. This team can terminate any activity that is deemed to endanger personnel. The safety team ensures that workers are adequately protected from hazards, including potentially hazardous material or precarious work environments. The objective is to ensure that no additional injuries occur after the initial impact.

Finance team   This team provides budget control for recovery and accurate accounting of costs. It would be a shame to overspend on the recovery effort and later fail due to insolvency. The recovery costs may qualify for special financial aid. It is often necessary to file claims early, before recovery funding disappears. Special tracking may be implemented to identify the response and recovery costs.

Legal team   The organization's lawyers may be able to provide assistance and advice to the emergency management team. This advice could include dealing with regulators, government bureaucracy, extensions on filing deadlines, and confidential matters.

Personnel team   Human resources will be a busy place. Employees and their families will need assistance with benefits. Time and attendance tracking will be necessary for the workers. A process for rapid staff augmentation will be required.

Business unit recovery team   Each business unit will have its own recovery team to focus on restoring its operation. This team may comprise the power users in a particular business unit. The business unit plan may be a smaller or larger scale than the plan of the head office.

Property and insurance teams   The property team assists with locating or rebuilding the office. An inventory of each facility, including space requirements and furniture needs, is used to help guide the selection of suitable offices for the interim need and long-term requirements. The insurance team works to get claims processed and paid. Insurance loss consultants may be hired to help increase the dollar amount of the insurance settlement.

External agency team   This team coordinates with fire, police, FEMA, FBI, and other government agencies.

Vendor team   This team provides coordination with key vendors. The organization may need to make special requests of vendors to facilitate recovery. It will also be necessary to ensure that the vendor does not close the line of credit or delay shipment of product.

Phase 7—Training and Awareness

Training programs need to be implemented to educate staff about the plan, its limitations, and the procedures they will be expected to execute. Training can take many forms, including seminars, workshops, video presentations, and individual training sessions.

Training is designed to increase the proficiency of every individual. Some individuals will require specialized training for assertiveness, crisis resource management, and medical procedures. An individual who is unable to fill a role for any reason should be moved to another support area. If it is a senior manager, the best use may be to fulfill an advisory role. Some individuals will not be mentally capable to lead under the heavy burden of crisis command.

Phase 8—Maintain and Test

Successful execution of the business continuity plan will depend on training and thorough testing. Without testing, the plan is sure to fail. Testing should begin with small processes and gradually build into testing larger functional processes. You need to focus on tests that support the core processes first. Every test should be timed and witnessed by a qualified observer. The objective is to record lessons learned and an estimate of the actual recovery time. By tracking these metrics, you will be able to benchmark improvement or reengineer the strategy.

Desktop review (paper exercise)   The simplest test is a desktop review. All the plans and documentation are laid out across the table and reviewed for obvious errors in consistency. Participants from each major area walk through the plans for a general review of accuracy. The purpose of the desktop review is to groom the document and eliminate obvious errors. After the errors are corrected, the next step is a functional test.

Functional (modular exercise)   In the functional test, actual procedures are executed by staff members. This provides an opportunity for hands-on training. During this training process, it is possible to view the effectiveness of both the procedure and actions by personnel. Functional testing is an extremely important component of preparedness. A functional test of the calling list, for example, could be used for notification of a company party. Another example is to use the business continuity procedures to train new staff members for their regular jobs. When you think about it, there are a number of opportunities for executing a small-scale functional test. An evaluator should grade the test exercise and make any recommendations for improvement. The first functional tests will start small, and then incorporate other functional tests with a growing scope. The final objective is to ensure that the full-scale business processes are properly supported.

Preparedness simulation   In the preparedness simulation, the staff is asked to react to a particular scenario as if it were a real event. The preparedness of each team is judged as well as the overall preparedness of the organization to respond. A preparedness simulation consumes resources and supplies. The objective is to carry out each activity to ensure that the staff is capable of responding properly. The next step after preparedness simulation is to perform a full operation test.

Full operation exercise   Testing should be planned and structured to ensure that the test does not create injury to persons or damage to the organization. Tests should be announced with warning to prevent panic. A well-known provision needs to exist to cancel the test if a real emergency occurs during the drill. Each drill needs to be preplanned, staged, executed, and subjected to a review. The lessons learned are recorded.

Figure 8.11 shows the life cycle of testing and exercising the plan.

It is strongly advised that all professionals adopt the terminology of *exercising* business continuity plans, rather than testing plans. The word *test* denotes passing or failing. A failing score will usually demoralize or alienate staff members. Nobody wants to be associated with a failure. A simple solution is to build on the concept of exercising for improvement. Athletes exercise before running marathons. The organization is no different.

Phase 9—Crisis Communications

The public and stakeholders are always interested to hear how an organization has succeeded or failed miserably in their endeavors. The planner needs to design an uninterruptible communications system with access via multiple delivery methods. Controlling communications with the public and the company's stakeholders is essential to surviving a crisis.

FIGURE 8.11   Plan test and exercise life cycle

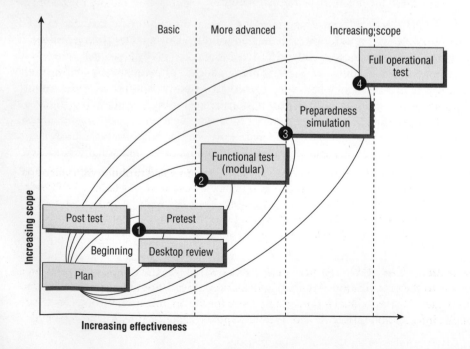

Buy-in from the highest level of the company needs to be obtained to enforce a policy that improper and unauthorized communications during a declared disaster is a terminating offense with possible legal repercussions.

Support plans need to be created for employees and their families. Be aware that trauma counseling may be required for employees, their families, and even corporate management during a crisis.

The business continuity planner must make sure all stakeholders, key customers, critical suppliers, and owners/stockholders are kept informed as appropriate during the crisis to avoid confusion or distrust. The time to build confidence is before the event occurs. During the event the focus is to communicate status information and immediate needs. The people need to feel that the situation is under control and being properly handled. Without timely communication, it is human nature to grow restless and distrustful.

Employee check-in aids   Provisions should be made for employee check-in after the declaration has been made. Individuals may attempt to check in and provide information concerning their status. Failure to account for personnel would be a serious problem. A common solution is to use 800 numbers answered by an operator in a message center. This could easily be outsourced to a telemarketing firm. The operator asks questions concerning the employee's status and whether the employee requires additional aid. Business travelers also can be accounted for through an 800 service. Another method is to implement a secure website database for check-in.

Prioritized calling list (call tree)   Outbound notification can be executed through a combination of live personnel and automated systems. Telephone numbers are sequenced according to the priority of the individual. Senior executives and recovery team leaders are of course high priority. A scripted message is delivered to each individual with a short explanation of the situation. The message should conclude with instructions explaining what the organization is requesting the individual to do.

Alternate communications   All business continuity planning exercises incorporate a worse-case scenario. The loss of communications would definitely be the worst possible scenario. It is important to plan for alternate communication methods. Each communication method needs to be properly implemented and monitored during a crisis. Alternate methods can be accomplished via private radio, wired Internet access, cellular voice/data communications, and satellite voice/data communications.

One of the authors of this Study Guide carried a satellite phone with voice and data capability. The phone was purchased several weeks before the Florida hurricanes for less than $300 on eBay. The satellite phone was the only dependable method of communication for six days. The phone's data kit made it possible to be on the Internet in less than 1 minute.

Public information officer (PIO)   As previously discussed, controls are necessary to prevent damage or loss to the organization. A public information officer should be appointed as the sole media contact. This individual is the spokesperson for the organization through the entire crisis. A public information officer should be a well-spoken individual with a professional voice for radio and a presentable appearance for television. This role may be fulfilled by the vice president of marketing or another senior executive. Occasionally, the PIO is contracted through a public-relations vendor.

The time to communicate actions is before the crisis. Then the staff will face a lesser challenge of communicating the level of success or status attained under the plan. All communications should be based in prewritten templates that have been vetted for proper effect. Don't make the company look foolish to the public.

Communicating with external agencies and public authorities is a key element to this phase as well. It is essential that accurate information is available to the proper authorities.

Phase 10—Integration with Other Plans

After all this work, the organization needs to reach out to their clients, business partners, and government agencies to compare the organization's plans and strategy with theirs. No organization is an island. Every business depends on someone else for revenue, investment, and support. The business continuity/disaster recovery plans need to be reviewed and modified to incorporate cooperation between different organizations. The strategies may be different or priorities may conflict. Depending on the scale of the issue, this may require you to rerun the entire process in order to create the next generation of planning.

Summary

Business continuity planning is an involved process of preparation. The focus of this preparation could be to rebuild in response to a disaster. Maybe the organization is more concerned about protecting a particular line of business or a highly prized customer.

Let's summarize with the points of interest that an IS auditor should look for. We have discussed the basic objectives to be fulfilled by management. It is the auditor's job to determine how well those objectives have been served. The auditor can use the following points for evaluation:

- Compare the results of the risk analysis and business impact analysis to the strategies selected. Does the BIA and risk assessment support management's strategy?

- Time delays are an absolute killer of business continuity plans. Has the client done a good job of documenting the RTO? Are the recovery time objectives well founded and realistic? Does the organization have the hardware and skills necessary to recover data in sufficient time to meet each RTO?

- Ask whether their document outlines a 0- to 100-hour timeline. This type of timeline sequences and prioritizes the recovery using RTO, RPO, and SDO. The presence of this document is a powerful statement in favor of the client. Absence of this document foretells a questionable future.

- Work backlogs exist every day in business. How does the organization intend to handle the backlog when the processing capability is significantly diminished? Manual methods are usually proposed because of the low cost; however, substantial testing would be required to prove the organization could manually keep up with the volume of work.

- An audit of the vital records inventory will tell an interesting story. Well-organized vital records foretell the future of a successful recovery.

- When was the last test's exercise? It would be valuable to review the exercise plan, results, and the schedule of future exercises. Plans must be exercised regularly to remain effective.

This concludes this chapter on disaster recovery and business continuity. The subject is far deeper and more broad than you will encounter for your CISA exam. Just remember that the next step after a control failure is a business continuity situation. According to the stories in the news, there is plenty of room for improvement.

Exam Essentials

Know the difference between business continuity and disaster recovery.   Disaster recovery is focused on rebuilding the organization. After obtaining the disaster recovery plan the organization can upgrade plans to include business continuity. Business continuity ensures that critical revenue producing processes continue.

Understand the requirements for business process resumption.   It is not necessary for all the business processes to be resumed immediately. The core business processes that generate revenue will be recovered first; supporting processes are recovered second. Noncritical, aka discretionary, processes will be recovered last if they are recovered at all.

Know the business impact analysis and the value it represents.   The business impact analysis will generate a blueprint of the current business processes. The BIA is used to define the recovery priorities and sequence timing of activities in the plan. Without the BIA, it would be impossible to generate a business continuity plan. Without the BIA, the best one could hope for would be a disaster recovery plan.

Understand the key terms describing business priorities.   The recovery time objective (RTO) defines the target time when the system will be back online. The recovery point objective (RPO) defines the amount of acceptable data loss that will occur due to the interruption. The service delivery objective (SDO) specifies the level of service at a particular time in the recovery plan. The recovery plan will specify multiple RTOs, RPOs, and SDOs during the recovery timeline.

Understand the business continuity plan development.   The business continuity plan should be developed in a modular format. The business continuity plan coordinates development. Individual procedure plans will be created by the team leaders representing the key stakeholders. The plan will require special security controls due to the sensitive nature of its contents.

Understand providing for personnel management.   In the business continuity plan and the disaster recovery plan, it is imperative that procedures exist to ensure the direction and control of personnel. Temporary personnel and contractors will be joining the recovery effort. Human resources will need to provide support for employees and employee benefits.

Know the emergency plan invocation process.   The emergency plan needs to be designed with a simple, easy to understand invocation criteria. The most effective method is based upon level of destruction, or the estimated magnitude of the outage. A senior executive is responsible for invoking the recovery process.

Know the types of alternate sites.   A recovery strategy may include redundant sites, hot sites, warm sites, and cold sites. The redundant site is always parallel to normal production and available within seconds. The hot site is preconfigured, just waiting for the backup to be restored before resuming processing, and is available within hours. The warm site will require equipment to be set up and shipped in and is available for processing within days. A cold site is no more than the building and requires everything to be shipped in and set up. The cold site will be available for processing within weeks.

Understand how to control communications and the media during the emergency.   All communications must be predefined and vetted before distribution. The public information officer (PIO) should be the only spokesperson to the media. Stakeholder communication should occur in a confidential manner. All communication must occur at regular intervals to promote trust and confidence.

Review Questions

1. Which of the following acronyms refer to the expected level of service during recovery?

   A. RTO

   B. SDO

   C. RPO

   D. ITO

2. A critical success factor is defined as which of the following?

   A. A measure or score of efficiency

   B. An asset to be planned

   C. Something that must occur perfectly every time

   D. Factor that is calculated for insurance purposes

3. Which of these is the most significant issue to consider regarding insurance coverage?

   A. Salvage may be dictated rather than replacement.

   B. Premiums may be very expensive.

   C. Coverage must include all business assets.

   D. Insurance can pay for all the costs of recovery.

4. The ultimate obstacles to business continuity are threats that may include which of the following?

   A. Natural disasters

   B. Missed targets

   C. Loss of profit

   D. All of the above

5. When planning team assignments, it is more important to remember that

   A. Nobody should hold more than one team assignment.

   B. The number of people or number of teams is not as important as making sure all the duties are performed.

   C. A single key person can be assigned to all teams for consistency.

   D. The number of duties is the same for each team.

6. What is the principal reason you might use a hot site?

   A. Expensive, but already configured for our use

   B. May not be available during a crisis

   C. Expensive, but we will have to install and configure new equipment

   D. Expensive and prevents us from using other warm or cold site alternatives

7. What does the term *MAO* stand for?

   A. Minimum acceptable outage

   B. Maximum acceptable outage

   C. Minimum available on-hand

   D. Maximum available overnight

8. In business continuity, why it is important to replicate every process?

   A. To ensure 100 percent full operational capabilities

   B. Market pressures

   C. Not important, only select processes will continue

   D. To protect the company reputation

9. Name one of the purposes of creating the business continuity plan.

   A. To maximize the number of decisions made during an incident

   B. To minimize decisions needed during a crisis

   C. To lower business insurance premiums

   D. To provide guidance for federal regulations

10. What does the acronym *EOC* represent?

   A. Emergency office complex

   B. Evacuate office center

   C. Emergency offensive controls

   D. Emergency operations center

11. News media attention should be

   A. Directed to a single designated spokesperson

   B. Used to create awareness of the crisis and warn the public

   C. Restricted to prevent any information from being released

   D. Allowed full access to interview staff

12. Continuity planners can create plans without the business impact analysis (BIA) process because

   A. Business impact analysis is not required.

   B. Management already dictated all the key processes to be used.

   C. Not possible; critical processes constantly change.

   D. Risk assessment is acceptable.

13. What should signal that the business continuity plan needs to be updated?

   A. Time and market conditions

   B. Personnel changes

   C. Significant changes in business objectives or direction

   D. All of the above

14. What is the best example of why plan testing is important?

   A. To prove the plan worked the first time

   B. To find and correct problems

   C. To show the team that is not pulling their own weight

   D. To verify that everyone shows up at the recovery site

15. What are the best examples of vital records and media?

   A. Specialized forms, financial records, how-to manuals, backup tapes

   B. Past annual reports, last year's cancelled checks, vacation forms, HR policies

   C. Preferred vendor lists, personal desk files, extra blank paper for copy machine

   D. Customer lists, office supplies, maintenance manuals, corporate seal

16. Which of the following should be considered when setting your business continuity strategy?

   A. Recovery time objectives

   B. Alternate sites available

   C. Testing time available at alternate sites

   D. All of the above

17. What is the process to activate the business continuity plan?

   A. Members of the organization call the recovery site to activate.

   B. Management designates decision criteria and appoints authorized personnel.

   C. The facility manager receives a severe threat warning.

   D. The senior manager on duty makes the decision.

18. What is the fundamental difference between disaster recovery and business continuity?

   A. Disaster recovery is focused on natural disasters; business continuity deals with man-made events.

   B. Business continuity is focused on ensuring that none of the services are interrupted; disaster recovery deals with restoring services.

   C. Disaster recovery is focused on rebuilding; business continuity deals with revenue to continue in the market.

   D. Business continuity is focused on protecting the IT investment; disaster recovery applies to the entire organization.

19. What indicators are used to identify the anticipated level of recovery and loss at a given point in time?

A. RPO and RTO

B. RTO and SDO

C. RPO and ITO

D. SDO and IRO

20. What are the five phases of business continuity planning according to ISACA? (Select the answer showing the correct phases and order.)

A. Analyze business impact, develop strategy, develop plan, plan testing, implement

B. Analyze business impact, develop plan, implement, plan testing, write the plan

C. Analyze business impact, write the plan, test strategy, develop plan, implement

D. Analyze business impact, develop strategy, develop plan, implement, plan testing

Answers to Review Questions

1. B. The service delivery objective (SDO) illustrates the expected level of service during recovery. The organization may have several SDO targets based on the different phases of recovery. RTO is the recovery time objective, and RPO is the recovery point objective. ITO is a distracter.

2. C. A critical success factor is also known as a showstopper. Critical success factors must go right every time in order for recovery to be successful. A key performance indicator (KPI) is a numerical score.

3. A. The insurance company may dictate salvage to save money. Salvage will increase the delay before recovery. Any replacement purchases by the organization may not be covered under reimbursement.

4. D. The concerns in business continuity include natural disasters, missed targets, and loss of profit. The goal of continuity is to ensure that important targets are not missed and revenue is not interrupted.

5. B. The most important point to remember when planning team assignments is that all the duties are performed, regardless of the number of people. In major incidents, the organization may need to hire hundreds of extra personnel to ensure that all the duties are performed.

6. A. The hot site is expensive but offers a better chance for recovery because it is already configured for use and ready to go.

7. B. MAO is the maximum acceptable outage that can occur before critical deadlines are missed or recovery is no longer feasible due to the amount of time lapsed. May be referred to as maximum tolerable downtime (MTD).

8. C. Only critical processes will continue. The other processes will be interrupted while the organization focuses efforts to restore critical processes. Plans will sequence recovery by using service delivery objectives (SDO), recovery point objectives (RPO), and recovery time objectives (RTO). A noncritical process might be shut down and never restarted.

9. B. The plan minimizes decisions needed during the crisis. Possible options would have been researched and decisions made in advance by management. The recovery staff is expected to follow the directions contained in the plan.

10. D. The EOC is the Emergency Operations Center, staffed by the emergency management team during a crisis.

11. A. All inquires and statements should be from the designated public information officer (PIO), the spokesperson for the organization. The PIO uses predefined scripts to deliver messages that have been vetted to ensure a positive image for the organization.

12. C. It is not possible to create business continuity plans without a current business impact analysis (BIA). The BIA will identify critical processes and their dependencies. The critical processes will change as the business changes with new products and customers.

13. D. The plan should be reviewed quarterly and updated at least annually. Updates should occur after each test, if personnel change, or upon changes in business direction. Plans are often updated for changes in key customers and products.

14. B. Plans are tested to train the staff in carrying out their work. The intention is to find problems and correct any mistakes. A secondary benefit is to demonstrate improvement in the response and recovery efforts.

15. A. Financial records and backup tapes are extremely important. How-to manuals will help aid the recovery effort.

16. D. The strategy will be selected based on information obtained during the risk assessment and business impact analysis. All options should be considered when selecting the business continuity strategy.

17. B. The purpose of planning is to establish decision criteria in advance. After the criteria are met, the plan will be activated by the appointed personnel. The alternate site invocation process allows a preauthorized manager to activate the alternate site. Invocation of the alternate site will cost money and should occur only when it is required.

18. C. Business continuity is intended to ensure that critical processes are restored in a timely manner and that revenue is not interrupted. With revenue, the organization will acquire the money necessary to survive.

19. A. The recovery point objective indicates the fallback position and duration of loss that has occurred. A valid RPO example is to recover using backup data from last night's backup tape, meaning the more recent transactions have been lost. The recovery time objective (RTO) indicates a point in time that the restored data should be available for the user to access.

20. D. Notice that business impact is always the first step. Then criteria are selected to guide the strategy selection. A detailed plan is written using the strategy. The written plan is then implemented. After implementation, the plan and staff are tested for effectiveness. The plan is revised, and then the testing and maintenance cycle begins.

Glossary

A

Access control list (ACL)   A table of user login IDs specifying each user's individual level of access to computer resources.

Accountability   Responsibility, liability. To be accountable is to be liable for the final result or to be held responsible for one's actions.

Accreditation   A formal approval by management based on perceived fitness of use. Approval may be granted for a system, site location, or function. Accreditation occurs after system certification.

Administrative audit   Verifies that appropriate policies and procedures exist, and that they have been implemented as management intended. This audit focuses on operational effectiveness and efficiency.

Administrative controls   The use of administrative policies and procedures in the implementation of preventative, detective, and corrective controls.

Advanced Encryption Standard (AES)   Symmetric-key encryption system designed by Belgian mathematicians. Also known as the Rijndael, Advanced Encryption Standard (AES) replaces the outdated DES data encryption standard used by the US government.

Agile development   A micromanagement methodology to force development within a series of short time boxes. The focus is on tactile knowledge in a person's mind, rather than the use of formal SDLC design and development documentation.

Antivirus software   A specialized software program used to detect viruses based on a database of known behavior (signature) or an attempt to append to a file.

Application   Computer software program designed for a particular purpose. Application software provides functions and stored procedures to solve a problem on behalf of the user.

Application layer   The highest layer of the OSI model, layer 7. The Application layer runs problem-solving software for the user. This layer provides the interface between the user and the computer program.

Artificial intelligence (AI)   An attempt to simulate human reasoning by using a computer program with a knowledge database and abstract procedures to measure cause-and-effect relationships.

Asset   Anything of value. May be tangible or intangible in the form of money, physical goods, products, resources, recipes, or procedures.

Assurance   A declaration or activity designed to instill confidence.

Asymmetric-key encryption   An encryption system using two different keys. Both keys are mathematically related. Asymmetric-key encryption is not time sensitive. The private key is kept secret by the sender, and the public key is freely distributed to anyone who desires to communicate with the owner. Also known as public-key cryptography.

Atomicity   A process used for database transaction integrity to ensure that the entire transaction is correctly processed or all the changes are backed out of the database.

Attestation   An affirmation by the signer that all statements are true and correct. The purpose is to certify that a declaration is genuine.

Attribute   In computer programming, an attribute is equivalent to a column in a database table. The attribute refers to a specific characteristic of a database entry.

Attribute sampling   A technique used to estimate the rate of occurrence for a particular attribute within the subject population. In compliance testing, attribute sampling answers the question, "How many?"

Audit   A systematic process of collecting evidence to test or confirm a statement or to confirm a record of transaction.

Audit charter   A formal document issued by management to designate audit responsibility, authority, and accountability. The absence of a formal audit charter document would indicate a control weakness.

Audit committee   A committee of the board of directors composed of financially literate executives. The purpose of the audit committee is to challenge the assertions of management by using internal and external auditors.

Audit objective   Specific goal(s) to be accomplished by the audit. This is the reason for the audit.

Audit risk   The possibility that material errors may exist that the auditor is unable to detect.

Audit scope   The boundaries and limitations of the individual audit. Normally particular systems or functions that will be reviewed during the audit.

Audit subject   The target to be audited. The audit subject may be a particular system, process, procedure, or department function.

Audit trail   Evidence that can be reassembled in chronological order to retrace a transaction or series of transactions.

Auditing standard   The mandatory examination procedures to be executed during an audit to ensure consistency of findings. The auditing standard specifies a minimum level of performance. Any deviations must be well documented, with justification as to why the standard was not followed.

Authentication   The process of verifying a user's identity. The user's claim will be tested against a known reference. If a match occurs, the user is authenticated and allowed to proceed. A mismatch will deny the request.

Authentication header (AH)   Used in the IPsec protocol to provide integrity, authentication, and nonrepudiation by means of encryption. The authentication header contains the security associations (SA) which are used for covert tunneling mode. The AH works with the encapsulated security protocol to hide both the internal IP address and encrypt the data payload.

Authorization   The granting of a right or authority.

Availability   A term that refers to the accessibility and functioning at the time frame required by the user.

B

Backdoor   A hidden software access mechanism that will bypass normal security controls to grant access into a program. Synonymous with trapdoor access.

Backup and recovery capability   The culmination of software, hardware, procedures, and data files that will permit timely recovery from a failure or disaster.

Balanced scorecard   A management tool that aligns individual activities to the higher-level business objectives.

Baseband   A single channel for data transmission. Coax cable is an example of a baseband technology.

Bastion host   A gateway host exposed to an external connection such as the Internet.

Batch controls   Used to ensure the accuracy and correct formatting of input data. The batch controls include sequence numbering and run-to-run totals. Batch count will count the number of all the items to ensure each transaction is processed. Batch totals can be used to verify the values within the transactions.

Benchmarking   A test to evaluate performance against a known workload or industry-accepted standard. Using the capability maturity model (CMM) is a form of benchmarking

Best evidence   Refers to evidence that specifically proves or disproves a particular point. Best evidence is both independent and objective. The worst evidence is subjective or circumstantial evidence.

Black-box testing   Tests the functionality of software by comparing the input and output, without understanding the internal process that creates the output. The internal logic is hidden from the tester.

Blackout   The complete failure of electrical power.

Biometrics   A technical process to verify a user's identity based on unique physical characteristics.

Bridge   A network device or software process that connects similar networks together. Network switching is based on a bridging process to join users into logical network segments. A standard bridge will forward all data packets to the other users in the subnet. A bridge operates at OSI layer 2.

Broadband   Multiple communication channels that are multiplexed over a single cable. DSL is an example of broadband transmitted on a different frequency and sharing the same physical wire with the voice telephone circuit.

Broadcast   A network transmission by one computer to all computers on the network. Ethernet uses broadcast technology to transmit data packets, which are seen by all the computers on the network.

Brownout   Low voltage for an extended period of time.

Brute force attack   An attempt to overpower the system or to attempt every possible combination until access is granted.

Bus topology   An early type of networking in which all the computers were connected on a single cable in a linear fashion.

Business continuity plan (BCP)   Organizational plan to continue core operations following a crisis or disaster. The objective of business continuity planning is to ensure uninterrupted revenue for business survival.

Business Impact Analysis (BIA)   The process of determining the actual steps to produce the desired product or service, as in use by the organization. The intention is to provide management with accurate information about how the business processes are performed.

Business performance indicators   Business performance can be measured by a variety of indicators, including return on investment (ROI), gross profit margin (GPM), capital gains, market share, production cost, and debt ratio.

Business process reengineering (BPR)   The process of streamlining existing operations in an effort to improve efficiency and reduce cost. Benefits may be derived by eliminating unnecessary steps as the organization has progressed through the learning curve, or by expanding capability for more work.

Business risk   The inherent potential for harm in the business or industry itself, as the organization attempts to fulfill its objectives. Business risks may be regulatory, contractual, or financial.

Bypass label processing   An attempt to circumvent mandatory access controls by bypassing the security control label. Examples include writing data to a read-only file, or accessing a file that would be off-limits because of its higher security rating.

C

Capability Maturity Model (CMM)   Developed by the Software Engineering Institute to benchmark the maturity of systems and management processes. Maturity levels range from 0 to 5. Level 5 is completely documented and optimized for continuous improvement.

Capacity monitoring   The process of continuously monitoring utilization in the environment against existing resource capacity. The objective is to ensure optimum use and expansion of services before an outage occurs.

Certificate authority (CA)   The trusted issuer of digital certificates using public- and private-key pairs. The certificate authority is responsible for verifying the authenticity of the user's identity.

Certificate revocation list (CRL)   A list maintained by the certificate authority, of certificates that are revoked or expired.

Certification   A comprehensive technical evaluation process to establish compliance to a minimum requirement.

Certification practice statement (CPS)   A detailed set of procedures specifying how the certificate authority governs its operation.

Chain of custody   Refers to the mandatory security and integrity requirements used in the evidence life cycle. The custodian of evidence must prove that the evidence has been kept secure with a high degree of integrity and has not been tampered with.

Change Control Board (CCB)   A management review to ensure awareness and management control of changes in the IT environment. A Change Control Board provides separation of duties.

Change control process (CCP)   A formal review of proposed changes using a systematic methodology.

Cipher text   An encrypted message displayed in unreadable text that appears as gibberish. The message is displayed in cipher form.

Circuit-level gateway   Refers to a proxy application firewall. No data packets are forwarded between the internal and external network, except by the proxy application. The proxy application is required to complete the data transmission circuit.

Circuit-switched   All communications are transmitted over a dedicated circuit such as a T-1 leased line telephone circuit. Circuit-switched is the opposite of packet-switched.

Clear text   A message that is completely readable to a human. The message can be clearly read.

Cold site   A physical location that can be used for disaster recovery of noncritical processes. The cold site is no more than a street address with basic utility service. The entire computing environment must be shipped in and then assembled. The cold site will be ready for production use in weeks or months.

Compensating control   An internal control that reduces the potential for loss by error or omission. Supervisory review and audit trails are compensating controls for a lack of separation of duties.

Compile   An automated process used by software developers to convert human-readable computer programs into executable machine language. Compiled computer software runs faster than interpreted program scripts. Compiled computer programs cannot be read by humans.

Compliance audit   A type of audit that determines whether internal controls are present and functioning effectively.

Compliance testing   The testing of internal controls to determine whether they are functioning correctly.

Computer assisted audit tools (CAAT)   The family of automated test software using a computerized audit procedure with specialized utilities.

Computer console   Physical access to the computer's primary input/output terminal, usually the video display and keyboard. Access to the computer console is a security risk that must be controlled.

Confidence coefficient   The quantified probability of error. The confidence coefficient of 95 percent is considered a high level of confidence in IS auditing.

Confidentiality   The protection of information held in secret for the benefit of authorized users.

Constructive Cost Model (COCOMO)   An early software project estimation technique used to forecast the time and effort required to develop a software program based on size and complexity.

Continuity of operations   Preemptive activities designed to ensure the continuous operation of core processes.

Control   The power to regulate or restrict activities. IS controls are used as a safeguard to prevent loss, error, or omission.

Control environment   A space designed to protect assets by using sufficient physical and technical controls to prevent unauthorized access or compromise. The computer room is a control environment.

Control group   Members of the operations staff responsible for collecting data from users for input to the computer system.

Control risk   The risk that errors may be introduced, or not identified and corrected in a timely manner. The risk of losing control.

Control self-assessment   A formal review executed by the user to assess the effectiveness of controls. The purpose of the control self-assessment is to induce ownership by the user and to facilitate improvement.

Corrective control   A control designed to minimize the impact of an error by repairing the condition or executing an alternative procedure. Examples of corrective controls include data restoration from tape backup, hot sites, and automated failover systems.

Cost of asset   The capital expense of an asset may be measured as total ownership cost (TOC). The cost of the asset is the cumulative total expense based on purchase price, delivery cost, implementation cost, and effective downtime.

Cracker   A malicious computer attacker who attempts to break into a system. Synonymous with the term malicious hacker.

Critical Path Methodology (CPM)   The path of execution that accomplishes the minimum objectives of the project. The critical path is the longest single path through a network diagram and the shortest time to accomplish the minimum objectives.

Critical success factor (CSF)   A process that must occur perfectly every single time in order to be successful. To fail a critical success factor would be a showstopper.

Cryptographic system   The implementation of a computer program using a cryptographic algorithm and keys to encrypt and decrypt messages.

Cryptography   The theories and methods of converting readable text into undecipherable gibberish and later reversing the process to create readable text. The purpose of cryptography is to hide information from other people.

Cyclical redundancy check (CRC)   A simple error-detection process whereby the contents are divided by a number prior to transmission. After transmission, the process is rerun to determine whether an error occurred. A value of zero indicates that the transmission was successful.

D

Data classification   A process of ranking information based on its value or requirements for secrecy.

Data custodian   The individual charged with protecting data from a loss of availability, loss of integrity, or loss of confidentiality. The data custodian implements controls appropriate to the desires of the data owner and data classification.

Data dictionary   A standardized reference listing of all the programmer's data descriptions and files used in a computer program.

Data Encryption Standard (DES)   A cryptographic symmetric-key algorithm implemented by the US government from 1972 to 1993. The DES standard was modified to use a triple process of encryption and decryption in an attempt to improve confidentiality (triple DES). DES was replaced by the Advanced Encryption Standard (AES). DES is commonly used in older devices.

Data integrity controls   Procedures to ensure the appropriateness and accuracy of information.

Data mart   A group of data selected from a data warehouse for analysis. The data selected is of particular interest to a group of people.

Data mining   The process of analyzing volumes of data to determine correlations that may be useful.

Data owner   The individual or executive responsible for the integrity of information. The duties of the owner include specifying appropriate controls, identifying authorized users, and appointing a custodian.

Database   A collection of persistence data items that are maintained in a grouping.

Database schema   The data structure and design of the database that represents a logical layout or schema.

Data-Link layer   The transmit-and-receive protocol between networked devices. Data-Link operates on OSI layer 2.

Data-oriented database (DODB)   A data collection designed around relevant information in a known format. The database and the program methods operate separately from each other.

Decision support system (DSS)   A database information system with scenario models designed to convey important facts and details to aid the decision process.

Decryption   The process of reversing encryption to convert unintelligible cipher text into human-readable clear text.

Defense-in-depth (DID)   A process of building layers of defensive controls for protective assurance. Also known as a layered defense strategy.

Demilitarized zone (DMZ)   See *screened subnet*.

Denial of service (DoS)   An attack designed to prevent the user from accessing the computer system.

Detection risk   The risk that an auditor will not be able to detect material error conditions (faults) that exist.

Detective control   A control designed to report items of concern including errors, omissions, and unauthorized access.

Dictionary attack   An attack used to discover system passwords by loading all the words found in a language dictionary into a password-cracking utility. The password-cracking utility will encrypt each word by using the same method as the operating system. Matching encrypted passwords are identified, and the originating word is displayed to the attacker as the unencrypted password.

Differential backup   A file backup method that copies every file that has been added or changed since the last full backup. A differential backup does not set the final archive bit flag.

Digital certificate   An encrypted computer file containing unique information about the identity of the individual and the issuer of the certificate. Digital certificates are used to verify the authenticity of a remote system. Digital certificates are required to enable Secure Shell (SSH) and Secure Sockets Layer (SSL).

Digital signature   An encrypted hash of an electronic file. The subject file is processed by using a hash algorithm such as MD-5 or SHA-1. The resulting hash output file is encrypted with the sender's private key. This encrypted hash file is known as a digital signature that is related to both the sender and the subject file. The signature is verified by using the sender's public key to decrypt the hash.

Disaster recovery plan (DRP)   A set of procedures for providing an emergency response following a disaster. The objective is to rebuild the organization to a state equal to that prior to the disaster. Disaster recovery does not provide for losses of market share and revenue. Business continuity is the next step above disaster recovery.

Discovery sampling   The process of searching attributes to determine the probability of occurrence. The intention is to discover whether a particular situation has occurred.

Discretionary access control (DAC)   A type of access control in which a person of authority decides to grant or revoke access for an individual. The decision may be based on need or desire.

Distributed denial of service attack (DDoS)   A particularly vicious form of denial of service attack that is launched concurrently from multiple systems.

Domain Name Service (DNS) An Internet protocol that looks up the servers IP address by using the server host name like www.CertTest.com. The Internet domain names and IP addresses are loaded into a server running the Domain Name Service.

Dry pipe A type of fire suppression system in which the pipes remain dry until seconds after the release is required. Most dry pipe systems utilize compressed gas to minimize the chance of leakage due to corrosion or freezing conditions.

Due care The level of care that a normal, prudent individual would give in the same situation.

E

Electromagnetic interference (EMI) Magnetic waves of interference generated by electricity. EMI generates interference with electrical transmissions.

Electronic Data Interchange (EDI) Used for e-commerce communication between two organizations using the Electronic Data Interchange standard. EDI mapping converts the names of data elements (data fields) between two trading organizations. Traditional EDI transmits data through a value-added network (VAN) operated by a service provider. Web-based EDI transmits data across the Internet.

Electronic vaulting A process of transmitting data to a remote backup site. This ensures that the most recent files are available in the event of a disaster. A common implementation is to transmit live data files to a remote server.

Elliptic curve Cryptography A new type of encryption using specific points on a three-dimensional random curve as the encryption key.

Emergency power off (EPO) A switch that shuts off computer room power in an emergency. The national fire protection act requires an emergency power disconnect to protect human life from electrocution. The EPO switch is located near the exit door.

Encryption The process of converting human-readable clear text into decipherable gibberish. The objective is to hide the contents of the file from other people.

Encryption algorithm A mathematical transformation procedure used to encrypt and decrypt files.

Encryption key A unique randomizer used by the encryption algorithm to ensure confidentiality.

Enterprise resource planning (ERP) An integrated database used for planning resource requirements of multiple departments.

Entity-relationship diagram (ERD) A diagram of data elements and their relationship to other data. The ERD specifies data names and data attributes to be used by the software program being developed. The ERD is created in the requirements and design phase to build a database schema.

Equal error rate (EER)   A setting used in biometrics, which provides a compromise between the false acceptance rate (FAR) and the false reject rate (FRR).

Evidence   A collection of verifiable information that is used to prove or disprove a point. The best evidence is both independent and objective.

Exception report   A report identifying data and transactions that may be incorrect and may warrant additional attention. Exception reports can be manual or automated.

Expert system   Specialized computer database software used to provide a recommendation based on the knowledge recorded from an expert. Expert systems possess between 50,000 and 100,000 descrete points of discrete information. The system uses an inference engine to identify possible conditions relating to the problem and their meaning.

Exposure   The adverse consequence that will occur if a potential threat becomes reality.

Extensible Markup Language (XML)   A universal program architecture designed to share information between different programming languages. XML uses three underlying programming specifications: Simple Object Access Protocol (SOAP) is used to define API programming interfaces; Web Services Description Language (WSDL) identifies the format to use; and Universal Description Discovery Integration protocol (UDDI) acts as an online directory of available web services.

Extranet   An Internet communication server used to exchange files between the organization and external business partners.

F

False acceptance rate (FAR), type 2 error   An error condition that allows an unwanted user to get access the system by mistake. This is less common overall due to the lower volume of attempts.

False positive   Generating an alert by mistake or error.

False rejection rate (FRR), type 1 error   Used in biometrics, False rejection means to reject access to an authorized user by mistake. This is the most common type of biometric authentication error.

Fault tolerant   A system that can continue to operate after a single failure condition has occurred. RAID systems are designed to be tolerant of individual disk failures. The success of the fault-tolerant system depends on the system being able to identify that the fault has occurred.

Feasibility study (SDLC phase 1)   An initial study to determine the benefits that will be derived from a new system, and the payback schedule for the investment required.

Financial audit   A review of financial records to determine their accuracy.

Fire control system   A fire suppression system using water or chemicals to extinguish a fire in the data processing facility.

Firewall   According to *The American Heritage Dictionary*, a fireproof wall used as a barrier to prevent the spread of fire. In information systems, the term refers to a combination of hardware and software used to restrict access between public and private networks.

Firmware   The solid-state memory chips on a circuit board containing a read-only program designed to operate the hardware.

Flowchart   A systematic diagram that details the procedures for data manipulation and data transformation in a computer program. The program flowchart is developed during SDLC design in phase 2.

Formal   Documented in writing and authorized by management.

Fourth-generation language (4GL)   An English-like programming language with integrated database support. 4GL programming tools allow the forms and database to be generated by using a drag-and-drop functionality. The 4GL does not create the data transformation procedures necessary for business functionality.

Full backup   The process of copying every file that exists onto backup media such as a tape cartridge. The full backup is used in combination with incremental or differential backup strategies to restore the most recent copy of data. The ability to restore files from a full backup is used to calculate the recovery point objective (RPO). Files that cannot be restored are lost.

Function Point Analysis (FPA)   A software estimation method used to forecast development, based on the number of system inputs, number of outputs, and complexity. FPA is used in the SDLC feasibility study to calculate resources and time required.

Function testing   A test run during software development to determine the integrity of specific program functions.

G

Gateway   A device running software to transfer data between two networking protocols. The gateway is an OSI layer 7 application. Examples include a mainframe gateway converting TCP/IP to 3270 sessions.

Generally Accepted Audit Procedures (GAAP)   A well-recognized set of agreed-on procedures for auditing financial records and information systems.

Guideline   A list of recommendations to follow in the absence of an existing standard.

H

Hacker   A malicious attacker of a computer system. A secondary meaning in computer programming is a programmer able to generate usable applications where none existed previously.

Halon   A chlorine-based gas previously used in fire suppression systems. Halon gas is now illegal due to the damaging effects of chlorine products upon the earth's ozone. Halon is still used on aircraft due to the severity of fires while in flight. Computer room halon is replaced by FM-200, NAF-S-3 and other products.

Hand geometry   Used in biometrics to verify a user's identity based on the unique three-dimensional geometry of the human user's hand.

Hashing algorithm   A mathematical process to create a message digest from a source file. The more common hashing algorithms are MD-5 and SHA-1. The purpose of a hash file message digest is to determine whether any changes have occurred to the source file.

Honey net   A fake network created to entice a hacker to attack. The purpose is for the attack to generate an alarm signaling the early warning of a hacker's presence.

Honey pot   An individual system set up to entice a hacker and generate an early warning alarm of the hacker's presence.

Host based   Software that is installed on an individual host for the purpose of monitoring activity on that specific host.

Hot site   An alternate processing facility that is fully equipped with all the necessary computer equipment and capable of commencing operation as soon as the latest data files have been loaded. Hot sites are capable of being in full operation within minutes or hours.

Hub   See *network hub*.

I

Identification   The process of determining a user's identity based on their claim of identity. The identity claimed by the user must be verified with an authentication process before access is granted.

Impact   The level of damage that will occur.

Incident handling   The systematic process of responding to an incident in order to determine its significance and impact. Proper incident handling will prevent negligent activities that could destroy meaningful evidence. A computer incident always has the potential of being a cyber crime scene.

Incremental backup   The process of backing up only the files that have changed since the last backup was run. Incremental backup uses the file archive bit flag to signal files that should be copied to the backup tape.

Independence   Independence in an audit refers to the auditor not being related to the audit subject. The desire is for the auditor to be objective and free of conflict because they are not related to the audit subject.

Information assets   Data that has a value.

Information processing facility (IPF)   The building that houses the data center.

Inherent risk   The natural or built-in risk that always exists.

Initial program load (IPL)   Computer systems are susceptible to compromise while the system is loading and before the security front control end becomes active. Computer software is vulnerable to configuration changes during the initial program loading. A system in IPL mode is also in supervisory mode.

Integrated audit   A type of audit that combines financial records review with an assessment of internal IS controls.

Internet   The shared public communications network.

Internet layer   The equivalent to OSI layer 3, the Networking layer, in the TCP/IP model.

Internet Protocol (IP)   The de facto communications protocol and addressing standard used on the Internet. IP is implemented with TCP for connection-oriented data transmission or UDP for connectionless transmission.

Interoperability   The ability for hardware and software systems from different manufacturers to communicate with each other.

Intranet   A private internal business network.

Intrusion detection system (IDS)   A technical system designed to alert personnel to activity that may indicate the presence of a hacker. An intrusion detection system is a type of network hacker alarm.

IPSec   A security-based implementation of the Internet Protocol. IPsec offers encryption during data transmission or the tunneling of encrypted packets through network routing with an ISP.

Iris scan   A type of biometric technique that uses the unique characteristics found in the iris of the human eye.

IS steering committee   A committee composed of business executives for the purpose of conveying current business priorities and objectives to IT management. The steering committee provides governance for major projects and the IT budget.

IT governance   A clearly stated process of leadership to lead and control the performance expected from the IT function. The focus of IT governance is control over the technology environment.

J

Just-in-time inventory (JIT)   A process of scheduling the minimum amount of inventory to arrive shortly before it is required in the manufacturing process. The objective is to reduce inventory on hand. The opposite of JIT is stockpiling inventory. JIT practices create a quandary with business continuity plans.

K

Key distribution   The safe process of exchanging keys to be used in a cryptographic system for encryption and decryption.

Key performance indicator (KPI)   A historical score of business process performance. Unfortunately, the score may indicate a failure has occurred before corrective action can be taken.

Knowledge base   A database of information derived from the knowledge of individuals who perform the related tasks. Knowledge-based systems are used for decision support systems.

L

Leased line   A dedicated communications line between two locations such as a T-1 circuit. Also known as a circuit-switched connection. This type of connection is charged by distance covered regardless of volume of data transmitted.

Least privilege   Granting only the minimum access necessary to perform the job function or role. Least privilege is implemented to improve confidentiality.

Local area network (LAN)   A computer network with boundaries that match the physical building.

Logic bomb   A programmed function inside of a computer software application designed to damage the system or data files on the occurrence of a particular event, date, or time. Logic bombs are extremely difficult to locate.

Logical access   Electronic access to a system without being physically present.

M

MAC address   A unique serial number burned in to the network interface card by the manufacturer. The MAC (Media Access Control) address operates in the Data-Link layer (layer 2) of the OSI model. The MAC address is used to tie the TCP/IP address to a particular computer.

Mainframe   A large-scale, traditional, multiuser, multiprocessor system designed with excellent internal controls.

Malware   A family classification of computer software designed to cause malicious damage.

Management oversight   A committee or reporting hierarchy to convey questionable situations involving management to the highest level of authority, often the board of directors.

Mandatory access control (MAC)   An access control system, based on rules that require the user to have an explicit level of access that matches the appropriate security label. The only way to increase access is by a formal promotion of the user ID to the next security level.

Manual reconciliation   The process of manually verifying that records match.

Manufacturing requirements planning (MRP)   A computer database designed to schedule the requirements of manufacturing design, purchasing, scheduling, and the manufacturing production process.

Masquerading   Pretending to possess an identity under false pretense.

Materiality   Materiality applies to evidence. It is materially significant if the evidence will have enough bearing to change the final outcome.

Message digest   A hash file of a fixed length created by a source file of any length. The purpose of the message digest is to indicate whether the source file has changed.

Message modification   The alteration of a message to change its contents.

Methodology   A systematic process of procedures to generate a desired outcome.

Metropolitan area network (MAN)   A type of limited-area network in which the boundary is equal to the city's metropolitan area.

Middleware   Utility software that operates on program interfaces and is invisible to both the user and the database server. Middleware performs an intermediary service between two programs.

Multicast   The process of transmitting data across the network to several specific stations concurrently.

Multiprocessing   Using multiple processors.

Multitasking   Running multiple tasks concurrently in a time-sharing mode by allocating a specific amount of resources.

Multithreading   To run several instances of a program concurrently for multiple users.

N

Network based   A hardware or software device that is watching the communications traffic flowing across the network to other systems.

Network File System (NFS)   A method of sharing disk systems across the network by using remote procedure calls. NFS was invented by Sun Microsystems to share hard drives with multiple users across the network.

Network hub   An OSI layer 2 device designed to relay electrical transmit and receive signals between computers.

Network layer   The OSI layer 3 function of network addressing and routing.

Network monitoring   The process of monitoring communications traffic performance and events by using packet analyzers (sniffers), Simple Network Management Protocol (SNMP), and the Remote Monitoring Protocol (RMON).

Network switch   An intelligent bridge running on OSI layer 2. The network switch converts shared traffic from all ports into filtered discrete traffic for an individual port. The purpose is to reduce network congestion by eliminating traffic that does not involve the specific station.

Neural network   A type of decision-making system that uses weights and the simulation of human synapses to make a decision.

Nondiscretionary access control   A method of access control based on job role and required tasks.

Nonrepudiation   A technical process to eliminate the opportunity for a person to claim they were not involved. Designed to protect the recipient from false denial by the sender.

Normalization   The process of removing duplicate, redundant data from a database.

O

Object   In object-oriented programming, the program object contains both data and procedural methods. Program objects are able to delegate to another program object.

Object code   The machine-executable instructions that are output from the programmer's compiling process. Object code is designed to run on the computer and is unreadable to humans.

Object-oriented data base (OODB)   A database designed for data with an unknown format and structure. OODB is very flexible and may be quite complex. OODB is good for organizing information like MP3 files with photographic images and other programs as items inside the database.

Objectivity   Impartiality, fairness. This term is used in relation to fair and unbiased information used in an audit. An auditor who acts in a manner that is fair and unbiased has objectivity.

Open Systems Interconnect (OSI)   An international reference model used to explain the functions in network communications.

Operating system (OS)   A computer software program that interfaces between hardware devices and the user's application. Operating systems provide the coordination of resources and the user interface.

Operational audit   A type of audit that reviews the internal controls used in daily operation.

Output controls   A combination of physical and administrative controls used to protect the confidentiality of system output. Examples of output controls include report distribution lists and physical security of specialized output such as payroll checks.

Outsourcing   The contractual arrangement to transfer ongoing operations to an external service provider.

P

Packet replay   An attack that replays a series of previously recorded legitimate network messages in an attempt to fool the recipient into believing that the attacker is a legitimate user.

Packet switching   A method of transmitting data through a variety of different paths en route to its destination. The user is billed by the data packets sent and not the route or distance traveled.

Packet-filtering firewall   A primitive type of network firewall that filters traffic based on source and destination addresses.

Paper test   A desktop review of printed documentation.

Parallel testing   Running two systems in parallel to verify the integrity of transactions and minimize risk during the system migration process.

Password   A short sequence of six to eight characters used in single-factor (weak) authentication. Passwords should be changed every 30 to 90 days. The password itself should not be a word printed in any language, but instead a set of alphanumeric characters that is memorable to the user.

Penetration testing   A type of test designed to gauge possible penetration through the system security mechanisms by exploiting known vulnerabilities.

Phishing   A social engineering technique designed to trick the user into divulging confidential information such as user ID, password, bank account information, and social security numbers.

Physical control   A type of control implemented by using barriers to prevent unauthorized access.

Physical layer   The lowest layer of the OSI model that deals with physical cabling and electrical signals.

Policy   A high-level statement by management specifying an objective that requires mandatory compliance for all persons of lower authority.

Postimplementation review   A review of the system after it is placed in operation to determine whether it has fulfilled its original objectives. New objectives may be identified that require the system to be modified to attain compliance with the new requirements.

Presentation layer   This layer of the OSI model deals with screen formatting and display properties. Presentation runs on OSI layer 6.

Preventative control   A type of control that seeks to stop a particular type of event from occurring. Preventative controls may be implemented by using administrative methods, technical methods, and physical methods.

Primary key   A unique entry into a database record that is required for the record to be valid. The primary key for user information might be the login ID. Without the login ID, the user's details would be invalid. Primary keys can be user ID numbers to prevent conflicts from using last names for people. Last names can change as users get married and divorced.

Private Branch Exchange (PBX)   The telephone switch that creates virtual private extensions for the users in the organization. The telephone switch is a technology resource that must be protected from hackers.

Private key   A file used as a randomizer in encryption algorithms. The private key must be kept secret from all other users in order to protect the confidentiality of encrypted files.

Procedure   A mandatory set of steps used as a cookbook recipe for a desired result. Procedures provide the day-to-day low-level execution necessary to support a standard.

Program Evaluation Review Technique (PERT)   A project management technique used to determine the critical path and to forecast the time and resources necessary to complete a project.

Project management   A management methodology used to plan and control the execution of a project to maximize its outcome based on limitations of time, resources, and scope.

Protocol   A formal specification of rules for interfaces and procedures used in communication.

Prototyping   A system development technique used to create initial versions of software functionality. The prototype is focused on proving a method or gaining early user acceptance. Prototypes seldom have any internal controls.

Proxy firewall   A type of firewall that prevents direct access to network resources. The user request is rerouted through a proxy application that will filter the request for security compliance and present the filtered requests to the desired application on behalf of the user

Public key   A variable used in the encryption algorithm that is mathematically related to the private key. The public key is freely distributed by the sender to parties interested in communicating with the sender. A sender and recipient would exchange public keys in order to encrypt the files for transmission.

Public-key infrastructure (PKI)   See *asymmetric-key encryption*.

Q

Quality assurance (QA)   A process of standards designed to ensure product integrity.

Quality control (QC)   The process of planning, testing, and reviewing to ensure that the product meets the minimum acceptable performance (level of quality).

R

Rapid Application Development (RAD)   A software development methodology that automates portions of the SDLC process. RAD does not provide the enterprise-level requirements planning necessary for a business system. RAD is designed to speed coding time in smaller software modules.

Reciprocal agreement   An agreement between two parties to help each other in the event of a disaster. Most reciprocal agreements are ineffective and unenforceable. The concept is popular because it does not bear any direct cost to either party. The reciprocal agreement ignores inherent conflicts that exist between two organizations. An exception exists regarding cooperative ownership of hot sites between financial organizations.

Recovery point objective (RPO)   Refers to a point backward in time to which the loss of data is acceptable. This means that work in progress since the last data backup will be lost.

Recovery time objective (RTO)   The estimated time to recover a system based on the organization's capabilities and maximum acceptable outage.

Redundant Array of Independent Disks (RAID)   A technical method of providing redundant disk storage space by using multiple disk drives. Previously known as Redundant Array of Inexpensive Disks.

Regression testing   The process of retesting a system after changes to ensure that the change does not create any additional undesired complications.

Regulatory controls   Controls placed on industry by the government.

Relational database structure   A type of database that splits information between multiple tables while maintaining a link between the data for related entries. A relational database keeps a relation between different data elements.

Remote access server (RAS)   A service that provides security and authentication for remote users.

Remote procedure call (RPC)   A program method in client/server computing that allows a computer to request services from another computer without having to develop specific procedures for each program.

Residual risk   The amount of risk that remains after all controls have been implemented and mitigation efforts have been completed.

Retina scan   A biometrics technique that maps the unique pattern of veins and arteries in the back of the human eyeball.

Reverse engineering   An engineering technique used to steal the secrets of a competitor for the purpose of developing your own product. Reverse engineering is usually a violation of the software user license agreement.

Right to audit   The contractual rights of an organization to audit a third-party service provider. The right to audit must be clearly defined in the contract along with the expected terms of the audit.

Ring topology   A networking topology that creates two paths between the senders and receivers. The most common implementation is an IBM token ring for a local area network. The public telephone company uses a fiber ring topology for redundant connection between central offices.

Risk   The likelihood that an unfortunate event will occur and cause a loss of assets.

Risk assessment   The process of reviewing risks, threats, and vulnerabilities to determine appropriate controls.

Risk management   The process of assessing risks in determining the organization's response. Acceptable responses could be mitigation, avoidance, acceptance, or transference.

Risk-based audit   The technique to determine the high-risk areas of an organization. Priority would be given to audit the high-risk areas first, before low-risk areas.

Role-based access control (RBAC)   A type of nondiscretionary access control based on job duties.

Router   A networking device that uses traffic routing to forward a message to its intended destination. Network routers operate on OSI layer 3.

Run-to-run totals   A process that tracks the total number of submissions to ensure that all transactions have been processed.

S

Screened host   A single computer host protected by a firewall and accessible by both internal and external users.

Screened subnet   A subnet of multiple computer hosts protected by a firewall and accessible by both internal and external users. A screened subnet is also known as a demilitarized zone (DMZ). War veterans will tell you that you can still get killed in a demilitarized zone.

Secure Shell (SSH)   An encrypted terminal session providing additional security for the user.

Secure Sockets Layer (SSL)   Session-layer security and encryption between a user and a server. SSL is a common form of security for virtual private networks (VPNs). This method uses private-key encryption with a digital certificate on the server.

Security Parameter Index (SPI)   A security specification used in the header of the IPSec protocol to identify encryption keys used in communication.

Security policy   A formal statement by management of the importance in implementing proper security controls. A second definition is a set of rules implemented to protect the organization.

Segregation of duties   The separation of transaction authorization from other normal work activities. The purpose of segregation of duties is to ensure that no changes are executed without being observed by another individual. The purpose of the control is to minimize fraud, error, and omission.

Service delivery objective (SDO)   The level of service to be available at a particular point in time. This may be full-service for all users or service for a particular core process only.

Service-level agreement (SLA)   A contractual agreement between the user and the service provider that outlines an acceptable level of support for business processing.

Session layer   Layer 5 of the OSI model, which manages service communication requests between systems.

Signature based   A technical method that relies on the database of known software behavior. Signature files indicate a particular type of attack for virus protection or intrusion detection.

Single sign-on (SSO)   A technical method that uses encryption to allow the user to simultaneously log in to all the network servers. The objective is to increase security with stronger passwords and to make the network easier for the user. Unauthorized access under single sign-on may allow the compromise of all network resources.

Single-factor authentication   A type of authentication that uses passwords alone or tokens alone to authenticate a user. There is no real assurance that the user is the intended party. Single-factor authentication is known as weak authentication regardless of the constructive strength of passwords used. The password indicates only that somebody has logged in by using that password string.

Sniffer   A packet analyzer that can decode data transmissions across the network. A sniffer can also display passwords in transit.

Social engineering   The process of gaining access by tricking a user into cooperating.

Source code   The original version of computer programs that are still in human-readable form. Programmers write program in source code. The source code is fed into a compiler that generates object code to run on the machine. Source code needs to be protected for integrity. The source code represents the original set of instructions and a tremendous amount of work.

Source routing   An old diagnostic protocol that allows the sender to specify the communications path to be used in spite of the network router settings configured by the network administrator. Source routing can circumvent firewalls and should be disabled on network devices.

Spiral model   A software development planning model that demonstrates the life cycle for multiple versions of software.

Standard   Specifies a minimum level of mandatory compliance to ensure uniform application of a policy.

Star topology   Uses a dedicated connection from the hub/switch to each node on the network. Star topology is the most flexible topology and is a higher cost due to the redundant use of cabling.

Stateful packet inspection   The technique used in third-generation firewalls to maintain a table of connectionless communications, also referred to as the state. Communication requests are monitored against the table to ensure that the request is in character with the transaction and is not a hacking attempt.

Statement on Auditing Standard (SAS)   A list of accounting standards put forth by the American Institute of Certified Public Accountants.

Stop-and-go sampling   A simple test used to prove that the likelihood of errors is low. It is used when few errors are detected and allows the auditor to stop at the earliest possible opportunity.

Storage area network   A special type of network used to connect various storage devices to servers. Storage area networks are usually attached by fiber optics.

Strategic   Describes a fundamental method or change used to direct the organization toward an objective. Strategic objectives are usually in a time frame of three to five years.

Strong authentication   See *two-factor authentication.*

Subject   The target of the audit or control mechanism.

Substantive testing   A type of test that seeks to verify content and its integrity. Substantive tests include verifying count balances and performing physical inventory counts. Technical methods include executing detailed system scans to detect the effectiveness of a particular security configuration.

Switch   See *network switch.*

Symmetric-key encryption (secret key)   An encryption algorithm that uses the same secret key shared between the sender and the receiver. Symmetric-key encryption systems are time sensitive and will operate only while both ends are using the same key. Symmetric-key systems are faster than asymmetric encryption because the key does not have to be derived through mathematical calculation.

System Development Life Cycle (SDLC)   A series of phases that represent the life cycle of software development. The phases are as follows: Feasibility Study, Requirements Definition, System Design, Development, Implementation, and Post-implementation.

T

Tactical   Describes the application of a procedure or method, hopefully in support of an organizational objective.

TCP/IP   Transmission Control Protocol running on the Internet Protocol. This has become synonymous with the Internet Protocol and accessing data across the network. Transmission Control Protocol is used for connection-oriented sessions on the Internet.

Threat   A potential danger that, if realized, will have a negative effect on assets.

Traffic analysis   A technique used by an intruder to monitor communications and determine which are the significant systems on the network. The objective is to build a map of network devices to be used for launching future attacks.

Transport layer   Layer 4 of the OSI model, responsible for the delivery of data transmissions across the network. Two common methods are the Transmission Control Protocol, which guarantees delivery, and the User Datagram Protocol, which does not provide any assurance of delivery.

Trojan horse   Malicious software that is intentionally hidden inside of a normal program. The concept is analogous with the Trojan horse story of ancient times.

Tuple   A row in a database, also known as the attribute of a particular data record.

Two-factor authentication   The processes of basing a decision regarding the user's identity on two pieces of information—usually, the user password and a unique physical characteristic of the user. Two-factor authentication is also known as strong authentication.

U

Unicast   A technical method used to transmit data to a single destination on the network.

Uninterruptible power supply (UPS)   An intelligent device that monitors commercial power and delivers supplemental battery power when necessary. The purpose of the UPS is to provide supplemental electricity for a brief period of time until the systems can be shut down. The UPS may have the capability to start an electric generator for extended runtimes during a power outage.

Unit testing   A testing technique to verify the functionality of an individual program module.

User acceptance testing (UAT)   A formal process of verifying that the system meets the user's requirements during the SDLC implementation phase.

User Datagram Protocol (UDP)   Provides for connectionless sessions with lower overhead by using Internet Protocol. UDP sessions are a best effort and will not ensure delivery to the destination.

V

Variable sampling   Used to designate a prorated dollar amount or weight of effectiveness to an entire subject population.

Virtual private network (VPN)   The method of providing secure access to the network for a remote user by means of encryption.

Virus A malicious, self-replicating computer program that spreads itself through the system as infected computer programs are executed. Viruses can destroy data or program files.

Vulnerability The weakness or path that can be exploited by a threat to damage an asset.

Vulnerability assessment The process of reviewing risks and vulnerabilities to determine the organization's current level of exposure.

W

Walk-through testing Used in disaster recovery testing to simulate the basic recovery process in order to clean any errors from the procedure.

Warm site A facility with basic utility services installed in some computer equipment but lacking all of the computer equipment necessary for recovery. A warm site needs to be built out before it can be used. It can be ready in days or weeks. A warm site offers a lower chance of success than a hot site.

Waterfall model An early software development model that cascades the completion of each phase into the next phase.

Weak authentication See *single-factor authentication*.

Wet pipe A fire suppression system with water stored in the pipes at all times. This type of is susceptible to corrosion and freezing.

White-box testing Testing that checks the integrity of transactions while allowing the programmer to view the logical paths through the software.

Wide area network (WAN) Computer networks providing users access in multiple cities.

Wired Equivalent Privacy (WEP) Symmetric-key encryption protocol originally designed to promote wireless security. Most WEP installations are totally compromised by the vendor's implementation favoring Plug and Play access over security.

Wireless Application Protocol (WAP) Loosely based on the OSI model and designed to display data on small screens with the limited resources of handheld devices.

Worm A malicious computer program that can travel independently through the network and infect systems.

X Y Z

XML See *Extensible Markup Language*.

Index

Note to the reader: Throughout this index **boldfaced** page numbers indicate primary discussions of a topic. *Italicized* page numbers indicate illustrations.

Numbers

1GL (first-generation language), 220
2GL (second-generation language), 220
3GL (third-generation language), 220
4GL (fourth-generation language), 221, 392
5GL (fifth-generation language), 221

A

accept risk response, 55
acceptable use policy, violation, 268
access control list (ACL), 382
accountability, 292, 304, 382
    in audit charter, 50
accreditation, **382**
    of computer system, **228**
Acquire Project Team process, 34
Act 302 statement, 12
Act 906 statement, 12
activation criteria, for emergency, 362–363
active attacks, **284–288**
Activity Definition process, 32
Activity Duration Estimating process, 32
Activity Resource Estimating process, 32
Activity Sequencing process, 32
Address Resolution Protocol (ARP), 162
addressed, 18
administration, representation on steering committee, 93
administrative audit, 12, 382
administrative controls, 382
administrative protection, **288–295**
    authority roles over data, **290–291**
    data retention requirements, **291**
    document access paths, **291–292**
    information security management, **288–289**
    IT security governance, **289–290**
    personnel management, **292–295**
administrator of computer, 154
Advanced Encryption Standard (AES), 321, 382
advertising, 348
advisory policy, 97
AES (Advanced Encryption Standard), 321, 382
Agile development method, 222–223, 382
AH (Authentication header), 383
AI (artificial intelligence), 221, 238, 382
air-conditioning for data processing location, 298
alarm systems, 296
alignment, 203
America Online (AOL), 342
American Institute of Certified Public Accountants (AICPA), 8
Analysis phase of evidence life cycle, 69
annual rate of occurrence, in risk management, 108
antivirus software, 382
Apple Mac OS, 149, 152
appliance, 151
Application layer (OSI), 166, *166*, 382

application processing controls, 260–261

application proxy filter, 313

applications, 382
  management plan, **98**
  security from, **304–305**

applications programmer, 129

ARP (Address Resolution Protocol), 162

artificial intelligence (AI), 221, **238**, 382

assembly language, 220

Assessment Test, xvii, xxiii–xxix

assets, 3, 382
  disposal, **265**
  insurance for protecting, **112–113**
  physical protection, **295–303**
  tagging and labeling, 265

Associate Business Continuity Professional (ABCP), xxi

associate level decision support system, 236

assurance, 382

asymmetric-key encryption, 322, 322, 323, 382

Asynchronous Transfer Mode (ATM), 182–183

atomicity, 383

attestation, 78, 383

attribute, 383

attribute sampling, 73, 383

audit, 383
  business requirements, 53
  vs. control self-assessments, **80**
  determining possibility of, **58–59**
  deviation from standards, 8, 51
  performing, **59–65**
    auditee communications, **60–61**
    data collection techniques, **61**, 63
    quality control, **60**
    reviewing existing controls, **63–65**
    staffing, **59**
  preplanning, **51–55**
  process overview, 49

  report on findings, **78–79**
  types, **11–12**

audit charter, 16, 383
  establishing and approving, **48–51**

Audit Charter (S1), 9

audit coefficient, 74

audit committee, 383
  role, **50**

audit objective, 383

Audit Reporting standard (S7), 9

audit risk, 57, 383

audit samples, 72, **72–73**

audit scope, 383

audit subject, 383

audit trail, 383

auditee
  vs. auditor, **6–12**
  communication with, **60–61**

auditing, xiii
  professional certifications, xxi
  purpose of, 6

auditing firm organizational chart, 24

auditing procedures, identifying omitted, 79

auditing standards, 8, 383

auditor
  vs. auditee, **6–12**
  as executive position, **12–20**
  internal and external, **18**
  replacement, 53
  responsibility, 6

authentication, 383
  methods, **305–310**

Authentication header (AH), 383

authority
  in audit charter, 50
  of project manager, **27–28**

authorization, 304, 384
  for changes, 132

automated working papers (WPs), 13

availability, 384

avoid risk response, 55

B

backbone, 169
backdoor, 384
backup and recovery capability, 384
backups, 13, 110, 360–361
  off-site storage, 130
  retired passwords for, 259
  safe storage, 303
  verifying, 262
badge access system, 292
balanced matrix organization type, and
  project manager authority, 28
balanced scorecard, 252–257,
  253, 384
Bank of America, 343
banking, cooperative recovery sites, 361
baseband, 384
Basel Accord Standard II (Basel II), xiii,
  8, 10
BASIC, 220
basic care, 55
bastion host, 384
batch controls, 384
batch processing mode, 261
BCP. See business continuity
  plan (BCP)
benchmarking, 384
  as BPR tool, **116–117**, *117*
best evidence, 384
best practices, vs. CISA exam, **347**
BIA (Business Impact Analysis), 120,
  121–123, *345*, **354–355**, 385
biometrics, 296, **307–310**, 384
  problems with, **310**
black-box testing, 226, 384
blackmail, 280
blackout, *53*, *297*, 384
board of directors, 21
Boehm, Barry, 208, 210
bonded evidence storage facility, 69
bonding, 361
boot strapping, 145

BPR (business process
  reengineering), 385
bridge, 168, 176, 384
British Standard 7799-1
  (BS-7799 part 1), 106–107
broadband, 384
broadcast, 385
broadcast domains, 161
brownout, *297*, 385
brute force attack, 286, 385
burglar alarm, 296
bus topology, **169**, *169*, 385
business continuity plan (BCP), 385
  planning phases, **345**, *346*
    business impact analysis, 345,
      354–355
    communication, 345
    create strategy, 345
    crisis communications,
      370–372
    emergency response, 345,
      362–365
    Initiation, 345, **348–350**
    integration with other
      organizations, 345
    integration with other plans, 372
    maintain and test, 345,
      369–370, *370*
    plan creation, 345, **365–368**
    Risk Analysis, 345, 350–353, *351*
    strategy selection, **356–362**
    training and awareness, 345, **369**
  purpose of, **341–344**
  uniting other plans with, *344*,
    344–372
Business Impact Analysis (BIA), 120,
  121–123, *345*, **354–355**, 385
business interruption insurance, 361
business needs, aligning software to,
  203–206
business performance indicators, 385
business process reengineering (BPR),
  114–126, 385
  benchmarking as tool, **116–117**, *117*

business impact analysis, **121–123**
business process controls to consider, **118–119**
goals, **115**
knowledge requirements, **119**
practical application, **119–121**
practical selection methods, **123–124**
principles, **115–116**
project risk assessment, **117–118**
reasons for, **114–115**
steps, **116**, **124–126**
business processes. *See* processes
business requirements of audit, *53*
business risk, 57, 385
business-to-business (B-to-B) transactions, 239
business-to-consumer (B-to-C) transactions, 239
business-to-employee (B-to-E) transactions, 239
business-to-government (B-to-G) transactions, 239
business unit recovery team, 368
buy vs. build decision, for software, 204
bypass label processing, 385

C

C programming language, 149, 220
CA (certificate authority), 385
CAAT (computer assisted audit tools), 386
cable
  automated tester, **187**
  for networks, **173–174**
  for star topology, 169–170
cable plants, 173
cache, 145
campus area network (CAN), 186
candidate key, 233

Capability Maturity Model (CMM), 105–106, *106*, 113, **199–200**, 385
capacity management, **266–267**
capacity monitoring, 385
cartridge tapes, 156
CASE (computer-aided software engineering), 221, 222
casualty insurance, 361
CCB (Change Control Board), 386
CCP (change control process), 386
CD-ROM, 157
CD-RW, 157
cell sampling, 73
central processing unit (CPU), 144, 146
central service unit (CSU), 181, 182
centralized database, **239**
CEO (chief executive officer), 21
certificate authority (CA), 325, 385
certificate revocation list (CRL), 325
certification, xx–xxii, 386
  of computer system, **228**
certification practice statement (CPS), 325, 386
Certified Associate in Project Management (CAPM), xxii
Certified Business Continuity Professional (CBCP), xxi
Certified Fraud Examiner (CFE), xxi
Certified Information Security Manager (CISM), xxi
Certified Information Systems Auditor (CISA), xiv
  job market for, xiii
  process to become, xv–xvi
  reasons to become, xiv–xv
  related professional certifications, xx–xxii
Certified Information Systems Auditor (CISA) exam, xiii
  preparation and taking, xvii–xx
Certified Information Systems Security Professional (CISSP), xx
Certified Internal Auditor (CIA), xxi

Certified Protection Professional (CPP), xxii
CertTest Training Center, 25
CFO (chief financial officer), 21
chain of custody, 68, 386
Champy, James, 114
change control, **133**
Change Control Board (CCB), 386
change control manager, 129
change control process (CCP), 386
change management, **206–207**, **262–266**, 263
   authorization for software change, 264
   software release, **263–264**
changeover techniques, for new software, **229**
charge-back, 96
charter, for steering committees, 91
chief executive officer (CEO), 21
chief financial officer (CFO), 21
chief information officer (CIO), 21
chief privacy officer, 289
chief security officer, 288–289
cipher lock, 295–296
cipher text, 386
circuit-level firewall, 313
circuit-level gateway, 386
circuit-switched, 386
circumstantial evidence, 65
CISA certification, xiv
   vs. best practices, **347**
clear text, 386
clients, 13
   expectations, 15
Close Project process, 31
closed architecture, 238
closed-circuit television, 295
Closing process group (PMI), 30
CMM (Capability Maturity Model), 105–106, 106, 113, **199–200**, 385
coaxial cable, **174**
COBOL, 220

COCOMO (Constructive Cost Model), 387
coding, 219
cold site, 359, 360, 386
colleague level decision support system, 236
collection phase of evidence life cycle, 68
collision, 162
command line, access to, 155
Committee of Sponsoring Organizations of the Treadway Commission (COSO), 8
commodity software, 198
communication, **15**
   with auditee, **60–61**
   in business continuity plan, 345
communications and media relations team, 367–368
Communications Planning process, 34
communications protocols. See TCP/IP
community strings, 188
compensating control, **132**, 386
competitive advantage, 98, 102, 343
compile, 386
compiling software programs, **223–224**
compliance audit, 12, 386
compliance testing, 8, 72, 73, 386
computer-aided software engineering (CASE), 221, 222
computer architecture, 145
   differences, **144–147**
   single processor vs. multiprocessor, **148–157**
      capabilities comparison, **153**
      data storage, **155–157**
      operating systems, **148–150**, 149
      port controls, **157**
      processing vs. system control, **154–155**
      selecting best computer, **151–153**

computer assisted audit tools (CAAT),
70, **74–76**, 386
computer console, 387
physical access, 293
computer operator, 130
computer room, *302*
physical access, 293
computers
life-cycle management, **112**
market share, *154*
typical roles, 150–151
Concurrent Version System
(CVS), 225
confidence coefficient, 387
confidential information, 290
printing reports, 261
confidentiality, **13–14**, 387
agreement, 111
of biometric data, 310
of records, 68
configuration management, 225
confirmed delivery, 164
conflicts, **17**
Constructive Cost Model (COCOMO),
212–214, 387
consultant, 22
consulting firm organizational
structure, roles in, **22**
context, 290
continuity of operations, 387
continuity planning, planning and
performance, **112**
continuous and intermittent simulation
(CIS) audit, 76
continuous online audit, CAAT for,
75–76
Contract Administration process, 36
Contract Closure process, 36
control, 387
control environment, 387
control group, 387
Control Objectives for Information and
related Technology (CoBIT), 119

control risk, 57, 387
control self-assessment, 387
vs. audit, **80**
controls
monitoring, **257–262**
application processing controls,
260–261
data file controls, **259–260**
maintenance controls, **261**
system access controls,
257–259
reviewing existing, for audit,
63–65
conversion, 76, **227–228**
core process, 356
corporate governance, 90
corporate organizational structure,
21–22, *23*
corrective control, 63–64, 387
for user account management
functions, 216
corrective counseling, 112
Cost Budgeting process, 33
Cost Control process, 33
Cost Estimating process, 33
cost, in project management, 26
cost of asset, 387
counseling
corrective, 112
trauma, 371
CPM (Critical Path Methodology), 387
CPU (central processing unit), 144, 146
cracker, **281**, 387
crash-restart, 286
CRC (cyclical redundancy check), 388
Create Work Breakdown Structure
process, 31
credibility, loss of, 280
credit-card number theft, 259
criminal evidence, 69
crisis communications, in business
continuity plan, **370–372**
critical function, 356

critical path, 37, 356
Critical Path Methodology (CPM), 387
critical success factor (CSF), **202–203**, 348, 387
CRL (certificate revocation list), 386
Crosby, Philip, 200
cross-network connectivity, 287
cross-over error rate (CER), 310
cryptographic system, 387
cryptography, 388
   elliptic curve, **324–325**, 390
   quantum, 325
crystal-box testing, 226
CSU (central service unit), 181, 182
cultural issues, and outsourcing, 100
custodian of data, 291
CVS (Concurrent Version System), 225
cyclical redundancy check (CRC), 388

D

DAC (discretionary access control), 389
Daemen, Joan, 321
Daisytek International, 342–343
damage assessment team, 366
data
   authority roles over, **290–291**
   collection techniques for audit, **61, 63**
   conversion, **227–228**
   purging from disposed assets, 265
data architecture, **231–236**
data bus, 145
data center, removing personnel from, 251
data classification, 388
data custodian, 388
   basic responsibilities, 20
data dictionary, 216, 388
Data Encryption Standard (DES), 321
data entry staff, 130
   in recovery process, 367

data file controls, **259–260**
data integrity, 110
data integrity controls, 388
Data-Link layer (OSI), 160–162, *161*, 388
data mart, 237, *237*, 388
data mining, 237, 388
Data-oriented database (DODB), 231, **232–234**, 388
data owner, 388
   basic responsibilities, 20
data processing locations, restricting physical access, **296**
data retention requirements, **291**
data set, 130
data storage. *See also* backups
   in computer architecture, 145
   safe storage, **302–303**
   single processor vs. multiprocessor, **155–157**
data user, basic responsibilities, 20
data warehouse, 237, *237*
database administrator (DBA), 130, 286
database schema, 216, 388
database server, 151
databases, **231–236**, 388
   centralized vs. distributed, **239**
   transaction integrity, **236**
   views, 304, *305*
DDoS (Distributed denial of service attack), 389
debugging software, **226**
Decision support system (DSS), **236–238**, 388
decision tree, 363
decoy target, 320
decryption, 389
defense-in-depth (DID), 389
defensive attitude, 15
defuzzification, 237
degaussing, 303
Delphi technique, 119

demilitarized zone (DMZ), *315*, 315, 389
Deming, W. Edwards, 200
denial of service (DoS), 286, 389
dense wave multiplexing, **174**
Dense Wave Multiplexing (DWM), 182
department directors, 22
DES (Data Encryption Standard), 321, 388
design area risks, in BPR, 117
design decisions, 7
desktop review, of business continuity plan, 369
detection risk, 57, 389
detective control, 63–64, 389
    for user account management functions, 216
Develop Preliminary Scope Statement process, 30
Develop Project Charter process, 30
Develop Project Management Plan process, 30
Develop Project Team process, 34
Development phase in SDLC, 211, **219–227**
Diagnose step in BPR, 126
dictionary attack, 389
DID (defense-in-depth), 389
diesel generator, 298
difference estimation, 74
differential backup, 361, 389
digital certificate, 389
digital envelope, *324*, 324
digital signature, *323*, **323–324**, 389
Digital Subscriber Line (DSL), 183
Direct and Manage Project Execution process, 30
direct evidence, 65–66
directional strategy, 90
disaster recovery, **340–341**
    brand name value, **341**
    financial challenges, **340–341**

Disaster Recovery and Business Continuity, certifications, xxi
Disaster Recovery Institute International, 340
disaster recovery plan (DRP), 389
discovery sampling, 73, 389
discretional process, 356
discretionary access control (DAC), 304, 389
discretionary action statements in regulations, 11
discretionary controls, 110
disk management systems, 155
disposal of assets, **265**
    information and media, **303**
distributed database, **239**
Distributed denial of service attack (DDoS), 389
DMZ (demilitarized zone), *315*, 315, 389
DNS (Domain Name Service), **177**, *178*, 390
DNS server, 150, 166
document access paths, **291–292**
document retention policy, 262
documentation
    of access points, **291–292**
    client's ability to find, 19
    of evidence, 67
    file archive for audit, 14
    preparing, **71–72**
    retaining, **14**
    reviewing existing, 61
    types, **3–4**
DODB (Data-oriented database), 231, **232–234**, 388
Domain Name Service (DNS), **177**, *178*, 390
DoS (denial of service), 389
dry chemical system, 300–301, *301*
dry pipe, *300*, 300, 390
DSL (Digital Subscriber Line), 183
dual-homed host computer, 314, *315*
dual power leads, 298

due care, *55*, 390
dumpster diving, 285
DVDs, 157
DWM (Dense Wave Multiplexing), 182
Dynamic Host Configuration Protocol,
    177–179, *179*
dynamic routing, 163

E

e-commerce, **239–240**, *240*
    types, *328*
eavesdropping, 284, 293
EDI (Electronic Data Interchange), 390
EEPROM (electronically erasable
    programmable read-only
    memory), 157
EER (equal error rate), 391
effectiveness metric, 254
efficiency, 114
efficiency metric, 254
EIA/TIA (Electronic Industries Alliance/
    Telecommunications Industry
    Association), 173
Eisner, Michael, 20
electrical power, 296–298
    conditions, *297*
electromagnetic interference (EMI), 390
electronic commerce, **239–240**, *240*
    types, *328*
Electronic Data Interchange (EDI), 390
electronic evidence, protection from
    tampering, 69
Electronic Industries Alliance/
    Telecommunications Industry
    Association (EIA/TIA), 173
electronic lock, 295
electronic vaulting, 390
electronically erasable programmable
    read-only memory (EEPROM), 157
elliptic curve cryptography,
    324–325, 390
embedded audit module (EAM), 76

embedded program audit hooks, 76
embezzlement, 76
emergency management team, 366
Emergency Operations Center
    (EOC), 364
emergency power off (EPO), 390
emergency response, in business
    continuity plan, 345, **362–365**
emergency response team, 366
emergency software fixes, 264
employee contracts, 111
employees. *See* personnel
encryption, **321–325**, 390
    digital signature, *323*, **323–324**
    elliptic curve cryptography,
        324–325
    private key, **321–322**
    public key, *322*, **322**, *323*
encryption algorithm, 390
encryption key, 390
encryption-key management, **327**
engagement letter, 16, 50, *51*
engagement manager, 22
enterprise resource planning
    (ERP), 390
entity-relationship diagram (ERD),
    215–216, *216*, 390
environmental controls, **296–301**
Envision step in BPR, 125
equal error rate (EER), 310, 391
ERD (entity-relationship diagram), 390
ERP (enterprise resource planning), 390
Ethernet networks, 162
ethical hacker, 282
ethics code of ISACA, **4–5**
ethics statements, 111
European Union, privacy laws, 102
Evaluate step in BPR, 126
event logs, 262
event monitor, online, **75–76**
evidence, 391
    focus on, *57*
    grading, **66–67**
    identifying, **65–77**

for IS audits, 70–71
life cycle, **68–70**, *70*
to prove point, 71
report on, 6
timing of, **67**
types, **65–66**
evidence rule, **18–19**, 61
evolutionary software development, 207, 208
exception report, 132, 391
excluded process, 124
Executing process group (PMI), 29
executive officer
  accountability, 50
  auditor as, **12–20**
  organizational cost of interviewing, 20
  responsibility for goals, **96–97**
executive performance review, 103
exit interview, **79**
expected error rate, 74
expert, 66
expert level decision support system, 236
expert system, 391
exposure, 391
Extensible Markup Language (XML), 391
external agency team, 368
external auditors, 18
Extranet, 391
extraordinary care, 55

F

face scan, 309, *309*
facilities plan, 100
failures, 17
Fair and Accurate Credit Transactions Act of 2003, 10, 259
fair audit, ability to perform, 6
false acceptance rate (FAR), type 2 error, 391

false positive, 391
false rejection rate (FRR), type 1 error, 391
fault tolerant, 391
feasibility study, 391
Feasibility Study phase in SDLC, 211, **212–215**
Federal Financial Institutions Examination Council, 10
Federal Information Processing Standards (FIPS), 106
Federal Information Security Management Act, xiii, 3, 10, 106
Fellow of the Business Continuity Institute (FBCI), xxii
fiber-optic cable, **174**
fidelity insurance, 361
fiduciary relationship, 6
fifth-generation programming language (5GL), 221
file server, 150
finance, representation on steering committee, 92
finance team, 368
Financial Accounting Standards Board (FASB), 8
financial audit, 12, 391
Financial Institutions Examination Council, 10
fingerprints, 307, *307*
FIPS. *See* Federal Information Processing Standards (FIPS)
fire
  detection, 299
  suppression, **299–301**
fire control system, 392
firewall, 267, 292, **312–315**, 392
  for land-based wireless connection, 184
firmware, 392
first-generation programming language, 220
fixed interval sampling, 73
flash memory, 157

floppy drives, 156
flowchart, 392
    for entity-relationship diagram, 216
focus, and strategy, *95*
"follow the sun" concept, 100
follow-up activities, **79–80**
Follow-up Activities standard (S8), 9
footprinting, 283, 284
foreign key, 233
formal, 392
fortification in place, 361
Fortran, 220
fourth-generation language (4GL), 392,
    207, 221, 392
FPA (Function Point Analysis), 392
FQDN (fully qualified domain
    name), 177
Frame relay, 183
fraud, 76, 280
full backup, 360, 392
full operation exercise, of business
    continuity plan, 370
fully meshed network, 171, *172*
fully qualified domain name
    (FQDN), 177
Function Point Analysis (FPA), *213*,
    213–214, 392
    getting fair estimate with, 213–214
function testing, 226, 392
functional organization type, and
    project manager authority, 28
functional review, of business
    continuity plan, 369
funding, 96
fuzzification, 237

G

Gantt charts, 37, *37*
gateway, 392
general manager, 21
Generally Accepted Accounting
    Principles (GAAP), 8

Generally Accepted Audit Procedures
    (GAAP), 392
generator, standby, 297–298
global economy, 101
    issues, **102**
goals
    of BPR, **115**
    executive responsibility for, **96–97**
goodwill, 341
grading, evidence, **66–67**
Gramm-Leach-Bliley Act 1999 (GLBA),
    3, 10
guards, 295
*A Guide to the Project Management
    Body of Knowledge (PMBOK)*, 25
guidelines, 4, 392
    relationship to other
        documentation, *5*

H

hacker, 154, **281**, 292, 393
    and constant connections, 183
    firewall and, 313
    maintenance login accounts and, 259
    modem access, 180
halon, 393
Hammer, Michael, 114
hand geometry, 308, 393
haphazard sampling, 73
hard changeover for software, 229
hard disk drives, 155
hard token, 306, *307*
hashing algorithm, 393
Health Insurance Portability and
    Accountability Act (HIPAA), xiii,
    3, 10
heat
    for data processing location, 298
    detection, 299
help desk, 131, **256**
heuristics, 236
high-availability servers, 328, *329*

HIPAA (Health Insurance Portability
   and Accountability Act), xiii
hiring personnel, 111
   risk in, 109
honey net, 320, 393
honey pot, 320, 393
Hopkins, Claude, 95
host based intrusion detection
   system, 319
host based software, 393
host traffic analysis, 283
hot fixes, 264
hot site, 358, 359, 393
HTTPS (secure hyper text
   protocol), 327
hub, 174, 176
human implants, RFID tags for, 184
Human Resource Planning
   process, 33
human resources
   planning and performance,
      111–112
   representation on steering
      committee, 93
humidity, 298
hybrid sourcing models, 101

I

IBM OS/MVS, 149
identification, 393
identification phase of evidence life
   cycle, 68
IDS (intrusion detection system), 394
IEEE (Institute of Electrical and
   Electronics Engineers), 173
ignorance, 283
illegal acts, detecting, **76–77**
immunization, 285
impact, 203, 393
impact metric, 254
implementation area risks, in BPR, 118
implementation metric, 254

Implementation phase in SDLC, 212,
   227–230
implementing standards, **109–110**
incident, 362
Incident Command System (ICS),
   363–364
   roles, 364
incident commander, 364
incident handling, 267, **294**, 393
   response, 110
incremental backup, 361, 394
independence, 6, 394
   of evidence, 66, 67
Independence standard (S2), 9
independence test, 6
   applying, 7
India, outsourcing to, 102
indirect evidence, 65–66
industrial espionage, 280
inference, 65
Information Assessment Methodology
   (IAM), xxi
information assets, 394
information assets protection
   administrative protection, **288–295**
      authority roles over data,
         290–291
      data retention requirements, **291**
      document access paths,
         291–292
      information security management,
         288–289
      IT security governance, **289–290**
      personnel management, **292–295**
   attack methods, **283–288**
      active attacks, **284–288**
      passive attacks, **283–284**
   encryption, **321–325**
      digital signature, *323*, 323–324
      elliptic curve cryptography,
         324–325
      private key, **321–322**
      public key, **322**, *322*, 323

intrusion detection system (IDS),
  317–321, *320*
network access protection, **311–317**
  firewall, 184, 267, 292,
    312–315, 392
  Kerberos single sign-on, 311, *312*
physical protection, **295–303**
  environmental controls, **296–301**
  safe storage, **302–303**
technical protection, **303–330**
  application software controls,
    304–305
  authentication methods, **305–310**
  control classification, **304**
threat, **278–288**
  employee betrayal, 282
  examples, 279–280
  hacker, 282
  identifying perpetrators, 281–283
  third parties, 282–283
Information Distribution process, 34
Information Evaluation Methodology
  (IEM), xxi
Information policy, **97**
information processing facility
  (IPF), **394**
information security management, 129,
  288–289
information systems audit, 12
  demands for, 2–6
  evidence for, 70–71
Information Systems Audit and Control
  Association (ISACA), xiii, 8
  Audit Standards, Guidelines, and
    Procedures, 117
  code of professional ethics, **4–5**
  IS audit standards, **9–11**, 60
Information Systems Security
  certification, xx
information systems security
  manager, 289
information systems steering
  committee, **394**

information systems, verifying
  integrity, 2
information technology
  balanced scorecard, **252–257**, *253*
  continuity planning, **112**
  operations, **250–251**
  organizational structure, 99
  performance indicators, 268
  representation on steering
    committee, 93
infrared light, 175
inherent risk, 57, **394**
initial preservation storage, 69
initial program load (IPL), 145, **394**
Initiate step in BPR, 125–126
Initiating process group (PMI), 29
Initiation phase, in business continuity
  plan, 345, **348–350**
inoculation, 285
input controls, **260**
input/output
  in computer architecture, 144
  control of physical access, 157
insourced services, 101
Institute of Electrical and Electronics
  Engineers (IEEE), 173
insurance, 361–362
  planning and performance, **112–113**
integrated audit, 12, **394**
Integrated Change Control process, 31
integrated development environment
  tools, **222**
Integrated Services Digital Network
  (ISDN), 182
integrated test facility, 76
integrity of information systems,
  verifying, 2
intellectual property, 110
internal auditors, 18
internal controls, documenting access
  points, **291–292**
International Organization for
  Standardization (ISO), 8, 158,
  200–202

international standards, **106–107**
International Telecommunication
    Standard X.25, 182
Internet, 394
Internet layer, 394
Internet Protocol (IP), 394
    address structure, 163
interoperability, 394
interrupt masking, 148
interviews, 61
    identifying potential, **19–20**
intranet, 394
intrusion detection system (IDS),
    317–321, *320*, 394
    firewall communication with, 313
IP address, 162
IP fragmentation attack, 286
IPF (information processing
    facility), 394
IPL (initial program load), 394
IPSec, 317, *318*, 327, 394
iris scan, 309, 394
Irregularities and Illegal Acts standard
    (S9), 9
irregularities, detecting, **76–77**
irrelevant evidence, 66
IS. *See* information systems ...
ISACA (Information Systems Audit and
    Control Association), xiii
ISDN (Integrated Services Digital
    Network), 182
ISO 9001 standard, 24, **201**
ISO 9126 standard, on software quality,
    201–202
ISO 15504, 200–201
IT department, separation of duties,
    131–132
IT director, 128
IT environment, familiarization
    with, 62
IT governance, 394
IT Governance Institute (ITG), 8
IT Governance standard (S10), 9

IT hardware recovery team, 367
IT operations manager, 128
IT recovery teams, 366–367
IT steering committee, **91–95**
    process, *94*

J

Jaz drives, 156
job accounting, 268
job market, for certified IS
    auditors, xiii
job rotation, 132
judgmental sampling, 73
Juran, Joseph, 200
just-in-time (JIT) inventory, 395

K

Kerberos single sign-on, **311**, *312*
kernel process for firewall, 313
key distribution, 395
Key Distribution Center (KDC), 311
key performance indicator (KPI), 113,
    348, 395
keyboard, 293
knowledge areas
    Project Communications
        Management, **34**
    Project Cost Management, 32, 33
    Project Human Resource
        Management, **33–34**
    Project Integration Management,
        30–31
    Project Procurement Management,
        35–36
    Project Quality Management, 32–33
    Project Risk Management, 34–35
    Project Scope Management, **31**
    Project Time Management, 32
knowledge base, 395

L

labor union environment, 58
  representation on steering
    committee, 93
LAN (local area network), 185, 395
laptops, and confidentiality, 14
laser, 184
last-mile service areas, 181
Latest Copy, 225
lawyers, **14**
layer 2 bridge, 168
leadership, **15–16**
leased line, 395
least privilege, 13, 257, 294, 395
legal compliance issues, **102–103**
legal department, representation on
  steering committee, 92
legal repercussions, 280
legal team, 368
liability, 68
librarian, 130. *See also*
  media librarian
licensing for software, **265**
life cycle, 198
lights-out operation, 251
local area network (LAN), 185, 395
location. *See also* sourcing locations
  selecting alternate, 352–353,
    358–360
locking security cables for laptops, 14
locks, 295
logging centralized system, 186–187
logic bomb, 285, 395
logic path monitor, 226
logical access, 395
  controls, 260
logical protection, 303
login accounts, 257–259
  maintenance, **259**
logistics team, 368
long-term plans, vs. strategy, 95
loss event, cost calculation, 107

M

MAC (mandatory access control),
  304, 396
MAC (media access control) address,
  160–161, 395
machine language, 220
machinery insurance, 361
magnetic hard disk, 155
magnetic soft disk, 156
magnetic tape, 156
mainframe, 151–152, 395
maintenance accounts, **259**, 286
maintenance controls, **261**
major software release, 264
malware, 396
man-in-the-middle attack, 287–288
MAN (metropolitan area network),
  186, 396
Manage Project Team process, 34
Manage Stakeholders process, 34
management control methods, **104–107**
management objectives, auditor
  verification, 90
management oversight, 396
  review, 220
managers, 22
mandatory access control (MAC),
  304, 396
mandatory action statements in
  regulations, 11
mandatory controls, 110
mantrap, 292
manual reconciliation, 396
manufacturing, representation on
  steering committee, 92
manufacturing requirements planning
  (MRP), 396
marginal process, 124
marketing and customer support
  team, 367
marketing, representation on steering
  committee, 92

masquerading, 396
Master Business Continuity
 Professional (MBCP), xxi
material evidence, 66, 67
materiality, 57, 396
matrix organization type, and project
 manager authority, 28
maximum acceptable outage
 (MAO), 356
maximum tolerable downtime, 356
media access control (MAC) address,
 160–161
media librarian, 130–131, 302
meshed networks, **171–172**
Message digest, 396
message modification, 287, 396
methodology, 396
metrics layer for IT scoring,
 253–256, *255*
 developing and selecting metric,
 255–256
metropolitan area network (MAN),
 186, 396
microcomputers, 152–153
 susceptibility to port access, 157
microwave, 184
middleware, 259, 396
midrange computers, 152–153
migrating data, 227–228
millions of instructions per second
 (MIPS), 153
minor software release, 264
minutes of meetings, notes as
 documentation, 19
minutiae, 307
MIPS (millions of instructions per
 second), 153
mirrored disk drives, 358
mirrored servers, 328, *329*, 358
mishandling evidence, 68
missing audit periods, 53
mission layer for IT scoring, 253
mission objectives, 21
mitigate (reduce) risk response, *55*

mobile site, *359*, 360
modems, 180, 182, 292
modular stages, 54
modules, in program coding, 219
Monitor and Control Project Work
 process, 31
monitoring, 292
 IT systems, 110
Monitoring and Controlling process
 group (PMI), 30
MRP (manufacturing requirements
 planning), 396
multicast, 163
multiplexing, dense wave, **174**
multiplexor, 181, 182
multiprocessor computers, 146–147,
 147, 396
multiprocessor vs. single processor
 capabilities comparison, **153**
 data storage, **155–157**
 operating systems, 148–150, *149*
 port controls, **157**
 processing vs. system control,
 154–155
 selecting best computer, **151–153**
multitasking, *148*, 396
multithreading, 152, 396

N

N-1 design, 172
naming convention, for ISO
 standards, 201
National Institute of Standards and
 Technology (NIST), 106
National Security Agency, 330
natural gas generator, 298
negligence, *55*
negotiable instruments, controls, 261
network access layer, 181
network access protection, **311–317**
 firewall, **312–315**
 Kerberos single sign-on, **311**, *312*

network administrator, 130
network analysis, 283
network based, 396
network based intrusion detection
    system, 319
network communications team, 367
Network File System (NFS), 396
network hub, 174, 176, 397
Network layer (OSI), 162–164, 397
network repeater, 175
network routing, 163
network services, **177–178**
network switch, 175, 397
networks
    cables, **173–174**
    design for redundancy, **328–329**, *329*
    devices, **174–177**
    diagram, 62
    expanding, **180–185**
    intrusion detection system (IDS),
        317–321, *320*, 394
    management, **186–188, 266**
    monitoring, 397
    physical design, *168*, **168–169**
    summarizing, **185**
    topologies, **169–172**
        bus topology, *169*, **169**
        meshed networks, **171–172**
        ring topology, *171*, **171**
        star topology, **169–170**, *170*
    wireless access solutions, **183–185**
neural-based learning networks, 319
neural network, 397
NFS (Network File System), 396
NIST (National Institute of Standards
    and Technology), 106
Nmap utility, 284
noise (electrical), *297*
nonaudit roles, 6
noncompetition agreement, 111
nondiscretionary access control, 397
nonrepudiation, 397
nonsampling risks, *57*

nonstatistical sampling, **73**
nonworking process, 124
normalization, 397

O

object, 397
object classes, *235, 236*
object code, 224, 397
object-oriented data base (OODB), 231,
    234–236
objectives, planning detailed for audit,
    54–55
objectivity, 397
    of evidence, 66, 67
objects, concept overview, *235*
obstruction, 76
off-site functions, 100
off-site storage, **302**
Office, 234
offshore, 100
omissions and errors insurance, 361
on-site functions, 100
online event monitor, 75–76
OODB (object-oriented data base), 231,
    234–236, 397
open architecture, 238
Open Systems Interconnect (OSI)
    model, **158 168**, 397
    Application layer, 166, *166*
    computer communications, *167*,
        167–168
    Data-Link layer, 160–162, *161*
    firewall generations in, *314*
    mnemonic for layers, *159*
    Network layer, 162–164
    Physical layer, 160, *161*
    Presentation layer, *165*,
        165, *165*
    security protocols within, *327*
    Session layer, 164–165, *165*
    Transport layer, 164, *165*

operating systems (OS), 397
single processor vs. multiprocessor, **148–150**, *149*
operation/rollout area risks, in BPR, 118
operational audit, 12, 397
operational plan, vs. strategy, *95*
operational risks, 57
operations management, **127–133**
auditor's interest in operational delivery, **133**
change control, **133**
compensating control, **132**
performance tracking, **132–133**
personnel roles and responsibilities, **128–132**
supporting IT goals, **127**
sustaining operations, **128**
ordinary care, 55
Organization for Economic Cooperation and Development (OECD), 8
organizational chart, *23*
for auditing firm, *24*
currency of, 128
organizational control strategy, **90–103**
executive performance review, **103**
IT steering committee, **91–95**
planning, **98–100**
policy, **96–97**
selecting IT strategy, **96**
sourcing locations, **100–103**
organizational objectives, IT alignment with, *91*
organizational plan, 99
OSI. *See* Open Systems Interconnect (OSI) model
output controls, **261–262**, 398
outsourced activities, 58, 101
outsourcing, 398
and cultural issues, 100
management, **114**
overwriting, 303
owner of data, 290

P

packet filter, 313
packet-filtering firewall, 398
packet replay, 287, 398
packet sniffer, 187
packet switching, 398
painting, 283
palm print, *308*, 308
PAN (personal area network), 185
paper test, 398
parallel operation for software changeover, 229
parallel testing, 398
partial mesh, *172*, *172*
partner, 22
passive attacks, **283–284**
password, 306, 398
retired, for backups, 259
for SNMP, 187
for system administrator, 259
for user login accounts, 258
patches, 264
PBX (Private Branch Exchange), 399
PEM (Privacy Enhanced Mail), 326
penetration testing, 398
Perform Quality Assurance process, 33
Perform Quality Control process, 33
performance management, planning and performance, **113**
Performance of Audit Work standard (S6), 9
Performance Reporting process, 34
performance review, **105–106**, 111
performance, throughput as measure, 153
personal area network (PAN), 185
personnel
check-in in crisis, 371
honesty of, 294
roles and responsibilities, 128
terminating, 109, 111
terminating access, **294**

personnel management, **292–295**
personnel team, 368
PERT (Program Evaluation Review
    Technique), 37, *38*, 399
PFSweb, 343
PGP (pretty good privacy), 327
phased changeover for software, 229
phishing, 284, 398
photographing evidence, 68
phreakers, 329
physical access
    and IT security, **293**
    restricting to data processing
        locations, **296**
Physical Building Security,
    certifications, xxii
physical control, 398
Physical layer (OSI), 160, *161*, 398
Physical Security Professional
    (PSP), xxii
physical security team, 366
ping command, 283
pipelining, 148
PKI (public key infrastructure),
    325–327, *326*
plain old telephone service (POTS), 182
Plan Contracting process, 36
Plan Purchases and Acquisitions
    process, 35
planning, **15–16**
    auditor's responsibilities, 16
    detailed audit objectives, **54–55**
    IT strategy, **98–100**
    and performance, **104–114**
        continuity planning, **112**
        human resources, **111–112**
        implementing standards, **109–110**
        insurance, **112–113**
        management control methods,
            104–107
        outsourcing management, **114**
        performance management, **113**
        performance review, **105–106**
        project management, 107

risk management, **107–109**
system life-cycle management, **112**
Planning process group (PMI), 29
Planning standard (S5), 9
policies, 4, 398
    relationship to other
        documentation, *5*
    types, **97**
policy, 398
Poly Version Control System
    (VCS), 225
port controls, single processor vs.
    multiprocessor, **157**
ports, 157, *158*
Post-implementation phase in SDLC,
    212, **230–231**
Postanalysis preservation storage, 69
postimplementation review, 398
POTS (plain old telephone service), 182
power transfer system, 298
PowerBuilder, 221
precision, 74
preparedness simulation, of business
    continuity plan, 369
Presentation layer (OSI), 165, *165*, 398
presentation phase of evidence life
    cycle, 70
president, 21
pretty good privacy (PGP), 327
preventative controls, 63–64, 399
    for user account management
        functions, 216
preventive control, 399
primary key, 233, 399
Prince2 model, 24
principles of BPR, **115–116**
priorities, 15, **16–17**
prioritized calling list, in crisis, 371
Privacy Enhanced Mail (PEM), 326
privacy laws, and outsourcing, 102
privacy, RFID tags and, 184
privacy viewing screens for laptops, 14
Private Branch Exchange (PBX), 399
private key, 399

private key encryption, **321–322**
private records, 289
privileged login accounts, **258–259**
problem management, **267–268**
problem operating system, 154
procedures, 4, 399
    relationship to other
        documentation, *5*
process controls, 118
process groups for PMI, 29–30
process maps, 118
processes
    Business Impact Analysis to
        understand, 121–123
    categories, 123–124
    measuring maturity, 105–106, *106*
    in project, 25–26
    relationships, *354*
    understanding before changing,
        120–121
processing controls, **260–261**
production processing, switching to
    new system, 229
Professional Competence standard
    (S4), 9
Professional Ethics and Standards of
    Conduct standard (S3), 9
Program Evaluation Review Technique
    (PERT), 37, *38*, 399
program scripts, 223
programming languages, generations,
    220–221, *221*
Project+ certification, xxii
Project Communications
    Management, 34
Project Cost Management, 32, 33
Project Human Resource Management,
    33–34
Project Integration Management, 30–31
project life cycle, 29
project management, **23–37**, 399
    certifications, xxii
    diagramming techniques, 37
    importance of, 36

planning and performance, 107
process framework, **28–36**
representation on steering
    committee, 93
for software, **207–210**
what it is, **26–27**
Project Management Institute (PMI).
    See also knowledge areas
    *A Guide to the Project Management
        Body of Knowledge
        (PMBOK)*, 25
    model, 24
Project Management Professional
    (PMP), xxii
project manager
    authority, **27–28**
    requirements, 27
Project Procurement Management,
    35–36
Project Quality Management, **32–33**
Project Risk Management, **34–35**
Project Scope Management, **31**
Project Time Management, **32**
project, what it is, **25–26**
projectized organization type, and
    project manager authority, 28
promotion policy, 111
property and insurance team, 368
property insurance, 361
proprietary architecture, 238
proprietary information, loss of, 280
protocol, 399
protocol analyzer, **187**
prototyping, **223**, 399
proxy firewall, 399
Public Company Accounting Oversight
    Board (PCAOB), 8
public information, 289
public information officer, 371–372
public key, 399
public key encryption, **322,**
    322, 323
public-key infrastructure (PKI),
    325–327, *326*

Q

Qualitative Risk Analysis process, 35
quality assurance (QA), 399
quality control (QC), 23, 399
    for audit, **60**
    for program coding, 219
    for software, **199–202**
quality control division, representation
    on steering committee, 92
Quality Planning process, 33
Quantitative Risk Analysis process, 35
quantum cryptography, 325

R

racketeering, 77
Radio Frequency Identification (RFID),
    184–185
RAID (redundant array of independent
    disks), 155–156, *329*, 329, 400
RAM (random access memory),
    144, 145
random sampling, 73
Rapid Application Development
    (RAD), **223**, 400
RAS (remote access server), 400
RBAC (rote-based access control), 401
RCS (Revision Control System), 225
read-only memory (ROM), 156
rebuilding after disaster, **341**
reciprocal agreement, 361, 400
recommended action statements in
    regulations, 11
reconciliation, 132
Reconstruct step in BPR, 126
records retention, 14
recovery point objective (RPO),
    356, 400
recovery time objective (RTO),
    356, 400
Red Button, 282

Redesign step in BPR, 126
redundancy, 267
    in hardware, 358
    network design for,
        328–329, *329*
redundant array of independent
    disks (RAID), 155–156, *329*,
    329, 400
reengineering, **218**
    return on investment from, 120
reference by context decision support
    system, 236
referential integrity, 233
registration authority (RA), 325
regression testing, 226–227, 400
regulatory controls, 400
regulatory policy, 97
regulatory violations, 77
relational database structure,
    233, 400
reliability factor, 74
remediation, 7
remote access accounts, 286–287
remote access server (RAS), 400
remote dial-up access, **316**
remote procedure call (RPC), 400
repeater, 176
replacement auditor, 53
report, on audit findings, **78–79**
request for information
    (RFI), **205**
request for proposal (RFP), **205**
Request Seller Responses
    process, 36
Required action statements in
    regulations, 11
Requirements Definition phase in
    SDLC, 211, **215–218**
research and development,
    representation on steering
    committee, 93
residual risk, 57, 400
respect, 15

responsibility
   in audit charter, 50
   of auditor, 6
retina scan, 308, *308*, 400
return on investment, from
      reengineering, 120
revenue, business continuity and, 341
Reverse ARP, 162
reverse engineering, **218**, 400
review meetings, for software, 230
reviewing existing controls, for audit,
      63–65
Revision Control System (RCS), 225
revolutionary software
      development, 207
RFID (Radio Frequency Identification),
      184–185
right to audit, 401
   in outsourcing contract, 114
Right to Work laws, 111
Rijmen, Vincent, 321
ring topology, **171**, *171*, 401
risk, 401
risk analysis
   in business continuity plan, 345,
      350–353, *351*
   process flowchart, *56*
risk assessment, 57, 118–119, 292, 401
   for BPR project, **117–118**
   worksheet, *352*
risk-based audit, 401
Risk Identification process, 35
risk management, 401
   planning and performance, **107–109**
Risk Management Planning process, 35
risk management strategy, **55**
Risk Monitoring and Control
      process, 35
Risk Response Planning process, 35
Ritchie, Dennis, 149, 220
RMON2 (Remote Monitoring Protocol
      version 2), **188**
role-based access controls, 304

roles
   in consulting firm organizational
      structure, **22**
   in corporate organizational
      structure, **21–22**
ROM (read-only memory), 156
root user, 154
rote-based access control
      (RBAC), 401
router, 168, 175, 176, 182, 401
router of last resort, 164
RPC (remote procedure call), 400
RPO (recovery point objective), 400
RTO (recovery time objective), 400
run-to-run totals, 401
Russia, outsourcing to, 102

S

S/MIME (Secure Multipurpose Internet
      Mail Extension), **326**
sabotage, 280
safe operations team, 368
safe storage, **302–303**
salami technique, 287
sales function, representation on
      steering committee, 92
salvage, 362
salvage team, 367
sampling risk, 57, 72
SAN (storage area network),
      185, 403
SANS Institute, 267
Sarbanes-Oxley Act of 2002 (SOX), xiii,
      2, 10, 12, 50
SAS (Statement on Auditing
      Standard), 403
SAS-70 report, 58, 114
satellite phone, 371
satellite radio, 183
SCCS (Source Code Control
      System), 225

scenario approach, for software
    decisions, **203**
Schedule Control process, 32
Schedule Development process, 32
scope
    of audit, restrictions on, **53**
    in project management, 26
Scope Control process, 31
Scope Definition process, 31
Scope Planning process, 31
Scope Verification process, 31
screened host, 314, *314*, 401
screened subnet, 315, *315*, 401
script interpreter, 223
script kiddies, **281–282**
SDLC. *See* System Development Life
    Cycle (SDLC)
SDO (service delivery objective), 402
second-generation programming
    language, 220
Secure Electronic Transaction protocol
    (SET), 327–328
secure hyper text protocol
    (HTTPS), 327
Secure Multipurpose Internet Mail
    Extension (S/MIME), **326**
Secure Shell (SSH), 317, 401
Secure Socket Layer (SSL), 317,
    327, 401
security. *See also* information assets
    protection
    awareness training, 292–293
    flash devices and, 157
    IT governance, **289–290**
    port controls, **157**
Security+ certification, xxi
security labels, 305
security policy, 401
segregation of duties, 402
Select Sellers process, 36
self-insurance, 113
semantic networks, 237
semi-quantitative measurement, 204

senior consultant, 22
sensitive function, 357
sensitive information, 289
server administrator, 130
server applications team, 367
service delivery objective (SDO), 357
service-level agreement (SLA), 113,
    256–257, 402
service ports, physical access, 293
Session layer (OSI), 164–165, *165*, 402
SET (Secure Electronic Transaction
    protocol), 327–328
severance plans, 109
shall, vs. should, 11
shared cost, 96
shopping cart databases, and
    credit-card number theft, 259
should, vs. shall, 11
signature based, 402
signature-based IDS, 319
signature detection, 285
signature dynamics, 309
Simple Network Management Protocol
    (SNMP), **187–188**
single-factor authentication, 402
single loss expectancy (SLE), 107–108
single processor vs. multiprocessor
    capabilities comparison, **153**
    data storage, **155–157**
    operating systems, **148–150**, *149*
    port controls, **157**
    processing vs. system control,
        154–155
    selecting best computer, **151–153**
single sign-on (SSO), 402
Six Sigma model, 24
skills matrix, 59
SLA (service-level agreement), 402
SLOC (Source Lines Of Code), 213
smart card, 306, *306*
smoke detection, 299
SNA gateway, 166
snapshot audit, 76

Sniffer, 402
SNMP (Simple Network Management Protocol), **187–188**
social engineering, 284, 285, 402
software
    changeover techniques for, **229**
    licensing, **265**
    portability, 149
    project management for, **207–210**
    release, **263–264**
    user training on, **228–229**
software baseline, **218**
software development, 198
    alignment to business needs, **203–206**
    compiling programs, **223–224**
    debugging, **226**
    governance, **198–199**
    program architecture, **238**
    quality control, **199–202**
    representation on steering committee, 92
    testing, **226–227**
software loading team, 367
software management plan, 98
source code, 224, 402
Source Code Control System (SCCS), 225
Source Lines Of Code (SLOC), 213
    getting fair estimate with, 213
source routing, 287, 402
sourcing locations, **100–103**
spaghetti bowl programming, 219
spamming, 288
SPI (Security Parameter Index), 401
Spice (ISO 15504) standard, 200–201
spike, *297*
spiral model of software life cycle, *210, 210*, 402
sponsor payment, 96
spoofing, 288
SSH (Secure Shell), 317, 401
SSL (Secure Socket Layer), 327, 401

SSO (single sign-on), 402
staff workers, 22. *See also* personnel
staffing, for audit, **59**
stakeholders, 26
standard terms of reference, **17**
standards, 4, 7, 402
    implementing, **109–110**
    international, **106–107**
    IS audit, **9–11**
    for program coding, 219
    relationship to other documentation, *5*
    understanding, **8**
standby generator, 297–298
standing data controls, 259
star topology, **169–170**, *170*, 402
stateful inspection, 313, 403
Statement on Auditing Standards (SAS), 8, 403
    SAS-84, 53
static electricity, 298
static routing, 163
statistical detection of network intrusion, 319
statistical sampling, **73**
steering committees
    charter, 91
    organizational structure, *92*
    process, *94*
    on software decisions, **202–206**
        critical success factor (CSF), *202–203*
        scenario approach, **203**
stock market, 3
stockpile of supplies, 362
stop-and-go sampling, 73, 403
storage area network (SAN), 185, 403
strategic, 403
strategic systems, 199
strategy
    in business continuity plan, 345
    selection, **356–362**

and focus, 95
vs. long-term and operational
    plans, 95
in organizational control, 90–103
    executive performance
        review, 103
    IT steering committee, 91–95
    planning, 98–100
    policy, 96–97
    selecting IT strategy, 96
    sourcing locations, 100–103
strategy layer for IT scoring, 253
stratified mean estimation, 74
strong matrix organization type, and
    project manager authority, 28
subject, 403
subnetworks, 162, 175
    for remote connections, 181
substantive testing, 8, 72, 74, 403
supercomputers, 151
supervisor review, 132
Supervisory Controls and Data
    Acquisition, 10
supervisory operating state, 154
supervisory user, 154
supplies, stockpile, 362
supporting process, 356
suppression, 76
surge, 297
surveys, 61, 63
switch, 176
symmetric-key encryption, 321,
    321, 403
syslog, **186–187**, 266
system access controls, **257–259**
system administrator
    login accounts, 258
    password for, 259
system control audit review file
    with embedded audit modules
    (SCARF/EAM), 76
system control parameters, 260
System Design phase in SDLC, 211,
    218–219

System Development Life Cycle
    (SDLC), 198, 208, **210–231**,
    211, 403
    Development phase, 211,
        219–227
    Feasibility Study phase, 211,
        212–215
    Implementation phase, 212,
        227–230
    Post-implementation phase, 212,
        230–231
    Requirements Definition phase, 211,
        215–218
    System Design phase, 211, **218–219**
system life-cycle management, planning
    and performance, **112**
system monitoring, **266**
systems analyst, 22, 130
systems architect, 129
systems programmer, 129
Systems Security Certified Practitioner
    (SSCP), xx

T

tactical, 403
tactical management, *103*,
    103–104, **127**
tactical plan, 94
tape management systems, 155
TCP/IP, 158, 403
    mnemonic for layers, 159, *160*
teams, for business continuity plan,
    366–367
technical protection
    application software controls,
        304–305
    authentication methods, **305–310**
    control classification, **304**
    encryption methods, **321–325**
    intrusion detection, **317–321**, *320*
    network access protection, **311–317**

network security protocols, 327–328
    self assessment, **330**
technological risks, *57*
technology plan, *99*
telephone
    high-speed circuits, 181
    security, **329–330**
Telewall, 286
terminating personnel, 111
    risk in, 109
testing, **73–74**
    in business continuity plan, 345, **369–370**, *370*
theft, 76, 279
third-generation programming language, 220
Thomas, Dave, 343
Thompson, Ken, 149, 220
threat, 3, 403
throughput, 151, 153
time, in project management, 26
time-sharing, 146
timing of evidence, **67**
tolerable error rate, 74
Top Copy, 225
top-down structured programming, 219
topologies for networks, **169–172**
    bus topology, *169*, **169**
    meshed networks, **171–172**
    ring topology, *171*, **171**
    star topology, **169–170**, *170*
Total Quality Management (TQM) model, 24
traditional systems, 199
traffic analysis, 283, 404
training, 265, 268
    in business continuity plan, 345, **369**
    on software, **228–229**
transaction integrity, in databases, **236**

Transaction Layer Security (TLS), 317
transaction log, 132
transaction processing controls, 260
transfer risk response, *55*
transfer switch, 298
Transmission Control Protocol/Internet Protocol. *See* TCP/IP
Transport layer (OSI), 164, *165*, 404
Transport layer security (TLS), 327
trapdoor, 285
trauma counseling, 371
Tripwire, 76
Trojan horse, 404
tumbler lock, 295
tuple, 233, *234*, 404
twisted-pair (UTP) cable, unshielded, 173
two-factor authentication, 404
Type 1 events, 79
Type 1 information, 306
Type 2 events, 79
Type 2 information, 306
Type 3 information, 307

U

UAT (user acceptance testing), 404
UDP (User Datagram Protocol), 404
unauthorized disclosure, 280
unconfirmed delivery, 164
undelete utilities, 303
Unicast, 163, 404
Unified Command System (UCS), 364
uninterruptible power supply (UPS), 297, 404
union employment, 111
unit testing, 404
Unix operating system, 149, 152
unmanned facility, 251

unshielded twisted-pair (UTP) cable, 173
unstratified mean estimation, 74
UPS (uninterruptible power supply), 297, 404
U.S. Federal Information Security Management Act (FISMA), 8
U.S. National Institute of Standards and Technology (NIST), 8
USB token, 306
Use of Risk Analysis in Audit Planning standard (S11), 9
user acceptance testing (UAT), 404
User Datagram Protocol (UDP), 404
user support team, 367
users
  of data, 290–291
  identification, 305
  involvement in business continuity planning, 355
  login accounts, **258**
  restricted interface, 305
  training, 265, 268
    on software, 228–229

V

validation testing of software, 226
variable sampling, 74, 404
vendor proposals, **205–206**
vendor team, 368
ventilation for data processing location, 298
version control, 220, **224–225**
vetting, 16
vice president, 22
violation, reporting, **294–295**
virtual private network (VPN), **316–317**, *318*, 404
virus, 285, 405
vital function, 357

VLAN (virtual local area network), 175–176, 185
voice pattern recognition, 309, *310*
vulnerability, 3, 405
vulnerability assessment, 405

W

walk-through testing, 62, 405
WAN (wide area network), 186, 405
WAP (Wireless Application Protocol), 405
war chalking, 287
war dialing, 286
"war room," 14
warm site, 358, 360, 405
water detection, **301**
waterfall model for software development life cycle, **208–209**, *209*, 405
weak matrix organization type, and project manager authority, 28
website server, 150
Wendy's, 343–344
WEP (Wired Equivalent Privacy), 405
wet pipe, 299, *300*, 301, 405
"what if" questions, for software decisions, **203**
white-box testing, 226, 405
white hat, 282
Wi-Fi radio, 175, 176, 183
wide area network (WAN), 186, 405
willful omission, 76
Windows (Microsoft), 149, 152, 234
Wired Equivalent Privacy (WEP), 405
wireless access solutions, **183–185**
  security issues, 286, 317, *319*

Wireless Application Protocol (WAP), 405
wireless RFID systems, **184–185**
wiring closet, 169
work location for auditing, security, 14
work schedule, 112
working process, 123–124
workshops, 61
workstation, 150
worm, 285, 405
WPs (automated working papers), 13

X

X.25, 182
XML (Extensible Markup Language), 391

Z

zero hour, in business continuity planning, 357
Zip drives, 156

=> all audit files / Material

=> sample email / follow up emails

=> Request list

Wiley Publishing, Inc.
End-User License Agreement

READ THIS. You should carefully read these terms and conditions before opening the software packet(s) included with this book "Book". This is a license agreement "Agreement" between you and Wiley Publishing, Inc. "WPI". By opening the accompanying software packet(s), you acknowledge that you have read and accept the following terms and conditions. If you do not agree and do not want to be bound by such terms and conditions, promptly return the Book and the unopened software packet(s) to the place you obtained them for a full refund.

1.License Grant. WPI grants to you (either an individual or entity) a nonexclusive license to use one copy of the enclosed software program(s) (collectively, the "Software," solely for your own personal or business purposes on a single computer (whether a standard computer or a workstation component of a multi-user network). The Software is in use on a computer when it is loaded into temporary memory (RAM) or installed into permanent memory (hard disk, CD-ROM, or other storage device). WPI reserves all rights not expressly granted herein.

2.Ownership. WPI is the owner of all right, title, and interest, including copyright, in and to the compilation of the Software recorded on the physical packet included with this Book "Software Media". Copyright to the individual programs recorded on the Software Media is owned by the author or other authorized copyright owner of each program. Ownership of the Software and all proprietary rights relating thereto remain with WPI and its licensers.

3.Restrictions On Use and Transfer.

(a)You may only (i) make one copy of the Software for backup or archival purposes, or (ii) transfer the Software to a single hard disk, provided that you keep the original for backup or archival purposes. You may not (i) rent or lease the Software, (ii) copy or reproduce the Software through a LAN or other network system or through any computer subscriber system or bulletin-board system, or (iii) modify, adapt, or create derivative works based on the Software.

(b)You may not reverse engineer, decompile, or disassemble the Software. You may transfer the Software and user documentation on a permanent basis, provided that the transferee agrees to accept the terms and conditions of this Agreement and you retain no copies. If the Software is an update or has been updated, any transfer must include the most recent update and all prior versions.

4.Restrictions on Use of Individual Programs. You must follow the individual requirements and restrictions detailed for each individual program in the About the CD-ROM appendix of this Book or on the Software Media. These limitations are also contained in the individual license agreements recorded on the Software Media. These limitations may include a requirement that after using the program for a specified period of time, the user must pay a registration fee or discontinue use. By opening the Software packet(s), you will be agreeing to abide by the licenses and restrictions for these individual programs that are detailed in the About the CD-ROM appendix and/or on the Software Media. None of the material on this Software Media or listed in this Book may ever be redistributed, in original or modified form, for commercial purposes.

5.Limited Warranty.

(a)WPI warrants that the Software and Software Media are free from defects in materials and workmanship under normal use for a period of sixty (60) days from the date of purchase of this Book. If WPI receives notification within the warranty period of defects in materials or workmanship, WPI will replace the defective Software Media.

(b)WPI AND THE AUTHOR(S) OF THE BOOK DISCLAIM ALL OTHER WARRANTIES, EXPRESS OR IMPLIED, INCLUDING WITHOUT LIMITATION IMPLIED WARRANTIES OF MERCHANTABILITY AND FITNESS FOR A PARTICULAR PURPOSE, WITH RESPECT TO THE SOFTWARE, THE PROGRAMS, THE SOURCE CODE CONTAINED THEREIN, AND/OR THE TECHNIQUES DESCRIBED IN THIS BOOK. WPI DOES NOT WARRANT THAT THE FUNCTIONS CONTAINED IN THE SOFTWARE WILL MEET YOUR REQUIREMENTS OR THAT THE OPERATION OF THE SOFTWARE WILL BE ERROR FREE.

(c)This limited warranty gives you specific legal rights, and you may have other rights that vary from jurisdiction to jurisdiction.

6.Remedies.

(a)WPI's entire liability and your exclusive remedy for defects in materials and workmanship shall be limited to replacement of the Software Media, which may be returned to WPI with a copy of your receipt at the following address: Software Media Fulfillment Department, Attn.: CISA: *Certified Information System Auditor Study Guide*, Wiley Publishing, Inc., 10475 Crosspoint Blvd., Indianapolis, IN 46256, or call 1-800-762-2974. Please allow four to six weeks for delivery. This Limited Warranty is void if failure of the Software Media has resulted from accident, abuse, or misapplication. Any replacement Software Media will be warranted for the remainder of the original warranty period or thirty (30) days, whichever is longer.

(b)In no event shall WPI or the author be liable for any damages whatsoever (including without limitation damages for loss of business profits, business interruption, loss of business information, or any other pecuniary loss) arising from the use of or inability to use the Book or the Software, even if WPI has been advised of the possibility of such damages.

(c)Because some jurisdictions do not allow the exclusion or limitation of liability for consequential or incidental damages, the above limitation or exclusion may not apply to you.

7.U.S. Government Restricted Rights. Use, duplication, or disclosure of the Software for or on behalf of the United States of America, its agencies and/or instrumentalities "U.S. Government" is subject to restrictions as stated in paragraph (c)(1)(ii) of the Rights in Technical Data and Computer Software clause of DFARS 252.227-7013, or subparagraphs (c) (1) and (2) of the Commercial Computer Software - Restricted Rights clause at FAR 52.227-19, and in similar clauses in the NASA FAR supplement, as applicable.

8.General. This Agreement constitutes the entire understanding of the parties and revokes and supersedes all prior agreements, oral or written, between them and may not be modified or amended except in a writing signed by both parties hereto that specifically refers to this Agreement. This Agreement shall take precedence over any other documents that may be in conflict herewith. If any one or more provisions contained in this Agreement are held by any court or tribunal to be invalid, illegal, or otherwise unenforceable, each and every other provision shall remain in full force and effect.

The Absolute Best CISA Book/CD Package on the Market!

Get Ready for ISACA's Certified Information System Auditor (CISA) Exam with the most comprehensive and challenging sample tests anywhere!

The Sybex Test Engine features:

- All the review questions, as covered in each chapter of the book.

- Challenging questions representative of those you'll find on the real exam.

- Two full length bonus exams available only on the CD.

- An Assessment Test to narrow your focus to certain objective groups.

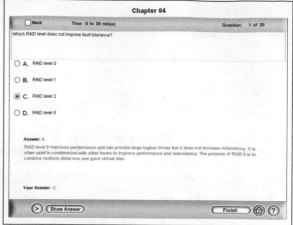

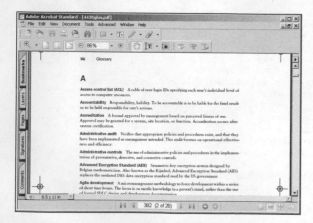

Search through the complete book in PDF!

- Access the entire *CISA: Certified Information System Auditor Study Guide,* complete with figures and tables, in electronic format.

- Search the *CISA: Certified Information System Auditor Study Guide* chapters to find information on any topic in seconds.

Use the Electronic Flashcards for PCs or PDA devices to jog your memory and prep last-minute for the exam!

- Reinforce your understanding of key concepts with these hardcore flash-card-style questions.

- Download the Flashcards to your Palm or PDA device and go on the road. Now you can study for the CISA exam any time, anywhere.

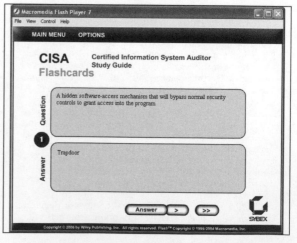